INVENTORS
AT
WORK

INVENTORS
AT
WORK

Interviews with 16 notable American inventors

Kenneth A. Brown

TEMPUS™

PUBLISHED BY

Tempus Books of Microsoft Press
A Division of Microsoft Corporation
16011 NE 36th Way, Box 97017, Redmond, Washington 98073-9717

Library of Congress Cataloging in Publication Data

Brown, Kenneth A.
Inventors at work / Kenneth A. Brown.
        p.   cm.
ISBN 1-55615-042-3 (paper)   1-55615-123-3 (cloth)
1. Inventors—Interviews.   I. Microsoft Press.   II. Title.
T39.B86   1988   87-24390
609.2'2—dc19   CIP

Printed and bound in the United States of America

 23456789   HCHC   89098

Distributed to the book trade in the United States by Harper & Row.

Distributed to the book trade in Canada by General Publishing Company, Ltd.

Tempus Books and the Tempus Books logo are trademarks of Microsoft Press.

Tempus Books is an imprint of Microsoft Press.

Acquisitions editor: Anne Depue
Project editor: Marie Doyle

CONTENTS

FOREWORD

Human beings are different from all other animals on the planet in their ability to shape and use tools. When they do so, they bring change to their environment. At every stage in our history, we have used this facility to develop artifacts and systems whose use has radically altered our society.

Hieroglyphics made possible the organization of an urban civilization in ancient Egypt. The alphabet permitted the recording and transmission of Greek philosophical and scientific thought. Printing freed youth from dependence on age when it made available the experience and the knowledge of a lifetime between the covers of a book. The railways churned up the European gene pool and opened the American West. Future developments in molecular biology may alter the physical appearance of the human population as well as that of the natural world around us.

As time has passed, the social effects of our new tools and systems have multiplied to become more complex and interdependent than ever before. As a result, we live with an accelerating rate of change that is beyond the grasp of most ordinary citizens. It is said that if today you discover that you have finally understood how some new development operates, then, by definition, such a development must already be obsolete.

All of this makes the business of organizing and running our society more and more complex and demanding. With increasing frequency, the electorate is called upon to make decisions about issues they do not properly comprehend—for example, nuclear power, genetic engineering, and surrogate parenthood.

To compound this already bewildering state of affairs, as the twentieth century draws to a close we stand on the threshold of an age of discovery whose products and their effects will make everything that has gone before seem simple and leisurely. In almost every field of science and technology, the introduction of sophisticated data-processing systems is likely to accelerate beyond measure the speed with which new knowledge can be manufactured and applied.

The consequences of such developments are so complicated as to be virtually incalculable. But some attempt must be made to forecast the potential social fallout of these new levels of innovation if we are to be able to use the radically enhanced power for change, which they will also bring, to benefit our own lives and those of others, human and nonhuman, on the planet.

This book is a valuable asset to such an endeavor because it deals with that special group of people who, throughout history, have been key to the advances that have brought us from the caves to the clone in less than a thousand human lifetimes. These extraordinary individuals are the inventors—the bringers of change. As this book so vividly shows, inventors have a unique ability among a species already unique: They can add one and one to make three. Why?

New research in neurophysiology suggests that the cerebral processes involved in memory and creative thought are intensely interactive. The brain may be structured in the form of a tremendous network of dynamic, interconnected systems capable a million times over of making mental associations that link one set of data to another in the most unexpected of ways.

The people interviewed in this book reveal their mental processes to be remarkably close to such a system. They all think laterally. Their best work comes from the exercise of making serendipitous and surprising mental associations. They all talk, in one form or another, about ideas "coming together" or "popping out" in ways that cause the resultant concept or innovative product to be more than simply the sum of its parts. When that happens, one and one make three.

Their perceptions of life are similarly oblique. Almost without exception, they look at the world in a highly idiosyncratic manner. In an age of mass experience and communal activity, they are refreshingly and sometimes sharply individualistic. For them, group activity and committee thinking are, at best, of secondary importance. Some of them express provocative views on the stifling effects of formal education on imaginative and creative thinking. All of them share the burning desire of Edison's: "to find a better way."

These are the people whose mental processes we must try to understand if we are to make sense of what we are about to experience during the next generation. Ken Brown's perceptive and engaging approach to his subjects and their work makes those processes readily and excitingly accessible to the reader.

There have been inventors since the beginning of recorded history—and they have at all times, in a sense, been timeless. The mind of an inventor lives beyond the limitations of contemporary reality. Each one of the people here has, at some time, created the future...made a new world for the rest of us to inhabit.

As our rate of change accelerates into the next century, we must become more like the people in this book—or suffer the consequences. We must learn to think as they do, not to become inventors ourselves, but to survive in a world where we will be called on to make those leaps of the imagination that until now only the innovative mind has made.

That is the single reason this book is so important. It lays the mind of the future open to scrutiny.

James Burke
London 1987

INTRODUCTION

This book actually began with what is now its middle. My first interview was with Roman Szpur, whose laboratory is only a few miles from my parents' home in Kettering, Ohio. I thought we would probably talk for about an hour; instead, we talked for two or three.

About halfway through my somewhat disorganized list of questions, Szpur asked, "Why don't I show you some things while we talk?" We spent the next two hours or so walking around his laboratory looking at inventions: medical electrodes, syringes, waffle-making machines, light fixtures, and lasers. Since then, I've decided that the trite but true maxim "Expect the unexpected" could have been coined by someone who spent time talking to inventors.

I spent the next six months traveling to Los Angeles, New York, San Francisco, Houston, Washington, D.C., and points in between, piecing together the interviews that make up this book. Between trips, I frequently stopped by to see Szpur to tell him about my latest interviews and to hear about his latest ideas.

Of course, not every inventor I talked to had a laboratory full of inventions and projects. Some were businessmen and executives; others were engineers, scientists, and professors. Inventors, like inventions, apparently come in all shapes and sizes. One trait they all had in common, however, was a seemingly limitless supply of ideas—a roomful of ideas in the mind.

There are few limits to an active mind and even fewer to human curiosity, and, on the whole, inventors seem to have more curious minds than most. They spend more time questioning: How does this work? Why does it work? Could it be done better? Perhaps this curiosity explains why inventors seem to have such an unlimited store of ideas.

Surprisingly, those ideas are not limited to the intricacies of invention and engineering. From the start, the interviews took on a broad scope. As I walked around Roman Szpur's laboratory in Ohio, we talked about topics ranging from economics to education. The fifteen interviews that followed were no less broad. Inventions can change society in both profound and subtle ways, and, as architects of change, most inventors are well aware of that fact. Accordingly, the interviews in this book cover a wide range of issues; the inventors say as much about social issues as about scientific ones. The interviews are also about some of the most important inventions of the past fifty years, including manned spacecraft and artificial intelligence, microprocessors and plastic soda pop bottles.

Of course, no selection process is perfect, and the "process" used to select those appearing in this book is no exception. It was not intended to be a definitive list of modern inventions, but to represent a broad range of invention in a variety of fields.

Inventors seem to have an intuitive feel for science and technology—an understanding of their work that is more akin to what one expects to find in an artist or a musician than in a scientist or an engineer. Like artists, inventors are continually creating and discovering. Each interview was a kind of small discovery as well: As my tape recorder turned away, I always found myself hearing a perspective or viewpoint that hadn't been revealed in my reading or research.

At the heart of even the most complex invention there is usually a basic, and yet startling, insight—a new way of looking at an old problem. Xerography, for example, is based on the attraction of oppositely charged particles. The geosynchronous satellite is based on the stability of a spinning object. These kinds of new and unexpected insights are important for solving problems of all kinds—social as well as technical. Perhaps this book can help illuminate that kind of creative thinking. Most of us spend our time thinking along conventional lines. We are easily fenced in. Inventors, however, seem more ready to explore the unconventional or unusual. They think more freely. Their world seems to have fewer walls.

PAUL MacCREADY

M AN HAS dreamed of flight for centuries. The first airplane flight was in 1903, but man would first walk on the moon before he would truly fly under his own power. On August 23, 1977, Paul MacCready's man-powered Gossamer Condor flew into aviation history by covering a figure-eight course around two pylons half a mile apart to win the elusive Kremer Prize. The Condor covered the mile-long course in six and a half minutes, at an altitude of little more than ten feet. Its average speed was just under ten miles per hour.

Established by British industrialist Henry Kremer, the £50,000 Kremer Prize for man-powered flight had eluded flight enthusiasts and aeronautical engineers since 1959. The prize prompted efforts from Britain, Canada, Japan, South Africa, Austria, and the United States. Designs ranged from craft in the tradition of Leonardo da Vinci's ornithopter with flapping wings to pedal-powered machines with two-man crews. Some flew successfully for a few hundred yards, but none were able to complete the turning, twisting course laid out by the Kremer Prize. Before the historic flight of MacCready's Gossamer Condor, some people had even begun to question whether or not the mile-long figure-eight course was even possible.

MacCready's pedal-powered Condor used a front-mounted canard like the Wright Brothers' 1902 glider to control climbs and descents. Turns were accomplished by twisting the plane's wing tips with piano-wire supports.

Early efforts were inspired by the thought of flying like a bird. While the Condor's wings are fixed, it is somehow fitting that MacCready came to solve the puzzle of the Kremer Prize by watching birds soar.

It is an almost poetically simple plane. Now hanging in the National Air and Space Museum in Washington, D.C., not far from the Apollo *space capsule and* Glamorous Glennis *(the Bell X-1, the first plane to fly faster than the speed of sound), the Condor looks more like a child's ambitious project than a realization of one of mankind's oldest dreams. Although its ninety-six-foot wingspan is wider than that of a DC-9, the Condor weighs only seventy pounds. It's not made of high-tech composite materials but of aluminum tubing, corrugated cardboard, balsa wood, piano wire, and Mylar plastic.*

MacCready began building airplanes as a child. He has won the National Soaring Championships three times and the International Championship in 1956. In 1978, his Gossamer Albatross, a modified version of the Condor, flew across the English Channel. In 1980, he built the first solar-powered airplane, which flew 163 miles from Paris to England.

MacCready received his Ph.D. in aeronautics from the California Institute of Technology in 1952. He now heads AeroVironment, an environmental and aeronautical consulting firm he founded in 1971. He has been named the engineer of the century by the American Society of Mechanical Engineers.

INTERVIEWER: *Was man-powered flight part of some long-term goal or dream for you?*

MACCREADY: One of the main points behind the Gossamer Condor was the prize money. I had the debt of a relative that I had to handle. Even if I had come up with the idea for the Condor and the prize was there, I would not have done it without that debt. Back then, I felt that I didn't have the time to mess with such things, but I had this strong economic motivation to take an interest in man-powered flight, so I charged around trying to figure out a way to solve it.

INTERVIEWER: *Everything just came together for you?*

MACCREADY: You can consider that man-powered airplane project as though the prize were created just for me. All the experiences I had in my background and my particular strengths and weaknesses turned out to be most helpful for that particular challenge.

My background may not be right for some challenges, but for that one it was just right: knowing the right amount of aerodynamics without a

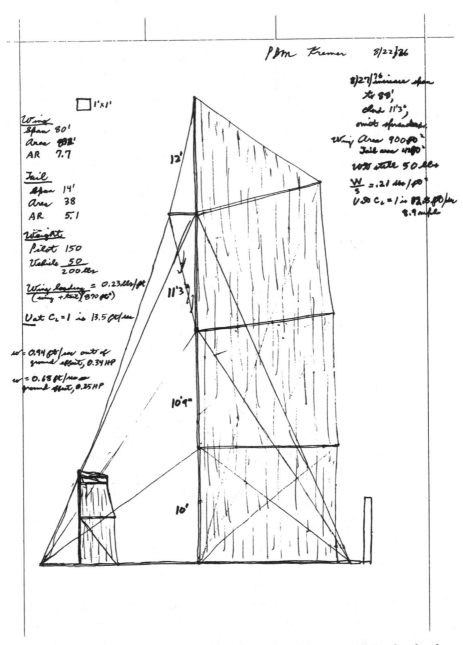

One of Paul MacCready's earliest notebook sketches of the Gossamer Condor, dated
August 22, 1976.

structures background, living in southern California, and having creative friends. All that I could draw on.

INTERVIEWER: *Was there anyone in your background who inspired you to become an inventor or work in aviation?*

MACCREADY: My father was very supportive and took me out to model airplane meets and bought model airplane engines for me as I was getting into that hobby. But he was a strong, pushy type in a way that I often found offensive. He was so goal-oriented that he occasionally tried to get me to cheat and push my way along, which didn't fit my personality and made it a bit awkward. Even so, he was very competent and helpful.

> *I'm delighted to work with other people who have much deeper talents and to communicate with them and maybe drag them along a little bit in their thinking.*

I was also the smallest kid in the class all throughout high school—not especially coordinated and certainly not the football-player type. All this made me socially uncomfortable and probably helped guide me toward model airplanes as a hobby. Looking back, I'm glad I had those limits.

INTERVIEWER: *Do you think that inventors have to be geniuses?*

MACCREADY: When it comes to my abilities, I think there's a lot less than meets the eye. I'm good at synthesizing concepts, seeing connections between this field and that, but I'm not an expert the way many other people are. On the execution of anything, I know people who are better at each aspect of it than I am, so having them around is very helpful.

INTERVIEWER: *How important do you think it is to have other people to work with and share ideas with?*

MACCREADY: I don't think of myself as a great intellect, and I do not have the technical background of somebody who's devoted his life to aircraft structures or airfoil design or computer programming. I'm delighted to work with other people who have much deeper talents and to communicate with them and maybe drag them along a little bit in their thinking. My special ability may be in putting a number of their thoughts together; I know enough about the subject to have a feel for what can and can't be done, and I do not feel threatened by working with brighter people who provide the key elements.

Even so, the most original ideas tend to be those which you come up with on your own, daydreaming, just letting your mind drift along. Sometimes you do best when you're trying to get a report out or you have to write a paper that forces you to attack a subject.

INTERVIEWER: *Do you work best under a deadline?*

MACCREADY: Oh yes. Isn't everybody a procrastinator? The stimulus often comes from the deadline. Say you're on a project and it's not working well, and you keep beating away at it and suddenly you find that "Hey! All the parts fit!" In that case it's not out of the blue; it's because you were forced into it.

The proposal effort on a new subject represents a very creative period. I need to get up to speed quickly on something that is not my specialty. I call somebody in Illinois and another person in Florida and talk to them about this item or that factor and suddenly, I find myself broadening and learning.

INTERVIEWER: *Was the Gossamer Condor that kind of broadening project?*

MACCREADY: It turned out to be a catalyst for other projects. Other unusual aviation projects evolved from it. Also, by getting on the lecture circuit because of it, I found that my perspective broadened a lot. I had to give considerable thought to the project's meaning and features; after the talk, I would have to answer questions from the audience, and sometimes co-lecturers provided new insights. All in all, the lecture circuit turned out to be a very good educational pressure cooker.

INTERVIEWER: *What traits or qualities do you have that help you to be a good inventor?*

MACCREADY: All three of my sons have had some manifestations of dyslexia, so I've learned quite a bit about the topic. And as I think back about myself as a youth, I recognize I had some similar characteristics. Even now, I can think a number, write it down, look at it, and notice that I've written another number.

That's a trivial matter, but perhaps it helps explain why English and history were hard for me in school and science and math were easy. Having that kind of mind means that you tend to have a short attention span and not be good at details, but have a facility for concepts, the bigger picture, and for seeing connections.

I find it enjoyable to jump around and pick up new fields. I'm not an especially good manager, even though I have to do it sometimes. I'm not especially proud or unproud of the way my mind works. Different people are different, and that is fine.

INTERVIEWER: *Do successful inventions spring more from creative ideas or from careful engineering and management?*

MACCREADY: Usually success doesn't come from the bright engineering idea. Bright engineering ideas are all over the place. The success comes from putting the management, the sponsorship, the associates, and the motivation together. Whatever gets it done. To quote Thomas Edison, it's the ninety-eight percent perspiration rather than the two percent inspiration that's important.

You've also got to get yourself into the right circumstances where you can spend time on some invention, and then you've got to have the motivation and resources to apply to the task. Given the right circumstances and pressure and support, most anybody can be pretty inventive. But if you get out of college, go into some narrow slot at a firm that pays you the best salary, and move up comfortably through the ranks, you've put yourself in sort of a comfortable straitjacket that inhibits the development of new approaches.

INTERVIEWER: *So you think that large corporations are not a good place to foster creativity and inventiveness?*

Telegram

```
        PNA003(0653)(2-065011G273)PD 09/30/77 0653
    ICS IPMIIHA IISS
     IISS FM RCA 30 0653
    PMS PASADENA CA
    WUB6406 UXS186 LGD934
    USNX CO GBLG 028
    LONDON/LG 28/27 30 1122
    TF2137937429
    PAUL B MACCREADY 1065 ARMADADRIVE
    PASADENACALIFORNIA(91103)
    THE ROYAL AERONAUTICAL SOCIETY LONDON ANNOUNCES YOU WINNER
     OF THE 50,000 POUNDS KREMER PRIZE HEARTIEST CONGRATULATIONS
          CLARK ROYAL AERONAUTICAL SOCIETY
    COL TF2137937429 1065 91103 50,000
    NNN
    NNNN
```

SF-1201 (R5-69)

Telegram congratulating Paul MacCready on the Gossamer Condor's successful flight.

MACCREADY: Actually I'm not the least bit negative about big companies. Through my lecture circuit, I felt I was practically an employee of IBM for a few years, and I also became involved with a number of other big companies. There is a hierarchy in most large companies, and typically you can't be as entrepreneurial as you could be in a smaller operation. But at a big company you get to deal with more important subjects, and you have larger financial and intellectual resources that you can draw on. What everyone would like to have is all the benefits of a big company with the flexibility of a small outfit.

INTERVIEWER: *Do you think you could have invented either the Condor or the Albatross if you had worked at a large corporation?*

MACCREADY: Well, a certain type of creativity springs from being in fields for which there are no big companies. I wanted to work for a big company when I got out of CalTech [California Institute of Technology]. None were in the field of weather modification, which I was especially interested in; therefore, I had to start my own company.

In the man-powered airplane, you're just a person, a real person. It's more intimate flying, more related to the birds.

I basically had no business talent, but when you're in a position like that, you charge ahead and you do it. Later this gives you the attitude that if you need to do something you just charge ahead and do it. If you want to start a company, you start it. It doesn't matter whether you have the capital or expertise. You have the confidence that comes from having done things in the past.

For me, having worked on sailplanes for a decade and finding that by working hard I ended up winning the contests gave me the confidence to charge in and achieve goals. Building model airplanes and finding that I did fairly well also helped. I wasn't better than anybody else technically, but I had the attitude that there are no barriers out there. If you want to build a battleship, you can go build a battleship. Somehow. So attitude is important, and it is engendered in a small company.

When it came to the Gossamer Condor, after I had come up with the appropriate technical approach, it was easy to have the attitude, "Okay, just go out and build it." I got a few things together and a few dollars here and there, and I did it. If I had worked for a big company like McDonnell

Douglas or TRW, I might have done a useful job for them or for me or for the world, but I would not have had the experience and the attitude that, if you want to go out and build a man-powered airplane, you simply go out and build it. That attitude is a very important ingredient.

INTERVIEWER: *I've heard that some of your ideas for the Condor came from watching a hawk soar. What's the story behind that?*

MACCREADY: Well, let me tell you the double story. In the late 1940s, I read an article called "Soaring Over the Open Ocean" by an oceanographer named Woodcock. It really stuck in my mind because this scientist had been out doing serious oceanographic work in the North Atlantic and began, as a hobby, watching various birds soaring out over the water.

But instead of just looking at the birds and thinking, How pretty, he began noting how they soared. Sometimes they soared in circles, sometimes in straight lines parallel to the wind, sometimes in straight lines perpendicular to the wind—and sometimes they couldn't soar at all. So, he thought about it and began measuring the temperature difference between the air and water as well as the wind speed each time he saw a bird soaring a particular way. Then, he plotted these variables on a scatter diagram and found that each type of soaring was always associated with a particular combination of wind speed and temperature difference.

And it became evident that these different soaring techniques were illuminating the flow patterns of the convective cells in the atmosphere, showing the very same convective cells (hexagonal thermals, longitudinal rolls, waves, or just plain turbulence), as the Benard cells one sees in a laboratory in the motions of a shallow fluid on a plate heated from below. What was going on in the lab in dimensions of millimeters was exactly analogous to what was going on in the atmosphere on a scale of kilometers.

I thought this was a wonderful research project. Woodcock didn't need a cyclotron or a huge radar. He just used some educated eyeballs, some insight, and he used birds as his free sensors.

When I went on a vacation in 1976, some thirty years later, I was daydreaming and thinking, Is there anything I can do that would kind of be like this project? And as we were driving through Arizona watching turkey vultures soar in circles, an answer dawned on me. If you measure the time it takes for a bird to make a complete 360-degree circle and if you estimate the bank angle, you can calculate the flight speed and turning radius for a bird.

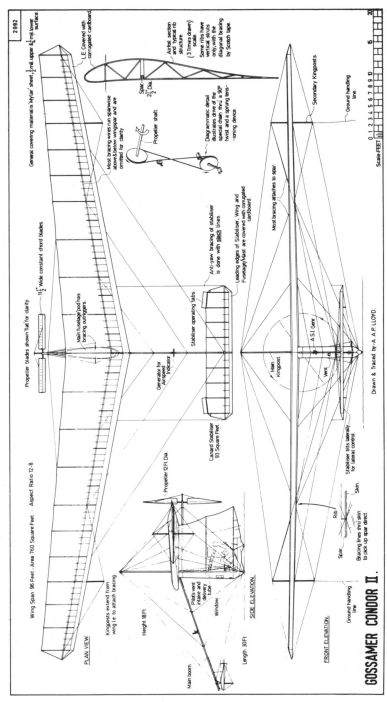

Schematic of the Gossamer Condor. (A.A.P. Lloyd)

And if you then look up the wing loading for that particular kind of bird, you can figure out the lift coefficient at which the wing is operating—something people have been wanting to find out for real birds gliding in the free atmosphere.

So, I did this type of bird study on that vacation and eventually wrote some low-grade technical articles on the subject. Then, I began thinking, How does this relate to hang gliders? How does this relate to sailplanes? I was considering some scaling laws to see how these relationships worked when it suddenly dawned on me that there was a simple and straightforward way of winning the Kremer Prize. What I realized was that by keeping the weight constant and increasing the dimensions in all directions, I could reduce the power required to keep a man-powered plane aloft. For the Condor, the calculations showed that, by taking something about the weight of a hang glider and increasing its wingspan to ninety feet, I could build a plane that a well-conditioned man could fly under his own power.

> When you do come up with a solution, you can always explain it logically, even though it's the absurd approach that gave you the solution.

INTERVIEWER: *So your unexpected insight was more important than a carefully ordered engineering approach?*

MACCREADY: When I first tried to win the Kremer Prize, all the ideas I came up with were the same as all the unsuccessful ideas that competent groups in England had come up with—the same linear way of approaching the problem. I had no idea how to do it. But through this lateral thinking process, through working on another subject, I could look back and suddenly the solution presented itself. After encountering the solution, you see how simple and logical it is, and you kick yourself for not having arrived at the obvious answer by the standard linear approach.

You have these jigsaw puzzles of ideas or challenges in your mind and you keep filling in pieces as you read something new or do some calculations. But until a puzzle is complete, it is not worth doing anything about. Suddenly I had found the last piece in this jigsaw puzzle of man-powered flight and I put it in and the problem was solved. Now, the project deserved being activated.

INTERVIEWER: *You mentioned lateral thinking. What do you mean by that?*

MACCREADY: Approaching the problem from an unexpected direction. The term "lateral thinking" was coined by Dr. Edward de Bono, a leader in the teaching of thinking skills. The way to describe this most succinctly, I think, is to picture yourself trying to solve a problem, any problem—whether it is in handling social relationships or in developing a device for cleaning a kitchen.

Say you have to move a couch out of a room but the door is too narrow and your only helper is a five-year-old kid who doesn't have much muscle. You try all possible approaches, thinking as creatively as possible, but nothing solves the problem.

You bring in some of your friends to help by brainstorming, and you still can't figure out how to do it. So, you enter the lateral thinking realm and try, for example, the random-word approach. You pick a noun, and you approach the problem from the standpoint of that word. This method may sound absurd because the word has absolutely nothing to do with your challenge. But that's the whole point. Previously, every approach you thought of came from the conventional way your mind works—the habitual thought patterns.

Say you pick xylophone. You approach the whole couch-moving problem from thinking about the characteristics of a xylophone, which has keys and rails and which you hit with little hammers. And the word begins with an X, which makes you think of crossed sticks and so on.

To your amazement, after you've been working on the problem for only about three minutes, you realize you are looking at it from different directions—different from those you would have ever come up with through ordinary thinking. Of course, the problem may not even be solvable. But more than half the time you find yourself thinking about rather good approaches that you would not have come up with through more linear approaches.

When you do come up with a solution, you can always explain it logically, even though it's the absurd approach that gave you the solution.

INTERVIEWER: *Does it seem now that you got the idea for the man-powered airplane in that way?*

MACCREADY: Oh yes. Using good linear thinking and standard aerodynamics laws, any aeronautical engineer can figure out the man-powered airplane in three steps and in less than one minute. All inventions are obvious once you have the solutions. You can justify how wise you were to go through this logical sequence. But that's not the sequence you went through to discover the invention. You were wandering out in left field when you stumbled onto it.

INTERVIEWER: Can creativity and inventiveness be taught?

MACCREADY: Yes. And enjoyably and quickly. As one avenue, consider Olympics of the Mind, now called OM. The technique is remarkably successful, and I strongly support it. It is utilized by five thousand schools nationwide, and it is growing fast. The schools help with coordination, but OM is not part of official curriculum and so avoids school politics. A group of five or six students is challenged to do some competitive project. They can do all the experimenting they want, but teachers can't provide answers.

It can be, for example, an engineering problem: You're given one ounce of one-eighth-inch-thick balsa sticks out of which you concoct a bridge to straddle a sixteen-inch gap. The competition is to see how much weight your bridge can support in the middle. If you're not much good, you can do twenty pounds. If you're really good, your bridge can support an unbelievable four hundred pounds.

Of course, the challenge doesn't have to be an engineering one. It could involve poetry or history. The important part is that it's hands-on. The students are not just reading about it or sitting in front of a TV set. They're actually doing things and doing them with a group of people. And, perhaps for the first time, they're working on a common goal, compromising and cooperating rather than each individual trying to get the best mark for himself.

The students become more inventive, and their perspective broadens. They become more secure with themselves, realizing they can go out and accomplish things. And they get motivated, which is probably the most important factor in the process.

INTERVIEWER: Is this a good time to be an inventor? Or has so much been invented that it's increasingly difficult to come up with anything new?

MACCREADY: With every subject I've ever had anything to do with, more challenges and solutions appear all the time, but I find that you have to be realistic in selecting goals. For example, I think we have more talent in this company, AeroVironment, for the development of small airplanes than many other aeronautical groups. But the field is not really worth pursuing. You can make a small plane for yourself but you can't produce it commercially because of the product liability problems. You may get a great idea for a buggy whip, but there's no future in buggy whips so you don't do it.

INTERVIEWER: Do you think creativity is being stifled in the United States?

MACCREADY: If there were no more technical creativity in the world than there is right now, I don't think very much would be lost. The most significant problems of the future are not technical.

For example, I'm disappointed when I talk with people in the aerospace field about the Falkland Islands War because they want to focus primarily on the issue of producing a better defense against the Exocet missile. If you bring up subjects such as how to facilitate better communications and problem-solving between countries so that the war wouldn't have happened in the first place, they're very uninterested in discussion. That's my real concern.

> *A lot of good, basic research is going on in classified areas. At the same time, it's disturbing that something like half the country's intellectual powers are devoted to military research.*

INTERVIEWER: So, your technical accomplishments have broadened your outlook?

MACCREADY: After the Gossamer Condor project, there were other programs, the lecture circuit, and involvement with museums and schools, all expanding my interests. The result has been an enthusiasm for thinking skills: how you teach them and how you get people's mental blinders off. This subject has a great deal to do with whether or not civilization will exist in fifty years. Technology doesn't offer the solution to this vital challenge; rather, it is just a tool and a tool which is on the way to becoming our master rather than our servant. It may be fun to play in the great technological sandbox—technology is what many of us get paid for, and it's delightful and challenging—but it should be viewed in perspective.

INTERVIEWER: *What do you mean by mental blinders? Do you think a broad and creative outlook is important for people in general as well as inventors and engineers?*

MACCREADY: Our political, religious, business, and educational institutions tend to perpetuate people having blinders on—the narrowing of minds rather than the broadening of them. And yet, with a little effort people can be made to view things much more broadly and rationally, so I am interested in that area. It's much more important than any of the technical areas I'm involved in. Engineering and inventing may be fun and remunerative, but they aren't that important when one worries about what's going to happen in five years or twenty years.

The United States is the most powerful country in the world. And what it does has huge reverberations throughout the world. I'm disturbed by the fact that so many people would slavishly follow the ingenious advertisement or the charismatic leader without thinking. If a charismatic President got enthused about some absurd military adventure, he could probably get most of the country behind him with three TV appearances. People don't say, "Hey, there are two sides to this issue; let's sit back and think about this one."

INTERVIEWER: *Your company does some defense work of its own. How do you reconcile that with your personal views?*

MACCREADY: Quite a gray area exists between defense work and non-defense work. If you make a truck, you can haul bombs and guns in it. If you work on the diffusion of chemical warfare agents (as did my previous company doing some good, basic research for a military sponsor), you can use the research to solve all sorts of air pollution problems.

There's a real "fuzzing out" when it comes to deciding whether a project is for this field or that field. There is one overriding factor: Projects don't get done unless they have financial support. For example, the "do-good" projects aimed at letting civilization reach a comfortable accommodation with the global ecosystem unfortunately are not remunerative. However, projects involving consumption of nonreplenishable resources are typically remunerative.

Gossamer Condor (above) and Gossamer Albatross (below).

In this less-than-perfect world you need some defense activities. You need police, and they need billy clubs and radios and helicopters and guns and so on. It isn't an absolute. I can't say I'm not going to do *any* military research, and I can't say that I'm going to devote my entire life to working on classified things. I'm sort of on the edge. A lot of good, basic research is going on in classified areas. At the same time, it's disturbing that something like half the country's intellectual powers are devoted to military research.

INTERVIEWER: *What about other problems? Do you see any high-tech quick fix for problems like pollution or energy?*

MACCREADY: I don't see them. There are certainly going to be quick fixes as time goes on, but that doesn't change the big problem. If you suddenly had a simple energy source it might change the time constant with which some things are happening in the world, but it wouldn't change the fact that five billion people are on the earth now and that there will be twelve billion in forty or fifty years and that each person will have higher expectations than those in the past.

With a lot of nonreplenishable resources disappearing and everybody elbowing each other harder, some real strife is going to occur. Technology may even speed it up. Such things as robotics, manufacturing, and advancements in agriculture will result in a smaller number of more professional people really running things.

A bigger percentage of the population in that situation will find that they are not qualified to contribute very much. There may be clothing, TV, and food for them, but not jobs. You wonder what they will be doing to keep themselves really interested in life. Fifty years ago people were coping with the depression or working on a farm, and they knew exactly what they were doing. If they could possibly get an education, they did, because they knew what that led to. But it's different now.

Technology changes the status quo, and a change in the status quo usually results in stresses that civilization is not well-prepared for because it still hasn't come into equilibrium with changes that happened in the past. So, I don't think technology helps particularly.

It's the most exciting time to be living in the world right now. But so is a balloon the prettiest when you put that last breath into it before it pops.

INTERVIEWER: *Is there anything you'd like to invent?*

MACCREADY: A lot of little "invention-y" things have been kicking around in the back of my mind for a long time.

I'd like to make a sailplane that could fly around at low speed in a thermal—something that could fly with a hawk, at the same speed, and with the same turning radius as a bird so that you could join the birds rather than charging around through them.

INTERVIEWER: *What do you consider your most important invention?*

MACCREADY: The Gossamer Condor was my most significant— achieving human-powered flight, which some people didn't think could be done. For eighteen years people had been pursuing it because of the Kremer Prize and not even coming close.

The challenge itself was a terrific invention. The gadget wasn't all that great and you could have made different configurations, any one of which could have won. The real genius was Henry Kremer, who put up the prize money and was assured that somebody was going to do this sometime. That was a very creative action.

As I look back at the Gossamer Condor—the approach, the testing, and the people that were involved, the managing of it all and so on—it was just one of these very special projects: family involvement, fun, kind of art-istic, kind of poetic, flying this silent airplane at dusk out at remote airports. It was all pretty special.

INTERVIEWER: *Has your perspective on the Gossamer Condor changed since those early flights?*

MACCREADY: The Gossamer Condor was a very important airplane. At first I was dumbfounded when the National Air and Space Museum wanted to hang it right near the Wright Brothers' plane and Lindbergh's plane. I thought, "That's absurd; the thing's ready to break! It looks like a plastic bag with some sticks of wood in it."

But as I look back, I'm much more enthused about it. I see it from a broader perspective. People can relate to it much more than they can to a big rocket or a 747. Some little kid can't quite picture building one of those or even being the pilot of one. But in the man-powered airplane, you're just a person, a real person. It's more intimate flying, more related to the birds.

The project itself gets you thinking more about what you can do with very little power and very little material. It is way out beyond the ordinary things of thought—that you can make an airplane with a ninety-six-foot wingspan, weighing only seventy pounds. Once you've done that, you think about things differently.

WILSON GREATBATCH

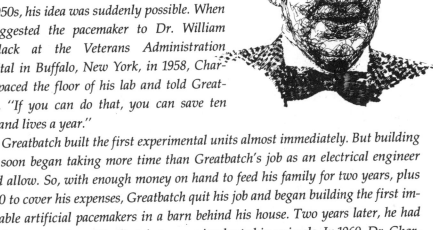

WHEN WILSON Greatbatch first learned about heart block in 1951, he knew that an artificial pacemaker could cure it, but he couldn't build one small enough to be implantable with the materials then available. However, when transistors became readily available in the late 1950s, his idea was suddenly possible. When he suggested the pacemaker to Dr. William Chardack at the Veterans Administration Hospital in Buffalo, New York, in 1958, Chardack paced the floor of his lab and told Greatbatch, "If you can do that, you can save ten thousand lives a year."

Greatbatch built the first experimental units almost immediately. But building them soon began taking more time than Greatbatch's job as an electrical engineer would allow. So, with enough money on hand to feed his family for two years, plus $2,000 to cover his expenses, Greatbatch quit his job and began building the first implantable artificial pacemakers in a barn behind his house. Two years later, he had built fifty pacemakers. The first forty were implanted in animals. In 1960, Dr. Chardack and his associates began implanting Greatbatch's pacemaker in patients. Today, more than three hundred thousand pacemakers are implanted worldwide each year.

Greatbatch's inventions have frequently come from combining disciplines. His pacemaker was a combination of engineering and medical electronics. In the 1970s, he developed an improved pacemaker battery and began working in the field of electrochemistry. He has also worked in biomass energy conversion and plant genetics. He is currently working on developing a treatment for retroviral diseases such as AIDS and adult T-cell leukemia.

Wilson Greatbatch was born in Buffalo, New York, in 1919. He served in both the Atlantic and Pacific theaters during the Second World War as a radioman. In the Pacific, he flew combat missions as a rear gunner in dive bombers and torpedo bombers off the aircraft carrier Monterey.

He received his bachelor's degree in electrical engineering from Cornell University in 1950 and his master's degree from the State University of New York (SUNY) at Buffalo in 1957. He has received honorary doctorates from Houghton College, SUNY Buffalo, and Clarkson College of Technology.

In 1983, the National Society of Professional Engineers (NSPE) selected the implantable pacemaker as one of the ten most important engineering contributions to society of the past fifty years.

Greatbatch is a fellow of both the Institute of Electrical and Electronics Engineers (IEEE) and the American College of Cardiology, as well as the British Royal Society of Health. His present company, Greatbatch Gen-Aid, Limited, has its offices in Clarence, New York. In 1986, he was inducted into the National Inventors Hall of Fame.

INTERVIEWER: *How did you get started on the pacemaker?*

GREATBATCH: I was a GI Bill student at Cornell University in the 1950s, and the only "honor" I graduated with was that I had more kids than anybody else in the class. I worked all kinds of jobs part-time while I was in school, and one of them was a job at the University's animal behavior farm in Varna, New York. I instrumented the animals for blood pressure, heart rate, and other variables. While I was working up there, a couple of brain surgeons came from Boston to do experimental brain surgery on some of the animals. These surgeons brought their lunch to work in a brown bag— just as I did—so we sat out in the sun and talked shop during lunch. During our talks, I learned about a disease called complete heart block. I knew I could fix that disease with an artificial pacemaker, but I couldn't build a pacemaker with vacuum tubes and storage batteries that was small enough—and in the 1950s, transistors weren't around yet.

Pacemaker is actually a physiological term. A section of the heart called the sinus node generates a little electrochemical impulse that gives the heart a shock every second or so and causes it to beat. The sinus node is like an electronic metronome—which is really what the circuitry in an artificial pacemaker looks like.

In diseases like complete heart block, the nerve which couples the auricle to the ventricle of the heart is disrupted. So, the impulse never reaches the ventricle, and the heart doesn't pump any blood.

Fortunately, the good Lord has put a safety mechanism lower in the heart. If the ventricle doesn't get any beats after a period of time, that safety mechanism will kick in with a randomly scattered pulse of its own. The ventricle may get one beat for every two or every three that it would get under normal circumstances. However, if you have Stokes–Adams syndrome in addition to complete heart block, that safety mechanism occasionally drops out too, and the heart doesn't beat at all. After fifteen seconds with no heartbeat, you faint, and after three minutes you've probably got some brain damage. After five minutes, you're dead.

> *The problem for a small inventor today is the FDA…. If I did today what I did twenty years ago, I would go to jail.*

INTERVIEWER: *How does the pacemaker actually work?*

GREATBATCH: The pacemaker consists of a pair of wires, either on the surface of the heart or held against the inside of the heart, which actually shock the heart and cause it to beat just like it would if the natural pacemaker was there.

I did not invent the first artificial pacemaker. It was invented by Paul Zoll, in Boston, and his pacemaker was an external pacemaker. I invented the implantable pacemaker.

The simplest form of the artificial pacemaker is the asynchronous pacemaker. It simply hits the heart with a shock once every second, regardless of what the heart does. Today, there's also a type known as the demand pacemaker, which only works when the heart doesn't. It not only drives the heart, but it listens to the heart electronically. As long as it "hears" a heartbeat, it doesn't do anything. But if a second goes by with no heartbeat, it will kick in a beat of its own on demand—which is why it's called a demand pacemaker.

INTERVIEWER: *When did you build your first pacemaker?*

GREATBATCH: I built my first pacemaker in 1958. Transistors were readily available by then, so it was possible to make a pacemaker small enough to be implantable. But it took me quite a while to find any doctors who were even interested in the idea.

However, I belonged to the local chapter of Professional Group in Medical Electronics [PGME], a division of the Institute of Electrical and Electronics Engineers, and about half of the people who came to our meetings were doctors. If a doctor had an instrumentation problem, the chapter would send out a team to help. Through that program, I met Dr. William Chardack at the Veterans Administration Hospital in Buffalo. His assistant was Dr. Andrew Gage, an old high school classmate. Dr. Chardack had a problem with a blood oximeter he was trying to build. Although we never solved his instrumentation problem, I told him about my ideas for the pacemaker. "You know," he told me, "if you can do that, you can save ten thousand lives a year."

I went home, and three weeks later I had put together a pacemaker unit. I built it in the barn behind my house. We brought it to the hospital and tried it out on an animal whose heart we'd blocked by constricting the auricular ventricular nerve bundle with a tied suture. We touched the wires to the animal's heart, and it started to beat. Dr. Chardack looked at the oscilloscope—he could see the signal on it—and he looked at the animal. He walked up and down the room and said, "Well, I'll be damned."

With that first pacemaker in 1958, Dr. Chardack, Dr. Gage, and I were so naive that we thought we could seal it against the body's fluids by wrapping it in electrical tape, but it only lasted for about four hours in the animal. Gradually, we learned that we had to cast the pacemakers in epoxy. Today they put them in metal cases. In the next two years, I built fifty pacemakers, forty of which we implanted in animals.

After two years of experimentation with animals, we felt we were ready for a real patient. The average life expectancy for a person with complete heart block and Stokes–Adams syndrome is about a year. The patient we installed the first pacemaker in was even worse off than this profile. He had already fallen twice and fractured his skull after passing out. He wore a football helmet all the time for protection. We did ten patients and published the results of our work in 1960. It just took off from there.

INTERVIEWER: *Did you ever foresee the tremendous impact pacemakers would have?*

GREATBATCH: Not really. When Dr. Chardack suggested that it could save ten thousand lives a year, we thought that if we could treat even that many people, it would be very worthwhile. Last year alone, however, three hundred thousand pacemakers were implanted worldwide. I'm a very religious person myself. When I work on something like the pacemaker, I don't ask, "How many are you going to sell?" or "How many are you going to use?" I ask, "Is this a good thing in the Lord's sight?" I felt it was.

INTERVIEWER: *Did you ever doubt that you would be able to make your pacemaker work or that you'd be able to make it small enough to be implantable?*

GREATBATCH: No, I really didn't. It was known that if you could deliver an electrical impulse to the heart, you could shock it and make it beat. Zoll proved that with his external pacemaker. It was simply left to us to build equipment small enough and reliable enough so that it could be sewn up inside the body.

The external pacemaker units were never completely satisfactory. To run them, you plugged them into the wall, and your world was the length of the cord.

Later, the Medtronic Corporation in Minneapolis started making hand-held, battery-operated pacemakers. They were much better, but there was still a wire going through the skin. One thing we engineers have never learned is how to seal wire to skin, and there was always an open wound around this wire that connected the external pacemaker to the heart. You had to put antibiotic jelly on the wound every morning and every night, you couldn't take a bath or a shower, and you couldn't go swimming.

The implantable pacemaker solved those problems, and with the batteries available then, we thought that if they ran for one or two years, it would be adequate. The first pacemaker we installed ran for twenty months. The larger sizes of lithium batteries we're building today should be good for ten years.

INTERVIEWER: *You mentioned the importance of transistors to actually building an implantable pacemaker. Would it be easier to invent a pacemaker with today's improved technology? Or would today's regulatory controls and legal liabilities make it even more difficult than it was in the 1950s?*

GREATBATCH: It would be much more difficult for someone like me to invent the pacemaker today. The problem is not really the liability. You can always carry a fair amount of insurance for protection, but the best protection against being sued is not to have any money. If you're a small, struggling inventor working in a cellar and you don't even own your own home, nobody is going to sue you.

The problem for a small inventor today is the FDA [Food and Drug Administration]. So many laws have been written that a small operator can't do something like the pacemaker. The regulations are so complex and the required testing is so expensive that a small company can't do it. It takes a big drug company to work in pacemakers today. The field is finished as far as the small operator goes.

> *A pacemaker is nothing more elaborate than a flasher that you see on a highway construction site.*

Of course, when I was first doing my work, the pacemaker was new and unheard of. There are still plenty of areas today that are new and unheard of that the FDA isn't regulating. You can work in those new areas without any problem, and I am. Right now, I'm working in molecular biology without too much concern from the FDA. But the fields I've been accustomed to working in, like pacemakers, are getting very restrictive. If I did today what I did twenty years ago, I would go to jail. Imagine making pacemakers in a barn and taking them to a hospital and putting them into patients! But we did it, and it worked. It was done very ethically, and a lot of people are alive today because of that work.

INTERVIEWER: *Are regulations and regulatory agencies like the FDA making it harder for advances and inventions in medicine?*

GREATBATCH: Actually, regulations don't bother me too much in my work. I must say, the FDA has probably done a pretty fair job in the last few years. They're mainly active in regulating fields that are mature enough that I'm not interested in them anymore.

I'm bothered more by the conservative attitudes of some of the larger medical institutions. For example, some of the work I'm doing in molecular biology with Ed Niles, a professor at SUNY Buffalo, may be applicable to finding a cure or vaccine for the AIDS virus. But if my partner and I want to challenge the systems we're building with the AIDS virus, it's a problem because current University and hospital regulations won't allow any AIDS cultures inside.

Roswell Park Hospital in Buffalo, New York, is the best cancer clinic in the country, but they won't allow any AIDS cultures inside the hospital. I think that's wrong. That's really a head-in-the-sand approach. They don't mind treating a patient with AIDS. If the AIDS is walking around, that's okay. But they won't allow any cultures in. I'd say the ultraconservative attitudes of some of our medical and research institutions hold us back more than any federal regulations.

INTERVIEWER: But while institutional and legal problems don't make invention impossible, do you think anything could be done to make invention easier in the medical field?

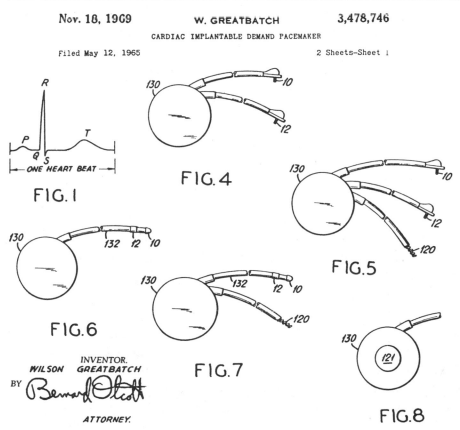

Patent drawings for Wilson Greatbatch's implantable pacemaker (dated November 18, 1969).

GREATBATCH: I think the liability crisis will have to work itself out one way or another. The concept of separate and several liability—that your liability is not related to your negligence but to your ability to pay—is a real problem. Lawyers today say, "Well, this person has been damaged; who can best afford to pay for it?" Liability insurance has skyrocketed in cost. People complain about the high cost of medical care, but a large part of the cost of that care is liability insurance. Europeans don't have that problem. You can't sue for malpractice under European law, and it's also difficult to do so under Canadian law.

Also, in the United States it's difficult for small business owners like me to accumulate capital. Most countries have no capital gains tax; if you put a company together and it's successful, you can sell it and use the money to start another company.

I ran into this problem of raising capital when I needed to put some more financing into my company, Greatbatch Gen-Aid, Limited. One of my options was to sell some stock I had bought. I sold ten thousand shares of it, but after the sale, I realized that the profit from that sale was considered taxable income. The government immediately wants a lot of that profit in taxes, which means I can't put that money into my company.

When I complained about this, people said, "Why don't you get an NIH [National Institutes of Health] grant?" But the NIH said, "Yeah, we'll give you the grant, but it's subject to certain restrictions."

But, their restrictions are such that I couldn't do much under the grant. When I told them, "I can't work under these restrictions," they said, "Well, what makes you—a little guy up in Buffalo—think that you can do this kind of research without our assistance or advice?"

It seems as though the government is saying that it wants all medical research to be done under NIH "guidance." It sounds a lot like Russia, you know?

INTERVIEWER: *Do you think there's too much red tape attached to federal grants for them to be useful to researchers and inventors like you?*

GREATBATCH: Oh yes, very definitely. I say—very capriciously—that if you're on a government grant, you spend half your time writing reports and the other half writing applications for the next grant. By the time you're finished with all that writing, you don't have time left to do any work.

Of course, it's not really that bad. Some projects need a big operation and government support to get them done. I couldn't build something like a satellite or a space vehicle or an artificial heart. But a small, self-financed operation like mine is quite feasible for pacemaker-sized projects.

INTERVIEWER: *Is funding for new ideas less of a problem inside a big company?*

GREATBATCH: You really don't find the right atmosphere in big companies either. Big companies are very ponderous, and most insist that you write out a proposal before you ever do the research—just like the government. Well, that's ridiculous. I don't even know what I'm going to do before I try it. I find that working the way I do—writing my purchase orders on the back of my business cards—gives me a great deal of freedom. I can completely reverse a project in midstream and say, "Well, I've been going the wrong way. I've got to go back and go the other way." If you try to explain that to a contracts administrator in Washington, D.C., or to a corporate vice president, they just don't understand.

The ideal situation is to build something that's so new and different and exciting that you ship it out and *then* sit back and say, "Now, what have we built?" I used to say that if you have to make drawings of something before you ship it, you're too big.

There are areas where this kind of fast response can really work. It worked for us in pacemakers, and it worked in lithium batteries. It would not work on a large project that requires five hundred people working together and communicating and so on. But there's still room today for the little guy with the big idea.

INTERVIEWER: *Are big ideas more likely to come out of a small company than a large one?*

GREATBATCH: I don't see how a large company can possibly come up with the sort of things we do. Mallory* was the biggest pacemaker battery company in the business for ten years, and they made most of the pacemaker batteries in the world. Now, they make none because we've beaten them out of the market with the lithium battery.

Another example is General Electric. Four different times in our history we've been up against General Electric: one time on aerospace medical

---

* P.R. Mallory & Co. Inc., now Duracell Inc., a business unit of Kraft, Inc.

work, one time on cardiac monitors, another time on pacemakers, and more recently on pacemaker batteries. They're no longer involved in any of those areas. Each time, we beat them out by fast response—and efficient research.

I don't see how a really entrepreneurial inventor can make it in a large company. I guess inventors can make it at a big company if they are working on a very large project—say, one that requires $100 million of investment. But I could not possibly have done the things I have done at a large company.

To work the way I want to, I don't want to ask anybody. If I have to ask someone if I can do something, I'm beat. If I get an idea late at night, I've just got to go ahead, get up at two o'clock in the morning, and go down to the lab—and not ask anybody.

I do, however, work in an interdisciplinary area, so working with other people is very important to me. I couldn't have built the pacemaker without Dr. Chardack and Dr. Gage working right along with me and contributing a lot of very good ideas. The electrode design was actually Dr. Chardack's, and he patented it himself.

INTERVIEWER: *Do you work best late at night?*

GREATBATCH: No, I don't. But I do get my best ideas at about four in the morning when I can't sleep. The development part of inventing, however, is just a lot of time at the workbench: I put something together, test it out on the scope, and see what it does. Then, I change it, put something else together, and test that out. The results of one experiment tell me what I should do next.

I almost never have an idea of what my inventions are going to look like in their final form. For example, I had no idea that the pacemaker would end up in a metal case. We originally encased it in plastic, which is gas-permeable, because the mercury batteries we used released hydrogen gas and required a permeable case. But, because water vapor inside the body is a gas, if you put a plastic-encapsulated device in the body, it's really working underwater. For the first ten years, we learned to make pacemakers work in that environment, but it wasn't the best way to go. Once we got rid of the mercury batteries, we were able to seal the pacemaker and keep water vapor out and the battery effluents in. Reliability went up quite markedly, but we didn't know any of this until we experimented.

INTERVIEWER: *Are carefully planned experiments more important to invention than the sudden burst of inspiration that sends you to your lab at four in the morning?*

GREATBATCH: I'm a proponent of the big jump. I like to throw something together, see if it works, and go on from there. Later, I might go back and fill in the gaps, but I might even let someone else do that.

One problem I have with the people I work with at universities is that they like to work step by step by step. And in their view, you don't start one step until you've finished the last one. But, there's usually a place in any project where you can say, "Well, maybe if I just built this thing, I could jump way over here."

An inventor can go three ways with an invention: sell the idea outright, license it to somebody and take a percentage of the profits, or build it himself.

In the pacemaker, for example, throwing a bunch of parts together and touching the wires to a dog's heart to make it beat—that was a big jump.

After that jump, I could go back and fill in different details: What kind of materials can be used in the body? What kind of circuitry can be used? A pacemaker is nothing more elaborate than a flasher that you see on a highway construction site. But you've got to redesign that flasher so that it will work off its battery for ten years instead of only a few nights. You've got to wrap it in something that the body won't reject, like silicon rubber or platinum or stainless steel. You have to find what's right and what isn't.

All those details are important, but if I've at least made the big jump, I know that I can make the heart go with a tiny pulse of electricity.

INTERVIEWER: *Is the problem with professors and research scientists that they are too well trained? Can someone be too well trained to be an inventor?*

GREATBATCH: I don't think the problem is too much training. The problem occurs when your training is too narrow and you get yourself on a rigid path of thinking and lose flexibility. I think some of the people I work with have this problem. They essentially lay out a research project ahead of time and call it an experiment. They may modify their projects somewhat as they're going through them, but they're rigid in what they want to achieve.

They do their experiment a certain way and see what the results are. And they wind up with either positive or negative answers, and that's the end of it. I don't care that much about the elegance of the experiment. I want to cure a disease.

If you keep an open mind, too much training can never hurt. I wish I had a Ph.D. in electrochemistry, for example. It would help me a great deal. In fact, I could also use a Ph.D. in microbiology. I could use Ph.D.'s in a number of things, but I actually don't have any. Well, I have three honorary degrees, but I never went beyond a master's degree as far as formal training goes. The rest was all osmosis.

At a basic level, I firmly believe that a broad background is helpful when it comes to inventing. I give credit for much of what I've been able to do to Cornell University, where I did my undergraduate work, and to the breadth of coursework they gave me in engineering. I had much more chemistry and physics and math than anyone would ever need in order to do just electrical engineering.

I also believe that engineering training is a very good foundation for anything a person may want to do in life. For example, many of the engineering principles show up in even sociology. The second law of thermodynamics is that you can't get something for nothing—which is pretty good sociology too.

INTERVIEWER: *Why did you pick electrical engineering at Cornell?*

GREATBATCH: I was always interested in electricity; it has always been fascinating to me. There's something going on that you can't see. You have to use a meter or a neon bulb or something like that to see what is going on. Trying to figure the mystery of electricity is a fascination for me. It's interesting that none of my children have shared that. I have five children, and none of them are engineers, and none of them are interested in electricity. My four boys are all mechanically inclined. They do beautiful wood and metal work, but they have to see what they're doing, and they have to have their hands on what they're doing.

When I went into the service in World War II, I planned to be an industrial arts teacher. I had been going to the Buffalo State Teachers College. When I joined the service, I was an amateur radio operator (a "ham"), so I became a radioman. When I got out of the service, however, I had the GI Bill, so I went to Cornell and became an engineer.

The GI Bill was absolutely the best federal aid to education that anybody ever thought of. Almost every engineer my age got their education under the GI Bill, and I think it should be kept in force. It wouldn't cost any more than we're spending now on federal aid to education, and it would give kids from minority groups a chance to get a college education.

Too often, we confine college training to the people who can afford it; it's given to many people who don't have the drive and aren't committed to their education. The policy in our company is to provide full tuition and books to all employees and their children, wherever they want to go to school. If the sweeper can get four kids into Harvard Medical School, we will pay the bill.

INTERVIEWER: *Can anyone be an inventor? Do you think inventors have any common traits?*

GREATBATCH: I think the most important factor is whether or not you have the curiosity—whether or not you look at something and wonder, What makes it work? Could I make it better? Inventing takes curiosity; it takes drive; it takes an inability to be discouraged. An inventor is the kind of person who really doesn't get interested in a problem until it looks impossible. That's not a usual trait, but I think it typifies inventors.

Some people don't have that outlook. Some people are more interested in fixing up the house and in their hobbies. Those things are probably creative, but they're not inventing. I get bored with things like that. Strangely enough, however, I'm a pathological gardener. I love gardening. It's the antithesis of inventing.

As far as my own inventing is concerned, people tell me that one of the big differences between me and other people in the field is stick-to-it-iveness. In fact, I think it's true of most inventors and most entrepreneurs. But while I can really stick to a thing when it looks impossible, I find the routine stuff boring. When I'm working on a project, it's all too easy for me to get bored once I've solved the basic problem. Sometimes I get interested in something else and don't finish what I started. When that happens, I need outside motivation—someone to tell me to keep on something and keep after it.

INTERVIEWER: *Did you start making pacemaker batteries because you wanted a new challenge?*

GREATBATCH: No, I did it because I believed we needed better pacemaker batteries. In 1970, after the pacemaker had been in use for ten years, the average pacemaker was coming out of a patient in two years. Eighty percent of the time, the reason was that the battery had failed. Not run down, but failed. The mercury battery couldn't tolerate the warm environment inside the body with its one hundred percent humidity. It's actually a very hostile environment; it's worse than the bottom of the ocean and worse than outer space.

> *An entrepreneur or inventor has to understand the business of patenting in order to get the maximum benefit from his inventions.*

So, we began to look for other power sources, and at that time, my pacemaker designs were one hundred percent licensed to Medtronic. I told Earl Bakken, the company president, "You're going to have to get a better battery before you ever get a better pacemaker, and I don't think that Mallory is going to build it for you. I think we're going to have to make a better one on our own."

He said he wouldn't do that. Mallory was his only source of batteries, and he didn't want to jeopardize that source. I said that I had to leave, and under friendly circumstances, I terminated my relationship with the company. I sold them all my patents and proceeded to become a battery designer and battery evaluator in my search for a better pacemaker battery. I looked at all different kinds of battery systems: rechargeable batteries, biological batteries, lithium batteries—everything I could think of—even nuclear batteries. I actually got very heavily involved in nuclear batteries with another company in Maryland and invested $200,000 in research and development.

After two years, I decided that the nuclear battery was the best battery anyone had ever seen for pacemakers. But while it was safe and efficacious, it would never go because of the regulatory requirements on it. Due to the critical nature of the isotopic material used to build the battery, a doctor was legally responsible for every patient at all times. The battery was made from plutonium 238, and if you wanted to, I guess you could make a sloppy atom bomb out of enough of the stuff.

INTERVIEWER: *Little, walking atom bombs everywhere.*

GREATBATCH: (Laughs.) I figured out that it would take thirty thousand pacemakers to make an atomic bomb. About six kilos is critical.

At the end of two years, I looked at the whole project, decided it was not going to go, and dropped it. I took a lot of criticism for doing that, but the company I had been working with lost $2 million before they decided to pull out too.

At the same time I was working on the nuclear battery, I was also working on lithium batteries. One day, I got a telephone call from Fred Tepper, who was working with the Catalyst Research Company in Baltimore. His company was making thermal batteries out of molten salt for the space program. These batteries had to be activated by a small explosive charge like a firecracker and were very short-lived. They only lasted about a minute and a half and were used in proximity fuses and things like that.

Tepper had also worked with lithium; his people combined it with an iodine cathode and found a way to make it work. Iodine is a rather unlikely material for a battery cathode because it doesn't conduct electricity. But if you mix a charge-transfer complex called poly-2-vinylpyridine, which is also a nonconductor, with iodine and hold the two at three hundred degrees Fahrenheit for three days, it becomes a black, sticky mess that does conduct electricity and can be used as a cathode. When you plaster lithium against that iodine-polyvinyl complex, you immediately get monomolecular lithium iodide, which acts as a crystalline separator.

One of the big problems with a mercury battery is that it has a fabricated separator that is attacked by the sodium hydroxide inside the battery, which eventually causes it to fail. Some people put as many as three separators in their batteries—the Swiss use five—to solve this problem. But adding more separators simply delays the end point and doesn't really improve the battery's reliability all that much.

But the lithium iodide battery has a crystalline separator which is spontaneously formed and therefore injury-proof. If you bang the battery or pierce it or do anything else that might damage it, the separator just reforms, which tremendously increases the reliability of the battery and the pacemaker.

Fred Tepper had discovered all this and, not knowing what to do with the thing, had called the NIH. Just by chance, he talked to a friend of mine who suggested that he give me a call. He did, and I talked to him on the phone for about ten minutes and decided he had something. I got on an airplane, flew down to see him, and signed a series of agreements with his company, Catalyst Research, Incorporated. At first, we just sold Catalyst Research's batteries. But later we began to manufacture them ourselves. Later on, I came up with an improved design of the lithium battery, which is what we sell today.

That lithium battery turned out to be the way to go. Today, I think every pacemaker in the world uses a lithium battery. Not all of them are my design, but pacemaker companies no longer use the mercury batteries.

Interestingly enough, Mallory wouldn't consider making the battery for us. I described our battery to them, and they said, "Well, what can you do with that? Will it light a flashlight?"

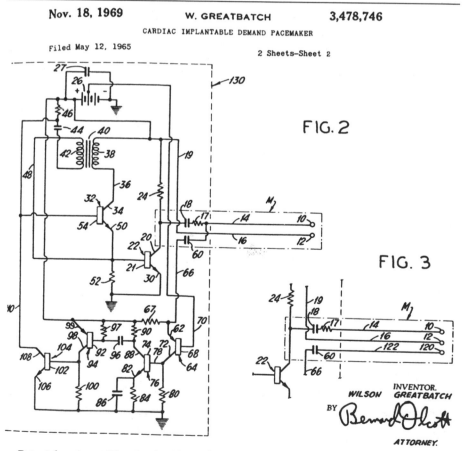

Patent drawings of the circuitry for Wilson Greatbatch's implantable pacemaker (dated November 18, 1969).

"No," I said, "it won't light a flashlight; it won't even work at room temperature, not to mention out in the cold. But at body temperature, it will give you a few microamperes for ten years."

"Well, what can you do with that?," they asked.

"You can run a pacemaker."

"Can you do anything else with it?"

"I don't know."

"Well then, we're not interested."

So, Mallory dropped the idea. This is an example of what I discussed before: small companies versus big companies. Today we're making sixty percent of the world's pacemaker batteries in my factory.

INTERVIEWER: *I've been told that foreign patent filings in some fields now outnumber United States filings at the Patent Office. Is there a creativity crisis of sorts in the United States? Are companies becoming less innovative or inventors less creative?*

GREATBATCH: I think it's evidence that the European countries are catching up with our way of doing things. I could not have invented the pacemaker in Eastern Europe. I don't even think I could have done it in Western Europe. You don't build something like a pacemaker in England, Germany, or France and take it to a local doctor to test it. Companies in Western Europe are not owned by the people who run them; companies are usually owned by financier families who hire a manager to run the company, and it's run for the bottom line. There's not much long-term investment.

But now, Europeans are doing things differently, and more foreign patents are being taken out over here. In the meantime, we're strapping our inventors with things like legal liability and the FDA regulations. While invention is not impossible, it's much more difficult today.

There's also getting to be a philosophy in our educational system, that you can't do important things unless you go with a big outfit or into a profession. In the last fifteen years, there's been a dearth of young people going into research. A lot of young people coming through college today could work in research but go to medical school instead so that they can become doctors and make a lot of money. They don't go to college with the right attitude. It's hard to generate any interest in the things I do, like medical engineering.

INTERVIEWER: *Does an inventor have to be a good businessman, in addition, to be a creative engineer or scientist?*

GREATBATCH: I don't think you need to be a good business administrator to be an inventor. I find that I can handle up to thirty people really well. I'm no good at managing more than thirty, especially when it comes to making people work who don't want to work.

My son, who has an M.B.A., is very good at management, and I've turned the running of this company over to him. We've got three hundred-plus people now, and it's a big operation that requires true business management. My son and I have real arguments sometimes. I say that you can't run a company like this unless you know your engineering. He says that a good manager can manage anything. He prides himself on not having the slightest idea of how the chemistry works inside our batteries. And I guess he's probably right.

> *I figure an inventor is doing well if he has one project out of ten that becomes a success. That one will pay for the other nine.*

But while administration may not be important, I think an inventor has to be a good businessman when it comes to marketing or selling an invention.

An inventor can go three ways with an invention: sell the idea outright, license it to somebody and take a percentage of the profits, or build it himself. I've done all three. Selling an idea is the least satisfactory because you can't really get a good price for something until you've proven what it's worth. By the time you've proven what it's worth, you generally know the field and the products so well that you could do a better job selling it yourself.

INTERVIEWER: *Do you patent your inventions?*

GREATBATCH: I believe very strongly in patents. I now have more than 150 myself. As a company, we believe very strongly in patenting things even though the cost has skyrocketed out of sight. We used to get a United States filing and ten foreign filings for $4,000. Today, it's more than $40,000, so we don't patent as much as we used to. I used to patent every idea we had, but I don't anymore. If it's not going to be used in our immediate future, I don't bother to patent it.

INTERVIEWER: *Where has the jump in rates come from? Is it rising patent fees or rising legal fees or a little bit of both?*

GREATBATCH: It's both. A lot of it is normal inflation. A lot of it is also the super-inflation that has taken place in the legal field. Legal fees have increased faster than the cost of living has increased. I don't think the cost of living has gone up by a factor of ten in the last twenty years, but the cost of patents has.

Even so, they're still worthwhile, and we still patent things. You can license out an idea, but companies change and people change, and soon a new executive comes along and asks, "What are we paying him for? We know how to do all this." If you have a patent you can say, "What you're paying for is claim five, six, and seven on patent number so-and-so. If you think you can get along without it, go ahead and try. We'll see you in court."

We patent inventions for two reasons. The first is not to keep someone else out of the field, but rather to make sure that someone doesn't stop us when we're all tooled-up to start manufacturing a product. We want to have patent coverage on our own processes.

The other reason we get patents is to describe something that we're licensing. There's no better description for a license than a patent, and a license always includes any patent that is derived from the original. That way, your license is not restricted to the seventeen-year time period of a patent. All the original pacemaker patents are expired now, but in many cases where we licensed things out, we've continued to patent improvements, and our package has lasted a lot longer. On the business end of it, I think an entrepreneur or inventor has to understand the business of patenting in order to get the maximum benefit from his inventions.

INTERVIEWER: *You mentioned earlier that you're now working in microbiology and genetic engineering. How did you move from electrical engineering to genetic engineering?*

GREATBATCH: Everything I've done has been a transition from one thing into another. Very rarely has there been a distinct break between projects, and I've only rarely been involved in diverse things. There's always been some connection.

Before I got involved in genetics, I was working in biomass energy conversion. It was a bit of a jump, but because the company was in the battery business, which is really a kind of energy business, I started looking at other kinds of energy, and I got interested in biomass energy conversion.

We found a hybrid poplar tree that will grow more dry material per acre than any other tree or shrub between Hudson Bay and Virginia, planted them, and started working on biomass energy.

Once we planted those trees, I became interested in cloning plants. We wanted trees which were genetically identical to their parents, but when you plant a tree from a normal seed, you have to wait thirty years to find out whether you got what you wanted. Genetic material like seeds and pollen carries only half the normal number of chromosomes and airborne or insect-borne pollen carries the other half, and you never know who the father is.

But if you plant a leaf, a root, or a cutting, that cutting has a full set of chromosomes. That's why you always get a plant with the same color when you plant a cutting from something like an African violet. It's harder to do that with trees, but we did learn how to clone poplar trees successfully, which was a big step.

INTERVIEWER: *Did you just want to grow poplar trees to do some basic experiments on biomass energy, or did you have larger plans?*

GREATBATCH: The plan for our biomass energy conversion program was to grow poplar trees on two fields of fifteen thousand acres each. The fields would be alternately cropped every other year. We planned to chip the trees in the field and burn them in turbogenerators to make electricity for a town of fifty thousand people. The trees would grow back on their own, because when you cut poplar trees off at the base, they grow right back up again from the stump—which is called coppicing.

Of course, turbogenerators are very inefficient in that you put in high-pressure steam and get out low-pressure steam. They only run at about twenty-five percent efficiency, so we planned to take the low-pressure steam and pipe it into stills to make wood alcohol for all the town's cars. We would then take the warm water from the stills, pipe it into town, and heat the town with hot water.

The trick to making trees grow fast enough for this biomass energy project is to fertilize the daylights out of them. We took the sewage sludge out of the town, composted it, and put it back into the trees. We had a complete cycle. We thought that if biomass energy really caught on, whole towns would be energy-independent. It could change all of society—places like New York City and Buffalo and Philadelphia would become obsolete. The whole country would revert to little towns of fifty thousand people scattered thirty miles apart, with about one-quarter of the land between the towns devoted to growing poplar trees. They would be completely energy-independent.

INTERVIEWER: *What happened to your plan?*

GREATBATCH: When the price of oil dropped in 1984, we couldn't grow wood chips profitably anymore. The economics killed it. We also needed a bottom line because I don't take funding from the government for any of our projects. Our bottom line was going to come from selling the composted sewage sludge to sod growers for fertilizer. However, it was going to take the EPA [Environmental Protection Agency] three years to give us a permit to sell the material, so I put the whole thing on the shelf.

> *An art is generally something that can be taught, and I don't think of invention that way. Inventiveness is a characteristic of a person.*

I figure an inventor is doing well if he has one project out of ten that becomes a success. That one will pay for the other nine. I've been lucky because three of my projects have been successes. Biomass energy conversion, however, was one of the seven that didn't work. Even so, I did have a lot of fun working on it.

INTERVIEWER: *You mentioned running cars on wood alcohol. Is that really possible?*

GREATBATCH: You can, but there are some complications. I had an old '67 Dodge pickup truck which I ran on one hundred percent methanol. It ran all right, but it wouldn't start cold. I had to squirt some gas into the carburetor to get it going. When I started that old truck, I had to have a squirt can of gas in one hand and a fire extinguisher in the other. My wife wouldn't ride in the thing.

If you tromped down on the throttle, the engine would die. But if you started slowly and came up to speed, you could get the truck up to fifty-five miles per hour on the highway, and it would run fine. It got about twelve miles per gallon instead of the fifteen miles per gallon it normally got on gas. Or as one fellow said, "About two miles per two-by-four."

The methanol also stripped all the lubrication off the cylinders, so we had to top-lubricate, and we had to add a teaspoon of soybean oil to every gallon of gas. When that truck went by, it smelled like burnt pancakes. But it ran, and we drove it around town for a while and people laughed.

We also planted forty thousand trees and developed a cloning laboratory. From the lab, we sold hybrid poplar trees and cloned raspberries as well. We also composted about two hundred tons of sewage from Akron, the town next to Clarence, where I live. I shoveled the first fifteen tons with my own hands. That's really getting knee-deep in your work. But as Confucius said, "He who chops his own wood is twice warmed."

INTERVIEWER: *When did you make the next jump into genetic engineering?*

GREATBATCH: From the biomass energy project, we had developed a sterile tissue-culture laboratory that we used on our next project. There's a fish called the arctic flounder that swims in water three degrees below freezing in the Arctic Ocean. The fish doesn't freeze because it has certain peptides in its blood which act like an antifreeze. These peptides, and the genes that control them, are well-known. We were approached by a fellow who had wanted to synthesize those genes and put them into orange trees to lower the trees' freezing point. Well, that sounded pretty interesting, so we got involved. It was a disaster, but it did get us into synthesizing genes.

INTERVIEWER: *And is that when you started doing AIDS-related research in microbiology?*

GREATBATCH: One Sunday, I was reading about AIDS research in the paper and thought, My god, some of the things they're trying to do in their research are exactly what we're doing. I called up the guy that we had been doing the fish work with, and he told me that yes, some of the things we were doing could be useful to AIDS research. So, that's when we got into cloning mammalian cells, and that's what we're doing now. It's all connected.

Now, I'm working with other people in molecular biology and actually synthesizing genes in a gene synthesizer—a machine that makes genes to specification. It's an amazing machine. We want to insert the synthesized genes into cells in such a way that they will intercept a retroviral disease. We want to design genes which can block the replication site in a virus. As far as we know, there's only one other group in the world that's approaching retroviral diseases in a similar fashion, and we're doing it a little different than they are. But time will tell.

There's never been a cure or vaccine for any human retroviral disease, but we have some ideas for things that might be able to block replication sites. I'm working with Ed Niles, a professor at SUNY Buffalo. Without him, I wouldn't know where to turn. The project will probably never work. It's tough to try to cure an "incurable" disease. The NIH hasn't been able to do it, and there's no reason why we should be able to do it. But if we don't try, we'll never know.

INTERVIEWER: *Is AIDS the only retroviral disease known right now?*

GREATBATCH: The big one right now is AIDS. I've been putting very little stress on it because it's in the news so much. To avoid publicity, I'd rather say we're just generally working on retroviral diseases.

Another retroviral disease is adult T-cell leukemia. It has much the same effect as AIDS and attacks the immune system of the body, but it is a true cancer. In fact, it's the first true cancer to be associated with a retrovirus. Right now, it's concentrated in Japan.

The cause of the disease was unknown until a few years ago when an American, Robert Gallo, discovered the retrovirus that caused it. The Japanese immediately started to screen for it and found it in a million of their people. It's largely confined to the southwestern part of Japan, and it seems to be found mostly in low-lying areas and isolated islands, which is sort of interesting. For a while it was thought that it might be mosquito-spread, but there's no evidence for that.

It's also begun to appear in New York City, and there's absolutely nothing being done to keep it out of the blood banks. Recently, the Red Cross decided to take thirty thousand blood samples from around the country and screen them for HTLV-1, which is the retrovirus that's associated with adult T-cell leukemia. They're trying to find out if they need a screen, but I think the need is pretty obvious. The Japanese have been screening for three years.

A lot of scientists feel that adult T-cell leukemia could become a bigger problem in the United States than AIDS. It hasn't been a problem yet because it has a twenty-five-year gestation period. So, it's a problem for our children's generation rather than ours. But, right now, AIDS is a tremendous problem.

INTERVIEWER: *I think a lot of people in the United States are under the mis-conception that AIDS is somehow a gay or homosexual disease, a problem that's limited to sexually active gay men.*

GREATBATCH: No, it's not just a homosexual disease. In Africa, it's a heterosexual disease. In the central African country of Rwanda, thirty percent of the young women reporting to the prenatal clinics in the capital city of Kigali are infected with AIDS. Their husbands are bringing it home from prostitutes. So, not only the husband and wife have the disease, but their kids are going to be infected as well. Seventy percent of the prostitutes in Rwanda are infected with AIDS. Some African countries may lose twenty-five percent of their population before this epidemic is through.

In the United States, the next biggest risk group after sexually active gay men is intravenous drug abusers who are infected by sharing needles. But the next group after that, virologists tell me, is sexually active teenage girls who don't use contraceptives. They're going to have to know this.

I've been talking to high school and college groups about AIDS. It's so much worse than anybody realizes. Some researchers say that thirty years can pass before you start to show symptoms of the disease. When you do, you've got a year, and then you're dead. AIDS is another black plague.

INTERVIEWER: *Are you focusing most of your efforts now on AIDS and other retroviral diseases?*

GREATBATCH: My work on this retroviral biology project is going to be long term. If we succeed, it will branch out into all sorts of things. I guess I'm pretty well committed to molecular biology for the near future. It's going to revolutionize both medicine and agriculture.

INTERVIEWER: *What do you think has been the most important invention of the past twenty-five or thirty years?*

GREATBATCH: The pacemaker is, without question, the most useful invention I've done. In general, I think the most useful inventions over the last twenty-five or thirty years have been medical ones: penicillin, the pace-maker, the polio vaccine, sulfa drugs, and things like that. The transistor transcends all of those, but that goes back some forty years.

In the future, molecular biology is going to be the outstanding con-tributor. At present, we're looking into somatic gene therapy. That means we're only changing genes in the nongenetic parts of the body; we're not going to be changing genes in the sperm or ovum. Whatever changes are made will die with the person. I think there's going to be some tremendous advances there.

We're also going to be able to control genetic diseases. We'll probably be able to generate blocking synthesis for a number of diseases.

Eventually, I think we're going to get into gene therapy—an area that people are avoiding now, and rightfully so, because your alterations carry on through the progeny. That's a field that has to be gone into very slowly because there are a lot of terrible implications about it. You could really do a lot of damage.

INTERVIEWER: *Do you think of yourself as an inventor?*

GREATBATCH: I do, but I guess I don't think of myself primarily as an inventor. When people ask me what I am, I say I'm an engineering executive or an entrepreneur. To me, invention is getting patents. Well, I do get patents. I get a lot of them. But that's not primarily what I do. The patents are a means to an end. I'm an entrepreneur. I do make new things, and I make them on a very minimal budget—I do all the things that entrepreneurs do. Inventing is simply a means to an end.

INTERVIEWER: *Medical inventions are very different from inventing a new type of fabric or a better lamp, because people's lives or their health depends on your work. Does that create any special pressures?*

GREATBATCH: It imposes an additional care, but after all, an automobile is in the same category. If you make a mistake in designing a car, you can kill people.

One of the reasons why it's so much harder to make medical inventions is that what you're trying to accomplish is so ethereal. Nobody really understands how the human body works.

Medical doctors are generally not scientists; they're really artists. They look at patients and try to solve their problems and cure them. But the kind of scientific information available to engineers is not usually available to doctors. They often have to work by the seat of their pants and by guesses and by gosh, and they still cure people. It's amazing that they cure people. I have a tremendous respect for them.

When you want to come up with a medical invention, you're in that same situation. You have to proceed by experiment and intuition, and very often the thing you come up with doesn't help very much. Millions of dollars, for example, have been spent trying to build a device that could automatically determine a person's blood pressure. After decades of work, however, there's still nothing as good as a cuff and a stethoscope.

If you want to invent a better carburetor, you can measure the engine performance, and you can come up with some solid information that remains constant. But when you work with a human body, you don't have that kind of information. The fact that you're working in such a variable system presents a major difficulty.

INTERVIEWER: *If doctors are artists, is invention an art as well?*

GREATBATCH: No. Not to me. Inventiveness is a very rational thing. From A, you go to B and you go to C and you go to D, and these steps are all very much spelled out. It's not like painting a picture, where you're being purely creative. A painting is purely creative. A piece of music is purely creative. An inventor doesn't work things out the same way. I think inventiveness is much closer to engineering.

INTERVIEWER: *Is it closer to an art such as woodworking or machining?*

GREATBATCH: I don't think it is. An art is generally something that can be taught, and I don't think of invention that way. Inventiveness is a characteristic of a person. It's responsiveness to curiosity; it's a stick-to-it-iveness, a stubbornness, and an unwillingness to accept other people's opinions, particularly when other people say something is impossible.

MAXIME FAGET

*E*ARLY ON *the morning of May 5, 1961, while Alan Shepard was preparing to become the first American astronaut in space, the California Highway Patrol reported that strange things were going on. Motorists were pulling off the highway and parking on the roadside. What they were stopping for, the CHP later found out, was to listen to Shepard's launch on their AM radios. "Even the simple act of driving overloaded the nervous system," explains Tom Wolfe in his book* The Right Stuff. *"They stopped; they turned up the volume; they were transfixed by the prospect of the lonely volunteer about to be exploded into hash."*

Exploding into hash seemed a likely possibility at the time. Six unmanned tests of the Mercury *space capsule had ended in disaster. Never mind that fourteen others had gone off without a hitch and that a trained chimpanzee had already executed the flight that Shepard was about to embark on. The launch still captured the public imagination.*

There was, however, more to the launch's appeal than just danger. Shepard would be flying faster and higher than any American had ever flown before. And he would be traveling out beyond the earth's atmosphere and into space—a mere fifteen-minute trip.

However, Shepard was not the first man in space. Some three weeks before, Russian cosmonaut Yuri Gagarin became the first man in space aboard the Vostok I. *But that was yet another facet of the* Mercury's *appeal. The Cold War was in full swing, and it was being fought with missiles; not nuclear ones, but manned ones.*

Not only had the Russians put the first man in space, they had also launched the first artificial satellite in 1957. According to the frantic logic of the day, they would be taking over space before the United States had even gotten off the ground. The Space Race was beginning.

More than a quarter century later it's almost hard to recall the irresistible and electric appeal of space. The Space Race has evolved into the Space Program. A simple launch no longer plays to a packed house and motorists parked by the roadside.

It's also hard to underestimate the impact that the Space Race had on American scientists and engineers at the time. Before the first Sputnik satellite went up in 1957, scientists at NACA, the National Advisory Committee for Aeronautics, were concentrating on high-speed flight. Planes like the X-15 were traveling at Mach 6. Someday, it was believed, those planes would simply fly into space—but that was not a pressing issue.

But after Sputnik, getting into space was all-important. When the United States was still getting its first satellite off the ground in 1958, Maxime Faget and a group of his co-workers came out with a groundbreaking paper on manned spaceflight called "Preliminary Studies of Manned Space Satellites, Wingless Configurations: Non-lifting." Faget's radical proposal for spaceflight was not a plane at all. As the title suggested, his craft was wingless. After a rocket had blasted it into space, it would drop back to earth like a stone. While some considered it an insult to aeronautical aesthetics, it was undeniably practical. After three years of work, his conception of wingless spacecraft became the Mercury space capsule.

Any space mission is a group effort involving tremendous teams of people. Over the years the size of the teams has grown, but if it is possible to trace the inspiration and inventiveness behind the United States space program to a single individual, Faget would be a likely source. From 1958 to 1961 he was the chief of the NASA Space Task Group's flight systems division and led the design work behind Project Mercury. He holds patents on everything from the capsule's escape launch system to the astronaut's formfitting couch.

Faget also holds patents on the space shuttle and was responsible for the design work on both the Apollo and the shuttle. He was the director of engineering and development at the Manned Spacecraft Center, which later became the Johnson Space Center, from 1961 to 1981. NASA moved quickly during Faget's first years. Within eight years of the first Mercury flight, astronauts were walking on the moon.

Faget was born in British Honduras in 1921. He received his B.S. from Louisiana State University in 1943. He worked for NACA from 1946 until 1958. He was then with NASA until 1981, when he left to join Eagle Engineering, an aerospace *firm. In 1983 he founded Space Industries, Inc., which is developing an industrial space facility to be used for scientific and industrial experiments in space.*

INTERVIEWER: *At the time the* Mercury *program started, the Air Force was pushing ahead with its X-15 and other X-aircraft and seemed on the verge of flying into space—an approach perhaps more like the space shuttle. If it hadn't been for the Russian successes in space, do you think the United States would have pushed on to orbital flight?*

FAGET: The conventional thinking was that airplanes were going to continue to fly faster and faster until they could get into orbit.

You've probably read about or heard of the aerospace plane. This is a proposed machine that would be able to fly into orbit. It would gradually gain altitude as it accelerated through the atmosphere. I really don't think that's possible in the foreseeable future. A number of things have to be invented—and I'm talking about real inventions, not just progress along known technical lines but real, completely new kinds of things that people haven't even thought of today—before it will be possible to fly an airplane in conventional and more or less horizontal flight until it goes fast enough to be at orbital speed.

> *The* Mercury *capsule was chosen because it was the only practical way to get man into space and stay within the weight constraints of the Atlas booster.*

When *Sputnik* went into space there were a number of people thinking, Well, let's do orbital flight. NACA was largely made up of aeronautical engineers, and I would say that there was a certain amount of resentment among the community to take something as ugly and unappealing, from an aeronautical aesthetics standpoint, as a missile and use that vehicle to fly mankind faster than he'd ever flown before. This attitude was probably strongest among the people who were involved with flight testing and with the test pilots.

INTERVIEWER: *Missiles weren't the right stuff?*

FAGET: Absolutely true. The test pilot community really looked down upon what they called the "guinea pigs" being put in those vehicles.

When I arrived at NACA, right after the end of World War II, we were flying at Mach 1 and Mach 2. It wasn't called NASA then; it was the National Advisory Committee for Aeronautics, a very long name. Several times, my branch held the speed record for man-made instrumented objects. Our business was to mount models on the front end of a rocket and see how fast they would go. We were flying at Mach 15 when NACA was turned into NASA. I was basically working in missiles because that was where very-high-speed flight was happening. But I was also one of a team of four people who did the preliminary planning on the X-15 at NACA.

We were right at the frontier of very-high-speed flight for both airplanes and missiles when *Sputnik* went up. It wasn't long after that before I got half a dozen people together and essentially created the idea of the *Mercury* space capsule.

The *Mercury* capsule was chosen because it was the only practical way to get man into space and stay within the weight constraints of the Atlas booster. It wasn't any more complicated than that. They didn't choose to do the *Mercury* design because they liked me better (laughs) or because they thought I was super smart or anything else. It was just the only way you could get a man into space.

The *Mercury* capsule was a very interesting project. In many ways no original technology was involved, and yet a lot of original thought was in the *Mercury* capsule.

INTERVIEWER: In 1958 your group came out with a paper proposing manned spaceflight—and that was before the United States had even launched a satellite. Was manned spaceflight an old dream of yours?

FAGET: No. Thinking about manned spaceflight and writing that first paper was a rather quick thing. In 1957 I spent much of the summer thinking about suitable configurations for hypersonic flight. All three NACA labs— Langley where I was, Ames in California, and the flight test center at Dryden, which used to be called Muroc—had been looking into what the next project should be after the X-15.

The X-15 was about two or three years from its first flight at that time, but it was well on its way. The previous airplane had gone Mach 3.1 or something like that, and the X-15 was designed to go Mach 6.

People said, "Gee, the least we can do is go twice as fast as the X-15 the next time. That's a good target because if you double that again you could go up to orbital speed." (Laughs.) Kind of a simplistic approach. Of course, doubling and redoubling speed is not that easy in airplane flight. But the people who had any experience at all in high-speed flight, be it in propulsion stability, aerodynamic heating, you name it, were all asked to think about doubling the X-15's speed on the next project.

And then a big convocation or meeting was held at Ames to discuss all the ideas these people had. Various laboratories had favorite ideas. The Lewis Research Center, which was doing propulsion research, also came to this thing with their ideas on propulsion systems. I had been thinking along

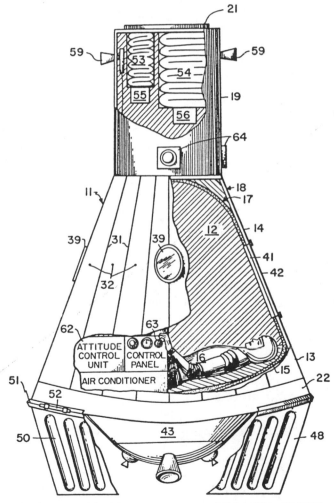

Patent drawing of the Mercury space capsule (dated June 11, 1963).

the lines of a kind of a flying airplane, although it wasn't a conventional-looking plane.

But just before we left for Ames, the *Sputnik* went up. And on the way out there we started talking. "Gosh," some of us said, "why do we want to go Mach 12? Why not just go into orbit?"

Of course, once you get into orbit you don't need wings. You can go as far as you want and stay as long as you want without wings. So wings, I had decided right away, were an unnecessary aspect of orbital flight. What you had to deal with was getting up into orbit and getting back down.

Harvey Allen from the Ames Laboratory was there. Harvey was a very prestigious scientist. Along with several others from NACA, he had been working more closely with the military on high-speed flight. There was interest in the military in flying at orbital speed, so they had been looking at orbital flight. Harvey said, "You don't need wings; just come down

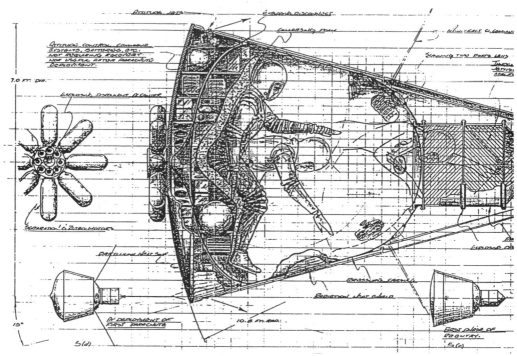

Early prototype drawings of the Mercury *space capsule.*

like a rock or a meteor."

Harvey was a very interesting guy. He'd go out into the desert and find these little meteors and study them because they had melted certain ways. He was trying to decide from the way they melted what kind of aerodynamic heating effects they had on them—thoughts like that.

What he had been promoting was simply the idea that the higher the drag during entry, the lower the heating. A very simple thought: If you've got lower drag, you penetrate to a much lower altitude before you slow down. Since heating is proportional to the density of the air, you get a lot more heating at lower altitudes. So he said, "Go for the drag. Don't go for the wing." A very simple message. I bought it right away.

It might have been Harvey Allen's invention, if you want to call it an invention. The idea of no wing and using drag to reenter was exactly what we did with the *Mercury*.

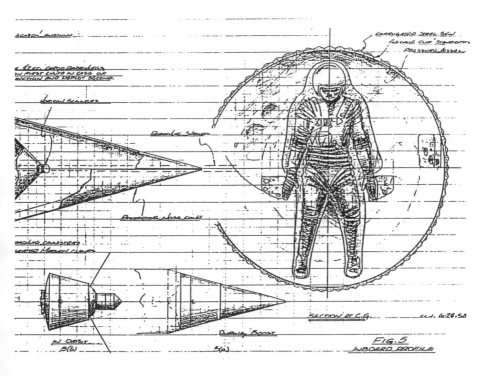

INTERVIEWER: *Have you been surprised at the speed with which manned spaceflight has progressed? Has the progress from* Mercury *to the* Apollo *to the space shuttle surprised you?*

FAGET: Well, we made some very rapid progress from a standing start to the time we had people walking on the moon. That was a very, very short time period. The first artificial satellite was put up by the Russians in 1957; less than twelve years later, in 1969, we had men walking on the moon. Now, that's pretty rapid progress.

But since 1970, the progress hasn't been that rapid really. It's gotten so the space program could almost be classified as a mature industry, although that's not a good description. Call it a maturing technology.

So, we made this tremendous peak in the first twelve years. And then in the seventeen years since, the total amount of progress has been at much more of a plateau.

In general, progress was made very rapidly. We went from a situation where outer space was only something that astronomers looked at or where we'd look at the moon over the water if it was a nice balmy night, to a situation where man could actually travel through space and walk on the moon. The space program has generated a great deal of knowledge about the universe in a relatively short period of time. I don't want to call it anything like the Industrial Revolution, but there has been a great impact on the way people think.

INTERVIEWER: *How did things change for you over the years as NASA became a larger and larger organization? Was it easier to be creative in the early days of the agency?*

FAGET: Shortly after I started working at NACA, I became a branch head, and that branch consisted of maybe twenty people. At that time NACA was strictly a research organization.

However, NACA did have engineering shops, and they could build models. They thought it was very important that you didn't just design an experiment and then put it out on public bid and have somebody else build the model. Think about it: If you're going to create something, you ought to do it yourself as opposed to getting a surrogate mother to have your child or using artificial insemination and that sort of stuff. It really takes all the fun and drive out of it (laughs). That might not be too bad an analogy.

But that's the way we did it. And when you worked for NACA you could be a project engineer in a matter of two to three years. As soon as they thought you could run your own project, they'd let you do it. Probably thirty percent of the technical staff at one time or another were project engineers. So, we had a tremendous number of projects going on at any one time.

We would build models in the shop, put them in the wind tunnel, mount them on top of an airplane, and test them. In my line of business we used to mount them on the front end of a rocket as a means of accelerating them up to fairly high velocities. We were using surplus World War II air-to-air rockets.

> *NACA was a great inspiration.... The management was very proud of the fact that ideas came from the bottom and worked their way up through the organization.*

We tested everything. When McDonnell Aircraft Company was building capsules for the *Mercury* project, the first delivery date they promised us was something like a year and a half after the contract date. An ungodly long time, or so it seemed.

Well, we figured we could make them a lot quicker than that by making boilerplate models ourselves, not perhaps in our back garage, but in NACA's back garage. We started flying boilerplate models of the *Mercury* shape within two to three months of having McDonnell in on the contract date. We also did parachute tests, escape rocket tests, and many other tests.

We also built a *Mercury* space capsule ourselves and put it on top of an Atlas booster. The Air Force was testing Atlases at the time, and we managed to get a surplus one.

In developing the Atlas, the Air Force put a great number into production so that they would have enough rockets to test. They had Atlas As, Bs, Cs, Ds, and so on. I think the first one they actually deployed was an Atlas E. Well, they were going to test some Atlas Cs the following summer, in 1959, and they found out they weren't going to need them all—that they were going to have a couple of surplus ones.

We found out about this in late November, and we got them to agree to let us have one the following August. We didn't have anything planned, but we recognized it as an opportunity to obtain early test data.

INTERVIEWER: *Sort of like borrowing a cup of sugar from your neighbor?*

FAGET: Oh, yes. (Laughs.) We built the test article to fly at full speed, with a complete heat shield, recovery system, stability system, instrumentation, and all that. We got it down to Florida with the idea of flying it in August—we had given ourselves something like eight months. We didn't quite make it. We made it in nine.

INTERVIEWER: *But that was still faster than the year and a half sponsored by McDonnell.*

FAGET: Yes, but you could only do that in the mode in which we were operating. We didn't need drawings. Well, we needed drawings, but we didn't have to take the drawings to the drawing review boards and get holy water sprinkled on them and then put them into some type of manufacturing flow like industry did. We had what you might call an engineering model shop capability. Within nine months of the time we thought of it, we had a horse to ride on.

COMPARISON OF NOSE SHAPES
WEIGHT, 2,000 LB;   DIAMETER, 7 FT

NOSE SHAPE				
$W/C_D A$	57	104	37	33
TOTAL HEAT INPUT, BTU	338,000	414,000	293,000	256,000
MAXIMUM HEATING RATE AT STAG POINT BTU/(SQ FT) (SEC)	125	215	166	64.5
C_{N_α}	.92	.97	.69	.24
C_{L_α}	0	.47	-.71	-1.32
C_{m_α}	-.16	-.09	-.22	-.13

Chart from a paper (ca. 1958) on manned spaceflight by Maxime Faget for NACA.

INTERVIEWER: *Developing or inventing the* Mercury *was unavoidably a group effort in some aspects. Was its success due more to group thoughts or discussions, or did each person come up with independent ideas that were incorporated into the whole?*

FAGET: I think my role in the *Mercury* project was the basic coagulation of ideas. That's certainly what I did—which is really what invention is...if you want to call the *Mercury* capsule an invention.

I will maintain to this day that it would be very difficult to design a more efficient spacecraft to do the job that the *Mercury* had to do other than the final design we came up with.

We had test data on file that one of our guys had done on blunt noses in missiles. So, I suggested a test program: "Why don't we find out what the best of all blunt noses would be?"

We started out with flat surfaces at the front end and went up to hemispheres. You can imagine a cylinder with a hemispheric front end, and you can imagine a cylinder with a flat front end. And, of course, you can vary the radius of curvature for a variety of surfaces between a flat surface and a hemisphere.

We had something like six different spherical radii that we tested for a fixed cylindrical radius. We put them in a heated jet so that we could measure both the heating rate and the drag. We wanted to find the least amount of heating divided by the drag.

It turned out, after doing all this, that the optimum was a one-and-a-half-to-one ratio—the spherical radius was one and a half times the diameter of the cylinder. And that's what we used on the *Mercury*. Why use anything else? That ratio of radii had the least amount of heating per unit of drag, and we had test data to show it.

By very lucky serendipity it also turned out that the heating was almost uniform across the surface, so selecting the material for the heat shield and deciding on its thickness were no longer problems. The problem with heating was that if the heating rate was too high in any one place, there would be some melting. With the one-and-a-half-to-one ratio we had a uniform solution that applied to all hot areas. And since the cone in the back was essentially flying in the wake of the nose during reentry, it stayed cool all the time.

I can tell you right now I don't think you could come up with a shape that could give you less heating per unit of drag than we did on the *Mercury*. I've thought about it a number of times. There isn't anything that would lead you to anything else. So, you can call that an invention, or you can call it a selection. But a knowledgeable selection. I considered it engineering. Just simple, logical engineering.

INTERVIEWER: *What about the escape rocket, which you also have patents on?*

FAGET: The escape rocket was kind of different. Originally we weren't too sure about the Atlas performance.

> *We don't design a prototype so that it won't work. But we do design it with the idea that ... it might fail.*

The Atlas was supposed to be a war missile, and the Air Force quickly figured that they didn't have to be much more than seventy-five percent reliable. They could then make them for half the cost if they were only seventy-five percent reliable, and they could kill more people per buck than if they were ninety percent reliable. Good military thinking. So, we had to have an escape rocket because it was damned difficult to get a launcher that was more than seventy-five percent reliable.

In order to be really sure that we could make it into orbit, in our original paper on manned spaceflight we suggested launching the *Mercury* with a two-and-a-half stage rocket, instead of a one-and-a-half-stage rocket. We planned to use the upper stage of a Polaris missile on top of an Atlas booster to push *Mercury* into orbit. Of course, integrating a Navy Polaris and an Air Force Atlas was going to be a damn tough job to do, and we wanted to avoid this if at all possible. Having that solid rocket stage of the Polaris on top of an Atlas booster meant, in a sense, that we had an escape rocket. We felt comfortable with that.

But when we went to the "bare Atlas"—with no Polaris—Robert Gilruth, who was my boss, said, "You've got to have a way to escape. How are you going to do it?" Coming up with that escape rocket for the *Mercury* was, I think, an invention. "Gosh," I said, "I've got to come up with a way to escape. I've got to have some stable way to get off this thing."

When we were testing experimental models at NASA, we normally put the rockets behind our models and pushed them. That approach was awkward when a model had a lot of wing. The whole thing would become aerodynamically unstable unless you put a huge tail on the booster rocket.

I had a guy working for me who had come up with a way of towing some of our models behind a rocket. His idea was to tow the model behind the rocket with a cable and cant the rocket nozzles outward so that they didn't blast away at the model. We tested his idea and it worked.

Now, for the *Mercury*, the escape rocket obviously wouldn't work on a cable. But it occurred to me that we could provide the propulsion and the stability needed to escape if we made the link between the escape rocket and the capsule a rigid tower instead of a cable.

INTERVIEWER: *The launch period was your biggest worry?*

FAGET: I've always been much more concerned about the launch period than the return-from-orbit period. During reentry, the concern is that the heating on the space capsule will get out of hand and burn up. It's easy, however, to put a lot of margin on the heat protection system.

But during the launch you have these powerful rocket engines firing, and so many things can go wrong. With the possible exception of the parachute landing, it's always impressed me as the most dangerous portion of the flight.

INTERVIEWER: *What worried you about the parachute landing?*

FAGET: I always worried about the parachutes on our space capsules— they're unpredictable. You have to understand that parachutes in a packed condition are a random assembly. No two will ever be packed exactly the same. You go through a packing sequence, and you try to get them exactly alike. But when you consider all the acres of cloth in a big chute, the risers, and the shroud lines, it's never going to come out exactly the same—no matter how hard you try.

Another problem was that the chutes were highly loaded when they first opened. The parachutes are reefed when they first open—a line around the shrouds keeps the chute from opening immediately. Little pyrotechnically operated cutters cut the reefing line, but all things have to work—the packing assembly, the reefing line, and the cutters—for the chute to deploy properly. So, parachutes were a big worry to me. I worked some in that area, and we had a very thorough test program for developing new parachutes.

It was really kind of bad for me. The whole mission would be over, the capsule would be coming down, and people would be cheering. But poor guys like me, who worried about the chute, would be saying, "Don't cheer! Don't cheer yet! Wait until it's in the water!"

In the *Mercury* and *Gemini* capsules we had backup chutes, but the primary chute always worked. We never had to use the backup chute. In *Apollo* we deployed three chutes at once. One time only two of the chutes worked, but we still had an acceptable landing.

Also, the *Apollo* kept getting heavier during its development, and we had to use a bigger chute. But we only had a limited amount of room, so we ended up having to pressure-pack it. What we did was pack the chute and then take these big hydraulic presses to push it into a smaller and smaller shape. We ended up packing those chutes to the density of mahogany. The weight of the chute divided by the packed volume was the same as the density of mahogany.

INTERVIEWER: *You also have a patent on the astronaut's couch. Was that more of an invention like the escape rocket, or was it a piece of engineering?*

FAGET: The couch was somewhat similar to the escape tower. When we were thinking of the estimated eight g's the astronauts would have to withstand during the launch, we made a literature search and found that during World War II the Germans had run human experiments for their fighter pilots to determine how many g's a man could take and still be useful—make decisions, turn switches, and tasks like that. They quickly discovered that the prone position was better by far than seated, but that supine was the best.

So, we did some of those tests and found that, by getting the legs up higher than the heart, plenty of blood got into the thorax and could then be pumped to the head when g's this high were encountered. You didn't want to get the head too high. The other idea was that by having a formfitting couch, you could cradle the soft parts of the body and minimize the distortion and pain of g forces.

INTERVIEWER: *Did the couch idea just come to you or was it a problem that you had been working on for some time?*

FAGET: The couch was an idea that suddenly came to me. In reading a short description of the German experiments, it occurred to me how we could do it. I had read somewhere that if you properly cradle an egg, you can subject it to very high g's, and the inside of the egg doesn't get hurt. Obviously, the inside of the egg is cradled in its container. So, if you treat the body as a fluid mass, like the inside of an egg, you can use a couch to help provide the support for it through hydrostatic pressure because the couch doesn't let it change shape.

Well, I came up with the idea for the couch, we tested it, and fortunately, the tests were very good. When we started the *Mercury* program, we thought the astronauts would only encounter a maximum of eight g's. Instead, for a worst-case abort, it could turn out to be eighteen or nineteen g's, and some people thought that would make the capsule unsafe to fly. Fortunately, we had some heroes waiting in the wings who were willing to test the couch at much higher g's and prove that it was safe to fly in the couch. They rode the couch up to twenty g's.

> *The explosion of the Challenger still goes down in my book as something that should not have happened.*

INTERVIEWER: *With all your patents on the couch, the escape rocket, the* Mercury *and the shuttle, do you think of yourself as an inventor?*

FAGET: I don't really think of myself as an inventor. Certain engineers have the capacity to do things that are needed, but I don't know if that type of invention is capacity or opportunity. I made a number of innovative things as an engineer that never got patented. In the culture of NACA there were very few patents.

I know we patented *Mercury* because management suggested we patent it. We kind of got together and wrote a patent. I put six other names on the patent besides my own because they were working in the group. Interestingly enough, when I first got the idea for manned spaceflight, I had a couple of people help me do the analysis. However, their names are not on the patent. Their names did appear on the paper describing it, and at NACA it was much more important to write a paper. It is kind of ironic that their names aren't on the patent.

INTERVIEWER: *Is there anyone in your background who inspired you to go into space engineering?*

FAGET: Both my brother and I got interested in aeronautical engineering at a fairly early age. He is two years older than I am, and we got to reading about it, and we'd talk about these things. So, at a fairly early age I decided I was going to be an aeronautical engineer.

The other thing that might have affected my life as far as space is concerned is that during the war, I was in the submarine Navy and was, from a mechanical engineering standpoint, absolutely intrigued with some of the very clever things they used on a submarine.

And then NACA was a great inspiration and training ground. The culture there really encouraged people to work on their own. The management was very proud of the fact that ideas came from the bottom and worked their way up through the organization. I guess after I got out of the Navy, I really started practicing engineering in a nice environment.

Beyond the cultural aspects of my background, my father was a physician and discovered a cure for leprosy, and his grandfather is recognized in medical history for finding the diagnosis for yellow fever. It may not sound like any great thing these days, but in those days yellow fever was an epidemic disease, and early diagnosis was important. Tropical-medicine textbooks still refer to the Faget Sign as a diagnosis for yellow fever. So, I guess there's a certain amount of inherited ability to be creative.

I think my father was more of an inspiration for me to excel. You really can't inspire people to be creative; either they're going to do it or they're not going to do it.

INTERVIEWER: *Do you think creativity is a rare talent?*

FAGET: I don't think I understand the process any better than anybody else does. I know that some people come up with ideas that they think are really great but that are absolutely worthless. I guess what I'm trying to tell you is that merely trying to be creative doesn't make you creative. It takes more than a desire to be creative.

INTERVIEWER: *How about deadlines? Do you find that you do your best work under pressure?*

FAGET: If you're talking about engineering problems and coming up with ideas, I've found that I tend to have those ideas more when I'm irritated than when I'm calm and comfortable. I guess there's a certain amount of psychological pressure involved that helps you generate ideas.

INTERVIEWER: When the Russians went into space first, it put a tremendous amount of pressure on NASA. Even testing was a major public event, and you had more than your share of problems. How was it working under that pressure? Was it a plus or minus?

FAGET: We created more of our own pressure than we felt from any external forces. We had a tremendous sense of urgency to do this thing, and we put together a program that was very rich in tests.

No one felt like every test had to be a success, like it is now in NASA. They fly something today and call it a test flight; but—by gosh—if it's a failure, it's terrible.

A test is not supposed to be that way. A test is supposed to find out if something works, not prove that it works. Qualification tests are for that. But a development test is only supposed to find out whether a model works or not or whether we're too close to a boundary condition or some other problem like that.

We hope it works. We don't design a prototype so that it won't work. But we do design it with the idea that something might be overlooked and it might fail. We had something like twenty different tests of the *Mercury* capsule without men, and six or seven of them were failures. Some of them were embarrassing in front of the public, but two or three months later we were going to have another test. We'd have a failure, and then a few months later we'd have a success. If we had a failure, we didn't shut everything down for a couple of years and put our tails between our legs and hide. We just kept going.

Also, by and large, only young people were involved in the *Mercury* program. I was in my late thirties, and I was one of the older guys on the job. So, there wasn't any honor at stake, so to speak. No one had a big, established reputation to protect, and NASA was young. It didn't feel like it had any reputation to protect either.

Overall, the whole *Mercury* program was highly compressed by today's standards. The McDonnell Aircraft Company signed the contract to build the capsule, and they delivered a man-ready capsule—the one that Alan Shepard rode in—in something like twenty-two months. From a standing start, they built a capsule that was ready to fly in less time than it takes to rebuild a couple of big, dumb solid rockets today.

INTERVIEWER: *To my mind, designing or inventing spacecraft is different from almost anything else. When all the tests were done and Alan Shepard was a few seconds from making the first United States spaceflight, what went through your mind? Did you ever wonder if he was really going to make it back?*

FAGET: I wondered about it. I always wondered whether there was going to be an explosion or something. In many ways, I felt more confident about the *Mercury* flights than I did when we first started flying the shuttle. Probably because I was younger.

> *Part of the problem that a space project faces today is that it has become too expensive to make mistakes.*

The other aspect that worried me was that the shuttle did not have an escape system, and I was very much aware of that fact. I really worried about it.

I never worried about solid rockets. They were something I had a great deal of familiarity with; they are simple, reliable, and easy to design, and they could be made rugged without sacrificing hardly any performance. I wasn't much involved with the design of the shuttle rocket because that was done at another center.

I particularly worried about the other propulsion system—the external tank fuel lines through the orbiter and the engines in the orbiter. Although they had been tested numerous times at full duration, the liquid fuel rockets were still not considered completely developed. We were still having problems, and we had some catastrophic failures on the test stand. Every time we fixed a new problem, something else would happen, and we'd say, "Well, that's a new problem." We would fix that, and then we'd wonder, "Is there something else we don't know about that might happen?"

Fortunately, the liquid rockets on the space shuttle never gave us any problems in flight. But they gave us problems on the test stand even after we had started flying. If some of the things had happened in flight that happened on the test stand, we would have lost the bird.

I was particularly concerned about the shuttle program during the first few years. I left NASA after the second shuttle flight, so I got further and further away from the program. I then stopped worrying about it.

INTERVIEWER: There had been so many successful flights of the space shuttle that most people took its safety for granted. No one really believed that something like the Challenger *disaster could really happen.*

FAGET: Well, the explosion of the *Challenger* still goes down in my book as something that should not have happened. I certainly thought that one of these days one of the shuttles would blow up. But I thought it would blow up as a result of something that was a surprise. Instead, it was something that had been thought about and then passed over. It shows that human beings are human beings no matter where you locate them. I'm not trying to criticize anyone by any means. I'm just trying to say that human beings have frailties.

INTERVIEWER: Is the combination of ambitious projects and limited funding stretching people too far at NASA?

FAGET: Space endeavors are handicapped because it requires a tremendous amount of energy and, consequently, a great deal of capital to do anything in space. People at NASA are more frustrated than overstretched.

NASA has the human resources and facilities to carry out several more programs than their present funding level will support. Clearly, they could accomplish more if the cost of space operations was reduced. I know that a great number of people in NASA would like to reduce costs. However, they must contend with government procurement procedures and regulations, which tend to stifle innovation. During NASA's early years, things were more freewheeling.

Strictly from an engineering standpoint, the cost of a spacecraft could be significantly reduced if the cost of launching it was reduced.

Today, launch weight is at a premium, and every effort must be made to keep the weight down. Consequently, many spacecraft systems are highly stressed or otherwise pushed to their practical limit. Doing this safely requires extensive analysis, testing, quality control, and other expensive procedures.

INTERVIEWER: The group process seemed to work very well in the Mercury *program. What kind of changes are necessary to bring NASA back to that level of productivity and creativity?*

FAGET: During the *Mercury* project, we had a fairly tightknit team consisting of only several hundred people. Within this group, there was someone responsible for each aspect of the program. During the *Apollo* and

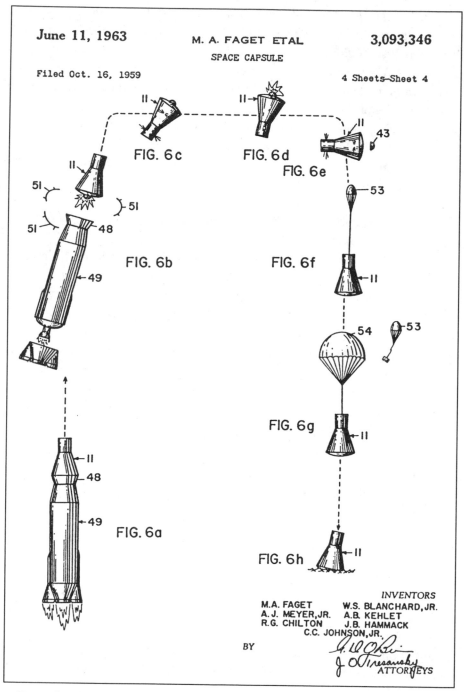

Patent drawings of stages of the Mercury *spacecraft from launch to splashdown (dated June 11, 1963).*

shuttle programs, responsibility was split among three NASA centers. I'm not sure NASA is willing to vest the responsibility of a major program in only one center. The fact is, NASA is planning to involve five centers with significant roles in the space station program.

NASA needs to put the entire program under one outstanding manager. In other words, go for quality not quantity.

Part of the problem that a space project faces today is that it has become too expensive to make mistakes. It takes a couple of billion dollars to design a launch vehicle within the current system. It's very difficult to bet on one person to build that billion-dollar system, but I'd say we've got to find a way to do that. It would be a risk, but there would be a chance of success. Now we use a riskless approach that has no chance of success.

INTERVIEWER: *Does the United States have to be willing to accept more risks to make new advances in spaceflight? Do we have to make more mistakes to continue learning and improving?*

FAGET: During the First World War the airplane underwent one of its most rapid rates of development. Like any good evolutionary process, there were a great number of attempts for improvement. They learned what was wrong as well as what was right. Now, we only allow ourselves to learn what's right; we never allow ourselves to learn what's wrong.

Today we have a completely different standard on the value of human life than they had in the old "scarf and soft helmet" days of World War I. If the plane didn't fly, the test pilot might have been killed. But the flaws were discovered, and progress was made.

It's also too expensive to make mistakes today. Airplanes evolved quickly during the First World War because they could be built in a matter of a few months by just a handful of people.

INTERVIEWER: *Is reducing costs then the key to advances in spaceflight? Do you have any inventions you would like to work on in this area?*

FAGET: I'm working on an industrial space facility (a man-tended space platform) at Space Industries right now. Overall, I think it's more satisfying to work on dynamic things, so I'd like to work on more advanced launch vehicles and projects of that nature. I'd also like to retire, so I have a few conflicts.

I believe engineers ought to try to work on things that are really needed as opposed to things that are just fun to work on. As far as I'm concerned, it's a lot more satisfying to work on things that are really needed.

Having been involved in spaceflight now for thirty years, I think the need at this time is for a better launch capability. We need to find and develop ways that would greatly reduce the cost of launching. I think we in the space business have failed to do that because we haven't used hardheaded engineering principles. We've been much more conscious of high performance than economy. Unfortunately, you need high performance to get into space. You've got to go really fast and make the propellant count. But the value of fuel is very small compared to the value of the weight that arrives in orbit. We've got to start looking at it from that standpoint.

INTERVIEWER: *Do you think the United States should pursue any projects beyond the shuttle?*

FAGET: When NASA built the shuttle, the genesis of that idea lay in the belief that we needed both a space station and a better transportation system than one that depends on parachutes to get back down.

When they got to figuring the costs, it was pretty obvious that NASA was not going to be able to do both at the same time. It was also pretty obvious that there was no point in having a space station without a transportation system.

We did build the transportation system, but we never got around to building the space station. I have a very simple thought about the whole problem. The way you will bring down the cost of transportation is to create the demand for a lot of transportation. And the space station will increase the need to fly up and back.

Of course, the space station needs to be productive—not in terms of absolute hard dollars and cents, but at least in intellectual and other returns. If the project is properly driven, I really think we can get the cost of transportation down.

The shuttle was a great project. Look at the size of the shuttle compared to anything that was flown before—it's a huge machine. But its cost of operation is not that low. We need a second generation shuttle. But to do that I think we're talking about another $5 billion to $10 billion in research and development, and we have to have a justification for that much money.

That justification can only be the need for more transportation or for a better transportation system.

I have a great deal of enthusiasm for the space station, and I hope it will be a success.

Going to Mars and things like that are great ideas, but they can never be accomplished as isolated projects. The infrastructure of the space station and a good transportation system are needed to make such a trip cheaper than it would be as an isolated project. Then we can get past this next hurdle and be on the road to doing real things in space again.

MARVIN CAMRAS

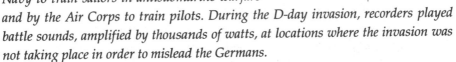

MARVIN CAMRAS *grew up building things. Interested in radio, he built his own crystal sets and a spark transmitter. Interested in telephones, he built his own telephone system to talk with his cousin. So, perhaps it's not surprising that when his cousin wanted an inexpensive way to record his voice to help his singing, Camras also built a wire recorder.*

Camras's recorder, developed in the late 1930s, used a revolutionary magnetic recording head to record symmetrically around the wire. Early versions of his recorders were used by the Navy to train sailors in antisubmarine warfare and by the Air Corps to train pilots. During the D-day invasion, recorders played battle sounds, amplified by thousands of watts, at locations where the invasion was not taking place in order to mislead the Germans.

After the war, Camras began to develop his recording techniques for home use at Armour Research Institute, today Illinois Institute of Technology (IIT) Research Institute. Through a rigorous testing program, Camras developed the first magnetic coatings that are the basis for modern recording tape. His coatings are also used in videotape, computer tape, and floppy disks for personal computers. While experimenting with high-frequency sound, he discovered high-frequency bias, which is used on almost every tape recorder today to improve sound quality.

He holds more than five hundred patents in electrical communications. Throughout the course of his work and research he also developed multi-track tape recording, magnetic sound for motion pictures, videotape recorders, stereophonic sound reproduction, and a variety of improved recording heads.

*Marvin Camras was born in Chicago in 1916. He received his B.S. in 1940
from Armour Institute of Technology and his master's in 1942 from Illinois Institute
of Technology (IIT). In 1978, he received an honorary doctorate from IIT. He spent
most of his career at IIT Research Institute as a senior scientific advisor. He is currently a professor of electrical engineering at IIT. Camras is a fellow of the Institute
of Electrical and Electronics Engineers (IEEE), the Acoustical Society of America,
the American Association for the Advancement of Science (AAAS), and the Society
of Motion Picture and Television Engineers (SMPTE). He was named inventor of
the year in 1979 by the Chicago Patent Law Association. In 1985, he was inducted
into the National Inventors Hall of Fame.*

INTERVIEWER: *When did you first start working on magnetic recording?*
CAMRAS: It was in the 1930s. My cousin, whose name is William
Korzon, used to sing in the bathtub, and he got to thinking that he could
become a great baritone or tenor like some of the Italian singers. He thought
he sounded every bit as good as the singers he heard on the radio, so he
wanted to take singing lessons.

He thought it would be nice to have some kind of disk recorder so that
he could listen to his singing, and he asked me for advice on what kind of
recorder to buy. I was a student in electrical engineering at Armour Institute of Technology, as it was called before it became Illinois Institute of
Technology. Recording in those days was done on records, but I thought it
was a waste of good records to record something only for practice. You
would make a record and probably listen to it once before you threw it out.

About forty years earlier, in 1898, a man named Poulsen* had done
some experiments proving that sounds could be recorded magnetically.
Machines of that kind were not available, but I discussed it with my cousin,
and we thought something like that would be ideal. However, the Poulsen
recorders used magnetic tape, which was awfully expensive, so I thought it
would be very nice if we could make our recordings on wire. The trouble
was that wire would twist and turn as it moved from spool to spool and
distort the magnetic impressions you had put on it.

* Vlademar Poulsen (1869–1942), Danish scientist who did early work in magnetic-wire recording (originally
known as the telegraphphone).

We sort of forgot about the idea, but then one day a thought occurred to me: Why not record symmetrically around the wire? Then it wouldn't matter if the wire turned because the magnetism would be the same all around. I thought of a recording head that could do that. It was different from the Poulsen principle because the Poulsen principle used a stylus, or straight bar, that touched the wire, and the wire would be magnetized only where it touched the stylus.

My idea was to have a magnetic head with a complete magnetic circuit. The wire would pass through the magnetic circuit and through a gap inside the circuit. That air gap would do the recording, and because that air gap surrounded the wire, it would be symmetrical. In other words, I would use the air space instead of a metal stylus to do the recording.

I was very excited about the idea. Of course, you never know if something like that will work or not. My cousin and I went to the flea market on Maxwell Street and bought some motors and various parts and

> *Invention is a one-person thing. This is recognized by the United States Patent Office. They don't issue patents to corporations.*

put something together that would pull the wire past the recording head. I used a lathe at school and made some spools and put together a machine that was the beginning of my wire recorder—and it worked.

INTERVIEWER: *It worked the first time?*

CAMRAS: Well, not exactly. The first time, I whistled "Yankee Doodle" and tried to listen to it on the playback. I could hear it backward when I was rewinding the wire, but when I wound it forward, absolutely nothing was on the wire. I wondered how that could be because I knew there was something on the wire—I had heard it. Then, it occurred to me that the head was magnetized, and while I was rewinding the wire, the head was erasing the recording. So, I demagnetized the head and was able to play the recording forward as well as backward. It was an interesting thing.

All this happened around 1937 or 1938, and my wire recorder attracted a lot of attention from the neighbors. We set it up in my cousin's house, and all kinds of people came by in the evenings. Everyone wanted to hear what

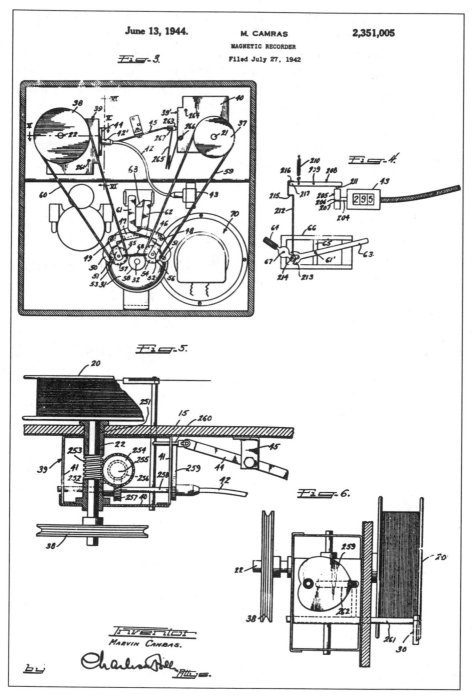

Patent drawings for Marvin Camras's magnetic recorder (dated June 13, 1944).

their voice sounded like. His house was always full of people who were admiring this wonderful thing that could record their voices on a wire.

INTERVIEWER: *What happened to your cousin's singing career?*

CAMRAS: After he heard his singing, he decided he didn't sound like the famous people on the radio, so he gave up.

INTERVIEWER: *Did you start trying to promote your recorder, or did other people come to you?*

CAMRAS: I showed my machine to some professors I knew at Armour, and they suggested I get a job with the Armour Research Foundation after I graduated. I did manage to get a job there. Thomas Poulter, who was there at the time and had connections with the Navy, showed some people in the Navy my machine, and they thought it was wonderful and absolutely what they wanted for dozens of uses. They gave the foundation a contract to start manufacturing the recorders, and we built them right there on the school premises using students for labor.

INTERVIEWER: *What were some of the military uses?*

CAMRAS: Dr. Poulter was interested in using the recorder to help train sailors in antisubmarine warfare. Ships would drop depth charges, which had to be set to explode at the right depth to catch the submarine. To train the crews for that, the Navy had simulated submarine attacks. They used an actual submarine, but not real explosives. The Navy used my wire recorder to record all the commands on the attack vessel as it zeroed in on the location of the submarine. They also recorded the sound of the depth charges when they exploded and all the depth pinging sounds. They used depth pingers, which were the predecessors of sonar in those days, for locating submarines. They would send a high-frequency sound wave down through the water and get a reflected sound back. The recording provided an excellent simulation of the battle, and they could play it over and over again to hear what they did right and wrong.

INTERVIEWER: *How did you make the transition from wire recording to the kind of plastic tapes used today?*

CAMRAS: I started working on other tapes in about 1945. The war seemed to be coming to an end, and people began to get interested in civilian uses for the magnetic recorder. I designed some wire recorders that were suitable for home use. I also thought it would be nice to have stereophonic recording as well as dictation machines that recorded onto a magnetic disk so that one could have instant access to any part of the recording without winding and rewinding.

To do that, I started thinking about coating disks and tapes, so I made some magnetic coatings that I could spread on just like paint. I spread them on paper tapes and disks, and this was the start of my work on magnetic recording tape.

INTERVIEWER: *What was the basic idea behind your invention of magnetic recording tape?*

CAMRAS: It had to do with the magnetic particles in the "paint." The magnetic particles in a recording tape are what's called acicular gamma ferric oxide—gamma Fe_2O_3. Acicular means that the particles are shaped like needles. They're also very, very small—a millionth of a meter, or micron size. I mixed these particles with a lacquer, or varnish, and then coated paper tapes and disks with them. While the coating was still wet, I subjected it to a magnetic field, and all the magnetic particles were aligned in a specific direction—the direction in which the recording would be made. These oriented particles are the basis for modern tapes.

I discovered these particles by testing thousands of different materials and trying to find the best material for magnetic recording.

INTERVIEWER: *How did you get started on stereo sound?*

CAMRAS: One of my original objectives in developing the tape was making it possible to record stereophonically. There had been experiments with stereophonic recording for movies and concert halls, but no one had ever considered it for everyday use in the home.

I thought it would be a wonderful thing for the home, so I built a stereo recorder and took it around to various places. I must have demonstrated it to dozens of manufacturers and record companies.

I demonstrated it once to RCA at the company's New Jersey headquarters. I told them that famous conductors like Arturo Toscanini ought to be recorded in stereo. Even though they weren't going to issue records in stereo or use it for anything, I thought it was important just to preserve it in that form. But they said, "We're not the least interested in anything like that. We think everything is fine just as it is." So, they missed recording some of the old masters.

Many years later when stereo was an established thing in the home, they re-recorded those recordings in what's called pseudostereo, which is not stereo at all. They played the monophonic recording in a room and recorded it with two microphones. They could have had the real thing if they had had some foresight.

INTERVIEWER: *Most people think that stereo simply means having two speakers.*

CAMRAS: Stereo means recording on at least two different channels with microphones that have a different coverage, or pickup. Each microphone hears the sounds a little bit differently—just as a person hears sounds a little differently with each ear. By combining these separate recordings, you get a spread of sound which makes it much more realistic. You have a sense of space, instead of hearing everything come from a hole in the wall—or one loudspeaker, you might say.

A scientific discovery or an invention doesn't have to please anybody. It just has to be in accordance with nature, and it has to work.

INTERVIEWER: *You also developed video-tape recording as well. What's the difference between the two?*

CAMRAS: They both use the same principle. With both audio and visual recordings, you have electrical signals that you record magnetically. When you play back the recordings, you recover the signals.

The difference, however, is that video recording requires frequencies that are three hundred times higher than audio. That's because the upper limit of hearing is considered to be about twenty thousand cycles per second, or twenty kilohertz. The upper limit of a television picture is six thousand kilohertz, or six megahertz, which is three hundred times as high. So, you would have to run a simple tape recorder three hundred times as fast to do video recording. Running a tape three hundred times as fast, however, means you would get only about six seconds of recording from a thirty-minute tape, which wouldn't give you much video.

No one has ever invented anything that gets away from that. To get that high speed, today's videotape recorders have a rotating head. The head rotates at tremendous speed—somewhere on the order of 120 miles per hour—and as the head rotates, it scans the tape. Because the head moves so fast, the tape can move rather slowly.

INTERVIEWER: *You have something like five hundred patents related to magnetic recording. What was your favorite invention?*

CAMRAS: I would say that my most important invention was the tape itself. According to the figures I get, something like $30 billion worth of tape and tape recording equipment is sold every year. That's a very large segment, you might say, of the gross national product. That figure includes audiotapes and videotapes as well as computer tapes and floppy disks, which also use my magnetic coatings. Inventing magnetic tape, however, wasn't especially exciting. It was a lot of drudgery, and it involved testing thousands of samples and setting up equipment and so on.

My most spectacular invention was what's called high-frequency bias. It's used on all audio tape recorders today. By accident, I discovered high-frequency bias in some of my earliest experiments. I was trying to record high frequencies, and I noticed that they did not record at all because the system was incapable of responding to them. On the other hand, the high frequencies I was trying to record—about ten times as high as what the ear can normally hear—seemed to sensitize the tape. When I tried to record the high frequencies, I could hear all sorts of low-frequency sounds that I couldn't hear through normal recording such as the so-called "microphonics" from the vacuum tubes which produced tinkling sounds in the output. I could hear those sounds when I was trying to record the high frequencies, but when I didn't have those high frequencies present, I couldn't hear them.

That made me think that there was something about these high-frequency sounds that was sensitizing the tape to low-frequency sounds. So, I tried to record my voice. I said, "Testing one, two, three, four." Those were the first sounds I ever recorded with high-frequency bias, and they came back so loud and clear that I knew something great had happened. I was very excited about it. It was purely an accident, you might say, because I was looking for something else.

INTERVIEWER: *Do you usually work on your own, or do you prefer to have other people around?*

CAMRAS: I generally work on projects by myself. I discuss them with others, and I attend conventions, but invention is a one-person thing. This is recognized by the United States Patent Office. They don't issue patents to corporations. Patents are only issued to individuals or a small group of individuals, although the rights are often given to the company for whom the inventor works.

INTERVIEWER: *Do you think it's better for an inventor to work independently or with an institution?*

CAMRAS: I spent most of my life working for the Armour Research Foundation and at IIT. All my patents were assigned to the Armour Research Foundation.

Where an inventor should work depends on what he's trying to invent. If you're trying to invent a new spacecraft or something like that, you absolutely need people who know about rocket engines, as well as people who know about computers and controls and so on. An important branch of electronics today is printed circuits, and if you're inventing something sophisticated like a new printed circuit, it's extremely hard to do it all on your own.

On the other hand, there are people like Steve Wozniak and Steven Jobs, who independently started Apple Computer Corporation. They started off very small with some new ideas. If someone wants to work as an individual, there are many things that don't require high-tech science or a group of people. All kinds of inventors are working on things like shoe polishers and can openers and new ways of pouring oil into your car. There must be a hundred patents on different kinds of funnels for putting oil in your car.

INTERVIEWER: *Have you noticed any traits that are common to inventors?*

CAMRAS: Inventors are generally an individualistic lot. They tend to be dissatisfied with what they see around them. Maybe they're dissatisfied with something they're actually working on or with an everyday thing, about which they say, "Gee, this is a very poor way of doing this." At least in my case, when I see something that is clumsy or inelegant, I always wonder why it was made that way. You might say that these first ideas lead to invention.

I think the mentality of an inventor is very close to that of other creative people. I think an inventor is very close to an artist or a composer or a writer. An author may invent characters in a novel, for example, but always with the purpose of creating a certain effect.

INTERVIEWER: *Is having a certain "effect" in mind important to inventing as well? Does it help to have a specific goal in mind, or can an inventor wait for an opportune accident to occur?*

CAMRAS: In most cases, you have to be working on something. Occasionally, an opportune accident happens, but usually you have to be working toward a specific goal. You can't generalize, however, because there are exceptions all the time.

INTERVIEWER: *Did you have any other "accidental" inventions besides high-frequency bias?*

> *A lot of things seem clumsy to me. I like to have things simplified.*

CAMRAS: Offhand, I can't think of anything special. I worked on developing rotating heads for recording video, but I don't think that was an accident. Usually, I have to have some objective in mind.

One difference between inventing and art, in this respect, is that science is answerable only to nature. A scientific discovery or an invention doesn't have to please anybody. It just has to be in accordance with nature, and it has to work. However, if you're an artist, you have to please critics or please a public. If you're writing music, you don't write it only to make sounds; you have to make sounds that will be recognized by people or please people. Of course, there is abstract art, but even abstract art has to give some pleasure to someone else who looks at it.

The results of an invention or a scientific discovery can be startling or pleasing, but you don't have to worry about pleasing people—although it can be an indirect goal. I wanted to make a machine for my cousin so that he could listen to his voice, but the apparatus itself didn't have to be elegant or pleasing to anybody in order to do its work.

INTERVIEWER: *Do you have anything you'd like to invent? Any problems that have been sitting around waiting to be solved?*

CAMRAS: Some things have always seemed clumsy to me. One example is the rotating head on videotape recorders. As I've said, they have to rotate at 120 miles per hour, but I've often thought that sometime in the future we might be able to use a magnetic field to scan the tape—in other words, have a recording head without any moving parts. The magnetic field would move at the high velocity that's required, rather than the recording head moving. That's one possibility I'm interested in. But a lot of things seem clumsy to me. I like to have things simplified.

Another example of complexity is the automobile engine, which has valves and pistons and hundreds of moving parts. It's amazing to me that they all can work together reliably. A more elegant solution is the Wankel engine,* which is a step toward simplification. It eliminates pistons and everything, but it has some problems of its own.

INTERVIEWER: *What sort of inventions have you worked on outside the recording field?*

CAMRAS: When I first worked with stereo recording, I experimented with stereo systems and studied how to place loudspeakers. I have a patented invention—that's long-expired—for loudspeakers that reflects sound off the walls of a room rather than having the sound come directly at people. Some modern systems use that idea. Most of my inventions, however, have been in the recording field. You might say this was my assignment at Armour. It was a field in which a lot of things could be done.

INTERVIEWER: *When you built that first wire recorder for your cousin, did you ever foresee the impact it would have?*

CAMRAS: No, it never occurred to me. At the time, we were doing it just as a hobby and for the sole purpose of recording his voice. We didn't see any special outcome or impact on the world at all. We had made something and it worked and it sounded good and that's all we expected.

INTERVIEWER: *Can anyone be an inventor?*

CAMRAS: I think little children tend to be creative, but the more education you get, the more the inventive spark is educated out of you. In our educational process, you have to conform. Educators don't like you to go off the beaten path. In math, for example, you have to follow the style that someone suggests. After you've gone through more and more education, you conform more and more. You might even say that you're discouraged from inventing. Pretty soon, you are thoroughly cleansed of any possibility of inventing. Of course, different people have different natures. Some people can invent in spite of their education.

---

* Invented by German engineer Felix Wankel, the Wankel engine is an internal-combustion rotary engine that has a rounded triangular rotor functioning as a piston and rotating in a space in the engine and that has only two major moving parts.

Perhaps creativity is a natural ability. You could ask, for example, "Can everyone compose music?" You might suggest that if we want good music, we should throw dollars at it and give money or grants to anyone who wants to try composing music. But I think that would be a waste. A good piece of music can only be composed by someone with natural ability. If you're going to sponsor a bunch of untalented people, in art for example, you're going to get a lot of scribble-scrabble. Many people think this is what's happening to modern art.

INTERVIEWER: *So, lavish funding is not going to turn a routine engineer into an inventor?*

CAMRAS: Right. But many people are eager to receive funds that are available. Our present senator from Illinois thought we ought to have what he called an "inventor in residence" for every educational institution in Illinois, just as there are artists or musicians in residence at conservatories.

But I don't think you can pay someone to sit in an office and think up inventions. It just doesn't work that way. Generally, an inventor needs some objective—and some talent. You don't become an inventor by sitting down and saying, "Okay, today I'm going to be creative." I think being inventive is something that just happens.

INTERVIEWER: *If schools in the United States have a tendency to destroy creativity or to shackle it, what kind of training should we have?*

CAMRAS: Well, you said United States, but I think it's even worse in other countries. I understand, for example, that in European and Latin American countries you're not supposed to use your hands for anything if you're a professor or an educated person. One ridiculous example is a collector of insects. A professor of entomology in those places has an assistant who runs along behind him with a net. When he says, "Catch that fly!" it's done for him even though he's perfectly capable of doing it himself.

That kind of attitude is taking hold in the United States as well. If you're an engineer or a senior person, you're supposed to have your assistants do things for you. I don't subscribe to that at all. Doing something yourself leads you to see what's happening. The farther removed you are from it, the less chance you have of inventing.

But to continue with your question...what can be done? I think an educational system for scientists and engineers should be grounded on principles similar to what you see in the arts. If you're going to be a musician, you don't just go to school and get years and years of music theory without being allowed to touch a musical instrument. You go to a music conservatory where you can practice your instrument as well as have instructors who can help you practice. Music involves a lot of theory. But that's not the main thing. The main thing is performing.

If you're an artist, you go to a place like the Art Institute of Chicago and spend your time painting. If you're an architect, you spend your time at architectural school working on many different models and putting things together and making drawings and actually doing things.

Some people can invent in spite of their education.

But in fields like science and engineering, students simply spend their time writing down all sorts of equations and copying things that the professor or instructor writes out on a blackboard. That's really not the best way to learn science.

In my own teaching, I run an actual experiment, in conjunction with the theory I'm explaining, every time that I have a class. I hook up various things and show the principles of what I'm talking about. The students like it. They'd like it even better if they could do it themselves, but we would need a laboratory to do that. I'm trying to get something like that established here at IIT, but it is very expensive. Look at the people who made the most important advances in science, including Nobel Prize winners. They usually had a hands-on approach.

INTERVIEWER: *A lot of inventors I've talked to dislike being called an inventor, particularly if they're involved in academics.*

CAMRAS: Yes, it's true. There's something about the term inventor. Even in the earliest days, when someone called me an inventor, I felt uncomfortable, mainly because I was a graduate engineer. I felt they should say I was an engineer or a scientist or a physicist. I'm still uncomfortable when people call me an inventor, even though I have invented many things. If anyone asks me, I say I'm a professor. I don't think I've ever said that I'm an inventor. The term inventor has a whole bunch of mixed connotations.

Cartoonists picture inventors as being sort of semi-crazy people who are wrapped up in doing all kinds of impossible things. In movies, an inventor is portrayed as someone who's mixing things up, but doesn't really know what he's doing. Every ten minutes or so, something explodes.

Thomas Edison, for example, is probably one of the greatest inventors who ever lived. But he was not highly regarded by the scientific community of his era. He got a lot of static, you might say, from the so-called scientists of his day who had never invented a thing in their lives. They thought the things he did amounted to misconduct as far as the rules of science were concerned. If they had had the chance, they would have run him out of the scientific organizations of the day.

A lot of the work that Edison did was experimental. He didn't always know the reasons why his experiments worked, but he continued to experiment, and that was not the way the minds of the scientific community worked. They wanted some scientific basis for going to the next step. They claimed he just mixed things together.

Actually, Edison was a very shrewd and intelligent person. He didn't do things as randomly as it seemed. Even though he couldn't write a mathematical equation to explain what was going on, he had some very definite ideas of what he was doing and what he expected to happen.

Edison was also a fairly untutored person. I don't think he even went to high school. He was a self-taught individual, and that went against the grain of people who had spent dozens of years studying scientific and mathematical theories. They were frustrated by the fact that they weren't the ones inventing things. Instead, the great inventions were coming from someone who never even went to school. But instead of thinking that something might be wrong with the type of education they received, they thought there was something wrong with Edison.

INTERVIEWER: *People seem to picture the inventor as an adult-sized version of the sixth-grader with a chemistry set playing around in the basement.*

CAMRAS: I guess maybe you've hit it—that concept of someone playing around and not knowing what he's doing. If you call someone an inventor, you're implying that he's just monkeying around. As a matter of fact, most inventions do fail. An inventor may try hundreds of things that don't work, and that gives most people the impression that he is somewhat crazy.

Reprinted from The Journal of the Acoustical Society of America, Vol. 19, No. 2, 322–325, March, 1947
Copyright 1947 by the American Institute of Physics
Printed in U. S. A.

Recent Developments in Magnetic Recording for Motion Picture Film*

Marvin Camras
Armour Research Foundation, Chicago 16, Illinois
(Received November 29, 1946)

Magnetic recording gives an ideal sound system for use in motion picture work. Equipment for making the record is light, simple, and inexpensive. The material can be edited by "cutting," or by erasing and re-recording. Sound can also be added after the pictures are complete. Conventional projectors are used with the magnetic system. Response comparable to optical recording is obtained with low distortion and noise. Recording heads, circuits, and mechanical drives for use with various systems are described.

THE use of magnetic sound on film for professional work has been discussed in a previous paper,[1] and it has been indicated that these systems are capable of excellent fidelity. For amateur work the standards need not be as high; however the system must be simple, reliable, and inexpensive. Attempts at amateur sound on film by conventional methods have been so expensive, inflexible, and poor in quality that they have never become popular. However, recent work with magnetic tracks on sixteen- and on eight-millimeter films has provided a sound system that is ideal for the home movie photographer.

One of the important developments that makes it possible to record good quality sound at the low film speeds used in sixteen- and eight-millimeter work is a special high coercive magnetic material which can be bonded into the film stock (Fig. 1). Measurements of magnetic properties indicates that a coercive force of 350 and a remanence of 500 or more can be obtained in

the finished product. These characteristics are obtainable with magnetizing fields of 1000 or below; thus the record can be erased quite readily. A number of other high coercive alloys tried were very difficult to erase. The new material has a fine grain size of a micron or less. It is not affected by photographic solutions, so that magnetic sound can be recorded simultaneously with the picture, or can be put on afterwards.

Magnetic tracks can be incorporated into the film in a number of ways. A sound film is shown in the diagram (Fig. 2). It is made by coating a magnetic track 0.045 inch wide and 0.0005 inch thick on the back of ordinary sixteen-millimeter film. We run film through the projector at the standard sound speed of 36 feet per minute.

Although the coating makes the film thicker on one edge than the other, we have experienced no difficulty in reeling. To insure symmetry we could coat the other edge with an equal thickness of "blank" material, or we could put an addi-

Magnetic Recording Material

Particle size	1 micron
Coercive force	350
Remanence	above 500
Magnetizing field	1000

Good bond to film base.
Not harmed by photographic processing solutions.

Fig. 1.

* This paper was recorded on 16-millimeter magnetic sound film prepared as described. It was presented at the Acoustical Society Meeting in Chicago November 15, 1946 by projecting the sound film, which had music, pictures of the slides, of the equipment in operation, and of the author speaking.
[1] M. Camras, "Magnetic sound for motion pictures," presented before the Society of Motion Picture Engineers, October 23, 1946.

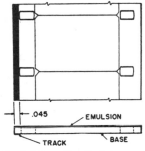

FIG. 2. Standard 16-mm film with single magnetic track.

322

INTERVIEWER: And even after an inventor has learned from those mistakes and come up with a successful invention, people often attribute it to luck. But aren't those mistakes part of the process?

CAMRAS: In physics, for example, there are theoretical physicists and experimental ones. After someone discovers something—say by accident—the theoreticians get busy and write their equations, and they get a good part of the credit for the discovery.

But few discoveries have been made theoretically, although theoretical physicists will deny that. Theoreticians say that everything has been predicted by their theories, but they're a flexible bunch. If they predict something and it's completely wrong or doesn't work, they're not unhappy. They just go along and try some new theory. If you have enough theories, maybe one of them will be correct. Those theories, however, are based on the work of experimental physicists whose input enables theoreticians to start their analyses.

I'm not saying that's bad. The world needs analysts too. But if you're one hundred percent analytical, you'll get nowhere.

Now, in mathematics that's okay. In mathematics you can start with unreal principles and build some very fine science around them. Of course, that science represents an ideal, rather than the real world. It is difficult to analyze real things because they're too complicated, so you simplify reality in order to handle it with mathematics.

When I started to school at IIT in 1936, there was a different approach. Teachers and professors felt that engineers should have an understanding of what they were drawing and designing. Machinery Hall, one of the original buildings on campus, was set up so that students could get some experience in pattern making, foundry work, machine shop, metallurgy, and other practical work.

But even when I started school, there was a movement among some of the more sophisticated professors to eliminate the kind of training we were being given at Machinery Hall. They felt it was the kind of thing that belonged in a trade school, not in college. There's only an essence of truth in that. It does belong in a trade school, but if you're going to be a designer or an engineer, you ought to be able to tell if what you're building will be workable. How can you have any feeling for whether or not your designs are going to be workable if you haven't had any experience?

People don't get much practical training anymore, and as a result we have some engineers designing very absurd things. That hinders progress. I think the training in Japan is more practical, and that's why they've made as much progress as they have—something which Americans and Europeans find discouraging because they like to think they have the best way of doing things.

INTERVIEWER: *Although your developments in the magnetic recording field were invented in the United States, that industry seems to have been taken over by the Japanese. Why do you think that's happened?*

CAMRAS: I think the Japanese people are every bit as intelligent as the people in the United States. They also work hard, and their labor costs are lower. How can we compete with people who are working for half or one-quarter of United States wages? Particularly when they can produce a product which is as good or even superior to ours at a fraction of the price.

> *An inventor may try hundreds of things that don't work, and that gives most people the impression that he is somewhat crazy.*

I know what happened to the tape recording industry in the United States, because Chicago was the center of the industry, and I used to visit the various companies we had licensed. Companies stopped making their own tape recorders when they discovered that they could import tape recorders from Japan and make three times as much profit as they could building their own and dealing with labor, city ordinances, and suppliers. It was easier to have someone else make it.

One by one, these companies started handling Japanese-made products and closing their factories. Of course, it put people here out of work, but the owners made more money than ever before.

At first, the Japanese worked with United States companies in this way because they were not familiar with American markets. But as soon as their products became accepted, they set up their own agencies. Why give a middleman in the United States more money than they were making themselves on the recorders? When they sold a recorder to a supplier here in the United States for $50, the supplier could sell it for $150. He made a profit of $100 while the Japanese who manufactured it were only netting about $25.

So, they set up their own marketing system. Today, Japanese companies like the Sony Corporation of America and Panasonic are recognized distributors in the United States.

INTERVIEWER: *How much of the problem is due to management in the United States? Few companies in the United States are run by men like Bob Sprague of Sprague Electric or Eugene McDonald of Zenith, who knew their businesses from the ground up.*

CAMRAS: I deplore the present system which has M.B.A.'s and people who know little or nothing about the product they are producing running corporations. I think corporations ought to be run by people who have come up from the ranks, who understand a product, and who know what they're doing. Instead, companies are run by people who have the objective of making money through mergers and financial manipulations.

Some Americans don't think that we need to make any products; they think we can have a service economy. "Service is not all that bad," they say. "Let's all service. We can take in each other's wash. You pay me for doing yours and I'll pay you for doing mine and we'll all earn money and live happily together."

Companies today have an acquisition department for one era and a divestiture department for the next. At first, they pat themselves on the back because they're acquiring all kinds of companies. Later, they sell off incompatible products that they didn't understand and didn't know how to make or market. Quite often, they sell them back to the original owners at a tremendous loss.

INTERVIEWER: *Is the problem that business people just don't understand how rapidly technology changes?*

CAMRAS: They don't have any feeling for technology at all because their basic training is in marketing and organization. They don't have a feeling for improving products or developing new ones. They leave that to the lower echelons, and the lower echelons get discouraged when they see all the manipulations going on above them.

INTERVIEWER: *Do you think business has become more glamorous and powerful than inventing and engineering today?*

CAMRAS: In the 1930s, engineers were heroes, and students aspired to be engineers. If you interviewed people in high school and asked them what they would like to be most of all, they usually said engineers.

I think the general public looked up to engineers and considered them the source of various benefits: They improved farming, built bridges, and created all sorts of new things.

But after the war, I guess this attitude faded away, and people decided they would rather make a quick dollar. Students today would rather be Wall Street types or lawyers who redistribute wealth from one group to another. That's okay, but you've got to have something to distribute in the first place.

INTERVIEWER: *Were you always interested in inventing and building things when you were growing up?*

CAMRAS: I was always making things with my hands. In fact, when I was five years old, people would say, "There's Marvin and his inventions!" But even then, the implication was that it was a crazy activity that I shouldn't be doing.

I made a telephone from scratch, for example, and used pieces of coal to make a microphone. Homes were heated with coal in those days, and I ground up some coal, put it between two plates, and made a microphone for the telephone mouthpiece. Coal is used in real telephones too, but I had to make mine out of everyday materials that were at hand. I wired it up and talked with my cousin over a telephone line. And it produced understandable sounds.

I also experimented with batteries, hooking them up different ways. With radios I built crystal sets, and I also used spark coils to build a spark transmitter. In the early days of radio, you had what was called "wireless telegraphy," which sent code by means of a spark transmitter. When I was building my spark transmitters, people were already getting regular radios, and my transmitter interfered with their sets. "That's probably Marvin, running his transmitter," they'd complain.

INTERVIEWER: *But while people thought you were doing something crazy or off the cuff, you clearly had to know what you were doing to build your own telephone or spark transmitter.*

CAMRAS: Some people never think about how things work. They don't understand them, and here's someone doing something they don't understand. They don't always think of it in a derogatory way, but they do think you're different.

I used to think that everyone was fairly similar, but some people just don't seem to have any inventive ability—even if they're not overeducated.

They just think along conventional lines, and it never occurs to them that something could be done differently from the way it's being done. They accept everything. To them, the TV, the Walkman, and other conveniences are just something one can buy; they're just there. Some people never consider how these conveniences originated or if there was ever a time that they didn't exist or how one would go about creating them.

INTERVIEWER: *What do you think the greatest invention of the past fifty or even one hundred years has been?*

Someone once said that Richard Nixon would still be President if it wasn't for tape recorders, so their benefit depends on whether or not you like Nixon.

CAMRAS: I would say that electrical communications has been the most important. Before radio and telephone and satellite communications, there was no long-distance communication except by Pony Express, and it took weeks to find out if something happened. Today everything is instantaneous. Some individuals even carry beepers so that they can be reached anytime, anywhere. There's also television.

Most of these things, however, have been perverted to entertainment. When Edison invented movies, for example, he thought they would be a great way to educate people. But it turned out that their main purpose became entertainment. In their early days, both television and radio were thought of as something that could carry information, but they have since become part of a tremendous entertainment industry.

Even though I know how large the entertainment industry is, I was amazed when I was out in Hollywood a couple of weeks ago. There are acres and acres of studios and thousands of actors and technicians in Hollywood who are there purely to create entertainment. I don't know what the real statistics are, but I think most people spend an average of five hours a day watching television—to say nothing of the time spent listening to the radio or with more traditional forms of entertainment like movies or the theater. We have become a nation of spectators.

INTERVIEWER: *How important was timing to the success of magnetic recording? Was it something people were ready for, or was it a long-standing need?*

CAMRAS: I think there's always been a need for recording. In the old days, you could keep records only in writing. Wouldn't it be interesting to know how the Greeks used to pronounce their language during the time of Plato or Socrates? But nobody knows. We have only a written record.

And, how did Paderewski* sound? Well, some people may still remember him, but how did Mozart sound when he played the piano? There was no way to preserve that. We have written notes and musicians who play them according to instructions. But is that the way Mozart really played his pieces, or did he have a different interpretation?

With a tape recorder you can record actual events, and with videotape you can record pictures as well as sound. It's a more perfect way of preserving performances.

Magnetic recording also has applications in the way data is stored in libraries. Books have been the way to store information. But to really look something up and do intensive research, one might have to spend weeks going through the Library of Congress. Today, the information in books is being transcribed onto computer tapes and computer disks with magnetic recording. Stored magnetically, information can be found almost instantly. It's an improved way to use the knowledge that's been stored in books. It seems to me that magnetic recording has helped our ability to store and use information in many, many ways. It's preserved information and made it more available—which, you might say, is the art of information itself.

INTERVIEWER: *Do you have any regrets about the way your magnetic recording techniques have been put to use? Has its importance as a historical record or an educational tool been compromised by its use for entertainment?*

CAMRAS: I've never thought much about it. People who want to use it can use it for whatever they want: listening to their singing voice to tell if they rate as opera stars or simply enjoying good music from a tape recording.

Someone once said that Richard Nixon would still be President if it wasn't for tape recorders, so their benefit depends on whether or not you like Nixon. (Laughs.) I'm glad tape recording is not a harmful activity because many inventions end up being used that way. The only possible use for some inventions, like weapons, is harming someone. I don't have any feelings for or against the way tape recording has been put to use. Overall, I think it has been beneficial. It's there for people to use.

---

* Ignacy Paderewski (1860–1941), Polish pianist and statesman.

BOB GUNDLACH

*L*IKE MOST *great inventions, xerography works so well that it's usually taken for granted. Even though the first fully automated photocopier—the Haloid Xerox 914—wasn't available until 1960, it's almost impossible to imagine an office or library today without one. The Haloid Company's xerographic copier was so successful that the company changed its name to Xerox. With exclusive patent rights, Xerox copiers were the only plain-paper copiers on the market for almost fifteen years. Not only did the patent monopoly turn Xerox into one of the world's largest corporations, it also turned the name Xerox into a generic term for photocopiers of all sorts.*

Xerography, derived from the Greek xer *(dry) and* graphos *(written), is really a photographic system based on physics instead of chemistry. While film photography depends on the reaction of chemicals to light, xerography depends on the attraction of charged particles.*

Inside every photocopier is a light-sensitive surface known as a photoreceptor. Usually cylindrical or drum-shaped, the photoreceptor can hold an electric charge—but only in the dark. When exposed to light, or the reflection from the white of a printed page, the drum loses its charge. In the case of a printed page, however, the drum will not lose its charge where the page is covered with ink. The result is an exact mirror image of the original page, recorded in a pattern of electric charges.

To produce a printed copy, the drum is then sprinkled with powdered ink carrying an electric charge of its own. The ink attaches itself to the charged pattern on the drum, and when the drum is rolled across a piece of paper, the "copy" is transferred to the paper. Finally, a device known as a fuser makes the copy permanent by melting the ink and fusing it to the page. Copies take only seconds, but it is an amazingly complex process.

"There almost seems to be a kind of black magic going on inside," says Xerox's Bob Gundlach. At last count, Gundlach had 133 patents in xerography—a fact that, by inference, makes him something of a wizard in the field.

Bob Gundlach joined the Haloid Company—later Xerox—in 1952 when the company was developing its first machines from inventor Chester Carlson's original patents on xerography. While the first Xerox machines were a triumph for Carlson, who had waited twenty-two years for his invention of xerography to be put into use, Haloid's first flat-plate copiers were cumbersome. Making a single copy took as long as four minutes.

Simplification was the key to success, and while Carlson and others were busy designing the company's first automated copier (the 914), Gundlach began working on the machines that followed it. Within a year, Gundlach had three patentable ideas, one of which was for the multiple-copy process. Another idea enabled the copier to reproduce solid areas; early Xerox machines copied only the outlines of solid figures, a technique which worked fine for print, but not so well for solid figures and shapes. It was a productive year for a twenty-five-year-old physicist who didn't think of himself as an inventor.

Eight years after Gundlach arrived, Haloid unveiled the 914. It could make a single copy in just under a minute. Ten years later, however, a $10,000 investment in Haloid stock was worth one million dollars. Today, Xerox copiers can produce 120 copies a minute.

Bob Gundlach was born in Buffalo, New York, and he graduated from the State University of New York at Buffalo (SUNY Buffalo) with a B.S. in physics. In 1975, he became Xerox's first research fellow, a position for which he wrote the specifications. In 1986, he asked for partial retirement from Xerox to work on his own inventions, among them such projects as a snowmaking system for ski resorts and a new type of backpack. His retirement, however, has been largely theoretical, and Gundlach spends much of his time heading Xerox's EXITE Lab, an experimental research lab created by the company to Gundlach's specifications, in East Rochester, New York.

INTERVIEWER: *Did you grow up thinking you would be an inventor?*

GUNDLACH: I have five aunts, one of whom is a palmist. When I was twelve years old, she read my palm and said, "Oh, Bobby, you're going to be an inventor." I didn't really take it too seriously at the time, but later I wondered if she could have planted the idea or perhaps perceived something in me that I wasn't aware of myself.

Actually, I grew up thinking I was going to be a chemist. My father was a cosmetic chemist and the inventor of Wildroot Cream Oil. He worked for a little company, the Wildroot Company, in Buffalo, New York, and I thought I was going to be a chemist like my father.

My favorite invention is always the next one.

But then I learned that you had to memorize too much to be a chemist in those days. So, I went into physics instead. Physics is very logical, and I like logical processes and figuring things out. I always liked puzzles.

I guess inventing is a lot like solving puzzles. You look at a challenge in as many different ways as you can. You look at it backward, you look at it upside down, you try it big, and you try it small. Eventually, things begin to happen in your mind as often as they happen in your hands.

INTERVIEWER: *Did you start studying physics with the plan to become an inventor?*

GUNDLACH: No, even when I first came to the Haloid Company, I didn't really think of myself as an inventor. I had been trained as a scientist and physicist. I had gone to the University of Buffalo [SUNY Buffalo] and received a bachelor's degree in physics and studied for two years in the master's program. I passed both my master's exam and my language exam before joining Haloid, but I went to work without finishing my master's thesis. One thing led to another, and I never did finish it. After a while, the thesis just didn't seem important any more.

Things began happening almost immediately when I went to Haloid. Within three weeks I had one or two inventions, and within the first year I had three patentable ideas.

The invention that really turned me on, the one that really inspired me and gave me enough confidence to say that I was an inventor, was the one that also excited Chester Carlson, the inventor of xerography.

I had been assigned to work on a simplification of our flat-plate reproduction equipment. It was on the market, but it took three to four minutes for an operator to make each image. Luckily, it wasn't just a copier, but made masters for offset printing from which you could then print 100 to 150 copies per minute.

You operated it by placing the xerographic plate on top of a tray of developer. You put developer in the bottom of the tray, and then you tipped the tray so that the developer would slide, roll, and bounce down over the xerographic plate. To get a really good copy, however, we found that you had to tip it in both directions. If you tipped it in just one direction, you got a very directional effect. And to get the best quality you had to tip it four times.

Haloid was trying to mechanize it, and our engineers had designed some fancy gears that would reciprocate the motion and tip the tray in both directions. But building those gears and adjusting the motion of the tray were so complex that the machine was too costly.

I thought I could simplify the whole thing if I could just make it rotate one way. I put a simple little baffle at one end of the tray so that it held the developer behind it and spilled it out only when the tray was rotated to a vertical position. Once you tipped or rotated the tray past vertical, all the developer rolled down the plate surface to the opposite end, and you just kept the tray moving in the same direction. Eventually, the developer rolled back down the tray again and behind the baffle. After one complete rotation, it was all back where it had started, but it had given the copy two-pass development in two different directions. A very simple invention.

One day Chet Carlson came by to check out my idea. When he looked at it, he said, "Bob, you're an inventor." Doubling my salary couldn't have given me a better feeling that day. Chet Carlson had said I was an inventor.

His comments on my first thoughts were a real inspiration. Of course, the xerographic method itself was also inspirational. Having a photographic method based on physics always seemed like a great game.

INTERVIEWER: *How close was Haloid to putting its first copier on the market when you joined the company?*

GUNDLACH: They had just begun the research on the first Xerox machine in 1949, and they put out their first product in 1950. That first product, however, didn't do much. It was really a contact-exposure device that

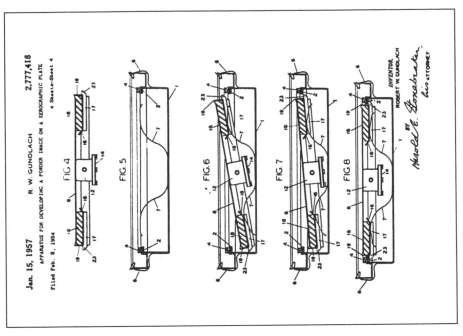

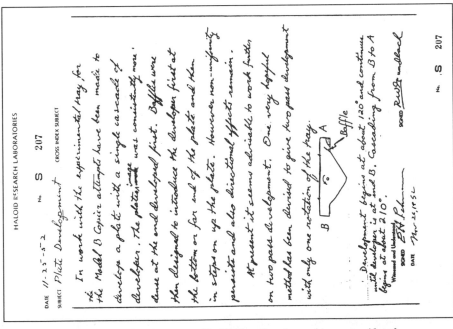

Patent drawings (dated January 15, 1957) and early working notes (dated November 25, 1952) by Bob Gundlach for the two-pass xerographic plate development process.

depended on transmitting light through the paper to make a copy. That immediately limited originals to one-sided copies. Secondly, if you tried to copy anything from carbon copies—which were on onionskin at the time—the transmissivity of light varied so much that the contrast was very low. As a result, the copy was almost unreadable.

It didn't take long for the company to change the first copier and add a camera to it. Instead of passing light through the paper, that camera-equipped machine worked like a present-day Xerox machine—by reflecting the light off the paper.

I think desperation is the mother of invention.

When you reflect light from a copy, it really goes through the ink twice: once on its way up to the surface of the paper through the ink and then back through the ink again as the light is reflected off the paper. By passing the light through the ink twice you really get a much better contrast, a greater difference between light and dark areas. In a contact-exposure device, light only goes through the ink once.

The camera was a big step forward. Xerography is inherently a very high-resolution, high-contrast process, and the use of a camera made it even more so. The high contrast tends to drive all dark grays black and make all light grays white, so it cleans up the background, removing fingerprint smudges and stains. At the same time, it also makes ink signatures darker. It's not just an advertising gimmick when we say that the copy is better than the original; it really can be more readable.

INTERVIEWER: *Did the speed with which xerography caught on surprise you?*

GUNDLACH: I think I can honestly say that it didn't. I had been with the company for only six months when John Dessauer, the company's director of research and development, asked me to write my views on xerography. I don't know where the paper is now—it's buried somewhere in my files—but I can remember saying that xerography was going to become a major industry.

But I, along with Chet Carlson, was frustrated at how long it took to put an automated copier on the market. For the first ten years the bread and butter of xerography was our flat-plate equipment. But it wasn't until we got the first automated copier, the 914, on the market that the stock—and the company's profits—really took off. I guess if I had known how fast the stock was going to go up, I would have invested in it more heavily. I didn't even know how to buy stock at the time.

INTERVIEWER: *Xerography has come a long way from the first flat-plate equipment. Did you ever wonder if it was really possible to bring the process as far as it has come today?*

GUNDLACH: No, I never doubted that we would be able to make it as good as we have today. Once we even had a group of people at Xerox assigned to determine the absolute limits of xerography. When they talked to me I said, "There aren't any. If you show me a limit, I'll invent a way around it." It was fun doing that, and I kept showing them. Every time they thought they had an absolute limit, I invented a way around it. A lot of people, however, say that if management had really understood the process better in the beginning—and all the difficulties involved in developing it— they wouldn't have invested in it. It's more complicated than they thought. There almost seems to be a kind of black magic going on inside that box.

But inventors have to be optimists. They're always gambling and taking chances. Many things can go wrong, but I tend to focus on the things that can go right.

As a physicist, I was also always fairly confident that we could do what we're doing today—that we could actually make xerography into a viable printing process and compete with offset markets. I guess I probably didn't appreciate how good you had to be to compete with offset printers.

At Xerox, when we first got our Xerox 9200, which makes 120 copies a minute, we installed it in our print shop. The print shop was run by a woman named Melvina Schmidt, who had been there for years. She didn't want to use it at first. In fact, she kept using the offset printers instead.

One day, some of the corporate people stopped by and asked, "Why don't you use this?"

And she said, "It isn't reliable."

And they asked, "Well, how often does your offset equipment break down?

"Never."

"Never?"

And she said, "Never. They occasionally come in and tweak the rollers and make sure the bearings are right. They replace something that's been worn or a spring that's been stretched, but these machines don't break down." (Laughs.)

And that's what we had to do with xerography. For the past two decades, I've been able to say that in the last three or four years, I've seen as big an improvement in the quality and reliability of xerography as I had in all the time before that. And I still feel that way today. I now see quality that is truly equal to offset printing—halftones as well as text and alphanumeric characters, color as well as black and white. All this has been done in xerography through better controls, through microprocessors, through monitoring exposure and developers, and through better development. A

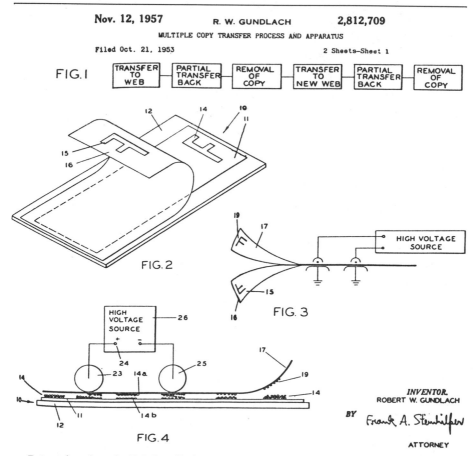

Patent drawings for Bob Gundlach's xerographic multiple-copy transfer process (dated November 12, 1957).

tremendous amount of physics is going on in the xerographic process, and the more you know about it, the more you can control it.

INTERVIEWER: *It looks very simple, but it is a very complex process, isn't it?*

GUNDLACH: I maintain that you need three million events for every square centimeter of developed image. You have to provide for that in the machines. You have to provide for toner particles to be brought in and out and made available to the image, on the order of three million events per square centimeter. That's about the size of my small fingernail. Three million events for every one of those. And we do it at two or three pages per second, and about six hundred square centimeters are on one standard-size page. Six hundred. But it happens. And, you know, the quality and reliability are still growing.

INTERVIEWER: *When we started, you mentioned your work on the flat-plate equipment. What were some of your other inventions with xerography?*

GUNDLACH: When we started to get into patent litigation, our attorneys asked me to break down my inventions into their different areas. I was surprised to find that I had about twenty-five inventions in development systems. I always felt that the development process was where the real opportunity was for improving quality and simplifying the machine. But I also had about five inventions on fusing systems—fusing the toner to paper, that is—and five or six on cleaning systems and quite a number on optical systems such as the first strip lens, which has now evolved into the selfoc optics, or strip lens, system. The selfoc system really makes the whole machine more compact and makes small, low-volume copiers possible. It eliminates that long focal length and all the space required for regular lenses. And I guess I have a number of patents on charging systems too.

INTERVIEWER: *What do you consider some of your most important inventions in xerography?*

GUNDLACH: I think one of them was developing a way of getting solid areas to reproduce. I don't know if you've seen some of the early images made by Xerox copiers, but they only showed the edges of characters. For typewriter-size characters that worked fine. But with a normal developer tray, the larger, solid areas came out with only their edges developed.

The reason that happened is that the xerographic process develops fields of charge, and fields are a function of differences in electric potential. The potential, of course, is the same over a solid area. The only place you have a difference is at the edges. It's sort of like a ball sitting on top of a mesa or a flat table. In the center of the table, it won't roll anywhere by itself because no unbalanced forces are acting on it. But at the edges of the table, there's an unbalanced force acting on the ball, and it can quite easily roll off the table.

I solved this problem by developing a close-spaced electrode that allowed the developer to flow through the space between the electrode and the plate but still drew out lines of force so that you got strong fields everywhere on the charged plate, not just at the edges of charge.

That was my first patent. It's hanging on the wall with my hundredth. And it was brought to the market about nine months after the invention. That's somewhat of a record in a large corporation.

In the first place, it was a rather small piece of hardware. It wasn't terribly complicated. We also didn't have to do the several hundred thousand print qualifying tests that we have to do today on any new process being incorporated into a high-volume machine.

These little parts were built for—maybe I shouldn't tell this—$18 a piece and rented for $10 a month, or $120 per year. Each one. Several thousand of them were on the market after the first year. So, that paid for my next hundred inventions as well as my salary for the next twenty to twenty-five years.

That might seem as though we were gouging the public, but it was one of the few inventions that made it to the marketplace and had a high return on investment. It may not have cost much to build, but it also had to pay for all the research costs on inventions that didn't make it to the market. If ten percent make it to the marketplace, I think you're doing very well. But that's somewhat discouraging to small inventors who haven't got a lot of resources behind them.

INTERVIEWER: *How many patents do you have outside the field of xerography?*

GUNDLACH: All but three of my patents are related to xerography. But I would trade my 133 patents on xerography for Chester Carlson's one patent—if his patent hadn't expired. Two of my patents are on a shadowless sundial. It's not very useful, but it's a nice hobby to work on, and it's been fun. I have some concepts on a backpack as well, but they aren't patented yet because they're tied up with attorneys while we decide who owns the rights to them.

I also have a patent on a snowmaking processes. It's ahead of its time, but its time is coming soon. My technique is to make ice, not snow, and then convert the ice to snow by shaving it with snow-grooming equipment. I've done the calculations and experiments to confirm the amount of energy required to shave ice to snow, and it's about one-tenth the energy consumed in the traditional refrigeration processes used today in making snow. I also think my technique can produce more snow per night than traditional methods.

At first, I thought of myself as an eager young physicist. But then I discovered I was accident-prone.

I've actually licensed a snowmaking corporation, Ratnik, Incorporated, that's only three miles from my house, to work with it. But the truth is that the owner has invested in the commercial conventional process, and I think he sees my system as a threat. Or at least he doesn't have a strong incentive to do the research and further development that will make this idea work. Snow groomers have improved so fast that today they can chop up boilerplate ice, or blue ice as we skiers call it, and turn it into fairly flaky powder. To make my system marketable, I need somebody to invest in making groomers work better on solid ice.

But I haven't really had the time to pursue my process with snow-grooming companies. I've written to them and said I have a snowmaking process. But they read the letter and immediately write back, "We're not in the snowmaking business; we're in the snow-grooming business." So, they really don't understand that they have a unique opportunity that the snowmaking companies don't.

INTERVIEWER: *What's your favorite invention?*

GUNDLACH: On the occasion of my one hundredth patent, Xerox put on a nice, big party for me and invited all my friends. One of them asked me that question, and I have always been grateful that he asked because it made me think about it.

I realized that my favorite invention is always the next one. I really don't get as excited about what I've already accomplished as what I'm doing and what I'm working on. I think most creative people, probably most productive people, are more interested in what they're doing than what they have done. I think it's important that you look to the future and that you're excited about what you're up to—not what laurels you can sit on.

INTERVIEWER: *Is there any particular situation in which you find you are at your most creative? Late at night or early in the morning, for example?*

GUNDLACH: I thought of my last invention while I was in the shower. Sometimes I think of them when I'm shaving. But most of my inventions come when I'm driving to and from work: I'm gearing up for the day, thinking about what I want to do and the projects I'm getting into. On the way home, I'm thinking about something I've been stuck on or some problem that's reached a barrier; I'm struggling to figure out a way to get around it and thinking of alternative ways to look at it.

INTERVIEWER: *Do you usually work alone, or do you find it helpful to discuss problems and ideas with others?*

GUNDLACH: I haven't had any good inventions in brainstorming with other people.

A few weeks ago, however, I was skiing in Utah with one of the scientists from our California lab, PARC Xerox, and together we came up with an idea. He presented me with a challenge, and I thought we could use a combination of one of his processes and one of mine and have a good solution to the problem. We're going to write a joint invention proposal for Xerox. Things like that often happen.

But I haven't had any really patentable ideas in formal brainstorming sessions. Sometimes brainstorming can help round out an understanding of a problem or present new opportunities, but I have to think about the problem afterwards, alone usually, before I'll come up with something. Other times, I have to go off and try some of the obvious ideas and fail. After I have a few failures, I get motivated, or perhaps smarter, and come up with some useful ideas.

INTERVIEWER: *Do you like to move on to new challenges once you've thought of an invention, or do you like to tinker with old inventions and improve them?*

GUNDLACH: I'm the latter type. I can never sit on an invention. I keep improving it. For example, I invented an electrostatic generator that can be made with five dollars' worth of equipment and that produces twenty thousand volts. Every time I worked on it I found ways to simplify it. It was

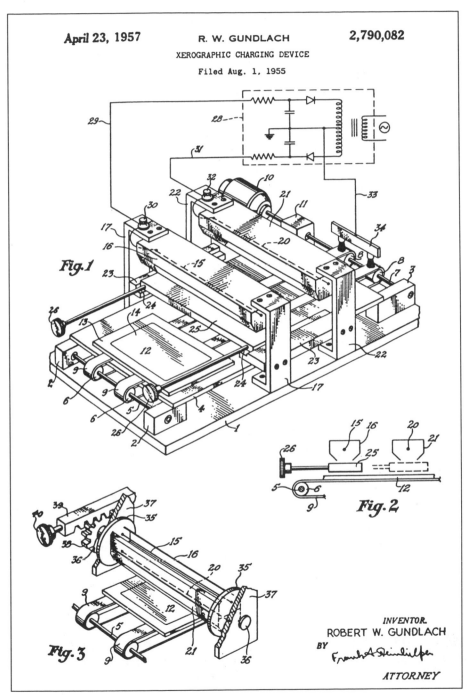

Patent drawings for Bob Gundlach's xerographic charging device (dated April 23, 1957).

thrilling to me to keep improving it and finding ways to make it simpler and more reliable.

That's the kind of perseverance that I think most inventors need. Many ideas don't work at first. I think failures are an important step in the process of invention for me. In fact, half the inventions that don't come from accidents probably come from failures (laughs). After I fail, I get even more motivated to prove that an idea can work. Or I learn from it and come up with a still better idea.

> *Good inventions are so obvious in retrospect that people say, "Why should he get a patent on that?"*

INTERVIEWER: *Is necessity the mother of invention?*

GUNDLACH: I think desperation is the mother of invention. For several years, I worked on a spirit-duplicating process that involved trying to use toner as glue. Spirit-duplicating is better known as the Ditto process. I think I developed a lot of my philosophy toward research and invention while working on that project.

The toner we use in xerography can actually be made sticky if you soften it or catch it at the right point in its melting cycle. You may have even seen it in xerographic copies yourself. Sometimes when you put a copy in a plastic file or a vinyl folder, the image will actually stick to it.

We had a process where we were trying to make use of this stickiness to transfer dye for making copies. It worked, but only for certain batches of these spirit-duplicating masters.

The problem is that the dye is actually contained in a wax, and it's a tough challenge to glue something to wax. But through that, I learned that it isn't just necessity that's the mother of invention, it's desperation that's the mother of invention. You can get pretty desperate when you try to glue something to wax.

INTERVIEWER: *Do you find that deadlines and pressure are helpful when it comes to invention?*

GUNDLACH: I think they can be helpful, but they can also be intimidating and constraining. If you know you've got a deadline, you might take fewer risks so that you can come up with something that works, even though it might not be as good as you can do. And yet, I put deadlines on myself sometimes to motivate me to think about a problem. I also have an internal pressure that keeps me going. I know people will be asking me what's new and that I have to be ready to show them something exciting. I get uncomfortable if I haven't invented something in the last month or two.

INTERVIEWER: *Are some people one-invention types?*

GUNDLACH: I've seen it happen, and I don't understand it. I really don't. Unless it's been an accident—a once-in-a-lifetime accident.

INTERVIEWER: *Do you think of yourself as an inventor or an engineer?*

GUNDLACH: I've come to think of myself as an inventor. At first, I thought of myself as an eager young physicist. But then I discovered I was accident-prone.

Also, although I manage this lab, the EXITE lab, I by far prefer to be thought of as an inventor rather than as a manager. The company offered me a manager's job twenty years ago, but I turned it down because I felt that would be a misuse of my time.

I'm excited about managing this group, partly because they're self-managing people who are self-driven and self-motivated and partly because I believe in this concept of having an autonomous lab which isn't driven by corporate policy to develop particular products.

I interpret the charter of this whole lab as the charter of a research fellow. I was Xerox's first research fellow, and I helped write the specifications for the position. It's agreed that people here at the lab should *not* be assigned to any particular project. Instead, they should work on those projects that they feel are important to the corporation. We fill gaps or explore new opportunities in imaging.

INTERVIEWER: *Can you invent things in your head? Or is hands-on experience in the lab also important?*

GUNDLACH: My friend Lew Walkup at Battelle [Memorial Institute] used to say that you should be able to invent in your mind and that you're admitting failure if you have to go into the laboratory. But I find that there's a synergy between the hand and the mind which is invaluable to me.

When Xerox offered me a dual-ladder role, first as a principal scientist and then as a senior research fellow, I gladly accepted those honors and the office with wooden furniture and a rug and the stock options, with the provision that they wouldn't take away any of my lab space. I wouldn't have given up the lab space to accept those honors or the stock options. The lab

XEROX CORPORATION

DATE Mar 22, 965 SUBJECT Induction Imaging   PROJECT No.

Because magnetic brush development is capable of extremely rapid response to fields of very short duration, we have demonstrated its use with conventional interposition development. We have, in fact, compared results by this technique with those of induction imaging at various relative humidities. Interposition development is done by exposing (Se µ Se plate) to a negative original, taping one end of paper to the plate and pressing it into contact using a biased (+360 volts) magnetic brush as shown:

The same brush is then moved over to the other half of the plate, which was exposed to a positive image, and moved from left to right with a bias of +120 volts while the paper is lifted from the xerographic plate, to give develop the induced image. The next page shows samples by both methods at various humidities.

WITNESSED AND UNDERSTOOD
SIGNED _Peter M. Keenan_   WORK AND RECORD
                                  SIGNED _R. Gundlach_
DATE March 26, 1965   DATE Mar 22, 1965

Bob Gundlach's project notes (dated March 22, 1965) on xerographic induction imaging.

space and the opportunity to get toner under my fingernails, to try out processes, and to do sloppy experiments was much more important to me. In
fact, I find that the sloppy experiments lead to invention more often than
methodical and quantitative ones.

In my own work I don't go for numbers initially. Eventually it might
help, but at first I just want to have a rough idea of something and to see if
it can work. I may want to find out some critical parameters, but I don't
need to know the precise optimum values of all the variables at first.

INTERVIEWER: *Research shouldn't always be carefully planned?*

GUNDLACH: Well, sometimes research is exploratory. I think that some
of the best things in research happen by fooling around. While working
toward a particular goal, I very often have an accident that leads me in
another direction. I think research should be organized with a freedom that
enables you to pursue accidents. Almost half of my inventions were total accidents or partial accidents based on an unplanned discovery. The importance of a goal, however, can't be minimized. You're not likely to invent
anything unless you're extremely motivated.

INTERVIEWER: *What were some of your accidental inventions?*

GUNDLACH: The one that comes to mind is the process for transferring
xerographic images to metal offset-printing masters. That was a true accident and resulted only because I was sloppy.

Like a lot of people, I had been trying to find a way to use the latent
image over and over again to make multiple copies. In xerography, we
create a pattern of charge on the plate called a latent image and then develop it. Normally, that pattern of charge is destroyed after you develop it
by transferring the toner powder to paper.

But if you could find a way of keeping that charge pattern or latent image on the plate after developing an image, you could use that latent image
to make maybe a hundred copies from just one exposure.

I took a lithographic plate into my darkroom and developed a powder
image and then transferred the powder image to paper in the dark by laying
the paper down on the plate and corona-charging it. I backed the paper with
the metal foil and pulled the paper and foil up together. The metal foil was
grounded, and it did what I expected it to do: It kept the plate from losing
its charge when you removed the paper.

But it also did something that I hadn't expected. When I was making the copy, I put the paper down crooked and got a beautiful "Page 15" transferred to the metal master where I missed covering the "Page 15" mark with the paper.

It turns out that transferring an image directly to metal was something that people had been trying to do for three years at Battelle. They had spent several hundred thousand dollars, and nobody had come up with a simple solution.

This was a very timely discovery because it enabled transfer of the xerographic image to metal offset-printing masters. At that time, Rank Xerox Limited* was just being formed and the European market was less receptive to paper offset masters. So, this gave us a viable product for sale in Europe.

INTERVIEWER: *Was that what led you to the multiple-copy process for plain-paper copiers?*

GUNDLACH: Well, that's another story. My boss had asked if there was a way of splitting the image between the paper and the plate and had suggested I try lower transfer fields—using less charge to make a copy.

Well, I tried that, and it didn't work too well. But eventually I got back to trying it on a day when he was out of town.

Normally, when you transfer charge from plate to paper in xerography, eighty percent goes to the paper and twenty percent is left behind on the plate. I decided that if you could transfer that eighty percent back to the plate, you would still have twenty percent left on the paper. By fusing and other enhancement techniques, you could get an acceptable image with that twenty percent. That would leave eighty percent on the plate—enough to make at least five copies from a single exposure.

In fact, I was able to make ten legible images with the process, each one a little bit lighter than the last. The process avoided making a separate exposure for each copy, which took three minutes in those days. With my process, I could make the first copy in three minutes and subsequent copies ten seconds apart. We thought it was a big boost.

INTERVIEWER: *Is it easier to be creative when the boss isn't around?*

GUNDLACH: Early in life, I discovered that most of the good things I had done happened when the boss was out of town. I think there is a good

* A fifty-fifty partnership between The Rank Organisation Limited and Xerox Corporation.

reason for that. I think it's because there's no intimidation then. I'm sure there's some of that in everybody. You don't have to account for what happened if the boss is out of town. If it doesn't work, you just throw it away. You don't have to explain it. If it does work, you can show it to your boss. Maybe he'll leave town more often.

If you want to invent, you have to be willing to risk, and sometimes you have to minimize risk by working on projects in secret. When the boss is out of town, you can go into that dark closet that is the source of endless ideas and start pulling out your most harebrained schemes. Sometimes you think that you've exhausted your last idea. But you really have an endless stream of ideas in there. You just have to be willing to go in and look for them and bring them out to the light of day.

> *What people are really risking in the case of invention is failure....*

INTERVIEWER: *Once your accident happened, was the solution obvious?*

GUNDLACH: As soon as it happened, the solution was perfectly obvious to me and to most people I told about it.

In fact, some said, "Well, that's not an invention, that's obvious." But I think that's the mark of a good invention. Good inventions are so obvious in retrospect that people say, "Why should he get a patent on that?"

To get a patent, incidentally, the law requires that your invention be new and useful as well as not obvious. It has to fulfill those three criteria. Well, if you can prove that it's useful and that it hasn't been done before, that in itself should prove that the invention is not obvious. If it was obvious, someone would have already done it. Once almost anything's been done, it seems obvious. You have to judge it beforehand. How long was the opportunity there? How long were people working on the problem without a solution? That's the proof that an invention wasn't obvious.

INTERVIEWER: *Maxwell's equations look obvious when you derive them in a college physics class, but they weren't obvious to a lot of people for quite a while.*

GUNDLACH: Those never looked that obvious to me, but I understood them anyway. But you can look back on some inventions, and they really do look obvious.

The wheel, for example, looks perfectly obvious to those of us who grew up with cars and wheelbarrows and whatever. But the Indians lived in America for at least ten thousand years and dragged everything—even though many of them lived in very mobile societies. They didn't use wheels, but what the French call a travois. They tied sticks to the back of a horse and dragged their tents and blankets and all their belongings along behind them. Even after covered wagons had proved that the wheel was useful, the Indians still used travois. The opportunity was there for a wheel in Indian societies all along, but they didn't use it. So, it couldn't have been all that obvious to everybody.

INTERVIEWER: *An inventor has to be creative, but he also has to have the technical skills to express his ideas. What kind of training do you think someone should have to be an inventor?*

GUNDLACH: Training is an interesting question because some people are so well-trained that it precludes invention. They're trained in what one should know to be an inventor or engineer, but they're afraid of being creative because being creative means taking risks. I think it was Mark Twain who said he never let formal education interfere with his learning. I feel that way myself. Maybe if you have a doctorate, it's a disincentive to your learning process. With a doctorate, you get a fairly intensive training in a fairly narrow time span. It takes away some of your motivation to continue learning, and in this fast-moving world, knowledge becomes obsolete in five years.

An inventor also has to take risks, and I don't know how you train people to take chances and risks. What people are really risking in the case of invention is failure, and our schools don't encourage failure. In fact, a student in school gets a big fat F for failure, and I think this is unfortunate. By training students not to fail, maybe we're also training them not to be creative. Unless you're willing to risk something, you're really not going to try something new. And you're not going to be very creative unless you're willing to risk something.

I'm sure schools could dream up a program to teach creativity and risk-taking. But we don't as a matter of course.

INTERVIEWER: *Is creativity more important than technical training?*

GUNDLACH: I would say that technical training is as important as creativity when it comes to being an inventor. I can think of several people who went broke because they were creative but not too well informed in the physics field.

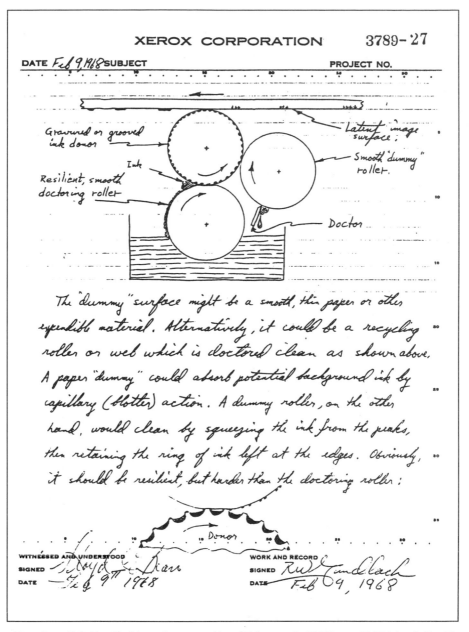

Page from Bob Gundlach's project notes (dated February 9, 1968) on a SLIC (simple liquid ink copier) development system.

William Heubner, for example, made revolutionary changes in the printing industry that brought him millions of dollars. But then, he had a fire in his printing press and saw smoke particles precipitated on the back of paper. After that, he set about trying to invent what he called the smokeprinting process.

If he had looked into it deeply enough, however, some back-of-the-envelope calculations would have told him that there was an inherent problem with the process and that it would probably never work. As an inventor I wouldn't say "never." People can dream up new things. But it's important to understand the fundamental constraints that exist in a given technology. If you want to succeed, you're going to have to invent ways around those constraints.

Smokeprinting depends on the conductivity of paper, which varies widely around the country and over time. It varies from a million to one between places like Louisiana in the middle of summer and Denver in the middle of winter. If you don't understand that, you can get fooled into thinking that you can develop images from the back side of a piece of paper through smokeprinting. That may work one-tenth of the year, but it generally won't work the rest of the year unless you dry the paper first—making it a much more complicated and impractical process.

Bill Heubner invested millions of dollars because he didn't understand the conductivity of paper. He kept pursuing a dream that had inherent limitations.

INTERVIEWER: *Are there any personal characteristics or traits that you think are common to inventors? What do you think it takes to be a good inventor?*

GUNDLACH: I've known a lot of creative people, and there aren't many common characteristics among them. I think one common characteristic, however, may be a good sense of imagination—more specifically, a good ability to visualize.

I picked this idea up from Lew Walkup at Battelle. When he would interview prospective inventors, he would ask them to visualize a cube such as the one we today call a Rubik's Cube. The question went like this:

Visualize a cube made of smaller cubes stacked together, three by three by three cubes. All the cubes are white. Then, paint the outside edges bright red. Now, how many cubes have no red paint on them? How many have one surface that's painted? How many have two surfaces painted, and how many have three? Then, he would ask people *how* they solved it. That was the key.

Some people solved the problem mathematically by writing down equations and solving them. But other people—the people who got the answers most quickly and who generally would make good inventors— visualized it. They just saw it in space. If you visualize it, you can count them. The cubes with a single side painted would be those in the middle of each side, and there would be one, two, three, four, five, six of them. Those with three edges painted would be the corner cubes, and there would be one, two, three, four, five, six, seven, eight of them. And so on.

INTERVIEWER: Are traits like stick-to-it-iveness and perseverance important to invention as well?

GUNDLACH: I think the one characteristic anyone who wants to be an inventor should have is a willingness to work. You also have to be highly motivated to be an inventor. Invention is an assertive act. It really takes a lot of energy and a lot of determination. Even after you have an invention, it probably won't go anywhere unless you have a lot of perseverance.

Look back, for example, at Chet Carlson, who invented xerography. He waited twenty-two years before he ever saw that idea come to the marketplace. Twenty-two years. He had the original idea, wrote it all down, and submitted a patent application before he ever got an actual reduction-to-practice.

After his patent application, he then worked on it unsuccessfully in his own kitchen and bathroom for about a year. Finally, he hired a helper, Otto Kornei, who was able to help him get a reduction-to-practice within three weeks. That first xerographic image was of the place and date, "Astoria 10-22-38." He finally got the process to work on October 22, 1938 in Astoria, New York, where he was living and working at the time. It was a small image, maybe a little less than two inches long, but it represented the copying process that we all know today.

When he started, he had no idea that it would take twenty-two years to get it on the market. He approached at least twenty major business-equipment corporations in America and received what he later termed "an enthusiastic lack of interest" from all twenty—as well as from the National Inventors Council and other federal agencies.

Eventually, he lived to see the day when an estimated two hundred million images were made by his process every day. And he would have been gratified to know that today it is up to three billion a day.

But it took a lot of perseverance and a lot of struggle to reach the point of marketability. The first positive response he got was from the Battelle Memorial Institute, a nonprofit research organization. Battelle agreed to pursue it if Carlson put up a certain amount of money to help research it.

Later, the Haloid Company read about it at a time when it was casting about, desperately looking for something new in the photographic business. Its primary business was in making photocopy paper. That process eventually became known as photostats because of Kodak's product in the area. Haloid could see that the field didn't have much future in it, so fortunately decided to pursue xerography.

> *If we had waited until we understood xerography absolutely, we probably wouldn't even have a product on the market yet.*

INTERVIEWER: *For a number of years, Xerox was the only game in town. Not only were there no United States competitors, there were no foreign competitors either. That's changed completely in the last five or ten years—particularly with the onslaught of Japanese products. But unlike the auto industry, Xerox hasn't been completely outsold or outmarketed by the Japanese. Has the competition actually been a positive thing? Has it helped keep Xerox innovative?*

GUNDLACH: There are some parallels between autos and copiers. In the 1950s, the United States auto industry decided there wasn't a high return on investment for improving the efficiency of cars, so they went for more and more power and bigger cars. It took Honda Motors to prove them wrong, and they proved it in a big way—in a way that hurt the American auto industry.

I think the same thing happened in copiers. It took the Japanese copier companies to prove that there was a market for smaller copiers. There was more money in big copiers, particularly those that went faster, and it was easier to justify them because there was a high return on investment. This was particularly true in the days when most of the machines were leased. Xerox did some very innovative marketing in its early days. Somewhat like the early mainframe computer companies and the phone company, we leased our equipment and charged by the copy. Customers didn't actually have to buy a machine.

As a result, there was a real focus in the company's marketing groups for getting the speed up because that made the meter turn faster, and the meter was the way we got money. We eventually pushed the copy rates up for machines like the Xerox 9700, which makes 120 copies a minute.

In the 1970s, a number of us in research had been urging the company to focus on reliability as well as speed, but it took the first IBM copier, which focused on reliability, to make the product planners more receptive to the idea. As soon as the challenge was set, however, there was a response, and Xerox did quite well in that area. There were always people in the corporation who knew how to make the copiers more reliable and wanted to do it, but they needed funding and support. Finally we got it, and competition was important in that sense. It does serve the public.

INTERVIEWER: *But before that happened, Xerox was embroiled in a bitter dispute with IBM and other companies over patent infringements in the field of xerography. How do you view that era in light of the stimulation and improvements that came about as a result of competition?*

GUNDLACH: I think competition is important, but I also think the patent umbrella was crucial. The fact that Xerox could invest in new processes with some assurance that it could get a return on that investment later was essential when it came to developing xerography. I don't think you could have convinced the corporation to take the risks involved in xerography if it hadn't had patent protection.

It was a little annoying to me in the 1970s when we began to get into lawsuits with people who wanted to infringe on our patents. We simply asserted our patent rights and said they couldn't do it. Their response was to say, "You're practicing a monopoly! You're violating antitrust laws by practicing a huge monopoly." Well, patents *guarantee* you a monopoly. They give you a legal monopoly for seventeen years, and I don't apologize for that.

Throughout the 1950s, we gave a number of these companies an opportunity to work in xerography, but they didn't believe in it. They didn't want to take the risks. As our attorney characterized it at the time, "Nobody wanted to help bake the cake, but they all wanted to taste the frosting once it was done." After early Xerox copiers like the 914, the 813, and the 2400 proved the markets and proved them in a spectacular way, everybody wanted to share in the rewards. I think we had earned a legal monopoly that was worth asserting.

INTERVIEWER: *Did losing the FTC [Federal Trade Commission] case have any impact on researchers and inventors like yourself? Did research pick up to meet the new challenge?*

GUNDLACH: Yes. At the time Xerox cut budgets in the patent department by forty percent. Following the FTC settlement, the general perception was that the legal system and society at large did not value patents as much and that the courts weren't willing to protect them.

There was also an immediate reaction to the FTC case in the research community. In fact, somebody did a good statistical accounting of it and found that invention proposals within Xerox had fallen by a factor of two. Just the perception that we weren't pushing patents as hard changed the activity and focus of the research people. They stopped submitting inventions and invention proposals. So, it's clear that researchers need to feel that patents are important to management.

I should add that, in the antitrust cases, the courts upheld our rights to assert our patent protection.

INTERVIEWER: *Do you have any thoughts or suggestions for improving the patent system? Are there any changes you would like to see?*

GUNDLACH: I think the costs have gone up too fast for individuals. For a large corporation, the costs are still manageable and justifiable, but the patent system is trying to pay for itself these days, and that has had some tangible impacts on invention.

In my field, xerography and imaging science, most of the patents are suddenly flowing in from the outside—more from Japan than from within America. I think that's a tragedy. I believe it's in the interest of our society to promote, induce, and encourage more innovation and creativity. On that basis, I could justify government support or subsidization of patents and the patent system. I think that's preferable to trying to make the system pay for itself on the backs of independent inventors. Ninety percent of all inventions never make it to the marketplace anyway, and higher fees just add to the burden and risks of the independent inventor.

INTERVIEWER: *It's easier to be an inventor with a large corporation than to work independently?*

GUNDLACH: Being an inventor is a good way to go broke if you're working on your own. Being an inventor in a large corporation is a very fortunate happenstance.

INTERVIEWER: *But can one be as creative in a large corporation?*

GUNDLACH: I think invention takes place in an environment that values invention. Most inventors, if you give them a good challenge, can be pretty creative.

In a large corporation, I think that it's important that the top management sets the standard for such things as quality, reliability, and affordability. Then the research and engineering people will make it happen.

Unfortunately, most companies try to do this by focusing on product programs rather than exploratory processes. I really have to say that most corporations spend an awful lot of money on engineering projects that never make it out the door. Xerox, for example, has a number of examples of products that were aborted just before they were scheduled to reach the market—usually for reasons that should have been obvious in the beginning. We've spent tens of millions of dollars on product programs that had to be canceled later. Often, it was because they were too late in getting on the market and the technology was out of date.

Exploratory research is relatively cheap in that sense. I think larger corporations should probably do more exploratory research and be more selective later. They should spend their engineering money on projects that have really proven themselves in the laboratory.

The problem is that it's hard to get corporations to spend money on anything except product programs. But product engineers can't afford to take the risks required to develop a really innovative product. There's almost an incompatibility between funding an exploratory project and developing a production machine. You want the product engineers to have options in proven technologies. But even though we can create new technologies in the lab, we don't have the funds to prove them in the way that product engineers want them proven.

INTERVIEWER: *Are the products of research too much of a gamble for most companies? Isn't careful lab work enough to prove that an idea or invention works?*

GUNDLACH: It's a fact of life that research is a gamble. When corporate managers and accountants discover that research is a gamble, they say, "Why don't we save money? If only one invention in ten is going to make it to the market, why don't we just support the ten percent that's going to make it? We can save ninety percent of our research budget." I guess most people understand the fallacy in that kind of logic. Nevertheless, we see evidence of it in the corporate world.

The problem is that research and science are rarely based on certainty. It's a matter of probabilities. Even most of the principles we accept—for example, quantum theory—are probabilistic. Nobody has ever really seen an electron, but we come to accept it because it explains so many things. It's an inferential conclusion that you reach, not a real proof. But you can work with things like that.

Architects, for example, still work with the assumption that squaring the sides of a building with a level will result in parallel sides on a structure. They know that the level tells what is straight up, so they build a building and assume that all walls are parallel. But, of course, the walls aren't parallel; they're all pointing to the center of the earth (laughs). For a building a few hundred feet high that's no problem, but if you made a skyscraper high enough, it probably would have an effect. I'm sure it's true that, unless they've compensated for it, the top floor of the Empire State Building is a little larger than the first floor. But that's something that we live with.

Approximations are usually valid, but you have to remember that we never work with certainties. Well, almost never.

INTERVIEWER: *Does that apply to xerographic processes?*

GUNDLACH: Yes, absolutely. We understand them functionally, but we don't understand them absolutely. If we had waited until we understood xerography absolutely, we probably wouldn't even have a product on the market yet.

INTERVIEWER: *Is there a lot of conflict between inventors and production engineers?*

GUNDLACH: I think there often is. I remember showing the head of our engineering department my baffle for simplifying the flat-plate equipment. Chester Carlson liked it a lot, but the head of the engineering department didn't at all.

I remember he said, "Bob, we hoped you'd give us physics-department support, like telling us the latitudes of toner to developer, the ratio of powders in the sand, and the speeds of development. Why don't you leave the engineering to us?" (Laughs.) That was a terrible blow to me—the realities of life.

That attitude is still true today. I've come to understand why it's true, and I accept it. But I don't think it's right.

An engineer, especially in product programs, is faced with deadlines, with vendors to be lined up, and with designs to be frozen. He views a creative inventor, who wants to keep changing things, as a thorn in his side, and I can't blame him. The engineer is trying to lock up a machine and meet a schedule, and the inventor walks in and says, "No, we shouldn't do it that way. I've got a better idea." But the engineer is already halfway down the road toward completion.

INTERVIEWER: *So, flexibility is a problem in a large corporation?*

GUNDLACH: Maybe this is what's wrong with a large corporation. They don't have the flexibility that's needed to change courses that quickly. There's a lot of inertia in a large corporation.

Corporations have some advantages in terms of marketing force and in doing things by the millions instead of by the hundreds. You can clearly get economies of scale. But in terms of modifying products as opportunities for improvement are perceived, it's easier for a smaller company.

We have, in fact, experimented with smaller groups and teams in bringing new products to the market to try and gain some of the advantages of a smaller corporation.

Our new engineering drawing copier, the Xerox 2510, was literally put out by a company within a company. It copies documents a yard wide. The group engineered and marketed the copier with a very small team and a relatively small investment. I think the return is going to be tremendous. But the changes that were made and the hidden problems that were discovered and fixed would have been almost impossible for a large group to manage. We would have had $40 million in obsolete equipment sitting in a warehouse somewhere if the 2510 project had been attempted by a large group.

INTERVIEWER: *But with Xerox's tremendous resources in basic research, it seems as though the company should have enough creative ideas to keep itself at least on par with the competition—if not far ahead of it.*

GUNDLACH: There's a difference between creativity and innovation. Innovation is the follow-through on the invention and the creation, and large corporations don't have as good a record as smaller ones do at innovation.

I read a year or so ago that the number of product innovations per million dollars is about twenty-six times as high for smaller corporations as it is for large corporations. Twenty-six times greater.

Large corporations, I think, get more conservative. They have more to lose. Maybe the Haloid Company, the predecessor to Xerox, was just more desperate. It was willing to risk a little more. I think it would be difficult for Chester Carlson to come into a company as big as Xerox is today and sell his product.

JEROME LEMELSON

WITH MORE than four hundred patents, Jerome Lemelson is one of the most productive inventors in the United States. He is also a rarity among inventors: He is a professional inventor. Many inventors also take on the role of entrepreneur and build companies around their ideas and inventions, but Lemelson has made a living solely from the royalties from his inventions.

Most of Lemelson's inventions are ideas: He invents in his head. Unlike other inventors who reduce their theories to practice in working models, Lemelson writes his ideas up in a patent. Critics claim that his inventions are little more than pieces of paper, but obviously the Patent Office has thought differently—several hundred times. With patents on everything from cut-out toys on the back of cereal boxes to manufacturing systems for integrated circuits, the scope of Lemelson's inventions is overwhelming. More inventions, of course, are on the way.

Lemelson, who usually does his own legal work, also writes his own patents. By his estimate, he has more than one million words in print in the form of patents.

Inventing has not always been Lemelson's sole occupation. After graduating from New York University in 1951 with a master's degree in industrial engineering, he spent several years working as an industrial engineer. In the mid-1950s, however, he decided to set out on his own. While he designed industrial robots and automated factories in his head and on paper, his income came from patents on toys and novelties. After receiving his first patent in 1955, Lemelson churned out patents at the rate of one a month for the next twenty years. In 1964, he licensed his first high-tech patent: an automated warehousing system.

Being a lone inventor presents problems of its own. Today, legal matters occupy almost as much time as inventing, as Lemelson tries to keep others from stealing his ideas. An independent inventor can be easy prey for companies who use ideas without licensing patents—through either ignorance or arrogance. Lemelson has been involved in more than twenty court cases, but he has lost more than he has won.

Jerome Lemelson was born in New York City in 1923. He lives in Princeton, New Jersey, and his company, Licensing Management Corporation—which he staffs, manages, and operates entirely on his own—has its offices in Manhattan.

INTERVIEWER: *You have more than four hundred inventions to your name. Do you have favorites?*

LEMELSON: I have a favorite invention. It's what's known as machine vision. I've gotten five patents in the field, and I expect to get a sixth one shortly. It's not my most successful, but I think it's probably one of my most important.

It started with a system I developed on paper in the early 1950s for analyzing image fields with a computer. At first it was relatively simple, but I've evolved it into a system that basically uses a television camera as the eyes of a computer. Video output from the camera is processed by a computer and then digitized and analyzed to determine what is actually going on in the image field. The concept is being used throughout the world.

In manufacturing, for example, machine vision can be used to tell a machine tool or a robot about an object it's supposed to work on. It can tell how the object is aligned, where it's located, which actions or commands are needed to pick it up, and so on.

Other uses for machine vision include such things as analyzing the terrain scanned by a satellite for reconnaissance purposes. It's being used by military forces throughout the world to provide eyes on the battlefield for military commanders. But it's really one of my favorite inventions because I feel it has applications that haven't even been thought of yet.

INTERVIEWER: *What's the story behind your development of machine vision?*

LEMELSON: It came about at a time in the 1950s when I was concentrating on automation in manufacturing. At the time, of course, computers were in their infancy.

One of my first inventions in the field had to do with programmed industrial robots. I designed and filed a patent application for what I considered a universal robot: one that could perform a variety of functions by simply changing its operating head. It could do such things as pick up and position units of work, perform machining operations on them, and then pass them on to the next machine. Given the proper sensors to measure and inspect a product, you could also program it to function as an inspection robot to do some basic quality control. Today, such a robot is known as the coordinate measuring machine—something which my patents indicate I was the first to invent. Coordinate measuring really amounts to sensing the surface locations of a machined piece of work with a touch probe.

I thought of using electro-optics, a light beam, to scan the surface of the work. There were no lasers available at the time, but light beams and photoelectric cells were available, and one of my patents has to do with measuring the dimensions of a two-sided object by interrupting a light beam. As a beam scans an object from one side, a photoelectric cell on the opposite side picks up the light as long as the beam

I don't know how many words I've published in the form of patents— probably a few million.

isn't broken by the object. When it begins to scan across an object, it will be interrupted for a time until it reaches the other side of an object. If the beam is moving at a constant speed, the length of time the interruption lasts can be used to tell the dimensions of the object being scanned.

From that, I later thought of using a television camera to do the measuring as well as to gather more information. A television camera could scan a piece of work or an image field in a thirtieth of a second or less. The video output could then be digitized and used by a computer to tell what was going on in the image field.

Then I got to thinking, My gosh, this can be used as the eyes of a machine. Through digitizing the image you could not only measure dimensions, but you could tell whether or not a part is present on a particular assembly, tell whether it is off-center or not, whether there are burrs on the edges or not, locate a hole, and detect surface imperfections on the part. You could even tell the color of a particular part or assembly and if the color was standard or not.

My ideas at the time also included comparing measurements and specifications with those recorded in the machine's memory to determine whether or not the parts were within tolerance. All in all, I had what I thought would be a wonderful way of inspecting products and maintaining quality control. Finally, I decided to incorporate a feedback loop into the system to use input from the image field to help control the robot and account for variations in its operation.

These things all developed in my mind over a period of years. I file my own patent applications, and this was one of the longest patents I ever got. Its length was something like forty thousand words.

INTERVIEWER: *You write up your own patents?*

LEMELSON: Oh, yes. With my income, I could have never have gotten my four hundred or more patents if I hadn't done it myself. Almost every patent I've received has been written by me. I don't know how many words I've published in the form of patents—probably a few million. I've also done the legal work for about eighty percent of my patents. It's been fun. In fact, it's still a thrill to me when the patent office allows a patent application and it's going to issue as a patent.

INTERVIEWER: *Are you still working on your machine vision concepts?*

LEMELSON: Well, as I said, I have five patents in the field and another one due to come out soon. I'm working on the seventh patent right now, and I have other advances beyond that in mind.

I really think the field is about to explode. General Motors is talking about employing more than forty thousand machine vision systems by 1990. It's a tremendous field in terms of its value to industry, and I have some basic patents in the field.

INTERVIEWER: *You have patents in everything from industrial robots to children's toys. How do you come up with your ideas? Do you pick out problems to work on, or do ideas just suddenly strike you?*

LEMELSON: A variety of mental procedures may come into play. I can't point to one particular manner which is responsible for the conception of ideas that eventually become patented inventions.

On a number of occasions, I've woken up in the middle of the night with the solution to a problem that had been on my mind. Sometimes I've also come up with ideas that were totally unrelated to anything I had ever done. There it would be—either a solution to a problem or the heart of the problem itself.

But I think that, more often than not, my ideas seem to come from constantly looking for problems to solve. It may be a problem I've experienced in everyday life, it may be a problem someone presents to me, or it may result from reading a magazine or newspaper article.

For example, I'll read an article on car theft, and then I'll think about ways to prevent it. I do, in fact, have a number of patents in that field.

INTERVIEWER: Do you ever specifically go out looking for problems to solve?

LEMELSON: There have been times when I've taken an interest in a particular field and have gone to the library to read up on it. Sometimes I start playing around with information obtained by reading and try to think about how I could develop something new in the field. At other times I just store the information in my memory.

I should add, however, that I don't attempt to force myself to come up with something new. There was a time when I tried that, but it just doesn't work that way.

The mind has to think about a problem subconsciously. We still don't know what goes on in the subconscious mind. There are many processes of short-circuiting, elimination, and so on at work. I'm sure these processes go on subconsciously. But there is a combination of things at work behind creative thoughts.

I think an important part of invention today is being able to discover the problem. You may immediately start thinking of ways to solve it, or you may forget about it for a while and the solution may come to you while you're working on something else. That's happened many times to me.

INTERVIEWER: Does one have to be selfish to be an inventor?

LEMELSON: Yes. In general, I think creativity occurs most often when an individual is alone and not disturbed by other people.

Even in "group creativity," members of the group generally don't work on the same problem. Each member of the group solves a different problem and contributes a portion of the total solution. That kind of group invention is a very important aspect of industry today as well as being important in the research and development community. But we shouldn't ignore the individual. Many of our greatest inventions came from individuals working alone or with a small group of assistants helping them. It's true that Thomas Edison had a staff of people working under him. Many of that group's greatest inventions, however, were really the result of Edison's initial efforts.

For the most part, I like working on my own. In the past, I have done some work with others, and I do have a number of consultants who help me out from time to time in development work. I also have an engineer out in Wisconsin who has helped me with some of my inventions.

INTERVIEWER: *Do you have a lab or shop that you work in, or do you prefer to work problems out in your head?*

> *An important part of invention today is being able to discover the problem.*

LEMELSON: Right now I don't have a lab. Years ago I had a shop where I made simple models of my inventions, mostly toys and gadgets.

That's where the consultants come in, and I have several working for me from time to time.

For example, I have a consultant in the field of speech generation and speech recognition who has done software and hardware development for me. I have another consultant who helps me with the details in some of my circuits when my inventions call for that. I've also hired people to help me develop products.

I really don't know if I will ever have a lab. I just moved into a new home which my wife and I redesigned, and I do have a shop and some laboratory equipment there. I hope to buy some more tools to use to putter around with some pet projects and do some development work. But development work can take up a lot of time and detract from purely inventing.

Most of my inventions are only in the form of patents, and many of them are quite detailed. I don't see a need for building models of everything I have invented or spending the time and money on models. I know they're helpful in promoting and licensing inventions, but they're not always necessary.

INTERVIEWER: *What do you think it takes to be a good inventor? Do you have a short list of qualities or traits in mind that you think are important?*

LEMELSON: I think the major trait is curiosity. You have to be curious, and you must have a desire to increase your knowledge, even if it's only in a limited field. You have to be willing to look for problems and find ways to solve them.

Optimism is also important—not overoptimism, but cautious optimism. People have always told inventors that their ideas wouldn't work. Even when the Wright Brothers had been flying their airplane for several years, people who hadn't seen it fly didn't believe it. People saw photographs of it and still didn't believe it. The remarks that were made in those years, from 1903 to 1907, were just incredible. To overcome that kind of negativism, you need a certain amount of optimism as well as determination and stick-to-it-iveness.

I think creativity and invention are a frame of mind. And, although they may be partially genetic as well, self-discipline and training also come into the picture.

Of course, you have to have some degree of peace of mind. If you're highly emotional all the time, you may conceive of an idea or two, but your emotions will interfere with the creative process.

INTERVIEWER: *Ideas and inventions seem to be fragile things. A number of inventors have told me that they often work on their inventions without telling anyone, to avoid the kind of negative feedback you mentioned. Have you ever done anything like that yourself?*

LEMELSON: It doesn't affect me. I had it happen just the other day. I was discussing a new development that I have in the field of magnetic recording with someone who's an expert in the field, and he had doubts about it. But I thought to myself, If it can be done, it will be done some day. I don't get discouraged very easily.

At the same time, I try to make as intelligent an evaluation of my ideas as I can. I try not to chase rainbows. At some time or another in his life, every inventor chases rainbows. This can vary from something extreme to a mild form of rainbow chasing.

By way of example, consider Thomas Edison. He had a number of projects that he probably wouldn't have gotten involved in if he had been able to sit back and look at them objectively.

Besides inventing the light bulb, Edison did a great deal of work in the field of electromagnetism. He also invented one of the first electromagnetic ore separators. When he discovered that he could use his separator to attract iron, he thought of ways to use it for separating low-grade iron from soil. He subsequently invested tens of millions of dollars to mine low-grade ore in Pennsylvania and almost went broke when the operation failed. Had he looked beyond the end of his nose and studied the process a little more and looked into the economics of it, he probably never would have gotten involved in it. But everybody chases rainbows.

INTERVIEWER: *You mentioned that inventing is still a thrill even after four hundred patents. Has it become any easier?*

LEMELSON: Yes, it has. In the beginning, problem-solving took a lot of effort. But as I matured and grew older, it became easier for me to solve problems and work out the details of an invention. Now, I consider it almost like eating pie. I'm not saying that it's the easiest thing in the world, but I just don't think about the difficulties any more. I move ahead with what I'm doing and as time goes by, the pieces fall together.

INTERVIEWER: *I've read in a number of places that foreign patent filings in certain fields at the United States Patent Office now outnumber those from American inventors. Do you think that means there are real problems with invention and creativity in the United States?*

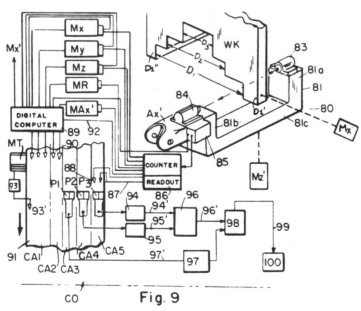

Fig. 9

Drawing from Jerome Lemelson's 1954 patent application that describes and illustrates a universal robot used to perform automatic production and measurement functions. Fig. 9 is the measurement head (81) of an automatic inspection robot (80) which is computer-controlled to cause a light beam to scan the surface of a workpiece or assembly (WK) and take measurements. Such measurements are computer-processed and recorded on magnetic tape (91); they can be used to operate an electronic display or to control a machine. One patent that issued from the 1954 parent application was for a computer-controlled coordinate measuring machine—the same type of machine that was employed to locate and measure the heat shield tiles on all the space shuttles made by Lockheed Corporation for NASA.

LEMELSON: Definitely. Last fall, for example, I interviewed a patent examiner in the field of information and handling—a field which I've done a lot of work in. He's been an examiner with the Patent Office for more than twenty years, and he told me that Japanese patent applications in the field now account for more than forty-five percent of the new filings. At the same time, those of American inventors—both corporate and individual—have dropped below that percentage. To me, this is frightening because it means that the system is not working the way it was intended to work.

INTERVIEWER: *Do you think the problem has more to do with industry attitudes and the business climate? Or do the problems lie with the patent system?*

LEMELSON: It's a combination of things. There are also problems with the way the legal system interprets patents. What I see happening, and I've been involved in the field of inventing for more than thirty-five years, is that the patent system has become extremely complex.

New products and patents are extremely valuable to corporations, which may invest a lot of money in developing new technology. The Xerox Corporation, for example, spent countless dollars developing xerography. But it worked, and as a result of their patents, they were able to grow to their present size. They had a monopoly on copiers for a number of years.

Xerox, formerly Haloid, was able to virtually create a new industry because of Chester Carlson,* an independent inventor with a good idea. But even with examples like Carlson, the independent inventor today still has an extremely difficult time convincing corporations that he has a product which deserves to be on the market. Most companies and industries have a tremendous resistance to ideas and technology developed on the outside. And by "outside," I'm talking about ideas from inventors, from other corporations, from research and development companies, from foreign countries—wherever ideas can be obtained.

I feel very strongly about this particular situation. It's often described as NIH—or the not-invented-here syndrome. Very few corporations will license outside inventions, particularly from individuals or small groups. Some may buy a technology that is hard to come by, but very few of them will look at an invention and say, "Can we profit from this item? Can this be a diversification of what we're already doing? Can we set up a new group

---

* Physicist who invented xerography.

or factory to do this and make more money for our stockholders and increase the gross national product?" This just doesn't happen very easily in our industrial society. Today, most corporations will wait for somebody else to develop the market. Once the market is established, they become "me-too"ers!

INTERVIEWER: *They don't want to take the risks required to get it going?*

LEMELSON: That's right; they don't want to take the risks.

I do, however, have some ideas of my own on how to increase innovation and productivity in the United States. At the outbreak of World War II, our government saw the need for ideas to help win the war, so they set up the National Inventors Council [NIC]. It was made up of representatives from both industry and science who reviewed ideas that were submitted by private citizens.

More than four hundred thousand ideas were submitted during the war. As I understand it, more than four thousand actually went into production and use. Those inventions certainly had an impact on winning the war, and a number of good inventions came out of the NIC.

I think we need something similar today, but it should be done a little differently. For instance, such a group should also have the ability to do some market research on different products and ideas.

How many inventions are out there approaching the magnitude of xerography? If not that, then how many would create one or more new jobs? Hundreds of jobs? I'm sure there are quite a number of them. The name of the game is really productivity and jobs, when you think about it.

If we're going downhill today—and we are—it's happening because we're being beaten by overseas competition. But the reason we're being beaten is because we're not using our innovative resources. The ideas of our individual citizens are not being exploited. I think re-instituting something like the National Inventors Council would do wonders for this country.

INTERVIEWER: *What about the NIH syndrome?*

LEMELSON: NIH is a major problem. How do you get rid of or reduce the NIH syndrome? Some corporations have set up product committees to review new products and inventions, but I don't know how successful that's been. Most of them will review new products and that's as far as they'll go. There aren't enough incentives. When you look at what's required to get a new product through all the red tape and the opposition, a major problem is that virtually a hundred people have to sign off on an idea. If any one of them says no, the idea is dead.

What scholars have discovered in studying innovation and product development is that new products require a champion—a person who will personally take responsibility for a product and move it along from stage to stage and be sure it doesn't get shot down. We don't have very many champions out there, and one of the basic reasons that we don't is because we don't train people as champions. We don't have enough product engineers training in our colleges and corporations. We also don't reward our champions. Most people in the field of product evaluation don't want to make ripples that could come back as waves and inundate them. There's no incentive for a person to become a champion.

At some time or another in his life, every inventor chases rainbows.

In the United States if a product fails, a champion may be degraded or lose his job. In Japan, groups champion products. If the product fails, the whole group is to blame, but no individual loses face or his job as a result of it. It's understood that some products are going to fail. And to that extent, they have a great advantage over us.

INTERVIEWER: *So, we need better protection as well as rewards to promote champions?*

LEMELSON: That's right. Let's take the individual level first. There should be more clearly defined and better rewards for the champion who comes out with a successful product. That person should be recognized and should receive financial rewards for it. If the champion fails, a cushion should be there—unless the failure was due to something that was drastically wrong. But you shouldn't threaten a person's position with the company because a product fails. Some guidelines for this sort of thing should be set up within the corporation.

Let's get to the corporate level. Most companies have a limited amount of money to invest in new products. What do they choose to invest in? Generally, it's something that comes from within the corporation. No one wants to pay for something if they can get it for nothing, and if they get it from their own employees, it's usually for nothing.

Now, I have conceived an idea that I haven't spoken to too many people about. I feel the tax laws should be changed to encourage corporations to license or buy outside technology. If a corporation increases its productivity, profits, or employment by licensing outside technology or a patented invention, some consideration should be given to rewarding the company with a tax break on its profits from that. They've done something that generally isn't done, and they're paying more taxes under today's system.

Now, conversely, if the product fails and they lose money, I think they're entitled to a *second* tax break. Losses could be cushioned in terms of a deduction on their total taxes.

If these two incentives—the tax break and tax deduction—were properly applied and administered, it could be a way of getting corporations to take a more serious look at licensing outside technology and outside patented inventions.

And I don't mean that we necessarily need more government. Even today, the level of government we have can do quite a bit to improve the incentives for invention at every level. The corporation can be helped as much as the individual inventor.

Foreign countries are already helping their inventors. Denmark, a small country with maybe four or five million people, invests $15 million to $20 million per year in developing the inventions of individual inventors. Sweden is doing this. France's government is investing in technology and the innovative ideas of its inventors. The British are also spending money in this field. Why can't we do it? This isn't socialism; it's common sense. The techniques we use today just aren't working.

INTERVIEWER: *How about the patent system itself? Do you think there are any changes that should be made there?*

LEMELSON: I think the drop in patent filings by American inventors also means that Patent Office fees are far too high. Fees today are set up to make money for the Patent Office, and that money goes directly into the United States Treasury.

But what the government doesn't consider is the effect of these high fees on the creativity of individual inventors and small corporations. Many of them can't afford these high fees. And this, in turn, has a direct effect on jobs and productivity as well as on future taxes. It's a matter of playing with dollars.

Let's say an inventor has an idea that has the potential of becoming a billion-dollar product. Just think of the money that can be made by the government in collecting taxes from the manufacture, distribution, and sale of the product—and from the income of the people who work on designing and developing it. The government should not focus on the few millions of dollars that the Patent Office can make on filing fees from individual inventors.

Inventors should be charged only a minimal fee, if any, during the prosecution of patent applications. Maybe they shouldn't even be charged when a patent is issued. If the product is put into production and the inventor collects royalties on it, then the government can tax the increase in income. But the government shouldn't create a negative incentive by setting the fees so high that it keeps many inventors from filing. Thousands of dollars are required to get and maintain a patent today.

Do you know what we're going to end up with in this country? We're going to end up with a lot of abandoned patents that were given to the public and to foreign companies because the inventors couldn't afford to maintain them.

INTERVIEWER: How much would you say it costs on average to get a patent today?

LEMELSON: There was a day that it cost me $30 to file a patent application. You could have twenty claims, and it cost $30 to obtain the patent. Those fees were a bargain, but that was a lot of money for an individual thirty years ago.

Today, depending on the complexity of an application, filing fees run anywhere from $170 to $300. Issue fees, I believe, are between $280 and $560. The maintenance fees are also rather high. I'm not really sure of the figures offhand, but over the lifetime of a single patent they are on the order of thousands of dollars.

When you add legal costs to these fees, the cost of obtaining a patent ranges from $3,000 to $10,000. If you consider the average income of a typical inventor who may have a dozen good ideas to patent, it's a real hardship to ask for this kind of money. I personally know several inventors who are not filing patents because of the fee structure.

This money would be better spent in developing the market for an invention, rather than in paying Patent Office fees. I'm not saying that the Patent Office should not charge a fee; but the fee should be extremely low. If they want to collect money, let them collect it after the invention is developed and marketed. Then, let the money go through the Patent Office and the Treasury.

INTERVIEWER: *In addition to the burden of high fees, does the legal system and its role in the patent system pose any additional problems? Are patent infringement suits, for example, becoming more of a problem?*

Foreign countries are already helping their inventors.... This isn't socialism; it's common sense.

LEMELSON: The founding fathers of the United States set up the patent system to serve as an incentive for individual enterprise and invention. It was intended to encourage individuals and groups to put their minds and money to work on solving problems and finding new products. Through the limited exclusivity granted to them by a patent, they could then put their money into a business and profit from these ideas. For the country it meant the creation of new industries and new products.

To a great extent, the patent system has continued to function along those lines—generally, the system works—although I have some reservations about the way inventors are being treated by the system itself.

There has been, however, a clash between the patent system, which decides what an invention is, and the legal system, which determines whether or not a patent is valid. The two standards are different. A patent is granted on the basis of what a government agency, the United States Patent and Trademark Office, interprets as an invention. Staff members there spend a great part of their lives setting the standard for patentability. They issue patents to both corporations and individuals. I think their standard should be honored—not some other standard in the mind of an individual who feels that just about everything that's ever been invented is obvious. Rather than apply or ask for the licenses to make a patented product, they decide to go ahead and produce it on their own—or challenge the patent in court. And that's where you have a clash between the patent system and the legal system.

INTERVIEWER: *Some companies decide it's cheaper to go to court than buy a technology?*

LEMELSON: That sometimes happens, but companies really should make an analysis of licensing. You have a lot of personalities coming into the picture. An executive, attorney, or patent counsel makes a decision to challenge a patent, and on the basis of that decision that person's reputation is on the line. I believe that has happened to me a number of times.

In the years before I was able to license my first high-technology patent, I invented toys and novelty items. One of the novelty items I invented and patented was a face mask that could be printed on the back of a cereal box. It was a constructional mask.

I approached a number of cereal companies with the idea, and none of them were interested. But, lo and behold, the largest of them decided to put it on more than forty million boxes without consulting me or licensing my patent. When I informed them of my prior disclosure to them, they told me, in effect, to go fly a kite.

To make a long story short, I went to an attorney and started litigation against them that lasted a number of years. By the time it was over, the company had invested probably $150,000 to $200,000 in legal fees actually fighting me over a toy face mask. It must have become the obsession of an executive in the corporation. I don't know why they squandered all that money without making an effort to settle the matter. If they had lost, according to their own claims, they would have had to pay me no more than $15,000 for the rights to the mask.

Instead, it took five years of pretrial work and hundreds of thousands of dollars in legal fees. This just doesn't make sense to me. I just can't understand it. Perhaps if the right executive had looked at it or someone had really analyzed the situation, the case never would have gone past the first stage. It was detrimental to the net worth of the company, and it was certainly detrimental to me. By my way of thinking, it certainly isn't the way you should conduct a business. But when personalities and egos are involved, a situation like this can get out of control.

INTERVIEWER: *Part of the reason for a case like this is economics, but I'm sure your personal feelings also come into play.*

LEMELSON: Oh, you definitely have personal feelings about the matter. Someone's stealing your ideas.

INTERVIEWER: *I'm intrigued that you work in so many areas. You work with computers, robots, and automation, but you also work with toys and games. Do you use the toys for fun or for a break from more serious projects?*

LEMELSON: That's part of it. It's nice to have a lot of knowledge in a particular field and focus your inventions there. But if you're going to be a professional inventor, I don't think you should limit your ideas or concepts to a single field. Many people ask me why I didn't concentrate on one field. If I had concentrated on one field, perhaps more of my ideas would have reached the market.

My very first inventions were in the toy field. I got to know a number of the leading toy companies in those days. That was in the 1950s, and they were easier to approach with ideas than larger corporations. They were looking for outside ideas because the lifeblood of most toy companies is based on new ideas and new toy products. I spent a lot of time developing toys and found that I did have a lot of ideas in the toy field.

The first invention I actually licensed was a wheeled toy that I licensed to the Ideal Toy Company, and it sold very well. If you were lucky enough to license a toy, the companies were willing to pay a decent royalty, and back then I'd always hoped to make an income through toys so that I could continue working on my high-tech ideas. The technical systems I was working on at the time were sort of overwhelming. While I hoped to license them someday, there was nothing on the horizon, and I could never have built them on my own because of the high cost.

I wasn't able to actually license my high-tech inventions until 1964. By that time, I had already spent fourteen or fifteen years developing and inventing new toys.

INTERVIEWER: *What was your first high-tech breakthrough?*

LEMELSON: The first was in 1964 when I licensed my patents in the field of automatic warehousing. They covered a computer or punch-card-controlled stacker crane which operated in and out of storage areas to pick up and deliver palletized products.

INTERVIEWER: *Were you always interested in those kinds of high-tech inventions when you were working on toys?*

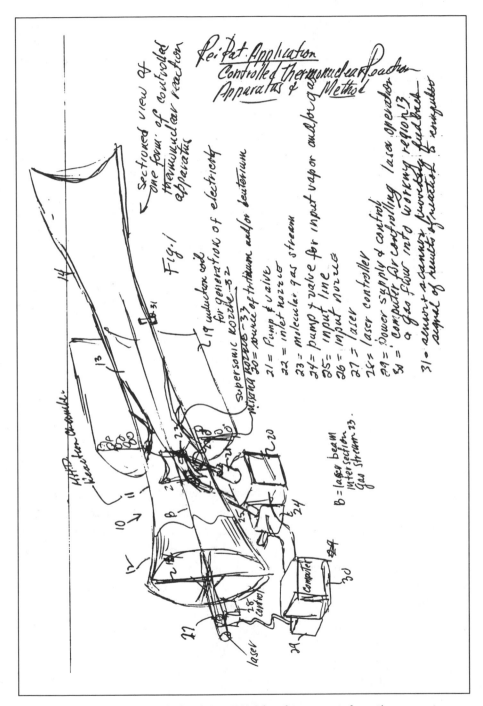

Jerome Lemelson's notebook sketch (ca. 1960s) for a laser-operated reaction apparatus. Although the form illustrated has not been patented, Lemelson has received a number of patents for inventions that employ lasers in chemical reactions.

LEMELSON: In my first few years as an inventor, I started to get ideas in the field of automation. It really got a boost when I attended a demonstration of a punch-card-controlled lathe. I don't remember why I was invited, but I went to see the demonstration, and it fascinated me.

I thought, Gee, here's a principle that I can apply to many different fields. It's not just limited to machine tools, but can be used for molding and extruding plastics, rolling mills, and manufacturing electronic circuits.

From that point, I started to think about automating production machinery. I got an idea for producing a universal robot that would not only handle products, but operate on them, measure them, and inspect them. These ideas later emerged as a flexible manufacturing system, which I was the first to patent. I envisioned it as computerized. Even though computers took up a whole room in those days, I believed that computers would come down in size.

At the time, however, I didn't know when that would be, so I used a programmer in my system which was about half the size of a present-day minicomputer. It performed the functions I wanted it to perform, and I wanted my machines to be automatically controlled.

By the way, I might mention that in 1960, the same year that integrated microcircuits were invented, I conceived of a way to manufacture them. I received several patents, which I licensed and which were actually in production at Texas Instruments for a number of years.

INTERVIEWER: *Just what is a flexible manufacturing system?*

LEMELSON: Let me explain what it is by first telling you what existed before flexible manufacturing. For example, a fixed production line was used in the machining of engine blocks and was called a transfer machine. Engine blocks were driven through the machine on conveyors, and fixed machine tools would operate on them as they passed through. But in the production line each machine tool could only perform one or two simple functions, and the transfer line always used the same machine tools in the same way on each engine block. Different machines had to be used to work on different parts of the engine block, and it was impossible to operate on different types of engine blocks without major changes in the transfer line, at a great cost in time and money.

But in the early 1950s when I was working on ideas about flexible manufacturing, I had visions of a machine line that would be highly flexible and capable of performing many different operations on many different units of work. When I say different, I mean that you could have an engine block pass along the machine line and be operated on one minute and a piston or an exhaust valve operated on the next. These "flexible machines" could perform different machining functions on each different part or product, if the functions were programmed into the computer.

Basically, a flexible manufacturing system consists of a series of computer-controlled machine tools which operate flexibly. They can perform many different operations on many different units of work or a number of different operations on the same unit of work. Several machines can even be used together and connected by conveyors to pass work from machine to machine, making use of machines that are not in use, while others are operating to boost productivity.

Many inventors conceive patentable ideas that are ahead of their time. The big problem is how far ahead.

You can, for example, have one flexible manufacturing system that may operate on fifty or more different parts or products. Today, companies are getting involved in flexible manufacturing cells which aren't as costly as a whole system. Eventually, one flexible manufacturing system may produce all of a company's output.

INTERVIEWER: *With flexible manufacturing, if a company wants to retool to build a new product, I assume they can reprogram their machines rather than buy new manufacturing equipment.*

LEMELSON: That's right. The Japanese have taken the lead in this. I believe that more than three hundred flexible manufacturing systems are in use in Japan, but the last figure I recall for the United States was that fewer than one hundred are in operation.

The Japanese have been the first to widely exploit flexible manufacturing even though the basic idea didn't come from Japan. It came from the United States. I own the first patents in the field, and they go back to the early 1950s.

INTERVIEWER: *When did you become a full-time inventor?*

LEMELSON: I would say my full-time efforts at inventing came about in 1957. That was when I terminated my last job as an engineer. Since then, I've had positions with several companies as the chief designer or vice president. I wasn't paid a salary with those positions, but I could devote my full time to inventing. My income came when a product was sold.

INTERVIEWER: *Did you always want to be a full-time inventor when you were working with other companies?*

LEMELSON: Not really. In the beginning, I wanted to manufacture certain ideas I had in the toy and hobby field and become financially independent. After that, I planned to get my own lab and machine shop and develop my ideas further.

I made several efforts to get into manufacturing, and they weren't very successful. I was working on a shoestring, and the money I had saved wasn't enough to carry me through. I finally gave up trying to put a product on the market. I thought that if I had a good product it would carry through on its own, but it just didn't work that way.

It wasn't until my last failure in business in 1961 that I realized I should become a professional inventor and spend most of my time at it. But it took me until 1964, when I licensed my automated warehouse patents, to be in a secure enough financial position to say, "I'm free to move ahead with full-time inventing."

INTERVIEWER: *Can inventions be too far ahead of their time?*

LEMELSON: My automated warehouse was actually that kind of invention, although it wasn't as far ahead of its time as I thought—or as my attorney thought. I went to a patent attorney with the idea in the mid-1950s, hoping that he would do the prosecution of the patent application on a percentage basis. "Jerry," he said, "I think you're twenty-five years ahead of your time. I can't afford to take anything on a straight percentage basis, but I'll charge you fifty percent of what I usually charge."

Well, I made a decision that if the system was going to be patented, I'd have to patent it myself. I eventually received fifteen patents in the field, and I wasn't twenty-five years ahead of my time; I was five. Five years after I filed my first patent application in automatic warehousing, a man in Cleveland started to develop the same system and became my first licensee in the field of electronically controlled warehousing systems.

I think many inventors conceive patentable ideas that are ahead of their time. The big problem is how far ahead. And it's a real problem when you come up with something that technology is already poised to overtake. In that case, you can be behind the times, and you don't even know it.

I'm working in a number of high-tech fields now, and I'm always worrying about whether or not the technology will advance so far ahead of me that I won't be able to license what I have already patented. I try to stay on the edge of technology as much as I can.

INTERVIEWER: *Have you come up with inventions that depend on pending technological advancements?*

LEMELSON: Yes, I have. Going back ten years ago when people were first talking about low-cost speech recognition chips, I started thinking about new products that could use them. I had already filed for a number of patents in the field by the late 1970s even though manufacturers didn't actually come out with the circuits and chips to do this until the 1980s. I still hope to license some of them.

One of the products I've patented is a talking thermometer. It's a simple idea, one that I've submitted to most of the thermometer companies in the United States. They've all turned me down. Last year I discovered that it's being sold in drugstores in Japan and that it's a successful product over there. So, now I'm going back to the people I previously approached here.

I think there's a need for a talking thermometer. The response has been that there are only a limited number of blind people who would buy it. But this product is not meant just for blind people, although it would certainly be a boon to a blind person to be able to take his own temperature. I really think somebody should say, "I'm not going to make a billion dollars on this product, but I'll do something for a number of deserving people— the blind."

But I didn't get that response. I went to some of the largest medical instrument companies in the country, and they all told me that there isn't a big enough market for it. But I also look at it as an aid to a person who may not be blind but may have bad vision. They might not have their glasses on, or they might want to read their temperature at night. It could be a substantial aid to a nurse. With both digital and voice indications of temperature, a nurse would have two inputs to reduce the possibility of errors. So, I believe there's a market for a talking thermometer, and I think it deserves to be on the market in this country.

INTERVIEWER: *It sounds like you are running into the same disinterest you talked about earlier as the NIH syndrome.*

LEMELSON: It's not restricted to small products like the talking thermometer, but it also pervades larger and more innovative products as well. It's so easy not to make ripples. If your company is moving along at a certain level, why stick your neck out? We appear to be playing big games of monopoly today. We're buying and selling corporations. We're not buying technology and selling new products.

Very few inventions are breakthroughs in any of the fields.

We really should think more in terms of the future. We all have children, and many of us have grandchildren. What's it going to be like for Americans ten or fifteen or twenty years from now? We really have to think more in terms of our nation's future.

INTERVIEWER: *Do you have anything you like to invent?*

LEMELSON: I really enjoy inventing products and systems in the art of information handling, particularly in the field of computer peripherals and electronic systems. I like inventing things of a technical nature, as opposed to toys or gadgets. I also like inventing things that make life easier or safer.

INTERVIEWER: *Do you have any inventions in mind which fit this category?*

LEMELSON: In retailing, for example, I've developed a transaction system that can be used in stores; it is an interactive transaction system. I've been working on such systems for many years.

In the machine-tool field, I've patented a talking micrometer that machinists can use. It provides speech playback of measurements made. Most micrometers use a Vernier scale. For a machinist using his eyes all day long, there's some eyestrain involved, and inspection is tedious. It's quite easy to make a mistake. Such a device would help a lot of people.

In the education field, I've got some patents that cover a book-reading toy. The software is printed matter read by a hand-held light pen. You get feedback in the form of synthetic speech such as questions and answers to questions or the speech equivalent of printed words. It can also be used to

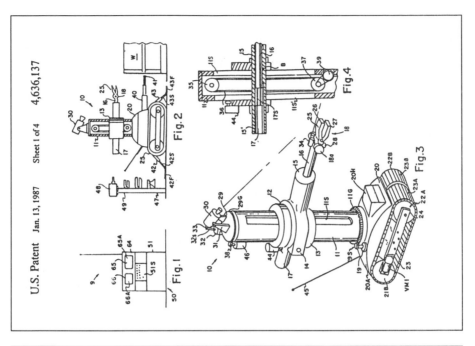

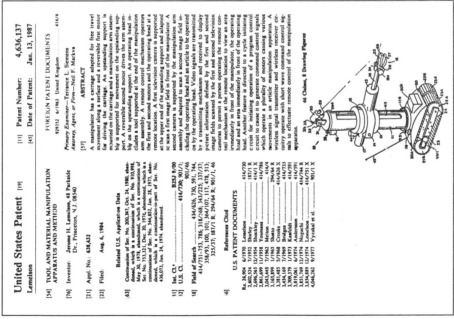

Patent drawings for Jerome Lemelson's free-traveling robot (dated January 13, 1987), which can be controlled at a select site by computer, or, via television cameras, by a remote operator at a console. This patent took twelve years to issue.

generate music. You can perform many educational functions with the system. I've invested quite a bit of time and money in it, and I think it deserves a place in our educational system today. Unfortunately, another company came out with a similar product at about the same time my development work was proceeding, and they killed the item by not presenting or promoting it properly.

INTERVIEWER: *You seem to be fairly interested in exploiting speech recognition technology.*

LEMELSON: Well, I have a number of patents pending in that field as well as a basic patent on a system which generates speech to indicate or monitor what's happening in a process. For example, my system can be used as part of a central monitoring station to verbally indicate a fire, where it is located, how far it has spread, and so on. Firefighters wouldn't have to rely on displays; the system would talk to them. In another form, the speech warning system could indicate and monitor forest fires. Used in hospitals, such a system could monitor intensive-care patients. Some medical companies are evaluating the invention now.

Also in the medical field, I have patented a system for storing a person's entire medical history—including visual data, X rays, and so on—on a single card. This idea's being evaluated by a number of companies.

I like to devote time to inventions in the medical field. I feel that inventions in the field of education and medicine are certainly of a higher level of importance than games and toys. But I will not deprecate ideas in the field of entertainment because that field is important to the well-being of the public as well.

INTERVIEWER: *What do you consider the most important invention of the past twenty to twenty-five years?*

LEMELSON: Invention or development?

INTERVIEWER: *Invention.*

LEMELSON: The greatest effect on the most number of people?

INTERVIEWER: *Yes.*

LEMELSON: Obviously, computers. And what will probably have the greatest effect on the most number of people will be the personal computer. It will change the way people think and act and communicate and obtain information or knowledge. It's definitely the revolution of the century.

INTERVIEWER: Will computers also change the direction of invention? Will inventing in the future be limited to those with a high-tech background, or is there still room for the creative thinker and tinkerer?

LEMELSON: I have never really given much thought to the future of invention or creativity. As for the impact of computers, I think they will make it easier for inventors who don't have a technical background to find information they need to develop their inventions.

More and more people are operating computers, and more and more data banks are coming on-line to increase the data-handling explosion. They are available to almost anyone who wants to subscribe to them whether they are involved in university research, are students, or are just individuals seeking information. A person who doesn't have a technical background can use this information to arrive at a point where he can get suitable technical assistance to help him develop his invention. In the future, the information explosion is going to contribute to creativity in a big way.

Nowadays, when someone gets an idea for a widget, the recourse is to go to a patent attorney who contacts a researcher to search the literature for $200 to $500 to find out if the widget was invented before. In the future, however, there may come a time when the patent system will have a data bank available on the telephone lines. This may not put the individual in a position to determine whether or not the idea is patentable, but it will certainly be possible to provide him with an idea of what exists in the particular area of his invention and use that information to decide whether to pursue the idea further.

In addition, information that is in the public domain in all fields of technology should be made available and will be made available to inventors through data banks and computer communications systems. Eventually, libraries will be set up this way. We may have a central library in Washington, D.C., or several of them throughout the country. Each library will have information in storage and electronically available to anyone who seeks it—instantly cross-referenced, on-line in the home or office.

INTERVIEWER: So, the inventor of the future will have better information to draw upon, but he or she will still go through the same processes and try to clear the same hurdles in realizing a new idea.

LEMELSON: A friend of mine once said that you have to be a prophet to be an inventor, but I don't agree with that. The average person can't just sit down and say, "Hey, ten years from now here's what's going to be in demand." Speculation like that is not the way to go about it.

I think the way to go about it is to ask yourself these questions: Is this particular function being properly performed? Is it being performed in the best way possible? Are there any problems with it? How can I improve upon it? The patent system contains patents, most of which are simply improvements over what existed before. And that's really the name of the game: improving on what's existing today. Very few inventions are breakthroughs in any of the fields.

STANFORD OVSHINSKY

*I*N THE *mid-1950s and early 1960s, while other scientists and engineers were opening the door to solid-state electronics with well-ordered crystals of silicon, Stanford Ovshinsky began studying amorphous materials. In 1968, Ovshinsky, a self-taught machinist from Akron, Ohio, published his ideas in the prestigious* Physical Review Letters *and unveiled his amorphous semiconductors. Crystalline structure, he stated, was not necessarily important when it came to making semiconductors. One could just as easily build semiconductors, and other microelectronic devices, with amorphous materials.* Established scientists were outraged. Ovshinsky's paper became one of the journal's five most frequently cited papers.

Ovshinsky's ideas, however, were backed by such prestigious scientists as Columbia's Nobel Prize-winning physicist, I. I. Rabi, Sir Nevill Mott of Cambridge University, Hellmut Fritzsche and Morrel Cohen of the University of Chicago, and MIT's David Adler. Proving these ideas to the rest of the academic community, however, took more than five years.

Some critics accused him of overstatement. Others took a more sophisticated approach to the critique, claiming that his amorphous Ovonic switch was not really a switch at all, and that the phenomenon Ovshinsky had observed in his laboratory was due only to heating from the electric current, not to any intrinsic property of the Ovonic material. It was, these critics claimed, an unreliable and unstable switch. Feelings ran so hot that when Ovshinsky presented his results at a meeting sponsored by the United States Army's research office in 1969, he was booed by critics in the audience.

Today, Ovshinsky has more than one hundred patents relating to Ovonic devices. Well-known United States companies such as IBM, Raytheon, 3M, and Standard Oil of Ohio, as well as Japanese companies like Matsushita and Canon, have licensed his ideas or worked with his company, Energy Conversion Devices (ECD).

Ovshinsky has put his Ovonic materials to use in new applications as well, ranging from new types of computer memories to photovoltaic cells.

Stanford Ovshinsky was educated in the public school system in Akron, Ohio. After graduating from high school and trade school, he worked as a machinist and later invented a high-speed, automated lathe. That work in automation directed his interest towards neurology: While director of research at the Hupp Corporation, a manufacturer of automobile parts, Ovshinsky started building switches and models that mimicked the actions of neurons.

Ovshinsky has worked closely throughout his career with his wife, Dr. Iris Miroy Ovshinsky, a biochemist whom he married in 1959 and who shares his interest in the workings of the brain. Together they founded ECD in 1960 in a Detroit storefront. Today, the company is headquartered in Troy, Michigan, with a branch office in Tokyo.

Stanford Ovshinsky is a fellow of the American Physics Society and of the American Association for the Advancement of Science (AAAS), and a senior member of the Institute of Electrical and Electronics Engineers (IEEE).

INTERVIEWER: *When you first came up with your theories on Ovonics, did you ever doubt that you'd be able to make it work?*

OVSHINSKY: No, I never did. I had a complete picture in my mind of how Ovonic materials were going to work and be applied, although I certainly didn't have all the details that I see now. I even had strategy charts of all the different things we were going to do. I knew we were going to build computers with these materials; I knew that AT&T was going to be interested in computers and that Texas Instruments and IBM were going to be interested in telecommunications. And that's exactly what happened.

I was also fortunate in getting some good scientists to support me very early on. I owe a particular debt of gratitude to that great man, Dr. I. I. Rabi of Columbia University, for having become a member of our board of directors and to Hellmut Fritzsche, who was later chairman of the Department of Physics at the University of Chicago. David Adler of MIT, Arthur

Bienenstock, head of the Stanford Synchrotron Radiation Laboratory [SSRL], and Heinz Henisch of Penn State [Pennsylvania State University] were also very helpful to me.

When I think of it all starting in a small room in the 1950s, I feel very good about it. My wife and I worked very hard.

INTERVIEWER: *It seems as though you are always showing people things they simply don't understand, turning conventional wisdom on its head. Has it been tough bucking the field? Did the rejections make you work harder?*

OVSHINSKY: I think it made me work harder. If you really want to do something that's basic and important and fundamental, you have to realize that people aren't going to accept it right away. That inertia doesn't only come from human institutions; it's in the brain as well. An organism is not made to respond quickly to change. Society is not meant to be in nonequilibrium conditions very often—for no more profound a reason than ensuring its own self-survival.

> *A new idea has to win its place against normal skepticism, a lack of desire to change, and even jealousy.*

So, a new idea has to win its place against normal skepticism, a lack of desire to change, and even jealousy. Not jealousy so much in a personal sense, but in the sense that people think, Gee, I ought to be smart enough to have thought of that one. Why does this upstart think he knows that? He doesn't have any formal training in this.

And on top of all that, my background is not a conventional background. I came into the study of amorphous materials by way of neurology. I did not have a Ph.D. or anything like that, so it was obvious I was going to have a hard time. Not because of my personality—fortunately I persevered—but because that's the historical way an idea has to win its place.

To understand the opposition I encountered, you have to go back to the deeply felt position that scientists had when my Ovonic switches first appeared. To them, semiconducting action was based upon the periodicity and the lattice structure of a crystal. It was dogma; it was truth; it was theology. And to say it was irrelevant was to be a heretic. Crystalline theory is

what they got their Ph.D.'s in. And, as a result, no one was trained to understand me; acceptance initially came from adventuresome and brilliant people who were open to new ideas.

INTERVIEWER: *What were the first Ovonic materials you came up with?*

OVSHINSKY: The term Ovonics originally applied to two classes of
material. The first class could be used as a switch, and the second could be
used as a computer memory.

The switches are made from a thin film of amorphous materials,
typically on the order of a micron in thickness. Generally, these switches are
made from films of chalcogenides. (In the 1950s, I also worked with copper
oxides, which are now important for their superconducting actions.)

In its "off" state, the Ovonic threshold switch acts like a dielectric, or
nonconductor, and keeps current from flowing. When the voltage is increased above a certain threshold, however, the switch becomes a conductor and conducts electricity like a metal. It's also a reversible switch; once
the voltage drops below a certain level, it becomes a dielectric again. The
Ovonic threshold switch is the fastest room-temperature switch ever invented. (Only the Josephson junction,* which works at several hundred
degrees below zero, is as fast.) It's a completely symmetrical switch and can
also be used as an AC switch. The amorphous material in the switch is
stable and undergoes no structural change.

INTERVIEWER: *How do Ovonic computer memories work?*

OVSHINSKY: The Ovonic memory device is another type of switch, and
the material it's made of is deliberately designed to be unstable to excitation
by light or electricity. It is structurally bistable: When it's subjected to excitation, the material undergoes a structural change. Information is stored
into that structural change like bits in a digital computer: One structural
condition represents "on," and another condition represents "off."
Although the memory switch is reversible, the structural changes are
locked in—the memory switch can remain in the amorphous "off" state or
the more ordered crystalline "on" state, without any voltage or holding current present.

These switches have been used for computer memories and are now
standard on IBM's personal computers in what's called an optical memory.

---

* An electronic fast-switching device consisting of layers of superconducting metal separated by a thin layer of
insulator; low current flows through the insulator, but increased current causes it to block the flow.

One form of that is switched by light, such as would come from a laser, instead of an electric field. The electrical memory was the first, and to my knowledge, the only nonvolatile EAROM [electrically alterable read-only memory] made.

Another form of Ovonic memory is an adaptive memory. It has the ability to learn. When you activate the memory in an adaptive system, you have a change of local order on the molecular level, and the structure of the material goes from amorphous to crystalline. That structural change into a more ordered state also stores information. There is also a change in electrical resistance corresponding to the change in structure.

INTERVIEWER: *I've heard that you developed your theories on amorphous materials through work in neurology. Solid-state physics by way of neurology is a rather unusual path. How did your ideas develop?*

OVSHINSKY: I started developing my theories about amorphous materials by thinking about the relationships between the surfaces of neurons in the brain and the storage and encoding of information. I was also interested in the relationship between information and the energy transformations that occur in the brain. It was obvious to me that what was going on did not involve crystallinity.

I wanted to find a way of duplicating in the lab the neuron's storage of information. And in trying to do this, I realized that I was in a field that was simply not explainable by conventional memory systems or by the conventional crystalline approach to solid-state physics.

In 1955, I started building small models based on my ideas of ordered and disordered materials and the conversion of disordered materials into more ordered materials as a means of encoding information.

Although my models were not crystalline, you could produce a crystalline structure from the amorphous state in response to energy and vice versa. And those energy transformations were very interesting.

So, early on, I took the position that energy conversion and information encoding were one and the same thing; in fact, they were opposite sides of the same coin.

INTERVIEWER: *When did you build your first Ovonic device?*

OVSHINSKY: In 1957, I started doing work beyond building models. Previously, I'd worked with passive amorphous surfaces, which I had made active by using an external force such as an electric field or a magnet. In 1957, I started to make my models active on a microscopic level—a chemical level.

To do that, I started working with the transition metal oxides, such as a tantalum oxide. Using thin films of those oxides, I was able to make the first Ovonic switch. I think I first mentioned this publicly in 1958. In fact, I gave my first talk on it in 1959 at the Detroit Physiological Society, one of the oldest societies of its kind in the country. I was also working on a memory version at the time.

I have a big list. I wish I had more years. I feel like I'm just getting started.

With my models, I was able to prove that by using thin films of noncrystalline material, it is possible to build analogs or devices realistic in size and function that could resemble neuronal action in the brain. And as I pursued this, it seemed to me that I was onto something very important.

At the time, the leading authority in the neurophysiological field, a fellow at MIT by the name of McCullough, considered the neuron to be like an empty bag. I didn't think that was true. I believed that both the internal structures and the surface of the "bag" were very important in encoding switching and transmitting information.

Everyone recognizes that the relationships between atomic orbits on the surface of a material are different from those in the bulk. These bonding configurations on the surface of a material are scattered at random, and the random sites are disordered. I thought that surface disorder was the beginning of a deeper disorder that would become three-dimensional as one went into the bulk. I was right, and those surface disorders, or more properly, differing local orders, did provide a way of understanding the properties of certain amorphous materials.

So, that's how it all started. My interest in disordered materials was very clear in the middle of the 1950s, and my inventions resulted in devices with unusual properties. Other people studying amorphous materials at the time—and there were very few, mostly in Russia—simply took measurements of different physical properties. No one else thought amorphous materials could be used to design new types of semiconductors or a new computer memory, or that they could be useful in energy conversion.

In 1960, my wife and I founded the company, ECD [Energy Conversion Devices], in a Detroit storefront. We called it Energy Conversion Labs at the time. We chose that name because I felt the work that we were doing could be applied to everything from photovoltaics to thermoelectricity to new kinds of batteries, sensors, memories, switches, transistors, and many other things as well.

INTERVIEWER: *What do you see as the future of Ovonics? Is there anything you'd like to invent?*

OVSHINSKY: Oh, I have a whole list of things I'd like to do. One of my favorite is three-dimensional circuits. They keep getting closer and closer to the brain models I've developed. We call them the nth generation electronics because they are not just the next generation. There are many new computing possibilities when you get down to those sizes and densities of circuits and interconnections.

I've also worked on superconductivity for a long time, and that's now a field that generates tremendous excitement. I feel we have an important contribution to make there.

I see Ovonic devices leading to new kinds of transistors, new kinds of integrated circuits, new kinds of computers, new kinds of materials and coatings. I also see amorphous materials as being a big factor in producing and storing energy.

I have a big list. I wish I had more years. I feel like I'm just getting started. Unfortunately, or perhaps fortunately, I feel as though I'm nineteen.

INTERVIEWER: *Do you see Ovonic materials playing an important role in energy production?*

OVSHINSKY: I really feel that the world needs to build new industries that are going to do some good. The old, declining industries are in bad shape. I think energy and information are going to be the two largest industries in the future, if they're not right now.

In my view, it's ridiculous not to use sunlight. It's not just a utopian dream anymore. We've advanced to the point where solar energy can be competitive with conventional fuels such as coal, oil, gas, and uranium. I believe that our work on energy is going to have a profound effect in the world. My idea is to develop photovoltaics into a giant, new industry that will help to do something about the greenhouse effect and make for a more peaceful world.

Energy that comes from conventional fuels is dangerous. Oil is a dangerous commodity whether it is in surplus or in shortage. Wars are being fought over it. Just look at what's happening in the Middle East. Nuclear energy is obviously an idea whose time has passed—you can also explode the whole world with it. Even coal is dangerous as a pollutant, and the fact that you have the greenhouse effect makes it even more dangerous.

INTERVIEWER: *Do you see yourself as a "big-picture" inventor? Do you like to come up with the general ideas and theories behind some new technology, Ovonics for instance, and then leave the nuts and bolts of application to others? Or do you like to work in all phases of invention?*

OVSHINSKY: I can't do just a big picture. I have to get down to detail. I have to see atoms and their relationships and change them in my own mind. I'm a visualizer. And, since amorphous materials are so process-dependent, I have to be able to develop the technology for manufacturing.

If you look at my inventions, you'll see that I'm as much involved in the machines that build the products—the nuts and bolts—as I am in the concepts, the basic claims, and the materials themselves.

INTERVIEWER: *Was your schooling a hindrance to thinking creatively, or did it give you some important nuts and bolts?*

OVSHINSKY: Teachers were largely a negative influence on me. I read very widely when I was a small kid, and that had the greatest effect on me. I could take as many books out of the local library as I wanted, and when I was only six, seven, and eight years old, I read everything in the sciences that I could get my hands on.

Later, when I worked in machine shops—that's where I came from really—I found that inventiveness and creativity could be put to use in the old arts of machining. Science could be applied to machine tools.

INTERVIEWER: *Was that where you made your first inventions?*

OVSHINSKY: My first invention was a high-speed center-drive metal lathe. It could run at very high speeds that no one ever considered before, orders of magnitude higher than anything else that had been done. This was in the early 1940s.

I used new physics in inventing that lathe, but I also did something that was very important in getting me started in this whole field of neurophysiology: I made everything automatic, what is now called robotics. I was intrigued by the "intelligence" and ability of automated machines.

It was a very important part of my life. My center-drive machine was used all over the world. It gave me the confidence that I was an inventor and that what I could do could be totally different from anything that had even been considered before.

It was a self-confirmation, a positive reinforcement. Once you're off and running and have a success like that, you think, Okay, I can invent...this is right...I love it...this is exciting...it's what I want to do. So, it's a commitment that you make, and it's also, in a sense, a calling that you answer. You wouldn't be happy if you weren't doing it.

I believe that our work on energy is going to have a profound effect in the world.

INTERVIEWER: *Are inventors becoming rare in the United States? Is there a shortage of creativity when it comes to solving problems?*

OVSHINSKY: Well, I think we have a culture which makes it difficult for creativity to express itself properly. But it's a problem that's never been solved in any part of the world, so it's not just simply the United States. But it is difficult to change society, and you've got to accept that and see what you can do about it.

INTERVIEWER: *Are new and different attitudes in the business community part of the problem?*

OVSHINSKY: American businesses used to be really oriented toward technology and science, toward manufacturing things, and we are losing that kind of base, the kind of "we-can-do-it" inventiveness that America is noted for, the Midwest spirit which is part of me.

You now have young people who are not exposed to that kind of environment and atmosphere. You have McDonald's and Wendy's; you have lawyers and professional people—all of whom are consumer-oriented.

An inventor can't really live alone. He needs money. The old warhorses who helped transform America after the Civil War may have been pirates, but they also knew that their fortunes would be made with new products and new ideas.

The financial community today, by contrast, has no real understanding of creativity. It's a different culture than they're accustomed to. They're very "bottom-line oriented," without understanding what makes up the bottom line. They come from a different background than the old guard, and they don't share the same concepts. They're not builders.

The idea of finance in American business today, in fact, seems to be buying and selling other companies—mergers, forced mergers, takeovers, and so on. The basis of finance today is not science and technology. Somehow, it's become a paper transaction which doesn't create new jobs or new industries.

I see it as a very bad change of our culture, detrimental to any kind of advancement of America's position in the world. What one needs is new products and new technology. That's what answers needs and gives you world leadership.

INTERVIEWER: *The old guard may have been supportive, but they also got their pound of flesh.*

OVSHINSKY: Well, yes. I remember many years ago negotiating with a son of one of America's wealthiest families. He was what they call a venture capitalist today, but we didn't call them that back then.

He was a young man, and he told me what his proposition was and laid out all the details. I thought about it a bit and said, "Well, gee, this all sounds rather confusing. My calculations indicate that I get nothing out of this deal, and you get everything. Why would it make any sense for me to do this with you?" He was very bemused. "Well, Stan," he said, "what you don't understand is that inventors were born to be screwed." And that, I guess, was a very important statement. He looked at history and had all sorts of rationalizations for it.

INTERVIEWER: *Do you feel that many of your inventions were things that people just weren't ready for?*

OVSHINSKY: They certainly weren't ready when I did my first inventions. But fortunately, things have changed. A critical mass has been reached, and we have a much more receptive audience out there. I never had that problem in Japan. Japan didn't care where the ideas came from as long as they were good and useful.

One of the biggest impediments to invention and its exploitation here is bureaucracy. The institutional resistance to new ideas is far harder to overcome than individual resistance—although one can't distinguish between them.

When one speaks of a revolution—even the transistor revolution—one thinks of something happening overnight, and it simply doesn't happen that way. Look at the transistor revolution: the number of people working in the field, the amount of money invested, and the inordinate amount of time it took to take hold—from 1947 to 1957. Some of the leading companies who you thought should have succeeded ended up failing.

With Ovonic materials, it was easy to see that I was going to have a hard time getting people to accept them because the field was so new. I wanted to use them in new forms of photography, for new types of computer memories, for new types of photovoltaic cells, and for superconducting devices.

As a company, we're building new industries rather than just one product. If I had focused on just one, I might have had success sooner.

INTERVIEWER: *Is your superconducting material a new type of Ovonic material?*

OVSHINSKY: It's something that uses the basic concepts of Ovonic materials with disorder playing a part and local order being important. It is related to my earlier work in chemically-modified ceramics. Fluorine is a key element, and that's what we use in some of our other materials.

INTERVIEWER: *When did you first start working with superconducting materials?*

OVSHINSKY: I've been working with oxides since the early 1960s, and I've been working with the new ceramics since they were publicized by Paul Chu and his colleagues in Houston in late 1986.

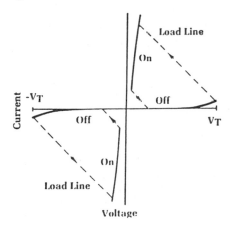

Illustration of the Ovonic threshold switch from Stanford Ovshinsky's controversial paper on amorphous materials.

INTERVIEWER: *You have achieved the highest temperature of superconductivity to date. Are you trying to go higher, and is the industry ready to take off?*

OVSHINSKY: We're at 90 degrees Fahrenheit now in our magnetic measurements and frankly, we've seen indications of superconductivity as high as 370 degrees Kelvin—which is much more than anyone's ever going to need. Our results of zero-resistance at 155 degrees Kelvin have now been confirmed by other researchers in China and Japan. We were glad to have that confirmation of our results from outside laboratories.

Invention as a whole is a very lonely art.

As for how quickly superconducting materials will catch on, it's very funny. It's a question I always ask because I know how long it takes to have an important new invention gain acceptance. With superconductivity, I think that the microelectronics part of it is going to move very fast. It will also move fast in areas like solenoids—the workhorse device. Applications like levitating trains, however, will take a long time to develop just by virtue of their size.

I feel we're in a good position to move into this field at ECD because we have the proprietary technology already in place for making thin films, strips, wires, powders, and devices that can carry a lot of current.

INTERVIEWER: *How important do you think a technical background is to being a successful inventor?*

OVSHINSKY: You must have a knowledge of technical subjects, but that does not necessarily mean a formal education. After all, I worked in the field of medicine, was published in medical journals, and I had nothing but a high school and trade school education. However, I am continually learning and educating myself.

I remember once sending back a medical paper of mine that had been accepted because they had addressed the acceptance letter, "Dear Dr. Ovshinsky." I wanted them to understand that I was not a doctor, in case that influenced their acceptance of the paper. They said that it didn't influence them at all, that the paper had been reviewed, that it was a very good paper, and that they recommended its acceptance.

What you have to do to succeed when you have a background like mine is to be like a minority person has to be in order to succeed: better prepared than others. You have to be even better educated. You must not make mistakes—either in terms of your words or in terms of your laboratory results. It's incredibly important that you are technically knowledgeable and proficient. Otherwise, even if you have a good idea, it will be destroyed—by the most sophisticated and sometimes malicious criticism. But criticism is what science is all about. You must be able to survive that, and you must be able to prove by legitimate scientific methods that you are indeed right.

INTERVIEWER: Is there any particular time or situation you find most productive? Do you get your solutions simply by keeping at something?

OVSHINSKY: No, no. I have to go through what I call my war dance to invent. First, I have to know what the problem is. Then, I do wide-range reading about the problem. And I have to work very hard thinking about it. I guess you could say it's like processing information into a computer.

Once that's done, I can do anything else—I can be at the beach, I can be walking in the woods—and suddenly, I will get the answers I want. Then, I hurry back to my workbench and try them out. These days, that means working with fellow scientists on my staff. I experiment and change things until I get what I want. It's a process that I force myself into whenever I have a problem.

INTERVIEWER: Have any of your inventions simply come to you right out of the blue?

OVSHINSKY: There's only one time that it happened that way, and even then it was as if my mind was prepared for the invention.

One of the big three automotive companies told our people that they wanted a transparent glass that generated electricity. They had discussed this with me before, and maybe I had already started thinking about it. We were in a meeting and our people were saying, "Now, that's a contradiction in terms. Obviously, if you absorb light, you're going to have some color. What's wrong with these stupid guys? Don't they understand it? That's the automotive industry."

Suddenly, when they said that, I just leaned over and said, "No, I understand how you can do it." And I did. We proved it experimentally, and now we have several patents on it. Something like that, a flash I guess, does happen, but I still think it couldn't have happened if I hadn't been challenged by some of the negative remarks our people were making about the request.

That work was part of our synthetic materials concepts. With amorphous materials you no longer have to worry about the crystalline lattice. You can design materials in two-dimensional and three-dimensional space—put atoms where nobody ever considered putting them before. It's opened up new fields of synthetic materials. Rather than just work with the materials we get from the mines, we can get new materials from the *mind*.

INTERVIEWER: *Almost everything you do is high tech, and as soon as somebody mentions the words high tech, most people think of Silicon Valley or Route 128 around Boston. What keeps you in Detroit?*

OVSHINSKY: Trying to define anything in terms of geography is all quite silly, really. Geography is just where you are. Nobody ever thought of California as an electronic state until Bill Shockley went there and started the semiconductor industry.* Nobody ever thought of Texas as an electronic state until Texas Instruments built up its solid-state empire. Detroit became an automotive city because Henry Ford and others happened to be here.

I like to use Einstein as an example. He was a Patent Office clerk when he did his greatest work. He did it without even having colleagues to talk to. Newton left London at the time of the plague and went to a farmhouse and did his greatest work all by himself—came up with theories that affect the way we all live.

I don't put myself in their company. I'm only using them as examples to show that creativity has nothing to do with where you're at. The magic of an area does not rub off on you.

INTERVIEWER: *Is environment important for an inventor?*

OVSHINSKY: I've been able to set up an environment here—an environment that I know is part of the inventive process.

With this company, I am able to think of things on my own and in my own way. I'm also able to try out my ideas without having to go through various committees. That isn't usually possible in a large corporation. And in a university, it's sometimes difficult to have the kind of laboratory you need at your disposal.

---

* Shockley Semiconductor was founded in 1955 by Nobel Prize-winner William Shockley in his hometown of Palo Alto, California.

In the last twenty-seven years, I've been very fortunate in building up a well-equipped laboratory with tremendously talented and superb people who are also very inventive in their own right. I also have a very good group of colleagues and collaborators that I can share ideas with. I know that environment is part of the invention process.

INTERVIEWER: *Regarding the actual creative process, do you find that it's important to have other people to share ideas with, or do you work better on your own?*

OVSHINSKY: I do it both ways. But because I work in advanced areas of science, I do find that there are few text-books to help me. To be able to flesh out my ideas with my colleagues and my wife, Iris, is very important. It's important to be sure that I don't have any artifacts in my experiments giving me misleading results; that theoretically, I'm not using any wrong

> *Criticism is what science is all about. You must be able to survive that....*

or misleading theory. In the early days, just talking it over with Iris was enough. But as we got involved in more sophisticated areas—like superconductivity or catalysis—I found I drew on a larger pool of colleagues, although the basic ideas are certainly my own. In some cases, my ideas become takeoff points, inspiring my colleagues as well.

For example, there's a well-known model in the field of amorphous materials called the Kastner–Adler–Fritzsche model. Some years ago, I was thinking about the bonding between lone pairs in semiconductors and came up with the idea that amorphous chalcogenides could have one- and three-electron bonds, along with their normal deviations. Well, those three scientists went ahead and made up a thoroughly acceptable and brilliant theoretical model using that concept in terms of what's called valence alternation pairs. Its implications were far beyond my original idea, and it's a beautiful piece of work. It's good to have colleagues because compatible colleagues can stimulate each other.

INTERVIEWER: *But is finding the original idea a solitary quest?*

OVSHINSKY: Invention as a whole is a very lonely art. Other people are important when it comes to making it happen and turning an idea into a

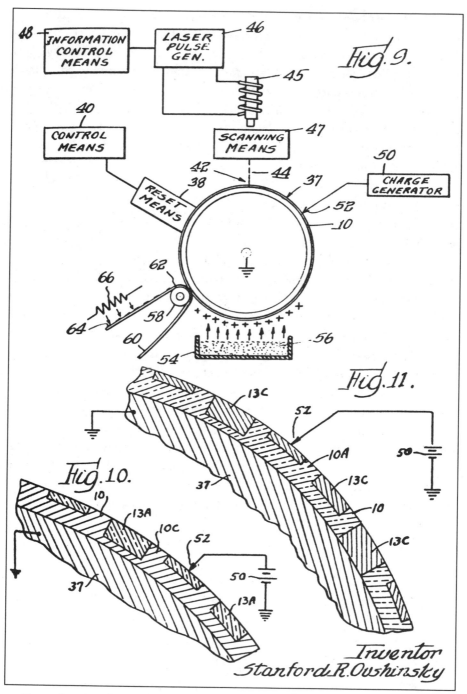

Patent drawings for one of Stanford Ovshinsky's devices for information storage and
retrieval (dated September 22, 1970).

successful invention. But the original idea is not the work of a committee. It is not the product of brainstorming or whatever other sort of term people want to use.

Ideas don't come out of a collective. People who say an invention is in the air or is a product of the times simply don't understand the process. I like one story about Einstein very much. Somebody once said that a committee probably could have come up with Einstein's famous relativity formula—but Einstein would have had to have been on the committee.

INTERVIEWER: *What do you think it takes to be a good inventor?*

OVSHINSKY: You must have what I call perfect pitch. One of my sons is a musician, and I've talked to him about perfect pitch. You have to know yourself whether or not an idea is really right. That's an intuitive feel like having perfect pitch.

INTERVIEWER: *Do you feel you have perfect pitch?*

OVSHINSKY: I've been inventing for a long time—since my late teens—and I'm sixty-four now. I know when it's right. I don't have to convince myself each time. On the other hand, I don't mislead myself either. You have to be very critical and not overly taken with enthusiasm, while at the same time, you must be enthusiastically driven. But somehow you must know whether or not you are right. And that's an intangible.

For example, I have many good friends who are much better at mathematics than I am. They've done calculations and shown them to me and I say, "It's wrong." And they say, "But I've spent a whole day on the computer." And I say, "It's wrong. Don't do that; don't publicize it. It's just not right." And I was right. Their calculations were wrong.

It doesn't mean that I'm better in mathematics than they are. That's ridiculous. But I think it means that I have a physical intuition, a feel that has been right and has been my saving grace. Maybe you can't teach people that, and maybe you can. At least you can sharpen it in people who have it.

It may very well be—or what I consider to be, knowing neurophysiology—that it isn't only the brain or the nerve cells that are important. It's the thresholds of the nerve cells—the connections they make—that are important. Obviously, my brain works differently than others'. I think other people think more logically, or at least with a different logic than I do. I'm very logical once I get to an idea, but my way of reaching a conclusion is based on my own form of logic, with many parallel paths operating simultaneously, perhaps subconsciously, based on a lot of information that I have already gathered.

For the most part, my inventions come from seemingly unrelated information. Therefore, I can only imagine that my brain works that way and that I make paths and connections where other people do not. There are a lot of people who may be smarter than I—so what is it that makes me a successful inventor? It's got to be that I process my information differently and draw upon my store, my environment, differently.

> I have a physical intuition, a feel that has been right and has been my saving grace.

INTERVIEWER: *Perseverance and dedication have certainly been important in your work. How important do you think they are to invention in general?*

OVSHINSKY: You must not be afraid of being alone. A lot of people may have good ideas and see different pathways and never have the courage to go against the crowd. Maybe they can't fight in defense of something that they believe in or persevere against great odds. A lot of people just don't want to do that. Why should they go through that?

I can't speak for other inventors, but I know that what has been important for me has been the ability to stand on my own and not cave in because other people don't agree with me. You have to be able to have a feel for a problem and know that you are right. And you have to work very, very hard. As I see it, many are called but few are chosen. Perseverance on a wrong approach is the bane of many would-be inventors. I think that one either has that critical intuitive "feel" or one doesn't.

INTERVIEWER: *Are some inventors exhausted after one invention? Is there a limit to one's inventiveness?*

OVSHINSKY: Many people are one-invention types. I have maybe one hundred inventions that are on the books by this time. I don't know the exact number.

But you have to judge my work like you judge an artist's: for the entire work rather than just this work or that. I'm proud of every one of my inventions, but I'm not a one-tune player. I cover a tremendous area from switching to memory to photovoltaics to superconductivity and so forth. I have wide-ranging interests, and I don't think of any field as closed to me if I'm prepared to study it and use my intellect and intuition.

INTERVIEWER: *Why do you think being an inventor is similar to being an artist?*

OVSHINSKY: You don't think they're similar?

INTERVIEWER: *I rather think they are in some respects. What I was getting at was that some of the inventors I've talked to say, "I'm an engineer, not an inventor." They seem uncomfortable with the title inventor and equally uncomfortable with being compared to an artist.*

OVSHINSKY: Well, that's one way of looking at it. I think you'll find there are all kinds of people. You can't denigrate any one approach. But I think they're afraid of the irrational. They want to be sure everything follows logic and that they came up with a solution because they used good engineering and that the answer was obvious. And that may be. How basic that is to an invention is questionable, I think, because a lot of good, logical thinkers are out there.

Now, I'm not saying logical thinking doesn't get an idea into the marketplace or into the Patent Office, but whether or not it's fundamental to invention, I don't know. I don't do that sort of invention. I do that kind of invention as a hobby—to make things a little better for someone. I consider that kind of invention—I hate to say it—trivial.

I think engineers feel that they have to be very literal, and they're afraid of criticism. They want to be sure that every solution follows some well thought out path—not so much for their own ego, but because they don't want to be derided. They don't want to live with the idea that this logical process isn't the way inventions really happen.

INTERVIEWER: *What makes a great invention?*

OVSHINSKY: In solving an engineering problem, you obviously go through certain steps. If you didn't have well-trodden paths and textbooks, you wouldn't be able to design machines and teach classes. But if you could solve all problems with textbooks, there wouldn't be any real invention.

If an invention follows a "one-two-three-four-okay-it's-solved" process, I doubt that it's much of an invention. It may have some importance, and you may have some pride in your problem-solving ability, but it's not the kind of thing that I consider a real invention.

A real invention is not just an extrapolation of the past: It is an absolutely transforming, bold, new step into the future.

MARY
SPAETH

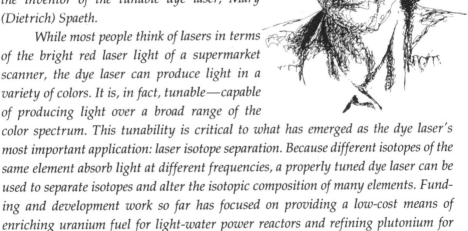

*A*LTHOUGH MORE *women are now pur-
*suing careers in science and engineering,
invention is still largely a man's world. There
are more than four million United States patents on file, but less than two percent of those
filings are by women. One of these exceptions is
the inventor of the tunable dye laser, Mary
(Dietrich) Spaeth.*

*While most people think of lasers in terms
of the bright red laser light of a supermarket
scanner, the dye laser can produce light in a
variety of colors. It is, in fact, tunable—capable
of producing light over a broad range of the
color spectrum. This tunability is critical to what has emerged as the dye laser's
most important application: laser isotope separation. Because different isotopes of the
same element absorb light at different frequencies, a properly tuned dye laser can be
used to separate isotopes and alter the isotopic composition of many elements. Funding and development work so far has focused on providing a low-cost means of
enriching uranium fuel for light-water power reactors and refining plutonium for
weapons applications.*

*Since inventing the first tunable dye laser in 1966, using a solid-state laser
pump and a fluorescent dye, Spaeth has been active in developing the process of laser
isotope separation at Lawrence Livermore National Laboratory (LLNL) in Livermore, California.*

*Located forty miles from the San Francisco Bay Area, LLNL has become a cen-
ter for both nuclear weapons research and antinuclear protests. The lab was started*

in 1952 at the urging of two Nobel Prize-winning physicists: Edward Teller, the father of the hydrogen bomb, and E. O. Lawrence, the inventor of the cyclotron. As Teller and Lawrence intended, the lab has played an important role in weapons research, providing the research and development behind the cruise missile, intercontinental ballistic missiles, or ICBMs, the neutron bomb, nuclear artillery shells, and the MX missile. The lab's O Group has also taken a lead role in the research and development of weapons for the controversial Star Wars, or Strategic Defense Initiative, system.

The lab conducts research in a host of other areas as well, ranging from biomedicine to controlled fusion for energy applications. However, it remains first and foremost a weapons lab.

On the morning I talked to Mary Spaeth, I arrived to find the lab gates blocked by several hundred protesters. Tiny wooden crosses dotted the roadsides near the lab. My visit in April happened to coincide with Good Friday, one of several yearly vigil days observed by protesters. Another occurs on August 6, marking the day the atom bomb was dropped on Hiroshima. Protesters and lab scientists have developed a prickly peace of their own. Neither side, as Spaeth says, wants to see a nuclear war, but their differences are a question of means—of how one goes about preserving peace.

Mary Spaeth graduated from Valparaiso University with a bachelor of science degree in both physics and mathematics. She received her master's degree in physics from Wayne State University. From 1962 until 1974, she worked for the Hughes Aircraft Company in Culver City, California, where she was a section leader and later, a senior scientist and project manager. While at Hughes, in addition to inventing the dye laser, Spaeth worked with ruby lasers and did pioneering research on passive Q switches for lasers. She also patented a resonant reflector used in most of the commercial ruby range finders produced by Hughes Aircraft.

Spaeth came to Lawrence Livermore National Laboratory in 1974. She has served as a group leader and as an associate program leader for laser development at the lab. In 1986, she was named the deputy associate director for the laboratory's Laser Isotope Separation, or LIS, program.

INTERVIEWER: When I talked to the Patent Office about inventors, I found that fewer than two percent of all patent filings are by women. Most of the inventors I've interviewed are men in their sixties and seventies, and my perception is that most women in the same age group weren't encouraged to go into science and engineering. Do you think that's true?

SPAETH: Yes, I think it probably is. I'm forty-eight. I think. I can never remember exactly. In my age group, girls were not encouraged to do that sort of thing. In my case, my father encouraged me to be a tomboy. In fact, before I was born, he told people that he wanted a girl and that he was going to raise her as a tomboy. And he did.

We had a shop in our garage, and I was given tools, carpentry-type tools, at a very early age—like two and a half or three—and I learned how to use them. My father didn't realize that doing this would make me very interested in science. In fact, I think he was sometimes disappointed that I ended up with such a big interest in science. It was sort of tomboy-ism gotten out of hand.

But because my father raised me as a tomboy, I never thought of myself as someone who couldn't do things—whatever I wanted to do. I was given footballs and baseballs and tools when I was growing up. I thought of myself more as a person than as a girl. I think that attitude had the biggest impact on me; it affected the way I thought about where I was going in life.

> *I thought of myself more as a person than as a girl. I think that attitude had the biggest impact on me; it affected the way I thought about where I was going in life.*

INTERVIEWER: *Do you think of yourself as an inventor?*

SPAETH: I never set out saying, "Okay, I think I will sit down here and invent something." I don't know that I'm really an inventor. I've done a couple of things that might be called inventions, but most of the things I've done have really been more in terms of making things fit together. I like to put big things together out of little things. That's sort of an inventive process in itself, but nobody gives you credit for that.

INTERVIEWER: *What is your most important invention?*

SPAETH: My most important invention and the one people know about is probably the tunable dye laser. It's hard for me to take a whole lot of credit for it because knowledge about this general area was growing so fast at the time. The knowledge base was out there, and the area was very, very pregnant. It was waiting for somebody to come along and say, "Oh, I see this, and I see that. Therefore, it must be true that…"

As it turned out, three different people actually worked on dye lasers in the same time frame that I did. Two of them accidentally made a dye laser when they were trying to do something else. When they saw this funny kind of signal, they followed it up and said, "Aha, this is a laser."

In my case, I never saw a signal, and I never made a dye laser by accident. I just thought about it. I knew about dye molecules, and I knew about lasers. When I put the things I knew together, I thought, Surely there's a laser there. All you have to do is put things together in the right combination, and you'll find the laser.

Among the three people working with dye lasers, I would say that I invented it and the other two discovered it. But if I hadn't invented it, the world still would have come to very much the same place it is today with dye lasers. I just fortuitously happened to be there.

It was fun getting an idea like that. At that point in time, lasers were not able to change color. All the lasers that were around then were one particular color or another. There were different lasers and different colors, but you couldn't take a single laser and make it change color. I did little things to my laser, and it would change color. That was amazing to me. In fact, for a while I didn't think it was a laser because it kept changing color. But I kept testing it, and since it still did all the other things a laser was supposed to do, I decided it had to be a laser.

INTERVIEWER: *Did you ever patent the dye laser?*

SPAETH: Yes, but only one of the original claims was granted. That patent on the dye laser is owned by the Army because that's who was funding my work at the time. I also have another patent on a component that is very important in making ruby range finders work. Hughes built a lot of ruby range finders using that particular component. I had been given a direct order not to work on it, but I worked on it anyway and saved them a lot of money over the years. Most of the concepts I've worked on over the years, however, aren't patentable. In fact, I was never much interested in patents. I was much more interested in getting things to work together. It's a struggle to get a patent. I was much more interested in something that works, rather than a piece of paper.

INTERVIEWER: *Before you came to Lawrence Livermore National Laboratory, you were with Hughes Aircraft Company. Did you work with Ted Maiman and the group who developed the first solid-state laser?*

SPAETH: I was at Hughes, but I was at Hughes/Culver City, and Maiman was at Hughes/Malibu. Even so, the Hughes community at both places was very heavily involved in lasers. Many of today's leaders in the laser industry came out of that little crowd of us that were at the two Hughes locations in the early 1960s.

My own background was that I had gone to school in nuclear physics, and the one important thing I learned was that I didn't want to spend one hundred percent of my time working in nuclear physics. I just didn't like it. Lasers were just being invented when I got out of school, and I was lucky enough to get a job where I could work with a very creative group of people who were doing pioneering work with lasers. My early years at Hughes were an exciting and challenging time. I feel very fortunate to have been part of that.

That early work eventually led me to the laser isotope separation process. The laser isotope separation process was invented many years ago, but it only began to be something that we could really think seriously about doing in the early 1970s. We did the work on the dye laser in 1966, so it had been around for about four years when I started to think of using it for isotope separation. The idea began to sound practical in the early 1970s because high-power, high-efficiency lasers were becoming available.

The reason I'm at Lawrence Livermore National Laboratory today and in laser isotope separation is that I'm very interested in making big things happen by fitting a large number of different ideas together. One of the

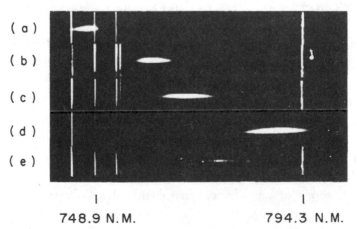

748.9 N.M.   794.3 N.M.

A photograph of the spectrograph output that measured the changing "color" of the first tunable dye laser. The vertical lines are calibration points. The different locations of the streaks indicate the different "color" of the laser (measured in nanometers) for different operating conditions.

words people use to describe this sort of approach is multidisciplinary. You know: making all different kinds of expertise work together to reach some common goal.

When I first began to think about laser isotope separation, work in this field was going on in two places: at Exxon and at Livermore. I got a job at Livermore, but I couldn't get them to hire me into laser isotope separation. My job was in laser fusion. After I was hired, it took about four months to convince them that I really ought to be doing laser isotope separation. Part

> *I was never much interested in patents.... I was much more interested in something that works, rather than a piece of paper.*

of that convincing process was getting a job offer to go to Exxon (laughs). I was really going to take it too. I was definitely going to go if they weren't going to let me work on LIS. Ever since then, which was 1974, I've been working on laser isotope separation.

INTERVIEWER: *How does that process work?*

SPAETH: There are ninety-two natural elements. Beyond those ninety-two are man-made elements such as plutonium and americium, which are made in nuclear reactors and in a number of other high-energy environments like particle accelerators and cyclotrons. Most of the elements have a number of different isotopes. In order to understand laser isotope separation, you first have to understand elements and isotopes.

If you look within the nucleus of the atom of a given element you will find a certain number of protons. The "number" of an element [on the Periodic Table] is actually the number of protons in the nucleus. But the nucleus not only has protons in it, it also has neutrons. The number of neutrons is roughly equal to, or larger than, the number of protons. However, you can have different numbers of neutrons in the nuclei of atoms of the same element. Atoms of the same element with a different number of neutrons are isotopes of that element.

All isotopes of one element are chemically very similar. In other words, you can have more than one type of boron—more than one isotope of boron—but each isotope of boron is chemically very similar to the others.

The isotopes of a single element can have very different physical properties from each other. These differences are important and valuable in certain situations. The isotope that "burns" in the nuclear reactors of electric power plants, for example, is one of the isotopes of uranium, uranium 235. It's an isotope that occurs in nature, but not very often. As mined from the ground, uranium contains 99.3 percent uranium 238 and 0.7 percent uranium 235. U-235 and U-238 are both isotopes of uranium. The uranium used in light-water power reactors needs to contain 3.0 to 5.0 percent U-235, much higher than the 0.7 percent U-235 that exists naturally. We say that it needs to be "enriched."

It's very difficult to take an element and separate it into its different isotopes. It's difficult because the atoms are chemically all very, very similar; as a result, you have to use physical means to separate them. In the past, most isotope separation techniques have made use of the fact that the weight, or mass, of an atom is different for the different isotopes. But, for the example of uranium, because these mass differences are very small, you have to do a lot of work to change the naturally occurring isotopic mixture into the mixture required to fuel our reactors.

Now we come back to laser isotope separation. The absorption spectrum of different isotopes—how they absorb light—is different from isotope to isotope. By different, I don't mean that one is in the red and the other one is in the blue. For example, the absorption spectra of both U-235 and U-238 might be in the blue, but they are still completely distinct. In other words, the absorption width of the line in the blue for one isotope is completely separate from the absorption width for another isotope—although they are both in the blue-light region. As far as your eye is concerned, these colors are very close together, but as far as a high-precision optical instrument is concerned, they are clearly separated. This is true for uranium, and it's also true for many other elements as well.

In laser isotope separation, we illuminate a set of atoms with light that has a color that is absorbed by only one of the isotopes. The light passes the other isotope without influencing it; it doesn't even "know" that it is there.

Let's say you have a uranium atom with an electron whipping around the nucleus. When a little bundle of light comes along, that electron absorbs it and this extra energy suddenly changes the shape and size of the orbit of the electron. The atom then has more energy. That little bundle of light has turned into energy inside the atom. By the way, these bundles of light are called photons.

INTERVIEWER: *The energy is absorbed?*

SPAETH: In simple terms, a little orbit is changed into a bigger orbit. When you give it another bundle of light, the electron goes into a still bigger orbit. If you give it yet another photon, the electron actually leaves the atom. By allowing the atom to absorb light like this, you can knock an electron off the atom.

Once an electron is knocked off the atom, you have something that is indeed unique. Now you no longer have a uranium atom that is very, very similar chemically to the other uranium atoms; you have a uranium atom that has an electric charge. It's positively charged because you knocked off a negatively charged electron.

Let's suppose you make a gas of naturally occurring uranium atoms. It will include both isotopes. If you can illuminate this gas with properly "tuned" light, you can knock an electron off one type of isotope but not off the other. Then, if you properly position a positively charged plate, the atoms with a negative charge will be pulled over to the plate. The atoms that are neutral don't "feel" the pull of the charged plate and they pass by undisturbed. Now you have physically separated the isotopes. With uranium, you would have a group of U-238s and a group of U-235s.

INTERVIEWER: *Does the dye laser fit into this process because you can tune it to the specific color required?*

SPAETH: Basically, yes. The dye laser is very important because the absorption bandwidths in the atoms are extremely narrow. It's hard to find a laser with a fixed frequency output that matches a particular isotope. But if you have a tunable laser, you can tune it anyplace, and you can "go after" any isotope that absorbs within the tunable range. If there's anything that I've contributed to laser isotope separation, it was recognizing very early that we really wanted tunable light. Of course, to be successful, that tunable light also has to be available at high power and it has to be made very cheaply. When I first came into the field, people were still planning on first selecting a color and then inventing a laser to produce that color. "No, no, no," I said. "That's the wrong way to do it. What you want to do is make a laser that can be tuned to anyplace in the spectrum." You see, that's sort of an invention, but nobody would ever consider it an invention.

INTERVIEWER: *Well, some people would. How did you actually build the first tunable laser?*

SPAETH: When I first worked on the tunable laser, no one, including myself, had ever thought of using it for laser isotope separation. I was simply interested in building that laser because it was a good idea.

Actually, I was working on another job that required using a very expensive piece of instrumentation. Some other people in my group, however, needed that instrumentation, and for two weeks I had nothing to do. I'd had this idea cooking around in my head for a long time, but because I didn't have any particular use or application for it I hadn't given it very high priority. But because I had two weeks with nothing to do, I thought, Well, I'm just going to try it and see if it works. So, I put the first tunable laser together with glass tubes and Duco cement, and I borrowed from a fellow employee, Dave Bortfeld, a big whumpin' laser, to serve as the pump to provide the input energy to drive my laser. It worked. It worked the very first time.

I don't want us to ever use nuclear weapons, but I surely want the other guys to know that if they start throwing them at us, they can expect to receive them back.

INTERVIEWER: *So, it wasn't just a theoretical model, but a working model?*

SPAETH: Oh yes, it worked.

INTERVIEWER: *What was the big breakthrough? When did you know it was working?*

SPAETH: Actually, I was very pregnant at the time, so Dave was helping me. I expected the color of the dye laser to be toward the red and outside of what's normally considered to be the visible band, but not outside by much. Some people can see more toward the red than others, and I figured, Well, look, this is going to be a laser. There is going to be a lot of light, so even though it's not normally within the visible range, I'm going to be able to see it.

Because I expected to be able to "see" the dye laser output, the first time that we operated it we didn't put up any electronic diagnostics. We decided just to look at the position where the beam should appear and see if it lased. We fired it up one afternoon, and we aimed it at something white and didn't see a bloody thing. We saw nothing. "Well, what happened?" I asked. "Was it that it didn't work or was it that our eyes didn't see it?" Because I was so pregnant, and it was the end of the day, I was very tired, so I went home. After I left, Dave decided to put up an electronic monitor, an instrument that could see further into the red than the human eye. That night, I was at home eating dinner when I got a telephone call. "It works!" he said. "It's there! When I put up the electronic sensor, it can see the beam." That was very exciting. I was pretty happy.

INTERVIEWER: *Was the pump the standard ruby-red laser everyone thinks of when the word laser is mentioned?*

SPAETH: It was a ruby laser. In 1966, it was still quite early in the development of lasers, and because people at Hughes had done all the pioneering work on ruby lasers, there were quite a few of them in our labs. In selecting the day for the first test, I had looked for a dye material that would absorb light at the ruby laser wavelength. Because the deep red color of the ruby laser provided the pump energy, the dye laser output had to appear deeper in the red, and so it was at a color that we could not see with our eyes.

INTERVIEWER: *Was the dye a colored material?*

SPAETH: We used two materials; both were dyes. One of the dyes was 1,1-diethyl 2,2-dicarbocyanine iodide, and the other was cryptocyanine. Right after we made the first dye laser, we had the second one working within a day or two.

I had tried very hard to buy a dye that would lase in the visible light range, but only a very small amount of the dye I chose was available in the world. The people at Kodak had sent the entire world's supply of this dye to a fellow in Germany, Fritz Schafer, who was working on similar concepts. He was one of the two other people who discovered the dye laser.

INTERVIEWER: *What kind of dyes can be used in a laser?*

SPAETH: The dyes used in a dye laser have a molecular structure that is very similar to that of the dyes used in clothing. Laser dyes are special, however, because they fluoresce—they spit out a photon of light after they've absorbed a photon of light. They are the same kind of dyes used in the bright orange jackets worn by highway workers. Those jackets are so bright because they fluoresce.

INTERVIEWER: *Like the orange used in some hunting jackets and hats?*

SPAETH: Yes, those colors. They're the ones you can use to make lasers. They're special dyes, but they're not that special.

INTERVIEWER: *Does the pump laser actually shine through the dyes to make them lase?*

SPAETH: One of the things that's not good about a dye laser is that you can't supply energy to it by plugging it into the wall. A dye laser has to get energy from another source of light. For our purposes in laser isotope separation, it makes sense to use another laser, a pump laser, as the source of energy for the dye laser.

INTERVIEWER: *So, is it correct to say that the laser light stimulates the dye?*

SPAETH: That's right, but it's not the right word. Actually, the light doesn't stimulate the dye; it energizes the dye.

INTERVIEWER: *We talked earlier about why there are so few women inventors and so few women in science. Has being a woman put special barriers in your way or created obstacles that male scientists and inventors don't have to overcome?*

SPAETH: I think it probably did to some extent. But, as I said, I've always thought of myself as a person, not as a woman.

In general, being a woman in this kind of a business has its pros and cons. You run into some people who say, "I will never work around a woman, I will never work for a woman, and blah, blah, blah." But after you work with them for a while and they find that you're competent and they understand that you can really contribute and that they need your help—soon they're your best buddies. All of that stuff they had to say at first really didn't apply once they got down to hard tacks.

There are all types of people. When I was at Hughes, there was an unwritten policy that said that a woman could not have a line-manager position. One reason I quit Hughes was because I could not get a line-manager position. The company will deny that, but in fact, I have been told by people I trust and who are in positions to know that it was an unwritten policy at the time, at least in the area where I worked.

In other ways, however, I could get my work done faster in those days. Some people would be so surprised to find that a woman could talk about technical stuff and understand it, that they would go out of their way to be helpful. That was particularly true in the machine shops. I could always get my parts out of the machine shops faster than the guys could (laughs).

I would talk to the machinists and say "Hey...," you know? That was very true when I was twenty-five years old.

INTERVIEWER: *I suppose the kind of work you do would be impossible outside of a large corporation or a government lab like Livermore.*

SPAETH: Yes, that's true for what I like to do.

The design of the dye laser system today still resembles the conceptual designs a few of us put together ten or twelve years ago. But it took hundreds of people to make it all come together. It could not have happened without those hundreds of people—each one contributing; each one making their own inventions.

There's no question in my mind that nuclear energy will fill a need in the future. The only question is when.

"Now, here's the general idea," I would say to someone working on the project. "It should look like this." They would take that general idea and go on to the next step of detail and tell someone working for them, "It ought to look like this." Then, somebody who worked for them would take it to the next step. It was an infrastructure of people who respected each other and who had a common understanding of the overall goal—but who each had a particular expertise—that built the dye laser system that exists today.

My particular expertise is more up front and lies in generally scoping the problem and saying, "This is the way we ought to do it. These are the ideas that have the capability of getting there in the long term." Then, that idea is taken over by somebody else who has the expertise in making the hardware. "Let's get this thing built. Let's make a system out of it." Then, other people say, "Now I've got that system, and I have to fix it. I have to modify what they've built and make it last a long time." Each person in that sequence has a different "kind" of mind. It takes a whole set of people working as a team to make something come out at the end. It's a long, complex process to take a concept and pursue it to the point of realization in a form that can really make a difference in the world.

INTERVIEWER: *What differences have you seen between working at a government lab like Livermore and a large corporation like Hughes?*

SPAETH: Although I've heard people say otherwise, in my particular instance I haven't sensed any discrimination at all here at the lab because I'm a woman. Now, I'm not saying that was the situation in the past, because other people have told me it was definitely not the same then. In the laser program, people were always equal. To a large extent, I think that has to do with John Emmet. He was in charge of the laser program when I arrived, and his view was always that you are what you can contribute, which didn't have anything to do with whether you were purple, female, or old or young. I've felt absolutely no discrimination at all since I've been with the laboratory.

I definitely felt discrimination at Hughes. But it had more to do with the particular individuals involved than with the fact that it was a private institution instead of a government laboratory.

There are, however, other differences between companies and a government lab, because of their missions. In many respects, the mission of this government institution is different from the mission of a private company. So, if the mission of this institution requires development of an invention that takes substantive resources, very often we can get the resources we need. In contrast, a private company may have to settle for inventions on a lower level, requiring fewer resources. A big company like Bell Labs, on the other hand, probably has even more freedom than we have in this institution.

INTERVIEWER: Yes, but even at institutions like Bell Labs, the staff still has to worry about having an end product of some sort to sell.

SPAETH: Well, we do here too. But if it takes a significant chunk of resources—and if we can see our way through the project to an end product that will help the mission of this institution—we have a respectable chance of getting those resources.

INTERVIEWER: Does it bother you that the Livermore Lab's major mission is weapons development? Does it bother you to know that your dye laser plays a critical role in the fabrication of nuclear weapons?

SPAETH: I believe in deterrence. I think everybody on both sides of the nuke and anti-nuke debate agrees, in principle. No one wants to have a nuclear war. The point of disagreement is in how we make sure we don't have a nuclear war—how we maintain individual freedoms in the world.

I'm one of the people who believe that if we don't maintain a powerful ability to go after those guys if they come after us guys, we put ourselves in great jeopardy. We jeopardize our ability to maintain a society where individual freedom is important. At a minimum, we need a bilateral disarmament where both sides put down their weapons together. I don't want us to ever use nuclear weapons, but I surely want the other guys to know that if they start throwing them at us, they can expect to receive them back. So, they might as well never start.

INTERVIEWER: *What are the applications of the dye laser? Is its most important role related to weapons?*

SPAETH: Today, the laser isotope separation process has two principal applications. One is to make enriched uranium to fuel nuclear electricity plants and to do it at a lower cost while using less electricity than the other methods. The other application is for plutonium. In order to have a deterrence, a nuclear force, you need plutonium. The Department of Energy "owns" a fair amount of plutonium that doesn't have the right isotopic mixture to be useful for weapons applications. It isn't safe enough (for the workers and handlers) to be used as weapons material. One of the things we can do is to reconfigure the isotopic composition of that plutonium and make it useful for the weapons program.

By the way, there are many other applications for isotopic separation in the future. The two I've talked about, uranium and plutonium, are the most economically driving. Other possibilities open up once the technology for them becomes available. Fifteen to thirty years from now, laser isotope separation could be providing materials for special applications, ranging from materials for construction in high-stress to materials that can improve performance or efficiency. For example, in mercury light bulbs you can improve the luminous efficiency by using mercury with a tailored isotopic combination.

INTERVIEWER: *What about the nuclear power industry? It seems to be bogged down now. Do you think it will make a comeback? Maybe bogged down isn't quite the right...*

SPAETH: I think bogged down is a good way to say it. Running the world takes energy and a lot of it. Today, a lot of that energy comes from conventional sources like oil and gas. But the world is using up those kinds of fuels—or at least depleting those sources which are available at a low cost. That's particularly true for the United States when you look at domestic energy sources. Like it or not, somewhere along the line the costs of more conventional sources of energy are going to skyrocket. Proper stewardship of our existing resources means that we should limit our use of conventional fuels like oil to areas where it is really needed—such as the need for "transportable" fuels like gasoline in our transportation system, and for fertilizers and plastics.

Somewhere along the way, we'll have to start relying on nuclear sources of energy. It may not be tomorrow, and it may not be in twenty years. But one hundred years from now this world will have to rely on nuclear power if it's going to have energy. There's no question in my mind that nuclear energy will fill a need in the future. The only question is when.

I liked to build things when I was growing up, and my dad was a good enough guy to buy me a jigsaw when I was three.

INTERVIEWER: *Do you have anything you'd like to do in the future?*

SPAETH: I'd love to be involved in a project to build a new city. It's very different from what I do around here. I'd like to be involved in city planning, in providing the environment in which people live their lives.

I think there's very little chance I will have the opportunity, but it's something I've always wanted to do. I've done a couple of housing developments on a relatively small scale—between ten and fifty lots—so I've had a taste of planning. But it's something you have to dedicate your life to. I couldn't do both jobs.

I liked to build things when I was growing up, and my dad was a good enough guy to buy me a jigsaw when I was three. I'm talking about a big one with a motor and the works. Although we didn't have much money, we had access to the leftovers from a venetian blind factory. Venetian blinds were made from wood then, so I built all kinds of things, mostly toys. I also built toy cities with houses and hospitals and station wagons.

INTERVIEWER: *Did you also invent things when you were growing up?*

SPAETH: People invent all the time. When I was a little kid, I used to re-cut cereal boxes. Whenever we bought cereal, I would very carefully cut open the cereal box and cut little grooves, holes, and tucks so that I could tuck the flap back in. Today, all cereal boxes come exactly that way. If I had only been smart enough when I was eight years old—I could have sold that idea to the cereal companies. But, of course, I wasn't.

When I was a little kid, I also made a sketch of what I thought an atom bomb would look like. I made it a few years after the atom bomb had been used in World War II. I had that sketch for a number of years, and when pictures of the atom bomb were published many years later, I found that my sketch wasn't far off. The atom bomb was pretty easy to invent, once you understood the basic principles.

Those things aren't useful; they're just interesting. You can say, "Hey, I invented something, but I was twenty years late!"

INTERVIEWER: *Can someone invent without a technical background?*

SPAETH: I think the answer to that question is that there are really two types of inventions. Some inventions can only be done if you are very well educated and have a highly technical background. But there are other things to be invented as well—conveniences such as a new way to hold a telephone—things that anybody with a creative mind can come up with.

I have a friend who has almost no technical training at all, and he definitely considers himself an inventor. He gets up every morning and says, "Well, let's see...I'm going to go out and invent something today."

JACOB RABINOW

A FEW *years ago, Jacob Rabinow was listen-ing to the complaints of a would-be inventor as part of his work on the National Inventors Council. Someone on the NIC, the inventor thought, had stolen her ideas for shark repellent. A lot of work had been done in the field, Rabinow pointed out. It was quite possible that someone had thought of her idea before. He had even had some similar problems with his own inventions.*

"Do you mean you have some patents?" she asked.

"Oh yes."

"How many?"

"A couple hundred," he replied cautiously.

"Nobody can invent that much! You must steal them!"

"Don't worry," he reassured her. "I only steal ideas on Thursdays and Fridays. This is Wednesday."

With his indefatigable sense of humor and his equally productive mind, Jacob Rabinow has emerged as a spokesman of sorts for American inventors. In his wide-ranging talks, he has spoken to grade school students on the mysteries of invention and testified before Congress on the problems facing contemporary inventors.

Rabinow is an accomplished inventor in his own right; his inventions include the first optical character recognition machine, or reading machine, to use the "best match" principle; the magnetic-particle clutch; the self-regulating clock; and the automated sorting machines used by the United States Post Office. Although he invented his first reading machine in 1954, versions of it are still used today to scan bank checks and credit card slips for computer processing. His magnetic-particle clutch has replaced traditional plate clutches on some Subaru cars, and it's also used in the drive mechanisms of some tape recorders and to control the flaps in Learjets.

Not all his inventions are patented. By his own estimate, he has some two thousand other inventions written down in the row of notebooks on a shelf in the living room of his home in Bethesda, Maryland. Some of those other inventions include a self-justifying typewriter, an automatic headlight dimmer for automobiles, a reflective lane-marker which lies flush with the road surface, and a pressurized canister for storing tennis balls. He invents for the challenge of it, for the fun of it, and also to win bets. Because he has spent most of his career solving technical puzzles, it is somehow fitting that Rabinow's most recent patented invention is a pick-proof lock.

Jacob Rabinow was born in Kharkov, Russia, in 1910. His father moved the family to Siberia in 1914. By 1919, the Russian Revolution was under way, his father's shoe factory was closed down by the Communists, and officers in the White Army occupied their home. His family traveled across Russia by freight car to settle in China; his father died of typhus shortly after they arrived. In 1921, Rabinow settled in Brooklyn, New York, with his brother and mother.

He graduated from the City College of New York with a B.S. in electrical engineering in 1933 and a graduate degree in 1934. With the depression in full swing, Rabinow worked odd jobs repairing radios and selling hot dogs. In 1938, he got a job as a mechanical engineer at the Bureau of Standards, one of the United States government's main research arms in the physical sciences. He spent the next sixteen years working in a variety of areas, designing bomb and rocket fuses and doing other defense-related work.

Rabinow also served on the National Inventors Council, an advisory board created by inventor Charles F. Kettering to aid the war effort. The council reviewed ideas from independent inventors and passed promising ideas on to other federal agencies for funding and development work. The council lasted from 1941 to 1974. Other notable members included Stark Draper of MIT, Marvin Camras, the inventor of audiotape, Chester Carlson, the inventor of xerography, and the trio of William Shockley, John Bardeen, and Walter Brattain, inventors of the transistor at Bell Laboratories.

After developing the reading machine in 1954, he left the Bureau of Standards and started the Rabinow Engineering Company, bought in 1964 by Control Data. From 1964 to 1972, he was a vice president of Control Data. In 1972, he returned as a research engineer to the Bureau of Standards, where he still works part time.

Jacob Rabinow is a fellow of both the Institute of Electrical and Electronics Engineers (IEEE) and the American Association for the Advancement of Science

(AAAS) and a member of the National Academy of Engineering. He has received many honors, among them awards and citations for his work as an inventor from the United States War Department and the Department of Commerce. In 1948, he received a Certificate of Merit from President Truman. In 1980, he was named Scientist of the Year by Industrial Research and Development magazine.

INTERVIEWER: Why do you invent?

RABINOW: When I see something that I don't like, I try to invent a way around it. My job is simply to design gadgets that I like. And I do it for the challenge. I don't invent gadgets just to make money, although I certainly like to make money from them if I can. Making money from inventions is really not that simple, but my inventions have certainly given me good jobs all my life.

> *Occasionally I invent things to win a bet.*

Let me give you an example that happened just this week. A TV camera crew from channel 9 in Washington, D.C., came to take some pictures of me in my laboratory. They were carrying a very large, heavy tape camera which was about a foot and a half long. The cameraman was using a professional tripod with a good head on it. But every time he wanted to change the camera height, he had to hold it up with one hand and adjust the tripod legs himself, or have his assistant move the legs up and down or stretch them out and clamp them. It's a hard way to position a heavy camera, but all tripods work like that, even those for ordinary cameras.

I looked at it and said to myself, That's silly. There should be a handle on top that you can turn to move the legs in and out so that the tripod gets higher or lower. I've never seen a tripod like that.

Even so, I'm willing to bet that the Patent Office has patents on file for adjustable tripods controlled from a single point. Maybe, but then maybe not. It's not easy to make a tripod like that. I started thinking, and I thought of using screws, all of which would be driven by a cable. I could set it up so that when you turn one handle, you turn three wheels which then turn three screws and make the legs move in and out. It would work, but a tripod like that would be expensive, and if the screws got dirty, it wouldn't work easily.

To get around that, I cooked up a tripod that would use cables instead of screws to move the legs. Cables are a rather interesting problem. Can you build a tripod so that by pulling a cable you can move the legs in and out? The answer is yes, you can do that, but you've got to get rid of the cable somewhere when the legs get short.

Well, I took a look at that problem, and I began to invent a new tripod. I wrote out some notes and did a sketch of the tripod in one of my notebooks. I have about two thousand inventions in my notebooks. I haven't patented all of them, of course.

When I get a chance, I'll look tripods up in the patent index in the Bureau of Standards' library under the heading "tripods, self-controlled." If I don't find the title exactly, I may go to the search room at the Patent Office and look through "tripods." Of course, the Patent Office might call them "supporting structures." God knows what they'll be called. I may even find that somebody's already invented my tripod.

If it hasn't been invented, I may approach some of my friends in the camera business and see if they're interested in it. I may do it. I may not. I may even build one for myself, maybe a little model.

INTERVIEWER: *Did a lot of your patented inventions come about through everyday challenges like that?*

RABINOW: I suppose so. For example, I invented a record player because I had a chance to study phonograph needles during the war, and I found out that the old-style record player never played correctly because the needles were not constrained correctly.

During the war, when I was doing research at the Bureau of Standards, we made records of fuses flying through space. We telemetered the data back from the shell or bomb and stored it by cutting it on records. Tape wasn't available yet, so we made records—regular cut records just like those you play on a phonograph.

I began to get curious about how needles played sounds. I was particularly curious as to why the needle was always tilted with respect to the record. I thought the needle should be perpendicular to the record to play the grooves more accurately. But if it's positioned like that, it grinds the record away, and the needle will chatter. It's easy to see why this is so.

If you take a pencil, hold it by the eraser end, and drag its point across a piece of paper while holding it perpendicular to the paper, you will find it oscillates. It will go "plup, plup, plup." But if you hold it at an angle, it won't oscillate.

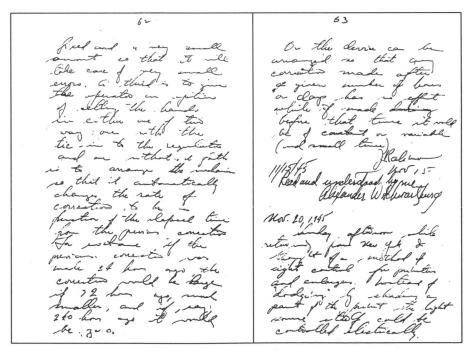

Pages from one of Jacob Rabinow's invention notebooks dated November, 1945.

I got interested in this. What are the mechanics of it? The pencil follows the paper and breaks loose, jumps a bit, and then it comes back in contact with the paper. You can see this just by looking at the marks it leaves on the paper. If you tilt the pencil, though, it becomes stable. Why? Because when it's at an angle and it grabs, it lifts a little and that reduces the pressure and it becomes stable. It's a case of feedback. In other words, it's a self-correcting system.

Well, I wrote and published some papers on this and noted the fact that the needle should be constrained differently. Old-style needles were tilted. That eliminated the oscillation problem, but it produced bad sound quality. I suggested that the needle be tied in the direction of the groove. Without this constraint, having it straight up and down, means that the needle goes back and forth along the groove and produces distortion. Soon after my paper, all the styluses of good phonograph cartridges were tied back so that they couldn't move back and forth along the groove.

Then, I began to think about how a record should be played. The arm that cuts a record moves in a straight line across the grooves, but most phonographs play records with a swinging arm that moves in an arc. The reason for the swinging arm was that before there were electronic amplifiers, phonographs used to have a horn to amplify the sound. Of course, there had to be joints so that the horn could rotate. But if you have an electric amplifier, you don't need that. You can move the tone arm in a straight line, and the distortion is lower. I built one and measured it, and—sure enough—it was lower.

I've got all kinds of patents on straight-line phonographs, and I've given lectures on the subject all over the world. The professional societies have all written papers on the subject. "You're right," they said. "Records should be played in a straight line. But who's going to tell the difference? The old style sounds good enough, and records are lousy anyway."

So, for fourteen years I couldn't get anybody interested in my record player. Finally, I put it on the market myself under the name RABCO. The company made straight-line phonographs, and I lost a pile of dough on it. I ran out of money before the idea caught on. Then the patent expired, and today everybody makes straight-line phonographs. In fact, it's actually easier to make a straight-line phonograph because it's inherently a straightfor-ward system. You don't need to make your tone arm swing through a big angle, and you don't need anti-skating devices.

INTERVIEWER: *Some of your inventions, like the reading machine and the magnetic-particle clutch, did earn money for you, didn't they?*

RABINOW: Yes, they did. I invented the magnetic-particle clutch because we were playing around with clutches at the Bureau of Standards. One day, I thought of using iron powder and some magnets instead of an electrostatic charge to stick the two plates of a clutch together. We did it, and an hour later we had a clutch. The Bureau gave me the foreign rights to it, and with financial help from my brother, I patented it in twenty-two countries and sold the rights on it for $100,000 and netted $26,000 in profit. It got me publicity and a medal and was worth doing.

The magnetic-particle clutch is a very simple device. You have iron dust, and it sticks to a magnet. When plates of the clutch aren't magnetized, the iron dust is almost like a liquid. When you magnetize it, the iron filings stick to each other and become chained up. Then the two plates are chained together. It's being used by Subaru, to control the flaps in Learjets, and in many other machines.

However, I usually don't make money on my inventions, but I do get good jobs from them. When I sold my reading machines and patents to Control Data, for example, I got a good job with the company. I had the know-how for making reading machines, and they wanted to get into that business because reading machines can be used as computer inputs. The reading machines can, for example, take a typewritten copy and read it for the computer. They can also read the impressions on a money order, or a credit card purchase. Checks today are now read across the bottom by read-ing machines, so they can be processed by computer. The Post Office is even beginning to read addresses with machines based on mine. Some day, hand sorting might be eliminated for maybe seventy percent of the mail. These machines are useful.

But, as I said earlier, I don't work on inventions to make money. I work on these machines because it's a challenge. I had some ideas about how to build a reading machine, and I built it because the bureau gave me permis-sion to fool around a little. The first reading machine I invented read very slowly, of course, and now it's in the Smithsonian Museum [National

Museum of American History] on permanent exhibition. I feel good about my work when I see that.

INTERVIEWER: *Do you have a lab at home to work on your inventions?*

RABINOW: When I built my house, I had my own company. I was also doing some consulting work. We designed the house with my lab right off the living room so that I wouldn't have to say good-bye to the family when I wanted to fool around. The sliding panels on the bookshelf actually open into my lab so that it's connected to the living room. Of course, I also have a workshop downstairs and a darkroom. I do a lot of photography. Some of my first patents were in photography.

> *Inventing is not a logical process. It's only a logical process after the fact.*

INTERVIEWER: *What areas of photography did you work in?*

RABINOW: I've worked on automatic focusing and various other tricks in photography. I did it because it was part of my job at the Bureau of Standards.

When we did some test bombing, for example, I was an observer at one of the targets and decided that the pilot of the airplane wasn't flying correctly. He was a colonel—the chief test pilot of the Army, no less—and I told my colonel to tell him he wasn't flying the plane correctly.

The pilot said, "You tell your damn civilian that I can see better with the seat of my pants than he can see with his eyes." To prove that he was wrong, I made this special camera that recorded his flight and showed that he didn't fly correctly. After that, he put a gunsight on his airplane and he flew correctly.

INTERVIEWER: *Do you like a challenge like that?*

RABINOW: Occasionally I invent things to win a bet. Let me give you an example of that.

In 1943, my wife and I were both working at the Bureau of Standards. My wife was working as a mathematician studying the whistles from bombs—the data records that I talked about earlier—and plotting curves of where they exploded. Also working with us was a mathematician by the name of David Gilbaird, who's now a professor of math at Stanford. His wife, Shirley, happened to be working as a secretary in the Department of Commerce.

One night, we were walking to their home to eat, and while we walked, Shirley told us she had to type everything twice. The first time that she typed a report on a regular typewriter, it came out with a ragged right-hand margin. Because they wanted to have justified margins, she then had to retype everything on a variable pitch typewriter so that she could adjust the line width. Of course, if she made a mistake, she had to do it a third time because there weren't any word processors around yet.

I said, "You know, there should be a typewriter that comes out even the first time you type." My friend the mathematician said, "That's impossible." And so I bet him a quarter.

By the time we had gotten to their home, I had figured out how to make a typewriter that came out with a justified margin the first time you typed something. It's not obvious. But there's one thing you have to realize immediately about this problem. If you put things on paper as you type, justified type is impossible. There's no way the machine can know how many words you're going to put on a line.

The rule is that you don't put anything on paper as you type. What I did was design a machine with a bunch of wheels. Each wheel had a complete alphabet on it, and there was a whole stack of wheels in the machine. If you're typing the word CAT, the first wheel spins to C, the second to A, and the next to T. Then you set a space and move on to the next word—and so on. When you finish a line, all the letters are set up, but nothing is on paper. You can even read the line if you want to by having letters on the wheels visible on the side facing you. So, you look through a window and see that you have the line you want. You press a shift key, and little springs between each of the wheels permit you to squeeze the line to the proper length. Once that's done, you can move the whole drum of wheels forward and print the line on the paper. That way, you can come out with a constant line length the first time, and you can do it fast.

I won the quarter bet. The next day, I went to the Patent Office to see if this was a new idea. Not only did I find it, I found a whole subclass called "justifying drum printers." They had them with springs and wedges and with visible lines to read from—they had them every way I had thought of. Why nobody did it, I don't know. Today, of course, you have word processors, so there's no need for them.

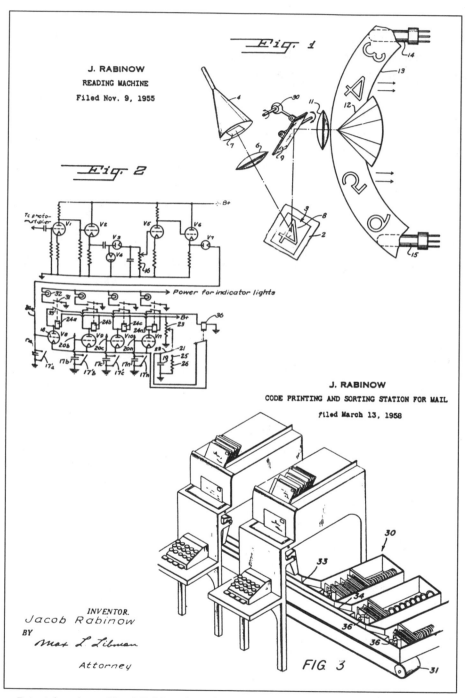

Patent drawings of Jacob Rabinow's reading machine (Figures 1 and 2) and mail-sorting machine (Figure 3).

INTERVIEWER: How did you get involved in inventing a sorting machine for the Post Office?

RABINOW: I became involved in the Post Office because of a dare. Sometime in the late 1940s or early 1950s, I designed a punch-card sorting machine for the Census Bureau. It could sort cards into as many categories as you wished; it had many hundreds or even thousands of output pockets. I had also invented and built, in 1948, the first magnetic disk file for computers. The basic patent belonged to the United States government. I owned the foreign rights, and I sold them to Remington Rand for the magnificent sum of $15,000!

So one evening, Sam Alexander, chief of the computer group at the Bureau of Standards, and I were giving a joint lecture on what computers could do for business. The session was before the Society for the Improvement of Management.

During my talk, I told of three developments: the reader, the disk file, and the sorter. I said that I had once read a statement by a postmaster general who said that letter sorting could not be automated because each letter is different. I said that while I had never been inside a post office, I was willing to bet lunches for a year that *something* inside a post office could be automated.

To make a very long story short, this interested some people and angered many more. Anyway, some two years after I left the government, the director of the Bureau of Standards called to say that some people from the Post Office were looking for me and had money in their hands. I told him to take the money and give me a subcontract.

My machines for sorting mail, all the new Burroughs machines, were invented on the contract, and I was paid a consulting fee. There are many types of sorting machines, but these are my babies.

The sorting machine picks up a letter from a stack with a vacuum cup and puts it in front of an operator.

Picking up sheets of paper with a vacuum cup is conventional in printing, and I knew that they could also be used to pick up letters. But I started thinking about picking up packages with them as well. Now, the vacuum cup has to be small enough to pick up the smallest object. The cup we were using was about an inch by an inch and a half—a little rubber thing that would touch the letter and pick it up. If you used a big cup, you might "swallow" a small letter or pick up more than one. So, the problem of picking up packages was very interesting. Packages at the Post Office can vary from two or three inches long to as much as seventy inches long. You can use a small vacuum cup to pick up a big package, but you have to figure out how to do it.

For example, can you pick up a coffee table, which probably weighs one hundred pounds, with a vacuum cup only a square inch in size? People will bet you money that it can't be done and that it can only pick up about fifteen pounds—in other words, an amount equal to atmospheric pressure.

Well, I've bet money on it, and I've bet lunches on the fact that I can pick up something as heavy as a table with a small vacuum cup. People say, "You're going to glue it." But I tell them, "No, this will be a vacuum cup connected to a vacuum hose, and it will pick up this table."

People forget how a vacuum cup operates. It isn't the vacuum cup that picks up an object; it's the air pressure on the opposite side. If you want to pick up a table with a small vacuum cup, all you have to do is pressurize the room to one hundred pounds per square inch.

That has some problems, of course. The walls would come off this room, the ceiling would come off, and you would have to pressurize yourself like a diver before you entered. All kinds of interesting problems arise, but you could pick up a heavy object.

Some people ask, "Is that useful?" And I say, "Yes." I have a patent on using a pressure chamber like this to straighten automobile bodies. You can straighten something like a bent door without ripping the upholstery off by using a mold with the correct shape of the door. Normal outside air pressure would act like a vacuum, so if the chamber's inside air pressure is one thousand pounds per square inch, you can use that force to straighten the automobile door.

Using this same concept, I also made for the government a machine to pick up small, heavy objects. We enclosed the whole machine in a steel chamber with one hundred pounds per square inch of inside pressure. The "vacuum" that picked up the objects was just a hose open to normal outside air pressure.

I've also thought of making a rug-cleaning device with much the same principle. You could roll a rug from one spindle to another in a round chamber with five hundred or one thousand pounds per square inch of pressure. Boy, you could just take the dust right out of the rug! The "vacuum cleaner," if you like, would just be a single line open to normal outside air pressure.

So, those are examples of how I come up with inventions. Sometimes I start with a funny idea and then I begin to think of uses for it. I invent by playing around with ideas.

I tell people that inventing is not a logical process. It's only a logical process after the fact.

> *Knowing what we know and permitting an atomic war to occur is inexcusable. If there are any gods out there, they must be laughing themselves sick.*

INTERVIEWER: *Do you think one of the keys is seeing how natural processes can be applied in new or different ways?*

RABINOW: I often solve problems that anyone should be able to solve. Once I invented something for Robert Burks, the artist who did the head of John F. Kennedy at the Kennedy Center for the Performing Arts in Washington, D.C. I'm a friend of his. He gave me a head of Kennedy that's similar to the one at the Center.

I was trying to solve for him the kind of problem that any kid in the world can solve and doesn't. You might be interested in this problem. Burks asked me, "Can you cut stainless steel figures? I want to do a figure of Mary McLeod Bethune, the black educator, seventeen feet high, made out of stainless steel, and then anodize it black."

"What's the problem?" I asked.

"Well," he said, "I'm going to make the model only three or four feet high, and I want to follow it with a profile follower, an electronic device, and cut a big statue."

This problem really becomes very interesting. If you have a cutter attached to an arm on the end of another arm that is twenty or thirty feet long, the thing will sag. The cutter has to be able to go all the way around the statue and cut it on all sides. It's kind of like a dentist's tool, if you want to think of it that way. What I wanted to invent was a way to keep this long arm from sagging.

What I thought was, Okay, I have an arm that sticks out thirty feet. I don't want it to sag, so I'll put the whole thing underwater—the statue and the tool. If I make the whole thing neutrally buoyant, I can make the arm go out a hundred feet, and it won't sag. It won't lift, and it won't lower. Its weight will be supported by the amount of water it displaces. It will just be floating neutral.

Well, I got a patent on that, and I got a three-column story about it in the International Edition of the *New York Times*, although I never built it. There are other ways of cutting statues, but it was a fascinating problem.

I like to use this invention as an example at talks and ask people what they would do to solve the problem. People always say, "Put ropes on it."

"But the problem then," I point out, "is that you'd have to connect the ropes to something else. I just want an arm with the cutter on it. And I don't want it to sag."

Eventually somebody will suggest making the arm neutrally buoyant. People finally figure it out if you suggest that they've all experienced a way of getting rid of gravity. Almost everyone has been in a pool.

Once when I was talking to a high school class, a student gave me a new idea. "Mr. Rabinow," he said, "why don't you put it into orbit? There's no gravity in space and you can do it there." Of course, then you've got other problems, but at least it's possible.

Putting it in water is interesting because of some beneficial side effects. The arm will not vibrate or jitter if it's underwater because the water dampens it. Most heavy-metal cutters also use a flow of water to take the cuttings and chips away from the cutter. With my system, you're already in water, so you can use a suction device to take the chips away.

The Ford Foundation offered us a lot of money to make a model. They wanted to use it to record profiles of the world's great statues on tape, in case they were destroyed. You remember a few years ago when the *Pietà* was damaged by someone who hit it with a hammer? So, there were some uses for my machine. The idea of putting it underwater was fun. I had no expectation that I was going to start selling water tanks with machines in them, but the challenge was appealing.

INTERVIEWER: *Do you take requests for inventions?*

RABINOW: Occasionally people ask me to invent things. During my ordnance days, I invented fuses for bombs and artillery shells. They wanted

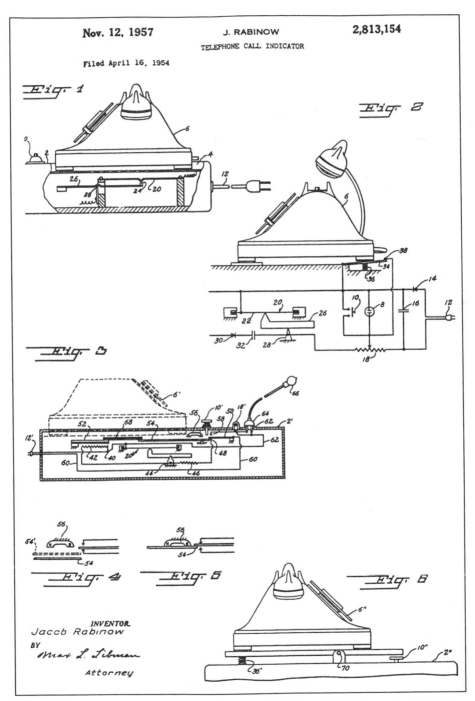

Nov. 12, 1957

J. RABINOW

TELEPHONE CALL INDICATOR

2,813,154

Filed April 16, 1954

Patent drawings of Jacob Rabinow's telephone call indicator (dated November 12, 1957).

something that would detonate at the proper time but still not go off if the shell or bomb was dropped or jolted. Strangely enough, some of my fuse ideas are now being used for air bags in automobiles. It's the same type of problem: You want something that will go off when it's supposed to. It has to be able to tell a real crash from a jolt or sudden stop.

It's often easier to invent when somebody comes to you with a problem. If you're good, you can attack the problem directly and come up with a good solution. If you're bad, you'll probably come up with a lousy solution. But you'll come up with a solution.

INTERVIEWER: *What do you think makes a great invention?*

RABINOW: What makes a great invention? I don't like to break my arm patting myself on the back, but speaking truthfully, I have to say I'm not so sure that I have any great inventions.

A great invention must be revolutionary. That means it has to be way ahead of its time. Television, for example, was a great invention, but it came about slowly through a succession of inventions: first a parallel system, then a scanning system, and finally the cathode-ray tube. Every great invention is usually a succession of minor inventions—maybe not minor, but inventions that did not individually solve the whole problem.

The transistor is certainly one of the greatest inventions of all time because it allowed us to build electronics that we couldn't dream of any other way: small gadgets such as a watch that tells the time and date for the next twenty years without reprogramming and costs only about two dollars. It also made modern computers possible. You could build a computer with vacuum tubes, but the ENIAC computer had eighteen thousand vacuum tubes and was practically as big as this house. When it came to computation, it didn't do as well as a modern pocket calculator.

Another great invention is undoubtedly satellite television. The fact that we can watch a tennis game being played in Australia is remarkable. It has changed our life and opened up new doors.

Einstein's Theory of Relativity is also a great invention. It *is* an invention. He did not discover the theory. He knew certain things were happening, and he invented a theory that could explain all those things. People may say there are other theories, but Einstein's was the simplest and the best and the most elegant.

Einstein's theory, for example, says that gravity is not a force but an acceleration. All physicists say that today. "We're not really attracted to the floor," Einstein said. "We're moving in an arc, and we appear to be attracted to the floor because it's constantly coming up to us."

After saying that, he started making some careful measurements and found his theories were correct. He predicted many things that are happening. He predicted that in three-dimensional space, the floor cannot be constantly coming up to us because that would mean the earth is expanding continuously, which is out of the question.

Einstein said that in fourth-dimensional mathematics you can show that space is curved. Then, if you move through that space in a curve, you get exactly the kind of gravitational effects we see on earth. Einstein worked this through mathematically, and everything checks out. Space is not a simple condition. The trouble is that we can't imagine it because our brains and our senses are three-dimensional. There is no way I can draw you a picture of four-dimensional space because your eyes don't respond to it and your brain doesn't respond to it.

Well, from these ideas follow things that are not obvious. If space is indeed curved, then light going through it will also bend. If you measure light, lo and behold, it bends! When there's a total eclipse and you look at a star whose light is passing near the sun, the damn star will appear to be in the wrong place because the light went around the sun and was bent. Einstein's theory predicts how much it will be bent.

The other thing he predicted as part of his theory was that things get heavier when they travel fast. As cyclotrons and particle accelerators began to move particles faster and faster, scientists did find that the things got heavier. And when they get close to the speed of light, they get infinitely heavy which means they can't travel at the speed of light. When you get them close to the speed of light, these particles get terribly heavy. You've got to pull them in like crazy. Who in the hell would have predicted that? These kinds of phenomena change life. Einstein's theories allowed us to develop atomic energy and the atomic bomb.

The Theory of Evolution is also an invention. Darwin theorized that life evolved through changes that happened accidentally. Survival of the fittest then decides what is left and what is discarded. It still bothers people to think that the complexity of the human being—the chemistry of the body, the physics of the eye, the complexity of the brain—all happened by a succession of accidents. Until somebody comes up with a better theory, however, that is the best explanation we have.

If you're religious, you might say, "Well, I don't have to know. God did it." Well, that's no answer. You'd still like to know how He did it and why He did it. If you like answers, the question is no different whether God directed evolution or Nature directed it.

INTERVIEWER: *If a great invention is revolutionary, what would you consider the greatest invention of the past fifty to one hundred years?*

> *My experience has been that you spend weeks building wooden models and then spend money on real models.*

RABINOW: Einstein's work opened the door to atomic energy, and there's no doubt that it has changed the history of the world. It may destroy us, but on the other hand it may stop wars. I can't imagine wars being fought with atomic weapons. You'd have to assume the people who would fight them would be insane.

Winning a nuclear war with Russia would mean sacrificing three-quarters of the United States. What kind of a victory is that? We have one city left and they have none? Big deal! Or we have two and they have one? So we won? It's not the kind of winning that makes any sense.

INTERVIEWER: *But conventional weapons are also deadly. World War II destroyed most of Europe and much of Asia. The fire bombing of Dresden killed more people than either of the atomic bombs dropped on Japan. What's changed since you developed weapons in World War II?*

RABINOW: I developed weapons for sixteen years, but I don't do it anymore. People talk about atomic war like it's the same kind of war we used to fight, only more so. The answer isn't that it's "more so"; it's different. And it's different in two fundamental ways.

When we developed weapons during the Second World War, we talked about their statistical effectiveness: If you dropped so many bombs, so many would hit and so many would do damage. If you shot bullets, so many would find their mark. You could therefore calculate that so many men with so many machine guns could kill so many people. It's bloody stuff, but you could predict a little bit.

The trouble with hydrogen bombs and atomic bombs is that the numbers stop meaning anything. If I fire a thousand missiles at Russia and they stop half or even sixty percent of the missiles, it doesn't make any difference. Forty percent of those missiles will still wipe out all of Russia and probably kill the entire population in this hemisphere. Suddenly, numbers don't mean much. If ten percent get through, I will still wipe out all of Russia's major cities. That would not have been possible in the old days.

The other thing that has changed is that for the first time in history, the governments at home are in more danger than the soldiers in the field. This has changed the game quite a bit. In the old days, soldiers were killed. If so many were killed but the line was held, the government at home was reasonably safe.

Now, for the first time in history, Washington and Moscow are in greater danger than the soldiers in the front lines of Europe. Neither country is likely to drop an A-bomb or an H-bomb on a group of soldiers. It's just not worth it.

If you're in Washington or Moscow, however, you're really up a creek. You can't go to a shelter because the H-bomb will squeeze the ground over you and crush the shelter with you inside. If you survive, the fallout will get you anyway. What will you breathe for the next two years?

INTERVIEWER: *Is the atomic bomb a great invention then because it's made war impossible? Or is it a tool we would be better off without?*

RABINOW: It may stop wars or it may destroy the human race. But knowing what we know and permitting an atomic war to occur is inexcusable. If there are any gods out there, they must be laughing themselves sick. A human race that kills itself! I mean, that's really a big joke. I don't think we're that stupid. At least I hope not.

INTERVIEWER: *What do you think of the Strategic Defense Initiative [SDI], or Star Wars?*

RABINOW: I think it's silly. By the time it's ready twenty years from now, the Russians will have developed new weapons. They're not going to sit there, knowing that we'll be able to stop all their big missiles in twenty years, and not do anything about it. They will change their arsenal to little missiles or submarine missiles or underground missiles.

Of course, the reason we're building SDI is not to defend the United States. This is fiction. It's to develop new weapons in general. SDI gives the

Army, Navy, and Air Force a tremendous amount of money to develop new weapons. Where else could they get this kind of money? They couldn't get it if they said they wanted to develop new weapons. But "defensive weapons" sounds good.

I think people like President Reagan, however, really believe that you can stop all weapons with an SDI system. But nothing in SDI can stop a submarine from coming within fifty miles of your shoreline and firing a missile at you.

The inherent problem with defensive weapons is that you can only build an effective defense if you can do it quickly. If you and I decide to start killing each other and I start putting this bulletproof shield around me, you've got to decide whether or not to shoot me before I finish. If I finish, I will probably shoot you. You can't wait. You'll certainly do something.

INTERVIEWER: *If atomic energy is the greatest invention of the past fifty years or so, what do you think the next great invention will be?*

RABINOW: I think the next great invention will be the discovery of the mechanism at work in the brain. Nobody understands how the brain works. They know it remembers a fantastic amount, and they know it does prodigious recall tricks, but nobody really understands how it works.

It's only a pound or so of material, but it stores a lifetime of experiences and recalls them at will. It recalls sounds. It can do original visual work, auditory work, and tactile work, and it can come up with new inventions. Nobody knows how it works. They know it's neurons, and they know it makes connections, but that's not very much.

Why, for example, can I think of a toy dog that I saw thirty years ago and apply it to an invention? Where is it stored? How is it stored? We know there are some five billion neurons in the brain and that they connect in many, many ways. The number of computations becomes astronomical, but we don't have any way of making computers do this. We know how computers work, but we don't know how the brain works.

INTERVIEWER: *Will that open up a Pandora's box of problems as did atomic energy?*

RABINOW: Frankly, I'm not happy about the possibility that we will discover how the brain works. I would like to know how the brain works, but I'm not sure it's a good thing for the human race to know. It's an apple that one shouldn't bite quite yet.

Understanding how the brain works would give a dictator the power to control people. Knowledge is control. I wouldn't want Hitler to have known how the brain works. I wouldn't want Stalin to have known. I don't even think I want any of the present-day rulers and leaders of the world to know how the brain works. They could very easily start exploiting that knowledge for their own advantage, and I don't think our ethics are as good as I'd like to see for us to have that sort of power.

An inventor has to be well trained. You're not going to combine ideas if you have none to start with.

We can now think to ourselves without other people knowing what we're thinking. I can think the President is smart or stupid. I can think that Stalin was a son of a bitch or a generous guy. I can think Hitler was a noble man or that he was an idiot.

But once they know how my brain works, they will be able to tell what I'm thinking. How? I don't know. And they'll certainly be able to change it. I would just as soon not give anybody the right to change my brain. That's not because my brain is so beautiful or so perfect. I just don't want anybody to change it. I worry about this.

INTERVIEWER: *You mentioned using a toy dog as the basis for an invention. What's the story behind that?*

RABINOW: This story starts in 1959 when I was driving home with my patent attorney, Max Libman. He's dead now, but he was my patent attorney for many years, and we were partners in everything we did. We were driving back from Cleveland, Ohio, where we had demonstrated an automatic headlight dimmer that I had invented.

As we were driving back, Max said to me, "You have nothing to do for the next several hours. Design me a gadget so that when the phone rings a light will light and stay lit. I have an answering service, and I'd like to know when I should call them to pick up a message. Now I call them, and if there's no message, I waste their time and mine. Other times I forget to call, and a message is waiting."

"Well, that's easy, Max," I said. "You take a microphone, and an amplifier, and you hook up a latching relay and arrange it so that when the amplifier makes a really loud noise it will pull the relay and light the light."

"You're a lousy engineer," he said. "I can do that without you. I know how to use a microphone, an amplifier, and all the rest of it. Give me something simple, something inexpensive."

I asked him to let me think. As we were driving, I kept thinking, What is it that I can do that will respond to a noise and light up? Then, I finally remembered something.

When I came to America in 1921, I was eleven years old and worked in my uncle's candy store on 125th Street in Manhattan. We sold candy and we also sold toys for Christmas. One of the toys I particularly enjoyed was a little cardboard box shaped like a doghouse. It was about four or five inches tall, and into the open door in front you pushed a toy bulldog. You held your breath, and the dog stayed in.

In the back of the box were two wires. The wires were part of a circuit that controlled an electromagnet that held a plate back against a spring. A long, thin piece of brass hung in the back of the doghouse, and as long as it touched the two wires connected to the electromagnet, the circuit stayed closed. But whenever you made a loud noise or yelled "Rex!" the back vibrated and shook the brass plate. That broke the contact for an instant, the spring-loaded plate was released, and the dog shot out. So, if you clapped your hands or yelled "Rex!" the dog jumped at you.

I thought that same setup would work with the phone. "Max," I said, "I can give you a telephone answering device that's simple." I went home and took a cigar box and made a loose contact just underneath the lid so that the circuit wire just barely touched the contact. Then, I wired it across a shunt and connected a resistor, in a series with a neon light. By using two resistors, I arranged them so that the neon light normally received seventy volts—which is not enough to light it. If the contact was broken for an instant, however, the shunt would be disconnected, and the voltage would jump enough to light the light. Even though the contact might be broken for only an instant, the light would stay lit because neon lights have what's called differential voltage. Once you light them at ninety volts, they will stay lit even at seventy. So, I made an answering machine light with two resistors and a lousy contact.

I brought it to Max's office on New York Avenue in Washington, D.C. We put it on the desk, and he called the operator and asked her to ring the phone. She did and the light lit, and he was very happy. I went home really proud of myself because the whole thing consisted of practically nothing.

When I got home, the phone rang, and it was Max. "You still stink as an engineer," he said. "I can't sneeze, I can't close the desk, and I can't close the door. Anytime I do anything in this room the damn light lights."

"Well," I said, "this will take a little fixing." We solved the problem by putting a little delay in the circuit so that not only would the current have to jump up to light the light, it would also have to stay up for a while.

Later, Max went to the Patent Office to look up the patents on this dog. He found that the patent for the toy dog was issued in 1918, and it was built exactly as I had drawn it. There was a bulldog in a doghouse, and it had the same two wires and the same shaped contact that I had drawn. I had remembered it exactly.

Look at the stunt that my brain did! I knew how that toy worked in 1921, and I remembered it in detail in 1959. Once, when I told this story as an example of information retrieval at a meeting, somebody said, "Oh, you looked it up in an index in your head under 'sound-operated devices.'" But that was impossible. One, I wouldn't have classified it under sound-operated devices when I was eleven. And two, I spoke Russian when I came to America, and I would have had to look it up in my Russian index and translate it. What really happens in situations like this, I think, is that you remember the picture of a thing, not the words.

It's interesting that the mind also remembers a smell. You smell something, and you say, "This reminds me of my mother's cooking." Or it's the perfume worn by a girl you dated thirty years ago. But you can't describe it. If I asked you what it smelled like, you would say, "Like that girl's perfume." There are no words to describe it. Professionals have words to describe a perfume; they describe it by names of flowers. But the brain doesn't remember a smell by words; the brain will just remember a smell. It can also remember a color or a behavior. For example, you may be looking at a person and say, "That's Joe. Look at the way he walks." What in the hell are you saying? You remember some kind of motion, and even though you've seen thousands of people walking you know that one is Joe. We have no idea how that's done.

INTERVIEWER: *Is the brain's ability to recall and combine different bits of information somewhat like invention itself?*

RABINOW: Invention to me is an art form. If you forget the mechanics and that I know how to do gadgetry, an invention is really putting together interesting ideas that people have not put together before—a toy dog and a telephone answering device or a vacuum cup and pressurizing a building. These things normally don't go together. This is what makes an invention.

A really good invention, in fact, is a work of art. A good piece of poetry, for example, is old words put together in a new way—and put together in a way that a sophisticated audience understands as good art. A good invention has the same qualities. It's not only old things combined in new ways; it's something that makes you feel good when you look at it. A good invention should evoke an emotional response. When I see an invention I like, I feel like smiling. I say, "That's beautiful."

> *I don't really think the Patent Office is the problem. The real problem is that American industry doesn't treat inventors well.*

When I tell artists that invention is an art form, they have a little trouble with it, probably because they know much less about my art form than I know about theirs. Everyone has been exposed to music and literature. It's relatively easy to explain why a beautiful poem is a beautiful poem. But it's a little harder to explain to a nontechnical audience that a differential gear in an automobile is a beautiful piece of work. It's not only useful—it's just beautiful. It's simple. It's clean. I don't know any other word to describe it, except a mathematical word called elegance.

INTERVIEWER: *What kind of inventions are you working on now?*

RABINOW: Lately I've been inventing locks, and I've recently patented a pick-proof lock. It started as a hobby. I made some models of locks to prove a few things to myself, and before long, I was trying to sell them to lock manufacturers.

I first make wooden models of my locks to show manufacturers how they work. The model for one of my latest locks is eight times the actual size. A manufacturer in Chicago was interested in it and wanted to see a real model. So, I had an instrument maker, who used to work for me, make a metal model in the actual size. It's the same as the wooden one, but much smaller. It also cost $1,050 unfinished. I had to finish it myself by putting in the springs and the key. It's hard to pick—not pick-proof—but hard to pick. I recently took it to Chicago, and they want me to design it for production. My experience has been that you spend weeks building wooden models and then spend money on real models. Finally, you get something that works, and you get patents. It's all very, very difficult. You'd like to have a magic wand to take you from the idea to the final model.

INTERVIEWER: *What's your favorite invention?*

RABINOW: It's not easy to say, but if I had to choose I would probably say it's my reading machine. It really reads very well, and it's very logical after the fact. It's probably as good as anything I've ever invented.

I built my first reading machine in 1954 while I was working at the Bureau of Standards. It looks at characters and scans them, comparing them point by point to matrices programmed into the machine. Unlike other reading machines at the time, mine compared each character it scanned with the whole set of characters to find the best match. A P, for example, would be compared with every letter from A to Z, either serially or in parallel. Call it a correlation machine if you like, but it selects the character with the least difference from the one being scanned. That kind of system allows you to be very accurate, as well as read degraded or damaged print. To the machine, a degraded B is still more like a B than anything else.

The clutch is certainly my simplest invention. I never understood why it wasn't done before. Why didn't someone think of using iron filings stuck to a plate? It just didn't happen.

Of course, my watch regulator was very successful, so I like that one. I don't know why someone didn't do it before. What is the big deal about coupling the rate regulator to the hands you use for adjusting the time? That way, when you move the hands forward, it gives the regulator a nudge, and you speed up the clock a little bit.

My regulator actually reduced the cost for making the clocks because the hand regulator disappeared. I eventually sold my patents on the self-regulated clock to manufacturers who used them for automobile clocks.

With my three-cent royalty per clock—I got a cent and a half and my attorney got a cent and a half—the clock was still cheaper than the older models because the old hand regulator cost more. My licensee also sold the rights on the self-regulator to others. No matter how you looked at it, it made the clock better and cheaper. Even so, companies didn't buy it for nine years. Chrysler, however, finally said they wanted it, and that's what sold it. It's just a simple device. A couple of stampings in there, and you have a gadget that kicks the regulator a little bit when you move the hands.

INTERVIEWER: *What do you think makes a good inventor?*

RABINOW: An inventor has to be well trained. You're not going to combine ideas if you have none to start with. An amateur can invent very well, but he will invent old junk because he doesn't know what's new. That is one of the tragedies of these self-styled inventors who come to us at the Bureau of Standards with an idea. They're nice people, but they have no training. It's as if they want to write but have never read a book.

INTERVIEWER: *So, an inventor has to have a background to draw upon?*

RABINOW: Well, invention, as I said, is not a logical process, and one invents by putting things together that normally don't go together. A lot of inventions, in fact, often seem obvious after they've been invented.

One thing that bothers me about the Patent Office is that very often they say something is obvious. They rejected one of my inventions for that reason—a road lane-marker that is flush with the road surface but can still reflect your headlights. Because it's flush, you can go over it with a snowplow without breaking the reflector or the plow.

The Patent Office, however, said my invention was obvious because forty years ago somebody invented a flush lane-marker—even though his didn't work properly. "His didn't work," the Patent Office agreed, "but forty years later, you know more than he did so you could invent one that works. The invention is obvious."

I think that's a silly argument. For forty years people have wanted to have reflective lane-markers and still be able to plow the roads and clear snow. I invented one that works, but they didn't want to give me a basic patent on it because it was obvious. I took it to court, and I lost the argument. The court also said that it was obvious. But it was only obvious after I did it. I eventually did get a patent on my lane-markers, but not a basic one.

The lane-markers are really very interesting because they're flush prisms. When you step back and shine a light on them, they will reflect your light back to you because the prism bends light. If I take a prism in my hand and shine a light through it, you will see a light on that table across the room. That light is coming from my light, and it's been bent by the prism. Now, if I turn the prism around and put bicycle reflectors along the corners, it will shine light back at me off the reflectors, even when it's flush with a roadway.

Well, I went to 3M with the idea, and they said "It's very clever, but it means a big investment."

"Yes," I told them, "it means you have to bury a bunch of them in the road and check them for a year or two. If you decide to sell them, you have to build a machine that grinds holes in the road and drops them into the roadway. But think of the market." They weren't interested. I went to other people and got the same response. Finally, I went to the Bureau of Public Roads in the Department of Transportation and they told me that they would test them if I gave them four hundred production models. I told them I couldn't afford to do that, so I have this kit of flush reflectors in my basement, and nobody has bought the idea.

INTERVIEWER: *What's the best place for an inventor to work?*

RABINOW: In a good laboratory, but in a small company.

INTERVIEWER: *Rather than on your own?*

RABINOW: I don't think you can make a living on your own. There are only two inventors I know who really invent full-time and live off their royalties. One is Sam Ruben, who invented the small mercury battery, the quick-heating vacuum tube, and the dry electrolytic condenser. The other inventor I know who truly lives off his inventions is Dick Walton in Boston. He invents things having to do with textiles. That's all. Others who claim to be full-time inventors really make their income from companies they started after coming up with a few key inventions.

It's more difficult to be an outside inventor. I'm an outside inventor. If I went to Sony and said, "Look, I know how to make this plug or socket on your tape recorder a little cheaper than yours," they would tell me to go away. I may be right, but they aren't going to change their tooling and give me a contract because I can make something a little better. Of course, if I worked at Sony as an engineer, the next time they made a new design, they might change the plug or socket to make it cheaper.

I really don't think you can make a living inventing on your own. I spoke to a group of inventors in February at the Patent Office as part of a Thomas Edison celebration. I talked and there were venture capitalists and other people to talk to the inventors and tell them how to start a business and so on.

I listened to the venture capitalists, and I said to myself, That's nonsense. Some of these inventors will make it, but many will not. Suppose they open a business, and they're successful? What's to prevent the Taiwanese from copying their product next year and doing it more cheaply? They can do this for two reasons: because their labor is cheaper and because they're second. The second guy can always make something cheaper than you can because he learns from your mistakes.

Nowadays, outside inventors are only getting five or six percent of the United States patents, and they used to get about forty percent. Foreign inventors are getting forty percent of the United States patents, and American companies are getting most of the rest.

INTERVIEWER: *Should the Patent Office be doing things differently to promote creativity and inventiveness?*

RABINOW: I don't really think the Patent Office is the problem. The real problem is that American industry doesn't treat inventors well.

I went to General Motors with my automatic headlight dimmer, and they said, "Beautiful, but we don't want it." I went to venetian blind manufacturers with my single-strip venetian blind, and they said, "It's gorgeous, but we don't want it." I went to computer people with the first computer disk file. "That's very clever," they said, "but who needs that much information storage?" This is the problem: They aren't interested in new ideas.

When a major company bought the rights to my record player, I saw how they were making my machines. "It's wrong," I told them. "If you do what you're doing, the record player won't work well, and it won't track properly. I've tried your way and I can tell you why. I've got sixteen patents and fourteen years of experience. Why won't you listen to me?"

The president said, "I'm not technical. My engineers want to do it that way." I told them what was wrong, and I was right. They eventually went out of the business of manufacturing record players.

Russia has these kinds of problems in spades because the whole country is one big industry. When I had the Russian Commissioner of Patents here to dinner with some of his staff, he told me they practically have to force industry to change and accept new ideas. When they ask the factory manager why he isn't making something in the new style, he tells them, "Look, I'm meeting my quota. All my suppliers know what they're doing, and all my workers know what they're doing. Leave me alone. I sell everything I make. I've even got a waiting list. Why should I change anything?" Sometimes they have to fire the manager to get a new product started.

INTERVIEWER: *Is that kind of inertia inevitable in big organizations? Do you see big business in the United States developing some of the same problems, or is our economic system too freewheeling for that?*

RABINOW: American companies are getting too big, and we are beginning to have some of the same problems. How do you make a change in a company like General Motors? How do you do it? If you make a new automobile, you can't just test it once. You've got to test a model in high altitudes. You've got to test a model in Canada. You've got to test it in Africa. You have to test it in a dusty atmosphere and so on. The fact that your one car worked well in Alaska proves nothing. It may overheat in Florida.

We used to have small companies. At Zenith, when you went to see the boss, you went to McDonald,* who was a radioman. If he liked your idea, he'd put it in a product. If it took three years, it took three years. But he was the owner.

Bob Sprague, who founded Sprague Electric, is another example. His company made sixty percent of all the capacitors in the world. Sam Ruben, whom I talked about earlier, came to him and said, "I have a dry electrolytic condenser that you might be interested in." Electrolytic condensers used to be made from glass jars with a liquid in them and aluminum in the liquid. If they had a failure in one spot, the whole capacitor went to pieces. It was a ridiculous arrangement for a radio.

Well, Sam Ruben had invented a dry electrolytic condenser, and it's used all over the world now.

Bob Sprague's people said Ruben's idea was no good. But Sprague also listened to Ruben and said, "I like it." They made more money on dry

---

* Eugene F. McDonald, Jr., Zenith Radio Corporation's founder/president.

INTERVIEWER: *I've been told that small companies outperform large* *panies when it comes to creativity and producing new products. Apparently you* *the same way since you told me a small company is the best place for an invent* *work. What's wrong with big companies when it comes to innovation?*

RABINOW: The thing you have to understand is that a new experie is much more risky for a large company than for a small one. Let's say I making a reading machine in my own shop, and I want to change my sca ner from one that uses blue light to one that uses a red laser. If I decide to d that, the next model I make will use a laser scanner because I'm only mak ing one model at a time. I could do that when I was making the machine on my own.

But when Control Data bought my company, we were using white light and blue light and using photomultipliers to scan. After we were started at Control Data, I decided it would be better to go to laser scanning because we could use a smaller beam and do some tricks with it. I went to Bill Norris, the president of Control Data and a good friend of mine, and said, "Bill, I'd like to switch to laser scanning."

"What does this mean?" he asked.

"Well, instead of 'invisible' blue ink on paper, we will use red ink. It means it will be a completely new type of reading machine."

He looked at me and said, "You're out of your mind. It took us three years to get your machine really rolling all over the world. We are making your page readers in quantities. We have sent service people from all over the world to classes to learn how to service them. We have the paper com- panies making the right kind of paper. The blue ink people know what kind of blue ink you want, and the black ink people know what kind of black ink you want so that you can read things well. Everything is running smoothly all over the world, and now you're going to change everything."

"Yes," I said, "it's better."

"That's not the question," he said. And he was right.

When you're big, you have to invest a lot of money in a new model. God help you if you make a mistake. A radical change will give you trouble. I even had troubles with this when I was building my phonographs. I knew some problems were developing with the design, but I could hardly afford to make the slightest change. I had parts in stock and was ordering others all the time. The bigger you are, the worse it gets.

electrolytics than they made on anything else for the next fifty years, and Sam Ruben made royalties on it as well.

One of Sprague's divisions in Milwaukee, Wisconsin, was run by a friend of mine named Harry Rubinstein who, incidentally, invented printed circuits. His division made five percent of Sprague's capacitors and twenty percent of their profits.

Rubinstein had invented the process they used, and he knew everyone in the plant. I was a consultant for them, and when we would walk through the plant, he would talk to each employee by his or her first name. "How's your mother?" And so on.

"How do you do that?" I asked.

"I give them their paychecks personally on payday, so I get to know them. That way I know them all."

When there were technical problems, he could also say, "No, don't do it that way; put it this way and clamp it like this." When they had trouble, they would come to him because he was both the chief engineer and the manager.

But when they retired him, they put a couple of youngsters in charge of the division who immediately put in three managers to run the plant. Rubinstein had run it by himself, and he was chief engineer. They put people in charge who didn't know the business, and they spoiled it. They tried to run the company according to some books they read, and today they're losing money.

INTERVIEWER: *What do you think the United States needs to do to make itself more competitive?*

RABINOW: What's wrong with us? There are two things wrong with us. The first is that unions have gotten the workers too much pay. The second is that United States has bad managers who don't know anything technically.

I was a member of a union, and if you quote me, I will say, "Yes, I said that unions have gotten too much pay." The problem with high pay is that you have to be competitive worldwide. You cannot protect a single industry at the expense of the rest of the public. If our steelworker gets $20 per hour and the Korean steelworker gets $3 per hour, we're in trouble.

Why, for example, does Kodak, which used to make beautiful cameras here in the United States, now make most of its cameras in Japan? Another example is the vise in my workroom. It's Sears and Roebuck's best vise, and it's a good vise. It's a heavy vise, and it has a split nut. In other words, you can slide it quickly in and out to put it in place. Once you start turning the handle, the nut will engage, and you have a vise. This is Sears' best. Eighty dollars or so, and it is very heavy. Made in Japan. Sears'.

All it is, is a bunch of metal. It's made with the same construction that's been used for a hundred years. I've seen older models exactly like this with the same half nut and everything.

Why does it pay to make it in Japan and ship it across the ocean? It pays because labor and management in the United States just don't give a damn. There's no excuse to have this $80 vise coming from Japan.

As soon as American companies find that it's cheaper to make their products overseas, they run to Japan or to Taiwan or South Korea or Singapore. AT&T, for example, closes a plant in the United States, and twenty thousand people lose their jobs. Later, AT&T opens up the same plant in Singapore. These companies don't really care where they make their money. Neither would I. If I had to make my phonograph in Tokyo or Singapore, I would. Patriotism has nothing to do with making money. Making money is an international game. I believe in it, curiously enough. If we start putting tariffs on products and commodities, our trade problems will only get worse. If we put a tariff on a product, we will be paying more money for the same thing that we could buy cheaply from, say, Japan. And a tariff doesn't mean Japan will necessarily buy that same product from us.

I have two or three friends who are high-level economists and they predict that our standard of living will eventually drop to a point where it is equal to that of other countries. Or, to put it politely, the standard of living in other countries will rise until it is equal to ours.

People say we will become a service economy. But what will happen to the workers? Lawyers will do well, doctors will do well, writers will do well, and tennis players and other people who entertain us will do well, but what about the workers?

One way or another, our labor force has to compete worldwide. Instead of cutting wages or protecting certain industries, we can make up for this problem by having products that other countries do not have. It means being ahead in biomedicine. It means having some electronic device like a CAT [computerized axial tomography] scan that other countries don't have yet. It means more inventions. It also means management has to be ahead all the time, but our management in the United States is not ahead all the time. Management has to compete worldwide too.

I worry when the Nakamichi company makes a good tape recorder and the guy who does it is Nakamichi. It bothers me that the honorary chairman of Sony, Dr. Masaru Ibuka, is a life fellow of the Institute of Electrical and Electronics Engineers. He's a member because he's a first-class engineer. Here's a guy who is one of a group of those who run enormous empires, but who also personally know electrical engineering. We don't have managers like that in the United States.

INTERVIEWER: So, to improve competitiveness, the United States would do better to hire managers with better scientific or technical training rather than whiz kids from business school or law school?

RABINOW: It's not just that managers need a better education; it's the whole system which needs to change. I've been a member of the IEEE's study group on productivity, and we could see all the problems coming several years ago. We could see Kodak not making its cameras here, radio equipment being made overseas, and so on. The problem isn't only cheap labor; it's the availability of competently trained technical people. For instance, my Bang & Olufsen turntable cost $1,000, and it's a museum piece. You couldn't get an engineer in the United States who knows how to build a machine like that.

My feeling is that we have to change the direction of the educational system in the United States so that bright kids will get to know math and science early in school. By the time they get to college, they should already have algebra and trigonometry and calculus. They should be able to do as well on math tests as Japanese and German students. Right now, we are not doing very well.

I have a friend who is teaching at a four-year accredited college that gives technical degrees. He's teaching a class of highly motivated young people, yet when he wrote on the chalkboard "$E=ir$ and therefore $i=E/r$," a student in the class raised his hand and said, "How did you get that?" This is a student who graduated from high school and wants to be an engineer. He wants to know how he got that! He doesn't even understand a simple rearrangement of variables in an equation.

What they have to do, my friend says, is give students special remedial courses in math. But you can't correct a poor background in trigonometry, algebra, geometry, and general math in one year. A student should have that training all the way along.

But the kind of changes I'm talking about won't happen because you start some new science courses. The whole educational system has to be improved, and I don't mean just rearranging courses. We have to have English teachers who love English so that kids will learn how to read. We have twenty-five million illiterate people in the United States—people who speak English well, but who can't read at all. We have teachers in public schools who don't even know how to write. We have science teachers who don't even know science.

My two daughters, for example, went to Walt Whitman, a very good high school in Bethesda, Maryland. They had a physics teacher who was really a physical education teacher, and he didn't know any physics. Every day when they came home, I had to unteach them what they had learned in class so that they could solve their homework problems. There's no excuse for that. Our kids should have good teachers who love their subjects and who inspire them.

Part of the solution, I think, is to raise teachers' salaries. We have to raise them not by a few thousand bucks, but by a lot, so that a teacher can earn as much as you or I do or as much as a lawyer or a doctor. That way, we will have a waiting list of good kids, bright kids, who will want to teach. If you are a brilliant science student, why on earth would you want to teach with today's salaries?

INTERVIEWER: *Do you think more money and better teachers would really create more inventors or more scientists and engineers?*

RABINOW: I think we should treat our science kids the way we treat our tennis kids. We take a bunch of tennis kids and teach them how to play the game when they're still young. I watched a class Saturday while I was playing tennis. The professionals were teaching a bunch of kids who were so small, they could hardly hold the racket.

On another court, I watched a fourteen-year-old girl play a sixteen-year-old girl in a tournament. They were so good, I had trouble playing my own game because I could hardly stop watching them. They were hitting balls with tremendous speed and tremendous accuracy. One of them is a national champion at age fourteen. The other one is runner-up in her division.

By the time they're eighteen, they will be world champions. That doesn't happen without a tremendous amount of inspiration and practice, as well as an early start.

Our values allow us to say that a kid should play tennis if he wants to. But if a kid wants to be a scientist, he should also be able to get the training he needs. He should be a brilliant scientist by the time he finishes high school. Brilliant kids in science should not just be an exception. If we took half the money that is being spent on defense for Star Wars and put it into education in science, we would be a stronger nation at the end of twenty years. We'd be better off defensively and economically. We'd be able to compete with the Japanese. We would have people in high places who know science. That would do a lot for us. We would have Nobel Prize-winners coming out of our ears.

STEVE WOZNIAK

*S*TEVE WOZNIAK *had no intention of starting a company when he designed the Apple II in the mid-1970s. He merely wanted a computer to impress his friends. In 1977, however, he founded Apple Computer with Steve Jobs. By 1980, their sales topped $100 million.*

The Apple II may not have been the first personal computer, but it was the first truly revolutionary one, and for several years it was simply the best personal computer anyone had ever seen. Other early PCs were largely tools for hobbyists and computer hackers. The Apple II, however, went several steps further. Like other PCs, it could be used by computer hackers, but it could also be used for bookkeeping, word processing, and a host of sophisticated computer games. The Apple II's unique features—color, sound, high-resolution graphics, and high-density RAMs—soon became the standard for the personal computer industry.

Wozniak designed his first computer at age thirteen. He met Steve Jobs at high school in Santa Clara, California. They became an unlikely pair. Wozniak was the thinker behind Apple Computer; Jobs was the driver. While Wozniak designed computers, Jobs set about marketing them. In 1976, they got their first order from the Byte Shop in Mountain View, California, for fifty of Wozniak's first Apple computer, the Apple I. They built their first computers in Jobs' garage. To finance their business, Wozniak sold two of his Hewlett–Packard calculators and Jobs sold his Volkswagen bus.

In 1977, Wozniak finished his design for the Apple II, and the company was incorporated. With $3 million in financing from a select group of venture capitalists, Apple Computer Corporation began its climb.

Outside the computer world, Wozniak is recognized more for his wealth than for his elegant computer and circuit designs. When Apple went public in 1980, Wozniak's stock holdings made him a multimillionaire. He has put his money to generous use since then. He has become a well-known supporter of the arts and of educational issues.

Steve Wozniak was born in San Jose, California, in the Silicon Valley, in 1950. He attended the University of Colorado in Boulder, and he later returned to the Silicon Valley to work for Hewlett–Packard, where he designed integrated circuits for calculators. In 1981, after a near-fatal plane crash, he took time off from Apple. During that time, he attended the University of California at Berkeley under an assumed name and earned a degree in computer science. He left Apple in 1985 to start CL 9, or Cloud Nine. His latest project is a programmable remote-control device for home entertainment systems.

INTERVIEWER: *How important was growing up in the Silicon Valley? Do you think you could have invented the Apple II if you had grown up somewhere else?*

WOZNIAK: I grew up in a kind of typical Silicon Valley neighborhood: A lot of "electronics kids" were running around, and all our projects were in electronics. We built house-to-house intercoms and walkie-talkies; it was all part of our life. I knew I was going to be an engineer from day one.

But, as far as the Silicon Valley is concerned, when I was growing up, computers weren't really around yet. This area wasn't known for computers. Microelectronics firms and chip makers were located here, but in 1964 when I was in the eighth grade, there were no chips you could afford unless you were involved in a military project. Then, you could buy two gates in a package for $50, which was equal to about $200 to $500 of today's dollars. It was totally out of this world.

But having local microelectronics companies around did help me some because they gave me diodes and transistors. They gave me surplus ones that I used in science fair projects, and that was a major step towards getting started. In the fifth grade, all it took was a phone call, primarily from my father, and I could get four hundred transistors.

There's a certain window in your life when you're very young and you get a few of these things in your hands. And then, for the rest of your life, they're familiar and they're friends and that's your thing. If you got a car that you started working on in the seventh grade, you'd probably be working on cars for the rest of your life.

INTERVIEWER: *Was there anyone in your background who really encouraged you to become an inventor?*

WOZNIAK: Tom Swift,* no question. He made it a good thing to invent and be a scientist. Winning science fairs at an early age or even entering science fairs was also important. If you enter a science fair and do something well, you get a lot of positive feedback from parents and teachers and the like. In your head, being an inventor becomes a good thing.

My father also gave me some direction because he was an electrical engineer. When the right times came around, he helped me with electronics projects. He would stand at a blackboard for no reason at all and teach me about transistors. He helped me learn things that weren't even taught in school. He also gave me some of the first books on computer programming, even though he didn't program himself. So, he influenced me a lot and gave me direction. I kind of wanted to be an engineer like my father.

> *I didn't have to understand a market of several million; nobody had a computer. All I had to understand was one person: myself.*

INTERVIEWER: *What do you consider your first invention? Was it the Apple?*

WOZNIAK: Not really. Whenever you solve a problem, whether it's mathematics in school or an electronics project, in a way you're inventing. Before I worked on the Apple, I worked on some electronics problems that were really kind of inventions. I built an adder-subtracter in the eighth grade, and I solved some circuit problems such as how to build a gate with two diodes. The two diodes wouldn't work, so I had to put transistors in there as well.

While I was in college, I invented my own version of a blue box.** In the three years just before the Apple, I totally designed a video terminal and a version of the video game Pong, which influenced some of the people at Atari who wanted to hire me. I also designed a movie system for hotel-room

---

* "The *Tom Swift, Jr.* books were a series about an inventor that was popular when I was growing up in the 1950s. They were sold alongside *Nancy Drew* and *The Hardy Boys*. I can recall always waiting until a new one I hadn't read yet came out!" —Steve Wozniak

** Electronic device that generates tones to "fool" and trigger telephone circuits. The original blue box was built by John Draper, alias Captain Crunch, who served a prison term for using his invention.

televisions back in 1970. Because I was interested in electronics, I was doing a lot of projects on the side even though I was working at Hewlett–Packard as an engineer on calculators.

INTERVIEWER: *Did you see the first Apple computers as filling a need or creating one?*

WOZNIAK: Filling a need. I knew I needed a personal computer. I was lucky. Back in those days, I didn't have to understand a market of several million; nobody had a computer. All I had to understand was one person: myself.

I needed a computer for my work at Hewlett–Packard to calculate a few solutions for designing gates and registers for the calculating chips. I even knew a few programs I wanted to write in BASIC. And, I also wanted to play the type of video games that send text to you and you type text back. It says, "I smell a wumpus. You're getting farther away." You type back, "Go left." That sort of thing. It was hard to visualize those sorts of games until the Apple II.

INTERVIEWER: *The early days of Apple have been described as a "ride on a rocket." Were you ever surprised at the way the personal computer market took off when the Apple was introduced?*

WOZNIAK: No, never once. I designed these computers to show off to my friends; I didn't have any plan to start a company. I knew from my electronics background that computers were going to sell at least a million units, even when they had sold only twenty thousand. I used to have a ham radio license, and I knew there was a large market for ham radios. And I also knew there were more computer people than ham radio operators.

In the beginning it wasn't a big shock. It happened so gradually that, by the time the market became as big as it is today, we already were very successful and already had a big, successful company. It was then that the personal computer industry went much further than we thought. Instead of being a $2 billion industry it was maybe an $8 billion industry.

I didn't think we would sell as many as we did or that the industry would become as big as it is today. If I had, I would have based all the decisions on building a product that consumers would like and that we could sell. And, we probably would have made the wrong decisions technically and built the wrong product.

INTERVIEWER: *Do you think you could have built the Apple from within a large company like Hewlett–Packard? Is it harder being creative inside a large company than when you're on your own?*

WOZNIAK: I don't see a major difference. A company works in a framework of conservatism where the only decision has to be the safe one. You have to be pretty sure of the result of anything you do. In that sort of framework, you can decide, Here's a few categories of technology we're going to pursue because they make good sense, and that's where the money will be spent.

Every once in a while, however, there's a rare event. And this rare event is the one that couldn't be calculated by the large company with very brilliant analysts who are employed to calculate such an event. These events happen maybe once a decade: A market springs out of nowhere and doesn't fit into the framework of existing companies. The existing companies can't be the ones to capitalize on it. And that's the rare occasion where

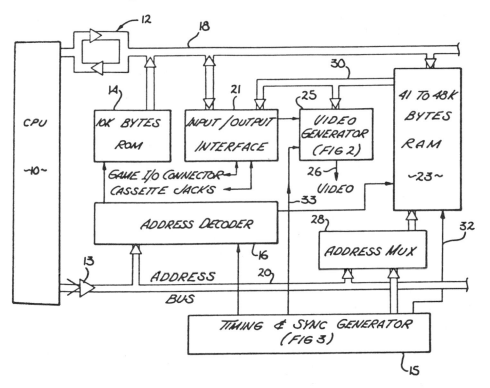

One of Steve Wozniak's Apple computer patent drawings (dated January 23, 1979).

entrepreneurs like me get a whole ton of credit—as if we discovered something amazing.

In my case, I would say that what I did was in some ways inevitable. All my life, all the little steps, all the right experiences in TV, video, circuits, building my own terminals, working at Atari, working at Hewlett–Packard—all these things converged. If you combined them all at that point in time, they were definitely going to be the Apple II.

INTERVIEWER: *Everything converged in the Apple II?*

I always stayed at the bottom in Apple. Being in a position where what I say is more important than what everyone else says is just not part of my personality.

WOZNIAK: Every single thing I stuck in there I had either worked with in the past or had been able to do a good job learning about before I used it.

For example, in the early days of microcomputers, the only two products to come out with color were the "Color Dazzler" from Cromenco and the Apple II. And it turns out that we both came out of the Homebrew Computer Club* in Palo Alto. It was a funny thing.

The same day I bought my first 6502 processor at the Wescon computer show in San Francisco, we had a club meeting in Palo Alto. Everybody came to that meeting. Some people from a company called Sphere brought a minicomputer connected to a color TV. They showed the first color graphics that probably most of us in that room had ever seen or only imagined that a computer could produce.

I just sat there thinking, I can't believe I'm seeing something like this. Probably, those people from Cromenco were sitting there just as I was: thinking what an unbelievable thing it was. For about two minutes everyone sat quietly, watching this TV draw color circles.

It was just one of those things. It's hard to explain. But if that hadn't happened to me, the Apple II probably never would have had color—or even been an Apple II.

---

* Founded in March 1975 in a Menlo Park, California, garage, the club began as an information-exchange group for people interested in computers and was the starting point for many Silicon Valley microcomputer companies.

Other projects I worked on also got worked into the Apple II: designing games at Atari, building terminals, working with TV and video, working at Hewlett–Packard. I had all the right experiences, but it was not planned. I never thought, Well, I'll do this and this and this, and then I'll be able to do the big combination. No plan. Every single thing converged.

INTERVIEWER: *When Apple went public, did your work situation change at all? Did this put any new pressures on you?*

WOZNIAK: No, that didn't change anything. I was at a desk even before then. It was something that happened before going public that changed things for me. When we starting working on a new computer, the Apple III, we built up our first large computer lab with fifty engineers, all managed in sub-groups with intermediate managers, a lab manager, and a division manager. By then, we had sort of structured ourselves so that I was just one more engineer with some ideas and some past experience. People grabbed me all the time to talk about their ideas, but I wasn't so crucial—I wasn't really needed. Whereas in the first couple of years, I was crucial. We had so few engineers then that everyone was crucial. And so I became disillusioned.

The funny thing was that I didn't even care all that much about starting a company. I really didn't believe all those prospects like being a $500 million company, because marketing people love to use all those big words.

It was very strange when the big day came. It was ultimatum day. I would have to quit my job at Hewlett–Packard. I loved Hewlett–Packard and had designed incredible stuff while I worked there. I was even a little insecure about getting my job back if Apple failed. When the big day came, I told Steve Jobs and Mike Markkula I wouldn't go ahead and start the company. It wasn't so obvious that we had to.

We were sitting in Mike Markkula's house, and I told them, "No. I'm not going to start Apple because I just want to design neat computers. I don't want to run a company because that's not my thing in life."

It was Alan Baum, one of my best friends for many, many years, a friend from high school, who called me on the phone the next day and convinced me that I could start a company and still be an engineer. I didn't have to be a manager; I didn't have to be a run-the-company person.

Once I had that clear in my head, I decided it would be okay to start a company. With my past and my background—what I was known for—I

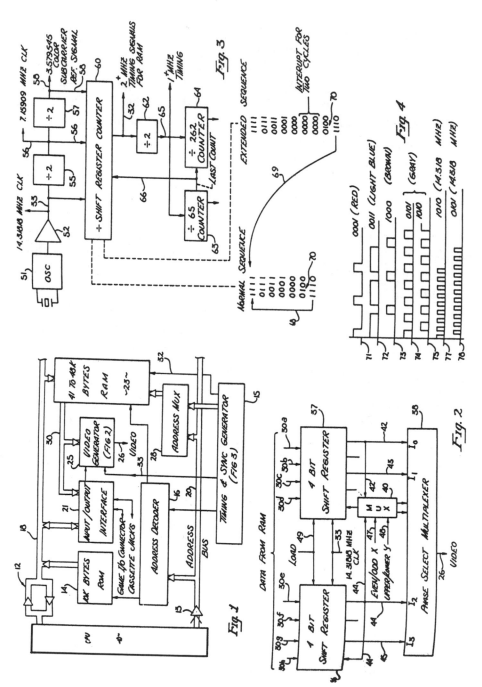

Drawings from Steve Wozniak's patent for the Apple computer (dated January 23, 1979).

didn't want to get involved in something like starting a company if it meant being put in a high role. I always stayed at the bottom in Apple. Being in a position where what I say is more important than what everyone else says is just not part of my personality.

INTERVIEWER: *Did Steve Jobs have a lot of input on the design of the Apple and Apple II?*

WOZNIAK: Not on circuits. Not on software. Only in the inspiration to start a company. He did not have the…well, he was a technician and not quite an engineer. He was not a computer designer; he didn't really know computer architecture; he wasn't really a programmer either. It wasn't until much later in his life that Jobs became competent at picking technologies.

I found that I had to be very, very good at the tools at the bottom of the pyramid, the primitives.

But he really made things go in the early days of the company. He was younger than I was….He had all this youngness in him. He wanted to challenge the world: Let's start a company….Let's just do it out of our garage!

He was able to manage projects, set up schedules, make sure that everything was done that needed to get done. He could persuade people to do things that normally couldn't get done.

On some decisions, like high-resolution graphics, he was important. I knew graphics were going to take over the world, but I couldn't see that high-resolution graphics, the display that every computer game today is done in, was really going to take off. Nobody knew what to do with it.

Steve and I had a discussion about it once, and I said, "Well, I've done it. It's three chips, but I don't even know if we should put it into the PC board." He said, "Yeah, we should put it in." He wanted everything in there. Well, thank god we did put it in there.

INTERVIEWER: *You never felt that anyone was close on your heels and about to come up with a similar product?*

WOZNIAK: Not at all. I knew that no one could talk to us about another product that was similar; the comparison would be a total wash. We never once had to compare the Apple or Apple II to any other product. For the first two years, all we had to do was show people what our computer had. Nobody ever came up and said to us, "Well, Commodore has this...."

In a few years, all those features we had—joy sticks, paddles, sound, color graphics, high-resolution graphics—became standard in every single personal computer.

INTERVIEWER: *What do you think it takes to come up with a good invention? You mentioned that everything converged for the Apple II. Is it just luck?*

WOZNIAK: You've got to have a pretty darn good idea in your head of an end goal. You can't just sit down and start using some tools you were taught and see where it takes you. You need one goal, and your goal has to coincide with something that somebody else wants to buy or something that will save them money.

INTERVIEWER: *Are there any particular traits that an inventor needs to have?*

WOZNIAK: It's very good if you can spread yourself over several disciplines.

Some people get down to one discipline. For example, I designed a certain part of a tape recorder amplifier; I took that as my job. I like to do these one after the other, maybe ten a year.

But in my experience, it has been very motivating to be able to whip out a piece of software for this task, build up a language over here, connect these chips together. When you can transcend different disciplines, several disciplines, you can make things much more optimal. And this is what makes something artistic. You make a better circuit when you know what kind of code is involved.

Getting good feedback is also important. I had the best in the world when I was developing the Apple II. When I had something, I would just take it down to the Homebrew Computer Club in Palo Alto.

I was shy. I was really shy. I would never raise my hand and say, "I have something I'm going to be showing." I would just set it up on a table, and a few people would gather around me by accident. I developed my own group that way, and I would just tell them what I had come up with. And the look in their eyes was the sort of feedback you don't quite get from a boss in a company. They knew that what I had done was important, and they knew why it was good.

It's very hard to get that kind of feedback, to know what you've done is important. When you design a product for a company, the feedback is:

"Now we have this product, and we're going to put our name on it, so it better be good."

INTERVIEWER: *Negative feedback is also a problem, isn't it? One inventor I talked to said he never tells anyone what he's working on because people can be so negative. Have you ever felt that way?*

WOZNIAK: Exactly, exactly! Right and left! Right and left! And I put up with it. I'm really patient and nice to people. But it's hard when you have an idea and you want to implement it the way you see it and everybody else tells you why it won't work. The funny thing is that sometimes they'll have very good logical reasons and they are right from some viewpoint.

But the trouble is that often a different approach makes no difference in the outcome. For example, I can use approach A, approach B, or approach C—it doesn't matter which I choose. In the end, the important thing is that I get it done. And in getting it done, the most important thing is confidence.

Anybody can point out a minus—"Well, that's not the way because it has a higher density of electrons," and this and that. The trouble is that it's not a fair way to judge an idea or an invention. Other people will look at a new idea and say, "Wow, that's great. Show me more later."

But it's a real problem when other people look over your shoulder and judge your invention before it's done. If you can wait to get feedback about a product until after you're done, you're kind of safe. You can take a whole bunch of lousy approaches as long as the final product is very good. You're only going to get feedback about the good product. People aren't going to know all the wrong approaches you took.

I can be judged on the outcome of the Apple. Boy, if somebody had been looking over my shoulder saying, "No, no, you ought to do it this way for that reason or that way for this reason," I know what I would have done: I would not have produced such a good product. The Apple had a rare purity for projects in this business.

INTERVIEWER: *How important do you think a technical background is to being a successful inventor?*

WOZNIAK: You must have a foundation in the basics, the atoms or the primitives, such as certain pieces of code or a few bottom-level code tricks. Based on those, you work yourself up a hierarchical ladder. You learn about a little processor, and then you learn that it has registers and an adder and a shifter. Then, you combine adds and shifts to make them multiply, and you combine some multiples to solve a larger problem. You go up and up a pyramid to the top where there is a real solution. I found that I had to be very, very good at the tools at the bottom of the pyramid, the primitives. Always. I had to master every little tiny tool and then work myself up a couple of steps. I always worked from the bottom up, starting with the tools I knew. I established a direction and made everything tight every step of the way, and I never made the whole project so large that one person couldn't do it. This way of working was a large part of my success and my ability to come up with good designs.

> *Maybe my learning is subliminal. I'm sure many other inventors have gone through this before. You think it out in your sleep.*

INTERVIEWER: Do you usually work alone?

WOZNIAK: Anything that I've ever been proud of or was acknowledged for later was always done on my own. As a matter of fact, in school I was always very much an individualist. To me, a teacher or a classroom didn't matter at all. I learned by reading in my bedroom or dorm room late at night or whenever I wanted to. Sometimes, I would do a whole course in a two-week cram.

Alan Baum is about the only other person I've done computer work with in my life. He and I went back and forth on some of the Apple II design. He would suggest a direction, suggest some code to start it with, and I would do some improvements on it because I was a good coder. We would work together like that. But that was about it.

Otherwise, all my life I've done things very much alone—in my little apartment, at midnight at Hewlett–Packard working on my lab bench on Apple projects, or just sitting in my house all alone writing codes. Even some of the work I've gotten done for this company, CL 9, has been like that.

For example, I wrote one set of code release for a custom microprocessor two summers ago when my wife was in Europe with the kids. I don't like to miss my family, and I would actually fly over on weekends to see them and fly back to the United States during the week. As it turned out, during those three weeks with just enough time alone and away from the family, I got a ton of work done. I could go for a year trying to get done what I accomplished in those three weeks.

In general, I spend a lot of time on anything I work on. I have to sit down and work out a problem on paper, working it out very carefully until I understand every line, every connection, how to improve this or that. It comes out very slowly.

The process sort of starts, and then it may continue over several days. I'll scrap things together, try this, try this—with no one around. Whereas other designers come in, and—blip, blip, blip—they whip it out and it's done. And it's beautiful. But I have to think out a design in a way that I know is optimal. My whole life has been this way—every electronics project I ever did. I was sort of known for it.

INTERVIEWER: Do inventors and other creative people need a certain amount of time alone to focus sharply enough on the work to come up with a new idea?

WOZNIAK: It's characteristic of artistic people that they spend an incredible amount of time working for what seems like very little. Even looking back at my own work, I can see some places where I spent a ton of hours working to save one tiny little bit of a part. I can question the worth of my work from a business standpoint. How can I say it was worth anything? But it was worth it for my motivation.

I remember once that I designed a PC board for our disk interface. I did a rare thing for an engineer: I laid out the board myself. At Apple, we had departments that usually did that. But I came in many nights in a row, working very, very late. I laid out the whole board, and then I got an idea to save one feed-through. So I took the board apart, I trashed maybe a week's worth of work, and then I started over.

And I did it another way that saved another feed-through. No big deal. Nobody in the world would ever know that I laid it out to have very few feed-throughs—three instead of maybe fifty. None of this would ever be seen, but for some reason it seemed important to me in an artistic sense. You can have a feeling that all these things are important, but you can't necessarily justify them logically. The effort comes from being so close to your art.

INTERVIEWER: Rather than just work on something and get it out of the way, you like to come back and keep refining it?

WOZNIAK: Almost always. With any idea I have, I'll go through and work it out, work it out. After I've found one solution, I'll go through it chip by chip. I'll go through our manual and look for something that's going to throw an idea my way—such as a slightly different mathematical algorithm. Even before I build a computer, I'll do that.

Once I have several pieces finished—the code is written, the circuits are built, and so on—I might accidentally stumble across something in the manual, and an idea will click suddenly. I don't know, maybe my learning is subliminal. I'm sure many other inventors have gone through this before. You think it out in your sleep. I don't do it too much anymore. I've only had one night in the last two years that went this way, where I woke up with the solution I was working on. I used to do it all the time—up until Apple was so successful.

INTERVIEWER: *Do you ever think of inventing as art?*

WOZNIAK: Not so much now, but that's because I don't have time to do that now. I got hung up with a bunch of artifacts in my life. Back then, yes. I understood that it was identical to, or close to being, a musician...

It's hard for me to think back now to why I thought that. I have to go back in time frames, back in time five or ten years when I knew. I can't even put it in its reality so that you can feel it right now. But when I was there, it was just so obvious that everything I ever read about an artist or a musician, such as the steps they went through, was exactly equivalent to mental steps I was going through. You know, the stages of turmoil and overcoming them to get a facet just right. Invention—like art—is kind of an idea that can't be seen, but you've got to express it some way. Back then, I knew I was like a musician or an artist. And I'm not right now. I only come close to it on occasion.

INTERVIEWER: *You find yourself sidetracked with other commitments?*

WOZNIAK: I wound up trapped by the world. You get very successful and get wealthy and all of a sudden, you have to live a wealthy person's life. I run a company. I have investments. I get calls all day for speaking engagements.

When I built the first Apple, I wanted to show off and impress my friends. This was before we decided to start a company. I even went over to people's houses and helped them to wire their own computers. It was important to give to and help people then. I was kind of poor or middle-class then. I lived in an apartment, and I had a normal, low-scale engineering job. But, you know, I was kind of happy forever. That was back in the days when I could even have a hobby. Hours were free.

Now, I have a personal life that's so complicated that for six hours every day I'm consumed with just trying to keep up with my personal banking, bills, this and that. Right now, I'm in the process of cleaning this up. I'd like nothing more than to be an eight-hour engineer, but it's not possible now. I've got to get rid of all that crap and say, "No, I can't do both."

INTERVIEWER: It's said that some writers have only one book in them and also that some painters have only one painting. Do you think that's true of inventors?

WOZNIAK: That will be largely true for me. If you are ever known in history as a good inventor, it's also probably true that you made a ton of money from your invention. And with a ton of money, you can buy yourself success on future projects. Basically, you can buy a project that's worth so much, put a few million dollars into it, and then get the credit for being the one to pursue a great thing. It gets to the point where you can't tell where the inventiveness was lost.

I knew all the time that what I was doing was very significant and that it was totally, totally different from every other computer coming out.

Walt Disney created his cartoons in the earliest days of black-and-white cartoons. People started watching them, they became popular, and Disney made enough money to start a small company. It wasn't very many years later that Walt Disney wasn't even drawing cartoons anymore. He didn't even sign his signature in the film credits; somebody in the art department signed it for him.

I suppose I'm sort of rare now in my current company because I still do some of the programming and circuit design. I'm trying to do even more of that kind of work than I am now. I'm trying to avoid just being a sponsor of ideas that I believe in.

INTERVIEWER: You would much rather be known for your hands-on work?

WOZNIAK: I'd much rather come up with a clever little code algorithm or a clever little arrangement that saves a diode or a transistor. I feel that I do my best work at night. But even though I've had a few all-nighters in the last couple of years at this company, some of them I spent wishing that this piece of code had been written at midnight like it should have been. The all-nighters I like aren't the ones when you stay up solving a problem because it needs to be solved, but when you stay, after everything's been solved, to put a little extra quality in, to add something here or there. Sometimes I wanted a code to be so perfect before I released it that I put in whole sections of code that were not even planned for the program and that nobody would even notice—so that it would be good and right. When something inside motivates you like that, you don't even notice time. You can go without sleep and not even sleep the next day.

INTERVIEWER: *Do you have anything you'd like to invent?*

WOZNIAK: Oh yes. Oh yeah, yeah, yeah. If this company, CL 9, makes it, I'd love to get into home video editing systems—very similar to TV station systems, but at a "home price." And, boy, there's a lot of tricky things coming about, and they're just getting here because memory chips have really fallen in price. No other reason.

INTERVIEWER: *Do you see people using this type of system to do more creative or professional-caliber projects in the home?*

WOZNIAK: Oh, no. It would be just for fun. Go into a TV studio with some new AMPEX equipment and just watch as they pop a few tricks up on the screen. Just think what fun it would be to be able to do that! And to realize that it could be done for a thousand dollars in the home. If not today, then within a couple of years.

INTERVIEWER: *What do you think the future holds for inventing?*

WOZNIAK: Are you referring to the idea that it's all been done before? Oh no, no, no, no! It always seems like so much has been done, but I'm sure people thought that way in Rome thousands of years ago. I've never had that impression. There will always be new inventions simply because there's a need inside us to express our creativity and inventiveness.

INTERVIEWER: *When you invented the Apple II, you were in almost unknown territory. Looking back on it, is there anything you would do differently?*

WOZNIAK: I might, unfortunately, do things differently and do them wrong. Today, I would have formulas that I didn't have then to guide me on product decisions. And it would have been terrible.

There were about ten things in the Apple II that none of the other computers were going to have for years. I had put in color, paddles, sound, better language commands, high-density RAMs—a whole environment that went so far beyond just a computer.

At first, a bunch of computer kits came out for hobbyists. And shortly after Apple, Commodore and Radio Shack planned to introduce these little black-and-white machines that were sort of computers. You could write a program in a programming language on them. You could write on a screen. But those companies built only the standard definition of a computer; they kept missing the boat.

Granted, they were doing it at low cost and selling them to people in their homes, but ours used no more parts and did much more. I knew all the time that what I was doing was very significant and that it was totally, totally different from every other computer coming out.

INTERVIEWER: *Artists often say they know when a painting is going to work or come together. Was there ever a time like that with the Apple II when it seemed like it all came together?*

WOZNIAK: When the two of us were first selling the Apple I, it was just a trivial little thing. We weren't making any money. We couldn't even pay ourselves salaries. But we were just doing it as a game to say we had a company.

So, I started thinking, What can I do to impress people even more? One of the keys to the Apple was that it was made with very few chips, and all of them were on one board. And I started thinking about how I could share memories here and there to make it with even fewer chips. I came up with a scheme: For forty microseconds video would be displayed on the screen, and then for twenty-five microseconds the processor would run. It was sort of a nice sharing.

Well, my computer kept dying on me; this machine that was to become the Apple II kept dying. It would work right away, and then after a few hours of usage, it wouldn't work. And I would pull out the microprocessor and put in a new one, and it would work.

I thought the problem was electrostatic discharge into the microprocessor. (When you walk up to something, such as a computer, you carry an electric charge on yourself. You don't even have to touch it, and you can zap that chip a little.)

I was blowing out these microprocessors because they couldn't hold themselves off for forty microseconds. Anyway, that one little accident, blowing out the microprocessors, made me search for a different solution. The one I found turned out to be very good for the computer: I looked up the memory speeds and discovered that the microprocessor and the video could run together, interleaving every other cycle. One of them would get half a microsecond, and then the other would get a half. This discovery really caused the speed of the computer, the ease to build it, the ease to understand it, the ease to write software for it—everything—to come together. But it was an accident that led me into it.

When I came up with the solution, I knew it was far out. I recognized that it was an outstanding design. It was going to be the finest of my life.

I recognized that with every little key I had hit upon, I had done something in so few parts that it was outstanding in an artistic sense. To me, an artistic design meant very few components doing the maximum job. I've always felt that way.

In college, I remember trying to write my programs in the absolute shortest way possible so that I could get them all on one card or on only three cards strung statement to statement to statement. I thought about which algorithm—whether a multiply and then an add later or an add and then a multiply—was going to save one character. These things became important in my life. And I don't know why. It's like some internal goal.

With the Apple, I was very lucky to have a situation where I could be that kind of artist. I was working on it only for myself. I had no financial restraints. I had no money, but the project was all mine. I had no schedules. I had no one telling me, "You've got to put this and this and this in and not the other three."

I remember being around other people when I was developing my designs for the Apple. When I would tell people what I was working on, what my direction was, how I used a certain chip a certain way, why I chose a certain chip, they would say, "No, no, no. I'm working on my own, and I do it this way."

And I would look at their design and *see* why it was so bad. Even in my head, I could see why it wasn't good: that it wasn't somehow an optimal, well-thought-out artistic design. For some reason, that just seemed important to me in an artistic sense.

RAYMOND KURZWEIL

"**M**OST COMPUTERS," *Raymond Kurzweil is fond of saying, "are idiot savants." Despite their tremendous memory and calculative ability, computers are usually— quite simply put—not terribly intelligent. They do not think for themselves. They must be carefully programmed and told what to do, even for the most routine tasks.*

Computers can, however, be made artificially intelligent, and Raymond Kurzweil is a leader in the field of artificial intelligence, or AI. As an inventor, he is credited with developing the first successful commercial AI product.

Using artificial intelligence technology, in 1976 he developed the world's first omni-font character recognition machine. Omni-font character recognition, or OCR, had been a classic problem among AI scientists: How could one develop a system capable of reading text in virtually any style of print or when print is degraded or smudged or marred by typographical errors?

For Kurzweil, the solution to that problem was more than an academic exercise. He put that OCR technology to use in a reading machine for the blind, which is known today as the Kurzweil Reading Machine. Coupling his work with OCR with his work in speech synthesis, Kurzweil invented a machine that could scan printed pages and read aloud. A set of eyes for the blind, the reading machine can read everything from phone bills to a full-length novel. It is regarded as the first commercial product to successfully apply AI technology.

Kurzweil has put AI to work in other areas as well. At the urging of singer/ composer Stevie Wonder, an enthusiastic user of the Kurzweil Reading Machine, he developed the first computer music keyboard capable of accurately reproducing the sounds of traditional acoustic instruments such as the piano, the violin, and the saxophone. Like his other inventions, the Kurzweil 250 uses artificial intelligence to accurately model instrumental sounds, vocal sounds, and even noises. His Kurzweil 250 is now used by popular musicians like Prince and Stevie Wonder. It has also found a place in the world of classical music. In 1985, the New York City Ballet's orchestra began using the Kurzweil 250.

Kurzweil's latest invention is called Voice Works—a voice-activated word processing system. By talking to Kurzweil's Voice Works, a user can actually "write" as well as edit a paper or report—it is essentially a computer that takes dictation. Versions of it are already in use by radiologists to dictate medical reports that were formerly transcribed from tape. He also has plans to apply the technology of Voice Works to create a writing machine for the deaf, providing a real-time readout of conversations and discussions.

Kurzweil is as enthusiastic about business as he is about inventing. He founded his first company, Kurzweil Computer Products, in 1974. After KCP was sold to Xerox in 1980, he founded two new companies in 1982: Kurzweil Applied Intelligence and Kurzweil Music Systems.

Raymond Kurzweil was born in 1948 and grew up in Queens, New York. His father was a conductor and professor of music; his mother is a successful illustrator and artist. By age five, Kurzweil had already begun to think of himself as a scientist and an inventor. By the time he was twelve, he had designed a software package distributed by IBM. At eighteen, he sold to Harcourt Brace World a computer program that used AI techniques to match college students to colleges.

Success, however, required as much perseverance as brilliance; in the mid-1970s, he was forced to sell his car and a collection of electronic gadgets in order to keep Kurzweil Computer Products alive. With the telephone company threatening to cut off his phone service, he went to a pawnshop with an assortment of tape recorders. When another customer's dog tore his pants, Kurzweil was offered $50 to cover the damages. It was enough to pay his phone bill, and Kurzweil was able to keep his tape recorders. Finally, he received more than $400,000 from the United States Department of Education and several national foundations to finance field testing and further development of the reading machine.

Raymond Kurzweil graduated from the Massachusetts Institute of Technology in 1970 with degrees in computer science and literature. Kurzweil, who also writes poetry and is an accomplished pianist, heads Kurzweil Music Systems, Inc. and Kurzweil Applied Intelligence, Inc. He was admitted into the Computer Industry Hall of Fame in 1982 and has received honorary doctorates from Hofstra University, Berklee College of Music, and Rensselaer Polytechnic Institute. In 1984, Esquire magazine selected him as one of the eight most influential young scientists in the United States. In 1986, he received an award for entrepreneurial excellence from President Ronald Reagan and was Honorary Chairman for Innovation of the White House Conference on Small Business.

INTERVIEWER: *Why did you develop the Kurzweil Reading Machine for the blind? It's a wonderful invention, but what led you to work on it?*

KURZWEIL: I came to it through the technology. I didn't actually know anyone who was blind. My specialty in computers was pattern recognition, and the reading machine involved solving some long-standing problems in the field.

Ever since Norbert Wiener talked about it in the book *Cybernetics* in 1948, omni-font character recognition has been a classic problem in pattern recognition. I saw that as an interesting challenge to take on, and a reading machine is one of the major applications of that technology. A functional reading machine must be able to read all sizes and styles of type—fonts, if you prefer.

I found working on the reading machine to be a rewarding project, and I feel a strong desire to work on other projects that apply artificial intelligence technology to the needs of the handicapped. I feel there's a very good fit there.

Right now, the threshold we're on in artificial intelligence is not creating cybernetic geniuses. We're not able to create computers with far-ranging intellectual capabilities. However, we do have the ability to create intelligence in a narrowly focused domain. If you can define a narrow problem, you can often devise an AI system to solve it. Reading a book, for example, requires intelligence. It's not a stupid activity; animals can't do it. Even so, it is a well-defined and fairly narrow activity. It's something that computers today are capable of mastering.

Now, a handicapped person is generally an intelligent person who is missing some very particular sensory or motor capability. But if we work with the natural intelligence of a handicapped person, a computer system with a certain amount of artificial intelligence can enable a handicapped person to overcome those disabilities.

In addition to the reading machine, other applications are out there for the technology we have developed. In fact, I am looking at ways to apply our speech-recognition technology to the problems of the deaf, and it has already been applied to the needs of quadriplegic persons and the voice-impaired. The kind of system that I envision would, for example, enable a deaf person to understand this conversation we're having right now. They would get a real-time readout of what we're saying. In person-to-person conversations or in conversations over the phone, this kind of system would enable a deaf person to overcome the principal handicap associated with that disability.

I don't really feel that the bulk of my training...took place in a formal way.

INTERVIEWER: *How did you start working on the reading machine?*

KURZWEIL: I started Kurzweil Computer Products in 1974. The purpose of that company was to solve the problem of omni-font character recognition. It was, as I said, a classic problem and a challenging one. How do you design a system with the ability to recognize printed characters in any print style? Also, to be effective it must also be able to deal with degraded print, including print that is smeared on the page, fragmented letters, characters or letters that are touching each other, and a wide variety of other common printing errors. A reading machine that would be truly useful to the blind had to be able to perform these functions with a high degree of accuracy and combine that technology with unlimited-vocabulary speech synthesis. That kind of speech-synthesis technology also did not exist at the time.

The year 1974 was actually a bad time to start a company. The availability of money for technological start-ups swings back and forth like a pendulum. In 1968, a great deal of money was available, but the venture-capital community was not as sophisticated then as it is today, and a lot of ventures failed. The result was that the pendulum had swung back the other way by 1974. According to statistics I have, about $1.5 billion in technological start-up funds were available in 1969 but only $15 million in 1974. Almost no money was available to start the company.

We did have about $33,000 in seed money from Johnson & Johnson. The rest of the money, about $200,000, was essentially raised from family and friends. We launched the reading machine in 1976 and were able to get some government contracts and foundation grants to purchase and evaluate the machine. In 1977, we started to get some serious venture capital, and we were beginning to get a track record. In 1978, we launched the KDEM, the Kurzweil Data Entry Machine, which is a version of the omni-font character recognition machine for commercial data entry.

By the end of 1979, we needed to expand, and we decided the best way to do that was to sell the company to Xerox. There was a certain synergy between Xerox's markets and our scanning capabilities. In 1980, Kurzweil Computer Products was sold to Xerox, with the understanding that it would remain an independent company with the same management that I had originally put in place. I stayed on as full-time president and CEO. In mid-1982, I worked out an arrangement with Xerox to start two other companies—Kurzweil Music and Kurzweil Applied Intelligence—while still retaining my position as chairman at Kurzweil Computer Products. Under the agreement, Xerox made a major investment in Kurzweil Applied Intelligence. They have since followed up with several other rounds of investment in the company.

INTERVIEWER: *What was the difference between having your own company and working under Xerox's wing? Did you start the other two companies so that you could work on more creative projects?*

KURZWEIL: My own goal is to expand the three companies I've started into major corporations. I'm interested in more than just the technology. Even though Kurzweil Computer Products is a subsidiary of Xerox, I still feel pretty much the same way towards it as I did when I founded it—I would like to see it grow into a large, successful company. There have been positive interactions with Xerox since the sale, particularly in the marketplace. But if you walk in the door of that company today, it's not Xerox. It's still Kurzweil Computer Products.

INTERVIEWER: *Was Marvin Minsky* an early influence on your thinking*

---

* Mathematician and educator at MIT in computer science and engineering.

*about AI? Did the experiences and formal training you picked up at MIT lay the
groundwork for later inventions?*

KURZWEIL: Formal training, I think, played a very small role. I don't
really feel that the bulk of my training in this field took place in a formal
way. I studied with Marvin Minsky while I was at MIT, but I had also corresponded with him while I was in high school. I don't know if specific
studies were such significant factors, but it was inspiring to work with him.
He is a historic figure. I'd known about him before I ever came to MIT. The
real value of being at MIT was having the opportunity to meet a lot of
talented people, whether they were professors or peers.

MIT was very oriented towards students who took initiative. For example, I took off one whole semester to get a company I had started off the
ground and received course credit for it. The company was built around an
expert system I had developed for matching high school students with colleges. It had several million facts on three thousand colleges in the United
States in its memory and a three-hundred-question questionnaire for students to fill out. Based on their answers, the expert system would give them
a list of fifteen colleges that they might want to look into. I sold that system
to Harcourt Brace World, which is now Harcourt Brace Jovanovich. It was
sort of my first business.

Somewhere along the line, of course, you do need to pick up certain
basics about your field of endeavor. But there's no substitute for practical experience when it comes to being an inventor or an entrepreneur. Practical
experience is really the essence of learning in these fields.

INTERVIEWER: *Did you grow up thinking you would be an inventor?*

KURZWEIL: Actually, I did. I felt I would be a scientist from the time I
was five years old. I even kept a notebook of inventions when I was five, six,
and seven years old. I still have it. The idea of inventing and being a scientist
was all wrapped up together for me. At the time, I was very interested in
building things—with my Erector Set, for example—and I also remember
trying to build a rocket.

At a very early age, however, I was fascinated with computers because
of their ability to actually do things and solve problems. Once I was exposed
to them, my interests really became quite focused, particularly on pattern
recognition—the primary area I work in today. Of course, computers were

not as ubiquitous back then as they are today, and personal computers didn't exist at all. But I was fascinated with them.

The science behind the technology I'm working on today still fascinates me. If I were to define what I do, I would say that I help develop technology to solve some previously unsolved human problems. That's where the excitement comes in—to have a blind person go to school because the technology can help him or her read or to have a musician create a new piece of music that wasn't feasible before.

INTERVIEWER: *Did your family inspire or encourage you to be an inventor?*

KURZWEIL: My father was a noted musician—a concert pianist and a conductor. My mother is an artist and a successful illustrator. But when I really think about it, the relative who might have had the most influence on me as a scientist was my grandmother Lillian Bader. She was somewhat of a famous scientist and the first woman in Europe to get a Ph.D. in chemistry. She traveled around Europe lecturing and also ran a major school that her mother had started, so she was actually both a scientist and an entrepreneur.

The immediate inspiration for starting to work on the synthesizer...came from some discussions I had with Stevie Wonder.

INTERVIEWER: *Are your inventions something you work on alone?*

KURZWEIL: I find that the projects I get involved with are increasingly interdisciplinary in their approach. Inventions like the reading machine are not the kind of product created by someone who goes down into his basement and emerges two years later with some brilliant breakthrough.

The projects I work on are a disciplined effort involving teams of people with different backgrounds. One of the key challenges I have in trying to lead these projects is to provide for good communication among people with very different backgrounds.

In speech recognition, for example, some of the technologists involved include linguists, signal-processing experts, VLSI [very large scale integration] designers, psycho-acoustic experts, speech scientists, computer scientists, human-factors designers, experts in artificial intelligence and pattern recognition, and so on.

Each one of these fields has very different methodologies and different terminologies. Very often a term in one field means something else entirely in another field. Sometimes we even create our own terminology for a particular project. So, enabling a team like that to communicate and solve a problem is a significant challenge.

If you look at the entire company, you bring in even more disciplines: manufacturing, material-resources planning, purchasing, marketing, finance, and so on. Each of these areas has also developed sophisticated methodologies of their own that are as complex as those in engineering. My challenge is to provide a climate in which people with different expertise can work together toward a common goal and communicate clearly with one another.

Because of the complexity involved, we often try to solve problems in groups. Very often I've found that fresh, novel ideas in a particular discipline do not always come from the experts in that field, but from those in other fields.

INTERVIEWER: *But do the ideas themselves come from the group, or do they come from each individual working independently on a specific problem?*

KURZWEIL: A great deal of group process is behind our inventions. Invention is increasingly interdisciplinary work. It involves teams of people. There are relatively few significant inventions that can be created by one or two people.

Generally, I play a key role in defining an initial architecture and algorithmic approach. Initially, I may even do some hands-on development myself. But the projects very quickly get complex enough that different people's expertise is required.

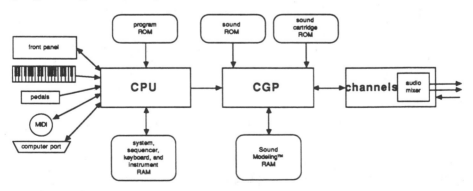

Diagram of the Kurzweil 250™ synthesizer. (Diagram by Don Byrd and Chris Yavelow.)

We do actually work as a group in this, but a lot of time has to be invested in bringing everybody's knowledge up to a working level in all aspects of a project. In going over a project we will take the key aspects of that project, signal processing, for example, and have them reviewed by all the scientists working on the project—the linguists, computer scientists, psycho-acoustic experts, and so on. I really try to encourage a lot of open communication so that we can tap the expertise and creativity of everyone in the group. We often have people who are at the top of their field working with us, and to keep attracting that level of talent, we have to encourage them to add their own creativity.

INTERVIEWER: *Is it important for an inventor to be a good visualizer?*

KURZWEIL: I think it's valuable to be able to understand the essence of problems without having to constantly refer to technical documentation. When you are talking over a problem, it helps if everyone involved can keep the essence of the subject in mind. You can't discuss a project if everyone is always rushing to a notebook and saying, "Let me spend fifteen minutes reading what you're talking about."

INTERVIEWER: *Do you see your role more as a coordinator?*

KURZWEIL: Coordination and leadership. I provide some key technical ideas and a climate that allows people to contribute. Those are my roles.

INTERVIEWER: *Are you also a hands-on inventor?*

KURZWEIL: I do both, at least to some extent. I am usually involved at a hands-on level with something. Over the past year, for example, I've been working on Voice Works, a voice-operated word processor. I've been coding some aspects of it because I think it's valuable to stay close to the technology. If I only hear about technical issues in a meeting, I don't get the same keen appreciation for what they mean. I try to have some hands-on experience to keep that perspective. But the companies I've started are now big enough and the diversity of issues they address is broad enough that I obviously can't get involved on a hands-on basis in very many areas. I probably spend half of my time on business issues and half on technology.

INTERVIEWER: *Has the business side of your inventions sidetracked you from more inventing?*

KURZWEIL: I don't think of it as sidetracking. If you define your task as creating a new technology and establishing it in a way that impacts the world, then business is essential. It takes more than just neat technology to accomplish that.

INTERVIEWER: *Besides coming from an artistic family, you have a degree in literature and write poetry. Do you see any similarities between inventing and being a poet or a painter?*

KURZWEIL: I think they're very closely linked. Creativity in both art and invention is a matter of coming up with new approaches and then developing them to the point where they really work. An artist may have a new idea for a genre of work or a new style, but it takes a lot of disciplined work to make those creative elements work.

Professionally, I have an interest in the link between technology and the arts. Kurzweil Music, for example, was created to apply computer technology to the creation of music. At the Kurzweil Foundation, we are developing the Cybernetic Composer, applying expert-system techniques to the composition of music. When that project is completed, a musician will be able to write out a melody or play a melody on a keyboard and then choose a variety of cybernetic accompanists. One cybernetic accompanist might provide the drum part. Another could develop harmonic progressions built on the original melody. With this system, you can create a piece of music—some elements you contribute yourself; others are provided by the computer's own capability.

INTERVIEWER: *But how "creative" or "original" is a piece of music if the composer's only contribution is little more than a melody line?*

KURZWEIL: A lot of creativity in the arts isn't unbridled creativity. A lot of craftsmanship is involved in creating music or a painting—craftsmanship that follows rules. Not all parts of the creative process are driven by inspiration. In fact, a lot of it is disciplined work using rules and methodologies known by the artist. Most people don't know these rules exist, but the artist, being an expert in the craft, learns them either by discovering them or by working with other artists.

It turns out that these rules are quite amenable to being programmed. Harold Cohen's work in teaching a computer how to draw, for example, attests to how many elements of drawing—from composition to the creation of the shapes themselves—can actually be programmed in the form of rules. There is still a kernel of creativity that's hard to capture with rules.

But at the same time, a lot of the methodology used to translate a creative inspiration into a finished product is highly disciplined. That's true of something whether it's a piece of music, a piece of art, or a piece of technology.

INTERVIEWER: *Did your interest in the links between technology and art lead you to produce your Kurzweil 250 Synthesizer?*

KURZWEIL: Well, there are two answers to that. I have a lifelong interest in music from my father as well as a nearly lifelong interest in computers. My father always felt that I would combine those interests someday, but he wasn't quite sure how. Music is, after all, very mathematical, and a well-known link exists between mathematical aptitude and musical ability. Many famous mathematicians and scientists were also gifted musicians. In one sense, Kurzweil Music and the Kurzweil 250 Synthesizer brought those two interests together.

The immediate inspiration for starting to work on the synthesizer, however, came from some discussions I had with Stevie Wonder. He was an avid user—one of the first—of my reading machine, and we got together a number of times because of his interest in that project.

People who want to do things the same way that they've been done for the past twenty years will find diminishing opportunities.

On one occasion, we happened to talk about music and musical instruments. Stevie made the point that he saw musical instrument development following two lines: acoustic and electronic. Acoustic instruments provided the sounds of choice for most musicians. Sounds such as those made by the piano, the violin, or the guitar were musically satisfying sounds. They were rich and complex and had a great deal of depth.

The problem with acoustic instruments, as Stevie saw it, was that you could not control them. You couldn't layer, sequence, or even modify them. You could only play them. In fact, you couldn't even do that unless you mastered the playing technique for a particular instrument. You could, for example, be a very gifted pianist, but that would not enable you to play a violin. Even if you learned to play the violin, you could not play it polyphonically—you could only play at most two notes at a time. And if you played both the violin and the piano, you still couldn't play both of them at the same time.

Electronic instruments eliminated many of these problems. With an electronic instrument, you could play several instruments at the same time, using a sequencer to record one part in a computer and then playing over it. You could even edit the sequence in the same way as you would edit a letter on a word processor. You could also take sounds and modify their shapes. And you could layer sounds; by pressing a single key on a synthesizer, you could generate ten different sounds at once.

Although electronic instruments gave the musician tremendous artistic power, the sounds themselves were not very interesting. They were relatively thin electronic sounds and very limited. "Wouldn't it be neat," said Stevie, "if we could take all those powerful control techniques and apply them to any sound—electronic or acoustic?"

With that kind of system, people who knew how to play the piano could also play the violin. They could play more than one violin line at the same time, and they could even play the violin and the piano at the same time. They could layer and sequence any acoustic or electronic sound.

So, Stevie's idea pretty much defined the goal of the Kurzweil 250. It was also the basis for Kurzweil Music Systems, the company I started along with Kurzweil Applied Intelligence, in 1982. Since introducing the K250, we've gone in two directions. One is to broaden the range of the instrument to provide more sounds and control techniques. The other is to bring down the cost of our technology so that the instrument's basic capability is available to the average musician.

INTERVIEWER: *How long did it take to develop a working model?*

KURZWEIL: We started to work on it in the middle of 1982. A year later, we built an engineering prototype, which we brought to the National Association of Music Merchants' trade show. We began shipping in the summer of 1984. Today, that product has undergone a tremendous amount of expansion and has really become a whole family of products.

INTERVIEWER: *What makes your synthesizer different from others already on the market?*

KURZWEIL: The essence of it is sound models. We essentially have a model of each instrument and the sounds it can create stored in the memory of the synthesizer.

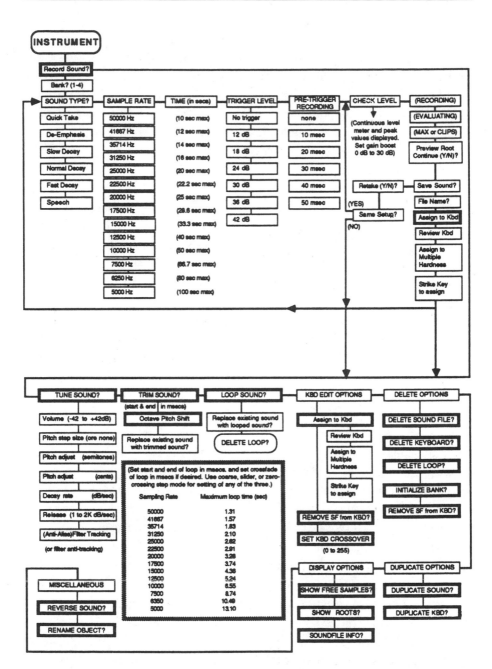

Flowchart of the Sound Modeling™ process for the Kurzweil 250™ synthesizer. (Diagram by Don Byrd and Chris Yavelow.)

We started by recording the original instruments with very high-quality digital recorders. Part of the art of creating these models was finding good instruments. We were actually unable to find a single Steinway grand piano that sounded good across its entire range. Some had a beautiful, deep, resonant bass, but were tinny in the treble or had a weak middle. We finally found five different Steinways that, together, gave us really beautiful sections across the entire keyboard. Those five pianos included one that Rudolf Serkin plays when he comes to Boston.

> *Computers have already had a tremendous impact on the world in spite of the fact that the vast majority of them are idiot savants.*

We recorded those pianos at many different pitches and at many different loudness levels. Hitting a note harder on the piano not only makes the note louder but also changes the entire time-varying spectrum of the sound. Well, we fed all this information into our computer system and very carefully shaped these sound models that describe how a piano sounds at different loudness levels and at different pitches.

All this information resides in the read-only memory [ROM] of the machine. As the keyboard is played, it essentially reconstructs what that instrument should sound like at the appropriate pitch and loudness levels and also captures all the time-varying effects of acoustic instruments. That's the most important characteristic of acoustic instruments, especially plucked or struck string instruments like the guitar and the piano. They're not static; they change their characteristics as the note progresses. All those dynamics are captured on the Kurzweil 250. The keyboard is also touch-sensitive so that—like on a piano—notes sound different depending upon how hard the keys are hit.

INTERVIEWER: *Do you think instruments such as the K250 will eliminate certain classical skills? Will musicians stop learning to play the violin, for example, because a synthesizer can produce the same sound? Will musicians' jobs be affected?*

KURZWEIL: Well, let's apply this whole issue of automation to music technology. It's just one small case in point in the debate about automation and jobs. People who want to do things the same way that they've been done for the past twenty years will find diminishing opportunities. They can point to people who used to get work making music in a certain way and find that some of those opportunities are drying up. But for every situation like that, there are several new opportunities that the technology opens up. I'll mention just a few.

Something like $10 billion a year is spent on making films such as corporate films, government films, and so on. The makers of these films by and large were using public-domain recordings for the background music because they couldn't afford to assemble an entire orchestra and create an original score—which is why the music from those types of films all sounded the same (laughs).

Since the advent of synthesizers, the filmmakers typically hire a musician with an instrument like the Kurzweil 250 to create an original score for the film. With a machine like the K250, it's feasible for even modest productions to hire a single musician to do that. That opportunity simply didn't exist before the technology opened up.

There is also a whole new field of music in synthesis. Musicians can now create and synthesize new sounds. Creating the actual sounds themselves, in fact, has become as important as creating melodies, rhythms, and harmonies. There are whole new areas of music production that involve coordinating all this musical technology. In fact, the demand for that type of musician is tremendous.

I don't believe that instruments like the Kurzweil 250 eliminate jobs. I know a lot of music groups, and I've found that they don't immediately halve the size of their group when they acquire this type of technology. Instead, they put out a richer and more interesting sound with the same number of people. This kind of technology makes music more exciting. In fact, there is more demand for music now and more interest in music. This new technology gives musicians additional choices, a more powerful palette of sounds, and a new means of controlling those sounds. But if you don't want change and you're not willing to learn new methods of creating music, you may find opportunities passing you by.

INTERVIEWER: *So, you don't see synthesizers actually replacing classical instruments like the violin or piano?*

KURZWEIL: I think we should distinguish playing techniques from sounds. When we used to think of creating flute sounds, we thought of flute

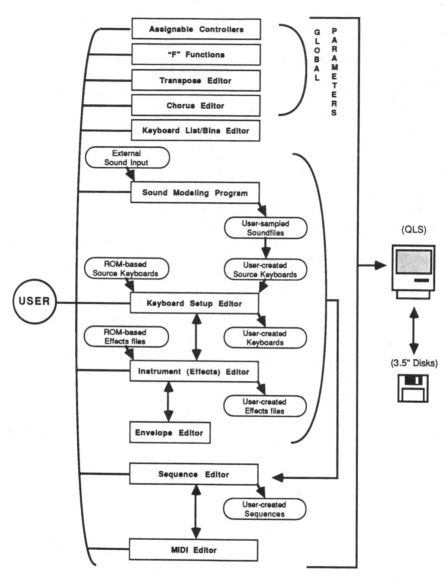

Illustration of user control on the Kurzweil 250™ synthesizer. (Diagram by Don Byrd and Chris Yavelow.)

fingering. In the same way, we thought you could produce violin sounds only by playing the violin. Technique was intimately involved with the type of sounds created.

We're now moving toward an era where the playing technique, or the method of controlling sounds, is to some extent being separated from the sounds being produced. It's quite clear that you can play on a piano-like keyboard and produce any musical sound: piano, violin, flute, synthesizer, and so on. New controllers are coming on the market that let you use other playing techniques, such as those you would use to play a guitar or a flute. Some controllers look just like flutes and have the same stops. You can play flute sounds with them, but you can also produce violin sounds or human voice sounds or piano sounds. In fact, some day there will be controllers that won't emulate any currently known musical instruments but that will be optimal in terms of human factors for "controlling" music. In terms of musical control, there will be a variety of ways for expressing musical ideas. When this is possible, any musician will be able to choose from the wide palette of sounds available.

Invention is not loner-type work, but involves collaboration.

INTERVIEWER: *When you first started working on projects like the reading machine or the Kurzweil 250, did you ever doubt that you would be able to make them work?*

KURZWEIL: I've always been confident in the ability of my companies to provide technical solutions to problems because I spend a lot of time thinking about a project before taking it on. The choice of a project is very important.

Einstein, for example, chose the wrong problem in his last twenty years. He spent his last years trying to come up with a Unified Field theory. It's now called the Theory of Everything, and its goal is to link all known forces into one set of equations. In retrospect, one can see that Einstein was destined not to solve it. It was just beyond the knowledge and experimental evidence of his time. Today, scientists are optimistic that they may be on the verge of solving it, but they still haven't come up with a complete solution.

It's important to pick a problem that can be solved in the end. At the same time, there's no point in solving a problem that twenty other people are going to solve as well.

In terms of developing a successful invention and a business, it is essential to have some unique and proprietary technology. For my own work, a project also has to be well matched to my skills and to the skills of the people I can attract to work on it.

The choice of the product is fundamental. I think the role of an entrepreneur is to understand both the technology and what it can reasonably produce in the near future. A successful invention is not simply a matter of creating some impressive technical feat. It includes solving a problem that meets a need.

INTERVIEWER: *So, it's important for an inventor to understand the needs of the market or the possible impacts of his invention?*

KURZWEIL: I think the essence of being an entrepreneur and an inventor is being able to grasp the potential impact of a new technology. You have to have the right vision—a product that's feasible, but sufficiently challenging and well matched to your abilities.

You also have to be able to articulate that potential to others so that you can gain support for your project—whether that support is getting somebody else to work on it with you or finding someone to invest in it. If you have a vision but can't articulate it, you're obviously not going to get the support you need, even if it's a good idea.

INTERVIEWER: *What do you see as the future for artificial intelligence and expert systems?*

KURZWEIL: Expert systems are not necessarily the same thing as artificial intelligence. Expert systems are one very exciting area of AI. AI also includes pattern recognition, robotics, natural language, and other areas. But in each of these areas, we're now able to create computer systems that can perform functions requiring intelligence. For example, understanding human speech requires a certain level of intelligence, but it is a narrowly defined task. Understanding what I'm saying now requires a certain level of intelligence. But, again, it's a narrowly defined task. Computers are now able to do many of these types of tasks. And that's a very significant development.

Computers have already had a tremendous impact on the world in spite of the fact that the vast majority of them are idiot savants. They are able to perform prodigious feats of memory and calculation, but, by and large, most still show little intelligence, if any. To give computers even a little bit of sharply focused intelligence is a powerful change. Such intelligence, combined with the computer's natural superiority in such things as memory and speed, is formidable. Right now, we're not yet on the threshold of having computers with broad, flexible areas of intellectual function. A computer cannot, for example, watch a movie and write a coherent summary of what happened. That task involves too large a diversity of intellectual skills for current computer technology.

It's a slow process, but computers are getting more intelligent, and their intellectual capabilities are gradually becoming more flexible. A computer, for example, can make a diagnosis in certain fields. In recent tests, its ability to make a diagnosis within at least one discipline was as good as a human doctor's. That diagnostic ability coupled with the computer's ability

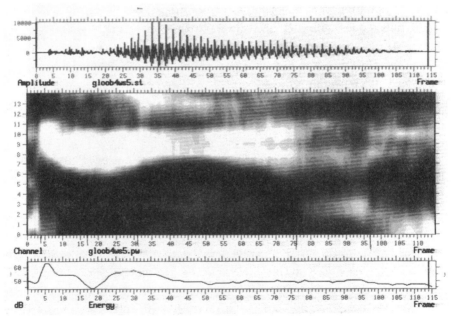

Waveforms used in analyzing human speech (part of Kurzweil Voice Works™ research).

to remember millions of facts and be tied into up-to-the-minute databases fed through a telecommunications network makes a powerful combination.

INTERVIEWER: *Do you think AI will ever get to the point of mimicking human intelligence? Will machines even replace people in white-collar jobs?*

KURZWEIL: Artificial intelligence is a continuation of the process of automation which began two centuries ago with the flying shuttle that automated certain elements of weaving. The first Industrial Revolution, which really happened over the course of the past two centuries, increased and leveraged our physical abilities. It enabled us to do things at a faster speed and with a greater capacity than human muscles alone were capable of.

Now, we are entering an era that can be thought of as a second Industrial Revolution. Machines are multiplying not just our physical capabilities, but our mental capabilities as well. We're now able to do things that our minds alone couldn't do. Consider the four-color map problem.* Mathematicians were never able to solve it because it's just too difficult to go through all the possible permutations of map types that are feasible. Yet a computer was able to methodically go through the thousands of different combinations quite effectively and solve that problem. Ed Feigenbaum** calls computers "power tools for the mind." I think that's true because computers have certainly been helpful to us when it comes to accurately mastering billions of pieces of information and keeping them highly organized. Computers also enable us to process and analyze those facts very quickly.

All this is a continuation of the process of automation. People used to think that automation would replace jobs and that jobs would go away. This is exactly what the Luddites thought at the beginning of the nineteenth century. They looked around and said, "Joe's going to lose his job because he spins wool, and Susie's going to lose her job because she makes cloth. These machines are coming along, and one person can do the work of twenty. One person will have a job running the machines, and the other nineteen people will be out of work." In fact, the Luddites predicted the demise of most employment. If we now look back at the last two centuries of automation and industrialization, however, we find the exact opposite of what we might have expected.

---

* Coloring a map using only four colors so that no neighboring territories or states have the same color.
** Head of the Artificial Intelligence Lab at Stanford University.

INTERVIEWER: *Are you saying that more new jobs were created although others became obsolete?*

KURZWEIL: For comparison, let's look at some statistics. In 1870, twelve million Americans had jobs, representing thirty percent of the population. Today, nearly 120 million jobs employ almost half of the population. Jobs have actually gone up on an absolute basis and on a per capita basis as well. If you look at the earning power of jobs in constant dollars, it multiplied by six in the past one hundred years. The per capita gross national product figure has also multiplied by about six or seven in constant dollars. That's a tremendous increase in real wealth, but people get lost in the year-to-year trends and political debates. We tend not to see these very strong trends of increasing employment and increasing wealth that have occurred over the broader period of time. We focus instead on whether the economy is up or down over the last two to five years.

Automation is constantly picking off jobs at the bottom of the skill ladder and creating new jobs at the more sophisticated end of the skill continuum. In fact, a lot of the new employment that has come about over the past century has been in education—providing the training needed for that higher level of skill. Today, three-quarters of the population has a high school diploma. A hundred years ago, only a small percentage of the population graduated from high school. We now have twelve million college students. We had only 52,000 a hundred years ago.

There have been recent studies indicating that this trend will continue. The problem is that people can always see jobs going away much more clearly than they can see them coming.

At the turn of the century, for example, about thirty percent of the population was working in agriculture. Today that figure is only about three percent. But although that shift was foreseen, no one could see where the new employment would come from. In the early 1900s, people were unable to say, "Obviously these people will find jobs in the electronics industry." People could not say that a major computer industry would spring up in fifty years or that an electronic publishing industry would start up in eighty years. We can't make predictions like that.

INTERVIEWER: *Do you think AI will be the basis for a new industry that will also create more jobs than it eliminates?*

KURZWEIL: Nobody really knows what kinds of new industries will be created in the future. But if we look back at the past century, we can see that technology created entirely new industries that hired millions of people. There's no reason to suspect that this trend is going to stop. Now, that's not to say that there aren't significant and painful dislocations along the way. Difficult problems are created by this process. You can't retrain all steel-workers as computer programmers.

If you look at the overall trends, however, society has benefited from greater wealth, a higher standard of living, better medical care, and better education through technological advances.

> *Competition can sometimes help you more than it can hurt you when you're a pioneer.*

INTERVIEWER: *So, you're saying that one has to take a broader look at the problems?*

KURZWEIL: The jobs that have been eliminated also tend to be the less creative and less desirable jobs. Many people today look at their jobs as sources of fulfillment and derive a certain amount of satisfaction from them. Overall, this is a positive trend.

I think all sectors of society have an interest in anticipating these changes and providing a means for these changes to occur without severe dislocations. Just from the point of view of American competitiveness, we need to strengthen our educational system. It's anticipated that today's children, once they become adults, will be changing the nature of their work quite frequently, and they're going to need the capacity to continue learning. We need to give our children the ability to keep learning so that they can develop new skills and change the nature of their work over the course of their lifetimes.

INTERVIEWER: *Are some of these dislocations absolute? Do you think the complexity of even basic jobs will be raised to so high a level that some people will be unable to compete?*

KURZWEIL: It's surprising the extent to which society can continue to raise its levels and standards and still maintain rising levels of employment. There is some concern that not everybody will be able to compete in the kind of world that further technical advances will bring about. Some find it

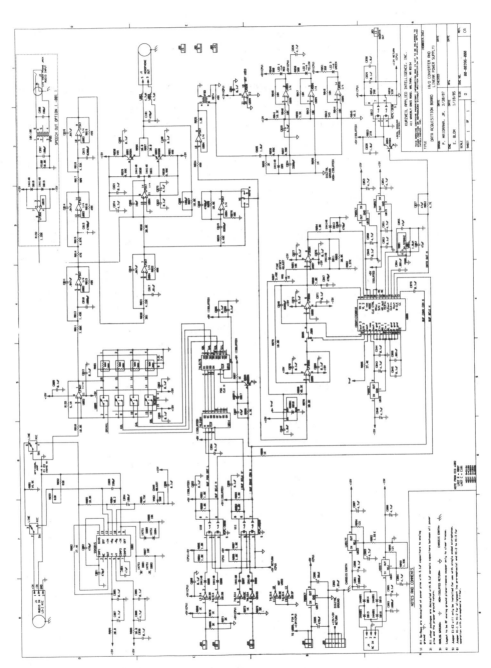

A schematic of the circuitry for the Kurzweil Voice Works™.

frightening to look into the future because we don't know what the future will bring. But, I do take some measure of comfort in the trends that one can see in the past.

Further technical advances don't mean that everyone will have to be a computer programmer or a scientist to be employed. It takes many different kinds of people to run the world. We have a need for teachers. We have a need for people who are good with children. We have a need for people who can be good bureaucrats in both business and government. Many types of skills will continue to be of value in the future.

The Industrial Revolution, while it brought many dislocations, provided enormous improvements in everything from health care to education. During the course of the Industrial Revolution, life expectancy doubled. Automation, combined with the related scientific and medical advances, has enormously improved our quality of life. I don't think there's any choice in the world we live in but to advance the technology, but we do have to be concerned about how we apply it. Technology is power, and power is a two-edged sword. We have to wield it carefully to provide for a better society.

INTERVIEWER: *Do you have any new projects you would like to work on, or is getting your three companies established your top priority now?*

KURZWEIL: Well, I'm committed to building the companies I've already started. I think they're broadly enough defined that they can continue to grow into very major enterprises.

Within those areas, however, I have a lot of ideas. I have a vision of combining a number of artificial intelligence technologies into an office assistant. The system I envision would combine a large vocabulary for speech recognition and synthesis so that you could have a two-way conversation with it. It would have a natural-language-understanding ability in that it would be able to understand what your sentences mean, and that understanding would be coupled with a certain problem-solving ability.

It would have access to your own private databases and the databases of your company, and would also understand all the available databases you could connect to through the telecommunications network. It would know the people you interact with and the kind of information and activities they could provide. You might, for example, ask it to conduct a little research project and gather some information for you. The project might involve gathering some information from your company's database. If it involved data from other companies, the computer would have to call up something like the Dow Jones database and gather some information from that.

The machine would make those calls on its own. It might come back and say, "I'm only authorized to spend $100 in connect charges for your requests, but I think this is going to cost $200. Do I have your authority to go over that allowance?"

The next day the machine might say, "Well, I've gathered the information about the five other companies, and I have the information on our own markets from our database. I need some additional information from our marketing director. I've sent her a request, and she's told me she will have the information by tomorrow. Assuming she gives me that information by tomorrow, I'll give you my final report then."

A system like this could provide a lot of different services in terms of gathering information and performing various tasks in organizing your work. It would require a variety of AI skills, combining speech recognition, natural-language understanding, and the ability to create reports with both language and graphics. It would also require problem-solving skills: the ability to figure out the type of information you're going to need to solve a particular request and the knowledge of how to get that information. A system like this can obviously have many different levels of sophistication. Crude systems like this already exist.

We did a joint project with a company called Artificial Intelligence Corporation that had a system combining natural-language understanding with a complex database. We added to their system our large-vocabulary speech-recognition capability so that you could actually talk to the computer. For example, you could ask, "What were the sales of our two western regions for the last three quarters?" It could understand the question, get the information, and present it to you. It's a very early prototype of the vision I just described. But I can see a system like this getting more and more sophisticated to the point where it could be a true office or executive assistant capable of performing a wide variety of functions—some of which might even take days to perform and involve interacting with other computers, other databases, and people.

I think this kind of system would be very useful. Very often at business meetings people need information, but it isn't available because it would take hours to dig it out. As a result, people estimate the data, and then they use that information—which can often be wrong—to make decisions. The problem is that they just don't have the time to get the real information. If we could plug into the information available in computer databases quickly and easily, we could make better decisions.

Take an area like medicine, for example. A tremendous amount of new knowledge is being created through research, but this knowledge takes a long time to filter to the doctors who can actually use it in their work.

The problem in situations like this is that very often people don't know what the information is or where it is. Computers can help solve this problem by organizing information and making it more readily accessible. We are developing much more powerful means of indexing information and more sophisticated search methods so that people can find the information that's relevant to their problem.

INTERVIEWER: *What kind of special talents do you think it takes to be an inventor?*

KURZWEIL: You certainly have to have an aptitude for technical work, but I think good communication skills are also important. Invention is not loner-type work, but involves collaboration.

I think it's also important to be able to imagine what the impacts of various inventions might be. One has to be able to assess how difficult or easy it would be for society to adapt to those changes. Some inventions, like the laser, which people thought would revolutionize science and industry very quickly, did not catch on for almost twenty years. The laser was revolutionary, but it wasn't until practical applications were developed for it that the importance of the laser began to manifest itself.

Other inventions, however, sometimes take off like a rocket. Personal computers and personal-computer applications spawned whole new industries within a matter of a few years. So, timing and a sense for what it takes to make a change in the world are important elements for an inventor.

Maybe the most important characteristic of all is persistence. A couple of guys I know, who are former vice presidents of Kurzweil Computer Products, started a company called Interleaf. They had a vision of using computers for electronic publishing. Today they're the leaders of that industry, but at the time they started, it wasn't a well-established concept. It took them a long time to get people to believe in the idea. If they hadn't been extremely persistent, they would have given up. In almost every case where you see some substantial success, someone was persistent.

INTERVIEWER: Has new technology changed inventing?

KURZWEIL: Yes. I think it's now feasible for people to start inventing quite early in life. The ubiquitousness of personal computers and their increasing power have made that possible. The latest PCs are not that expensive, but they are as powerful as mainframes were a few years ago. You don't need a half million dollars of equipment to have a software development laboratory. A teenager can create a winning software product on his or her own.

INTERVIEWER: Do you worry about competition in your line of business and invention? IBM, for example, has set up a group to do many of the same things your company does in speech recognition. Does that put a lot of pressure on you?

KURZWEIL: I've never really been all that concerned about competition. Competition is not a bad thing. I tend to get involved in companies that are trying to create both a market and a product. Competition can sometimes help you more than it can hurt you when you're a pioneer. IBM, for example, has given the field of speech recognition credibility and helped promote the concept.

I strongly believe that the success or failure of my companies rests on bringing excellence into our work. If we do good work, we'll be successful. *That's* the challenge—not the competition.

ROMAN SZPUR

*I*N 1938, Roman Szpur thought he "had the world by the tail," designing electrical layouts for a hospital in the Polish city of Lwow. When the Nazis overran Poland in 1939, however, Szpur ran for his life and made his way across Europe, along the north coast of Africa, and finally to the United States. He enlisted in the United States Army in 1942 after working odd jobs and learning English.

In the Army, Szpur was first shuttled between the Air Corps and the Signal Corps because of his valuable language skills, and then his superiors began to notice his talents as an inventor. When a bomb that he designed to cut telephone lines was patented, Szpur was transferred to the Air Corps' Wright Field in Dayton, Ohio—now Wright–Patterson Air Force Base—to work on weapons. By the time he retired to start work on his own projects, Szpur was the chief of weapons techniques at Wright–Patterson.

As chief of weapons techniques, Szpur developed the first non-lens focusing system for lasers. Capable of concentrating a laser's already intense light into even more powerful bursts of energy, the technique opened the door to such things as laser surgery and other precision laser work in medicine and industry.

After helping to set up a factory in Germany to build his laser-focusing system, Szpur built his own laboratory in Kettering, Ohio, in 1967. Now an independent inventor, Szpur has come up with a variety of inventions ranging from the stress-test electrode and the first "wet" medical electrode to a waffle-making machine.

Szpur was born in McKees Rocks, Pennsylvania, and raised near Lwow, Po-land. Now seventy years old, he still works eighteen-hour days, often seven days a week, at his laboratory. He holds forty-four patents.

INTERVIEWER: *Were you always interested in inventing and building things?*

SZPUR: I was raised on a small farm in Poland, and I was very curious about Mother Nature. I don't know where this curiosity came from; it was just always there. For example, there was a big flour mill in my home town with two big diesel engines. I was just thirteen or fourteen years old, but I was so impressed that I would have given anything just to sweep the floors there, just to be close to those engines.

Well, my father made a deal. He paid the mill so that I could go up there and work. Every day I went in the morning with my lunch in a brown bag, and I cleaned the floors and polished the engines. The floors were black and white tiles like you see in the movies. I had to clean them so that I could see myself in them. Every part of the engines was brass or nickel or black metal. The engine room was big, at least 100 by 150 feet. Maybe more.

Those were the olden days. With the diesel, you know, you have the first stroke with compressed air and then ignition starts. The flywheels on the engines were at least thirty feet in diameter, so it took a while to carry through. It sounded like POW, POW, POW. The engines drove the belts that powered all the machines that were grinding the flour—very, very fine flour that was exported out of the country.

I knew the man in charge of the engine room, and when the engines were not running, he would show me different things: how to grind a rod, how the lubricating system worked, and how they started the engines.

INTERVIEWER: *What was your first invention?*

SZPUR: When I was in the sixth grade, I was very curious about electricity and made a little DC generator. We were poor and, of course, I didn't have access to a machine shop. So, to make the generator, I saved the lids and bottoms of shoe polish cans and cut them with scissors into the various shapes I wanted.

I did, however, have access to a blacksmith's shop because the local blacksmith was curious about what I was doing. I once used his shop to make a horseshoe magnet out of a big file. I bent the file into the shape I wanted, and then I magnetized it against a big magnet we had in the laboratory at school. The sides of my generator were wood, and it had a pulley and a hand crank. It was rather crude. It was pretty weak, but I did manage to actually light a one-and-a-half-watt bulb with it. I became a hero in the sixth grade.

My teacher got a lot of enjoyment out of the generator and could see that I was thinking. Obviously, I was heading for school, so I went to a mechanical high school in the city of Lwow near my home. Our high schools in Poland were practical ones. We started by making scrapers for scraping the mud off shoes. Believe it or not, and I'm taking you back to before 1936, we made electric door locks in the school's electrical department. We made furniture. We also made pianos and very good brass band instruments. As a result, the school was always winning competitions with army bands.

I thought I was going to go back to Europe and get even with Hitler. But fate had it differently.

Joining the band, however, was not my goal. Even though we were required to take music in school, I made a decision as a kid that music and singing were items that I absolutely didn't need. So, I rebelled against those requirements, and the school decided that, if all my other grades were excellent, I could get an unsatisfactory grade in singing and music and still move ahead. Finally, after I studied two years in the mechanical high school, I was moved to more advanced schools at the government's request. I ended up at the technical school, which is higher, and graduated from there in electromechanics.

INTERVIEWER: *Did you go to work immediately, or did you continue your schooling?*

SZPUR: I went to work for an electrical firm designing the electrical layouts for the big hospitals in larger cities. I thought I had the world by the tail. I was making good money. I could wear a topcoat and hat, and I had a briefcase. I could send more money home to my relatives than a professor. But then the war came, and I had to run for my life.

INTERVIEWER: *Were the Germans after you because of your technical background?*

SZPUR: No, I was Polish, and that was enough. My parents did not escape, and they were taken to Siberia and kept there by Stalin until Khrushchev came to power. I never got to see them again. I escaped across the border and was arrested in Rumania and put in prison. Eventually, I made it to Greece, then to Africa, and finally to the United States.

INTERVIEWER: *What did you do when you first arrived in the United States?*

SZPUR: I had to learn English from scratch. At first I washed dishes. Later, I wrote for a Polish newspaper and worked at a radio station in Springfield, Massachussetts. I spent my time and money learning English because my goal was technology.

INTERVIEWER: *When did you get your first United States patent?*

SZPUR: It was while I was in the military. Because the United States was at war, I had enlisted in the United States Army Air Corps. I was in the Army for four and a half years, and they shuffled me back and forth from the Air Corps to the Signal Corps because I speak several languages. At the same time, I was also submitting plans for bombing and demolition devices. That's when I invented a bomb for destroying telephone and railroad wires.

Anyway, that evidently got to the Patent Office in Washington, D.C. One fine day, a telegram came to Fort Myers, Florida, where I was stationed with the Signal Corps, saying that I was to be transferred back to the Air Corps at Wright Field in Dayton.

INTERVIEWER: *Did you get involved with research right away?*

SZPUR: Yes. When I transferred to Wright Field, I was the first enlisted man to work in the laboratories. And the amazing thing was that they gave me a choice of which area I wanted to be involved in: bombing or fire control. Fire control, of course, is the aiming and firing of guns, not putting out fires.

I spent one day with the bombing people. That was in the days of the famous Norden bombsight.* When I spent a day with the fire control people, however, I saw the P-61** and its remote-control turrets. I knew that's what I wanted to work on. The gunner sat at a periscope with upper and lower sections. As he tracked a target, both sections followed him. There was no computer between the gunsight and the turret, but that kind of remote-control system was really my dream. When I was in electrical

---

* A precision optical device that incorporated gyrostabilized automatic pilot to keep the bomber straight and level during the bomb run. Invented by Carl L. Norden.
** A fighter plane designed for night flight.

engineering, I had set a goal for myself: I wanted to be able to turn a dial a degree or a minute or a second of an angle and have another system follow my commands precisely. So, here was the first opportunity to work on this goal, and I was sent off to General Electric to work with the scientists developing the system.

INTERVIEWER: *What were your plans at the time?*

SZPUR: I thought I was going to go back to Europe and get even with Hitler. But fate had it differently. The United States government decided that I was not to be let out of the country and that I was going to work on development. After learning at Lowry Field in Denver and training others in the use of the GE fire-control system, I was brought back to Wright Field. Some of my first inventions were for the computers used in B-29s—the same computers that were later introduced into B-47s and B-52s. I have some patents and awards that were given to me for those inventions.

When my enlistment ended, I had a one-day vacation, and then I joined the Air Force and became a government employee working in research. My next experiments at Wright Field were with magnetic guns. We cut wire into pieces, accelerated the pieces with magnets, and then fired them like bullets. It was hard to do because the technology was not advanced at the time. Even so, I did drive three- or four-inch-long pieces of wire through some boards. Today you can accelerate objects to the speed of sound and beyond with magnetic guns.

INTERVIEWER: *I've been told you did some work with lasers while you were with the Air Force.*

SZPUR: When I resigned from the Air Force in 1963, I was working with lasers and heading up an Air Force project to develop lasers. Dr. Ted Maiman, who built the first solid-state laser at Hughes Aircraft Company's laboratory in Malibu, California, was in charge of the project on the contractor's side. Some important breakthroughs were made on that project. While the Russians had a gas laser, no one else had a solid-state laser at the time. About a million times more power is available from a solid-state laser than from a gas laser. Industry started running after solid-state lasers right away, and in 1962, Dr. Maiman left to form the Quantatron Corporation and then the Korad Corporation.

I stayed with the project a little longer because I wasn't satisfied with it yet. I was going after focusing the laser's power even further. We were getting about one watt of energy from the laser's coherent radiation, but I thought it would be a beautiful thing to squeeze time. I wanted to keep the level of energy the same, but squeeze the time to one billionth of a second. It turned out to be fantastic.

INTERVIEWER: *How did you manage to focus the laser to that intensity?*

SZPUR: I developed the first non-lens focusing system for lasers. If you have a watt of energy in only one millionth of a second, you can focus it with a glass lens; but if you have a watt of energy in a billionth of a second, the glass lens blows up like a grenade. After developing the non-lens focusing system, I resigned from the government and got an offer and money from a Wall Street firm to set up a laboratory and do what I wanted.

Everything I develop is simple.

One thing I was still going after, believe it or not, was to find how I could focus this energy down to a width of two and a half microns. Living cells in nature are five to thirty microns in size, and if you take an "energy knife" of two to three microns, you can cut them in half. Then, one half can be married to a half of something else, and you can start building new things. Once this idea was developed, I went to Germany to set up a factory to make Remet focusing units for Spacerays, Incorporated. The company was concerned with production and marketing—which I don't give a hoot about and don't worry about. I like to look into new areas, so I decided to resign and start my own laboratory. When I resigned, I bought a piece of land here in Kettering and built myself a hobby shop.

INTERVIEWER: *What was your laboratory's first invention?*

SZPUR: I first developed a door burglar alarm. The alarm is mounted on the door, and a screw in the top of the door frame breaks the circuit when the door is closed. If anybody moves the door, it closes the circuit, and this thing screams bloody murder. In one year I sold $16,000-worth of these burglar alarms. But the alarm was a simple thing. After that, I developed the magnetic mixer.

INTERVIEWER: *Could you explain how the magnetic mixer works and what it's used for?*

SZPUR: An injectable drug that is going to be given into the bloodstream must be manufactured in a sphere. If you mix something in a sphere, everything participates. If you mix something in a flat-bottomed

AMERICAN REVOLUTION BICENTENNIAL
1776 – 1976

№ 3981304

THE UNITED STATES OF AMERICA

TO ALL TO WHOM THESE PRESENTS SHALL COME:

WHEREAS THERE HAS BEEN PRESENTED TO THE

COMMISSIONER OF PATENTS AND TRADEMARKS

A PETITION PRAYING FOR THE GRANT OF LETTERS PATENT FOR AN ALLEGED NEW AND USEFUL INVENTION THE TITLE AND DESCRIPTION OF WHICH ARE CONTAINED IN THE SPECIFICATIONS OF WHICH A COPY IS HEREUNTO ANNEXED AND MADE A PART HEREOF, AND THE VARIOUS REQUIREMENTS OF LAW IN SUCH CASES MADE AND PROVIDED HAVE BEEN COMPLIED WITH, AND THE TITLE THERE-TO IS, FROM THE RECORDS OF THE PATENT AND TRADEMARK OFFICE IN THE CLAIMANT(S) INDICATED IN THE SAID COPY, AND WHEREAS, UPON DUE EXAMI-NATION MADE, THE SAID CLAIMANT(S) IS (ARE) ADJUDGED TO BE ENTITLED TO A PATENT UNDER THE LAW.

NOW, THEREFORE, THESE LETTERS PATENT ARE TO GRANT UNTO THE SAID CLAIMANT(S) AND THE SUCCESSORS, HEIRS OR ASSIGNS OF THE SAID CLAIMANT(S) FOR THE TERM OF SEVENTEEN YEARS FROM THE DATE OF THIS GRANT, SUBJECT TO THE PAYMENT OF ISSUE FEES AS PROVIDED BY LAW, THE RIGHT TO EXCLUDE [OT]HERS FROM MAKING, USING OR SELLING THE SAID INVENTION THROUGHOUT [THE] UNITED STATES.

IN TESTIMONY WHEREOF *I have hereunto set my hand and caused the seal of the* **PATENT AND TRADEMARK OFFICE** *to be affixed at the City of Washington this* twenty-first *day of* September *in the year of our Lord one thousand nine hundred and seventy-six, and of the Independence of the United States of America the two hundredth and first.*

Attest:

Attesting Officer

C. Marshall Dann
Commissioner of Patents and Trademarks

First page of one of Roman Szpur's patents (special Bicentennial form).

container, the mixing rate is different in the corners of the container than in the center. In the old-style mixers, a glass rod went down into the round-bottomed flask and had a ninety-degree turn near the end. The rod end had a head like a nail head. A paddle, shaped like a half moon with a hole in it, was attached to the rod. This mixer was hooked to a bracket on the wall which powered it. The whole rod and paddle assembly whirled around to do the mixing. If the glass rod broke, they would have to throw the whole thing out and start over again. Some companies told me that they had loss rates as high as sixty percent. When I told them that, because of developments in chemistry, Teflon was available and that I could solve the problem, the response I got was a lot of garbage about how my plan would not work.

I took the Teflon, and I learned how to shape it around iron. If you take something like a U-shaped paddle blade and you let it spin, it will find the center of rotation for its mass, not for its dimension. If you put it in a flask with nothing but air in it, it won't work. But if you put it in a flask with a liquid, no matter what the liquid is, it will act as a bearing. Then, when you put the flask in a fluctuating magnetic field, the magnetic flux spins, and this poor thing has no choice but to follow.

INTERVIEWER: *The blade sits on the bottom of the flask and then spins without being directly connected to anything?*

SZPUR: Yes, it's just sitting there. Someone gave me a hard time that liquids turn differently north of the equator than south, and that it wouldn't work everywhere. So, I made one that goes counterclockwise. I've got the whole market. Today when you buy injectable drugs, when you buy Bausch & Lomb's contact lens solutions, when you buy an expensive perfume—it's all made on my machines.

INTERVIEWER: *I've also been told you invented the first "wet" medical electrode. What exactly is a "wet" electrode?*

SZPUR: There are many different types of electrodes for monitoring the heart, for measuring stress, for reducing pain, and so on. A wet electrode has the gel already on it. When a nurse snaps a cable onto an electrode, it gets pressed down and that can squeeze the gel out. My electrode is designed so that the gel will not squeeze out. Everything I develop is simple. The backing used for packaging has concentric rings that make a seal. It makes no difference if the electrode lies around for months. It will not dry out.

INTERVIEWER: *How much of a market do you see for your electrodes?*

SZPUR: At first, I'm going to go after about four percent of the market. In the United States, I would say that the electrode market is about $600 million a year, so four percent is a pretty good bite.

INTERVIEWER: *You also have a patent for a type of outdoor light or floodlight. What differentiates your light from other light fixtures?*

SZPUR: My light is shaped like a cylinder so that it will never get dirty. Nature cleans a cylinder. That's why trees are round. It's not for strength, as they tell you in school. Cylinders are strong, but trees and other such living things are cylinders because the wind will scrub them at any angle it blows. It's the same with my light. Flat surfaces on a lighting fixture are no different than your windowpanes—with

> *If I'm spending my money, nobody, but nobody, can stop me from expediting my decisions.*

the snow settling in the corners. That tells you right there what's happening. These lights are used outdoors and also indoors in places like electric power plants where the coal dust is always flying or the air quality is bad. Nobody else's fixtures survive. Mine do.

INTERVIEWER: *Are there any inventions of yours that you feel have been ahead of their time, that the public wasn't ready for?*

SZPUR: A lot of medical breakthroughs are coming with the laser. Some are already in place, but others have been held back because of regulations and other worries. Procedures such as using lasers to treat cancers or unclog blocked arteries are coming.

But you'd be surprised how many things people are not ready for. People are pretty negative anyway. I think it has to do with the way we are brought up. Nobody wants to be dumb. Nobody wants to be stupid. Your mother and father always say, "Don't be dumb." It's inbred, so when you're going to step into a new area or invention, you have to prepare yourself that you might make a mistake. You might make several mistakes. But if you work on your own as I do, nobody knows if you make a mistake. I pay for the whole operation. I don't ask anybody for a decision on my experiments,

so who's going to know? My wife will not know. My friends will not know.
It's up to me.

The majority of people, if you tell them what you're going to do, will
start passing judgment before you even do it. If you succeed and make it,
they say, "He stole it. He never worked for it." If you fail, they say, "Didn't I
tell you he was dumb?"

INTERVIEWER: *Is there anything you'd like to invent?*

SZPUR: It just so happens that I am dumb enough to think that I can get
the free ions out of salt water. In the process of doing so, I will get the salt
and all the minerals that come with the ion. But I'm really after the ion itself,
the free electron, and I'm going to use it to produce electricity.

INTERVIEWER: *What makes you think it will work?*

SZPUR: Let me explain. If you were to take a glass of water and stir in a
tablespoon of salt, obviously it would dissolve, and you would say, "Of
course, the water has dissolved it." If you add another tablespoon and
another until the salt doesn't dissolve anymore, you reach saturation.

But let's not go to saturation. Let's just say the salt is dissolved. You've
stirred it up, put the spoon on the table, and walked away. When you come
back the next day, the glass is sitting there, the water is there—and when
you look at the bottom, there's some salt.

What excites me is that the salt is back from the water and real crystals
are sitting on the bottom of the glass. Would you explain to me what happened to the mechanical energy you put into the salt water by stirring to
dissolve the salt? Where is it after the salt separates from the water? Well, I
already know because I measured it. The energy is still there.

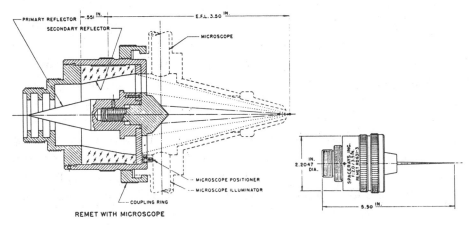

Schematics of Roman Szpur's Remet laser-focusing device.

Now, air moves the oceans, rocking them and dissolving salt, metals—all these things—in them. I know how to take this energy out. I'm actually going to take electric power out of the oceans and light the lamps. And at the same time, I'm going to get metals out of the seawater, scrape them off my machines, and sell them. My invention would even work in Third World countries. There wouldn't even be any moving parts in it.

I'm working right now to get the money together to start on this saltwater research.

INTERVIEWER: *You prefer to finance it yourself?*

SZPUR: Yes. I'm not going to take government money. I don't want private money. I want my own money. If I'm spending my money, nobody, but nobody, can stop me from expediting my decisions.

If you are the president of a company, regardless of how nice it is, you have a vice president. You are going to ask him, "Jim, you're my vice president; should we do this?" Now, Jim doesn't want to be wrong. My god, that's the last thing he wants. So, he's not going to be negative; he's just going to be neutral. And that's what's happening in big corporations.

INTERVIEWER: *Do you believe that big corporations are not a good place for an inventor to work?*

SZPUR: Big corporations don't have what it takes. The Russians are a good example of how things should be run. A lot of good science is coming out of Russia. Don't listen to these stories that say good science isn't being done in Russia. They know their plants must be run by technocrats, people who know what's going on, who came from the bottom up. The Japanese are doing this. You find a Japanese president of a company like Nissan or Toyota, and you're going to find that he worked his way up through the factory, and he knows which bolt and which screw goes where and why. If you go to General Motors, the president has a master's degree or a doctor's degree in administration.

The man who gets his master's degree in business administration doesn't know a thing about what the man in the shop is doing, so he doesn't make decisions. He's either negative, or he lets problems slip by. And that's the way the government works. Small, independent research needs to be protected.

INTERVIEWER: *Do you think small, independent inventors are more productive than those with the government or with corporations?*

SZPUR: Yes. In the free enterprise system a person will be a good, hard worker for money. But it's never going to be the same as when I decide that I want to work on something. Because I have a dream, I put in eighteen hours a day—not eight, eighteen.

In an article I recently clipped from the newspaper, I read that the government gave the Boeing Company $55 million to develop windmills to generate electric power. After a few years of work, they've decided they don't work, so now they're going to sell them for scrap.

> *Because I have a dream, I put in eighteen hours a day—not eight, eighteen.*

If the government was smart, they would have spent something like $10 million, not $55 million, and advertised the project to American inventors. You, the inventor, could submit your idea in writing to a government committee or go to Washington and let the committee look you over in person. If they like your idea, they could give you some money—with the condition that you will return the money if you succeed, but that they won't take the invention or the rights to it. If you don't succeed, you should be required to show them what you did, because learning why an idea fails is just as important as knowing why it works. Nobody does this. Money to burn. The government just dishes it out—$55 million for windmills that are now scrap. A good researcher would not be satisfied with that kind of situation. To just pour money out doesn't do anyone any good.

INTERVIEWER: *But inventors do need money to keep their projects going. What do you think the government should do differently?*

SZPUR: I think there should be a rebirth of old concepts such as giving inventors a tax break. Under the new tax laws you would spend your money to get patents, and then you pay Uncle Sam every year after that for the patent. If the invention is in the medical or health field or related to defense, the inventor should get a tax break. He's not going to take this money with him when he dies. Chances are, as an inventor, he's going to invest in a new invention, and a new benefit will come out of it. What the government is doing now is detrimental to the country. I've been told that foreign applications now exceed American among the patent filings at the United States Patent Office.

Right now the IRS [Internal Revenue Service] is only interested in how much you spend to develop an invention. It doesn't matter that you worked on a thing eighteen hours a day for several years. Your labor doesn't count. Zero. You cannot deduct it.

INTERVIEWER: *Do you think a tax break would be an incentive for inventors?*

SZPUR: Yes, it would. I learned about taxes the hard way. In October of 1965, I sold part of my stock because I wanted to know how it felt to have a quarter of a million dollars in my pocket. I found out that it was nothing. I was still the same man. But I was dumb. I didn't know about taxation; my bookkeeper handled that, and I hadn't asked him before I sold the stock. The next day when I told him what I had done, he wanted to kill me. He told me, "You are the dumbest person under the stars. December is coming, and you sold the stock. Do you know what the tax is going to be? I don't even want to tell you. You are going to be sick." They took more than half.

INTERVIEWER: *How else do you think the United States should go about changing its handling of inventors, besides overhauling the tax system?*

SZPUR: I would recommend that a study be made. I am very curious about why Russian men and women invent and then give their inventions to the government. I don't have a complete answer, but I know that it works. The Russians put the first rocket on the moon, and we can't take that away from them. I know that Russians care very much for their country and that "Mother Russia" is part of their cherished history, but so did we in Poland, and I don't remember ever wanting to give everything I invented to my country. Based on the results of this study, we should try to implement some changes in the United States.

INTERVIEWER: *You seem fairly critical of government research and suggest that it's not the best place for an inventor. Even so, you worked for the government for twenty years or more. Clearly you got something out of it.*

SZPUR: Well, at Wright Field I had it my way. I have to admit this. I was producing things that were useful, so I was successful and had my way. But I didn't have too many friends among the bureaucrats. I was always rippling the water.

If you find yourself in the right place with the government, there is a lot of opportunity. In the late 1950s and early 1960s, they did not pin me down to work on this or work on that. The philosophy was—at least among the people from the Pentagon that I was exposed to—that I didn't have to have a mission immediately.

INTERVIEWER: *Why did you decide to leave the government?*

SZPUR: I decided to resign from Wright Field for a very simple reason. When I came to the United States, I got off the boat and went to a restaurant to wash dishes and cook food, and I worked like hell to learn English. Then, I got into military service. When I got out of the military, I was a civilian for one day before I became a government employee. So, I never saw what the free enterprise system of the United States was like. When 1963 came along, I decided that I was going to try it. It was a bad time, professionally. The government said I was dumb to quit.

INTERVIEWER: *Do you have any regrets?*

SZPUR: No, I have no financial problems. I can handle a certain level of expenditures. It's nice to pick up the phone and say, "Order me this" or "Order me that," instead of saying, "Hey, can the company afford this?" or "Is this in the program?" or "What do you think so-and-so is going to think about it?" I can move fast.

I also have no health problems because I am stimulated every day. And, believe me, if you are happy with what you are doing, you will be healthy.

INTERVIEWER: *Do most of your inventions come from a perceived need? Or are they requested by someone else?*

SZPUR: I don't take on that sort of thing. However, if you walked in and showed me something that I'd never heard of, I would be very curious. For that, I might try to make a deal with you. But I don't want to have anybody come in and give me money to develop something. If you work with someone else's money, you're doing what they want.

INTERVIEWER: *You could easily retire if you wanted. What drives you to keep inventing? Is money or recognition important?*

SZPUR: I don't work for money. It's always been there, but I was never focused on making money from my inventions. As for recognition, maybe some people like to be congratulated, but who cares if Mr. Smith calls me up and congratulates me? That doesn't mean anything. I do get tremendous satisfaction if a young person works in my lab and is curious. That makes my day. Because then I have a chance to share what I know.

INTERVIEWER: *How important are your patents to you?*

SZPUR: I have forty-four patents right now—some in this country and some in foreign countries. Some still have to be licensed. Others don't have much time to run, so I have to work on them and update them and claim further extensions. They are like an instrument for making money.

INTERVIEWER: *What talent do you think is more important for an inventor: practicality or creativity?*

SZPUR: Practicality. If you think you want to crack a nut, you have to learn about that nut. You have to know all about it. It may be a gadget or something mechanical. Go to the library and get the background on it. Get everything you can possibly dig out, and then take a good look at all the information before you really start investing your money.

Learning why an idea fails is just as important as knowing why it works.

INTERVIEWER: *Where do you think the future of invention lies? Is the future limited to high-tech discoveries?*

SZPUR: Not so! Not so! What I do here is high tech, but there is room and place for other types of discoveries as well. Stimulation in the schools is where invention comes from. It's important to make physics attractive to students because it encompasses almost everything. With a background in physics, they can go into chemistry, electrical engineering, pneumatics, hydraulics, everything. Still, the most important thing is stimulation. If you think you have a good idea, your curiosity will drive you. You will not eat well. You will chase your idea.

When I grew up in Poland, I spent my time in the libraries. By the time I was seventeen, I had read everything that Jules Verne wrote. Everything. I also read everything about Henry Ford and Thomas Edison. All these books were translated into Polish. We were encouraged to be inventive. Why is this not done over here? Why is it so important who won the World Series? I'm not knocking sports down, but the whole damn school system is directed towards sports. How many athletes are there? Baseball players today get a million dollars a year for hitting a ball with a stick. It's a disgrace. They can't write, they can't read, and they get a million dollars. How do you expect inventions to bloom in this country?

INTERVIEWER: Is the United States becoming too "technically illiterate" for invention to flourish?

SZPUR: There's no training. Look at the curricula in most universities. The quality of science and technology classes should be kept up, not dragged down.

How about giving students a little stimulation, teaching them about unknown phenomena—natural occurrences that are still not understood by science? Why aren't things like that taught in the United States?

You can even ask a well-educated man and he won't be able to answer a simple question: What colors can you get out of mixing black and white? The answer you'll get is always "gray," but it's not true. You can get colors. No one has explained this phenomenon since it was discovered in the 1700s by a Frenchman. He used what's known as a Bantham disk—a disk with a black-and-white pattern on it, but when you spin it, you see colors.

The Bantham disk is one of, I think, nine unexplained natural phenomena that still exist. I keep a disk here in my laboratory, and when kids come here and see it they ask, "How does it work?" And I have to tell them, "Nobody knows. But maybe you're going to figure it out some day." Now, that's stimulation. And discovering the answer to that puzzle may lead to a new invention. My salt-water project, for example, is based on a natural phenomenon that's been observed for years.

When I was at Wright–Patterson, a very bright young man with Ph.D.'s from Stanford came to work with me. One day, when the cadets from the Air Force Academy were going to come in, I told him, "You should make a Bantham disk." He said, "What's that?" I said, "There was a Frenchman named Bantham in the 1700s who experimented with black and white and developed the Bantham disk. The disk is round; half of it is black, and the other part is divided into three sections. In each section, there are three rings of alternating black and white which gradually go to black. When you rotate it, you get colors."

"Oh yeah," he said. "I understand you're from Poland." And I said, "Yes." And he said, "Maybe you should go back there." So I said, "You smart ass. I'll tell you what—we are going back into the shop and make one of these disks, and we're going to watch it." It was about three o'clock then. I had him take the sheet metal blades off a floor fan, and I went into the drafting room to make the disk. When we finished, it was about nine o'clock or so.

When we turned it on, he just stood there watching it go around saying, "I'll be a son of a bitch. I'll be a son of a bitch." And I said, "Back to Stanford! You are going back to Stanford!"

MARCIAN E. "TED" HOFF

*I*N 1969, Ted Hoff revolutionized microelectronics by inventing the microprocessor—the
*computer on a chip. With most of the computer
industry focusing on large mainframes, the initial response was lukewarm. Some people at
Intel Corporation even wondered if there would
be a market for it. When Intel unveiled the microprocessor a year later, its usefulness was
readily apparent to designers and engineers. By
1975, more than 500,000 were in use.*

*The first microprocessor, Intel's 4004,
was not much larger than a pencil point; it
measured only one-eighth of an inch by one-*
sixth of an inch. A square inch could hold forty-eight of them. In spite of its small
size, each tiny silicon fleck contained the arithmetic and logic circuitry of a full-sized
computer—more than two thousand individual circuit elements. It was a long way
from ENIAC, the first all-electronic computer. Built by Presper Eckert and John
Mauchley at the University of Pennsylvania in 1946, ENIAC was as large as a house
and contained fifty thousand vacuum tubes. However, twenty-four years later, the
microprocessor put more computing power into a tiny chip of silicon.*

*Computers were already powerful tools by 1969, but Hoff's microprocessor
helped to make them all-purpose tools as well. With the microprocessor, computers
could be made small enough and inexpensive enough to run everything from wrist-
watches to pocket calculators. With the microprocessor, computing power was no
longer limited to the mainframe computers of business, government, and universities. It opened up a whole new field to the computer industry. Within ten years,
making the tiny silicon chip would become a multimillion-dollar industry, centered
in California's Silicon Valley.*

Ted Hoff was born in Rochester, New York, in 1937. He graduated from Rensselaer Polytechnic Institute in 1958 with a B.S. in electrical engineering. He did his graduate work at Stanford University and received a master's degree in 1959 and a Ph.D. in 1962. After six years as a research associate at Stanford, he joined Intel in 1968 as the manager of applications research. After leading the design team that produced the first microprocessor, he was named the first Intel fellow. In 1982, he left Intel to become the vice president of research and development at Atari, Inc. He left in 1984 when Warner Communications sold Atari. Since that time, he has been working as a consultant for a variety of Silicon Valley firms.

In 1983, he was named Inventor of the Year by the San Francisco Peninsula Patent Law Association. He has also been recognized by The Economist *as one of the seven most influential inventors since the end of the Second World War.*

INTERVIEWER: *How did Intel's program to develop a microprocessor begin?*

HOFF: Intel was a very young company when I started working there. I joined Intel as employee number twelve in 1968. In 1969, we were approached by a Japanese company named Busicom to work on a set of calculator chips. I was assigned to work with the Japanese engineers on the project. In particular, my job was to help find supplies and to help with the integration process.

In the course of working with them, it began to look as though there might be some problems with the project. At that time, Intel was a small company, and this calculator was going to involve six, eight, or even ten very complicated chips. I was talking to some of Intel's managers about the project, and they encouraged me to help the Japanese engineers simplify the design if there was any way to do so.

A couple of things about the design that they had brought with them made it unique. One was that they were using a read-only memory to customize what was actually the chip for a whole family of calculators. In other words, it wasn't one calculator they were building: There were going to be a half-dozen models.

The first thing that struck me when I looked at the design was that they were not using the memory very effectively. One thing led to another, and finally I proposed that they simplify their logic. I suggested that they reduce the number of chips in the calculator and essentially implement the more complicated steps not in logic, but as programs in memory. I defined an architecture and an instruction set and so on, and then I demonstrated to the Japanese engineers that the kind of tasks they were trying to get the calculator to do could be performed this way. They essentially said that they knew how to design calculators (laughs). In other words, "Don't bother us! We know what we're doing. Go away!" (Laughs.) Fortunately, some of the people at Intel, particularly Bob Noyce, who was president at the time, kept encouraging me. "You just keep looking at it," he said. It was nice to have a backup mode.

> *You've got to keep that small-child idea—always wondering why a thing works a certain way or what happens if you put two things together.*

Well, we continued with that work, and I was joined by another fellow, Stan Mazor. My original proposals were made in July and August of 1969. I believe Stan joined Intel around September. The two of us then continued to refine the basic ideas. Around October, we finally made a presentation to the Japanese management and presented both approaches: the one their engineers were working on and this new approach.

I don't know if we called it the microprocessor approach then, but at least we called it the general purpose computer approach. Even then, we were telling the Japanese engineers, "Look, this has applications that go way beyond calculators. This thing can be programmed to be a calculator; it could be a terminal; it could be a controller for elevators..." They went with it. "We like your approach," they said, "and that's the one we'll back up."

That was pretty much my role in the microprocessor. I defined the architecture and the basic concepts behind it. Some of the things that were unique about the architecture allowed us to put the first 4004 microprocessor into sixteen lead packages, whereas the original set was going to be in forty lead packages. There were a lot of economic benefits to doing it that way. Our work was then turned over to the design group, which did an excellent job of converting architectures to actual circuits.

The product became available early in 1971—at least we had working parts then. But you have to remember that it was still available exclusively to Busicom, the Japanese calculator company. Under the terms of the contract, it couldn't be sold to anyone else. There were some negotiations over this, and I tried to get our marketing people to negotiate for the rights to sell it to other people. Finally we did. I also developed some support tools, because again marketing was very reluctant to commit to the support of a complicated circuit like this. In November of 1971, the part was finally announced.

INTERVIEWER: Was that idea of putting the logic and the circuitry on one chip something you thought about before you came to Intel?

HOFF: I had always wanted to build my own computer, so that was probably one aspect of it. Another aspect was that I was working with a very small and relatively inexpensive computer at the time.

I had a Digital Equipment Corporation PDP8. That machine probably cost in the $10,000 to $15,000 range, which was quite inexpensive as computers went in those days. One could program that computer to act like a scientific calculator. In fact, I think I'd even had discussions with some of our own marketing people about why people paid so much for a scientific calculator when, for about the same amount, they could buy a general purpose computer—something that could be a scientific calculator today but something else tomorrow. Their argument was, "Well, you don't want it to have that much flexibility in some cases. Sometimes a tool is too flexible, and it becomes less useful if it's too flexible." We had various discussions about that.

It seemed that the PDP8 had a remarkably simple instruction set, yet I could do so much with it. The calculator design I was working on, however, had the relatively simple function of a calculator but very complicated logic. That's when I said, "If we've got a read-only memory in there, let's use that read-only memory effectively." One of the keys to doing that was to put in the equivalent of a subroutine—in other words, the ability to call a routine from different places in your program—so that we would think of these subroutines as building blocks. By doing that, we moved things out of hardware and into subroutines. And instead of executing things in parallel, we executed them serially. It's a slower process. But, for a calculator, the interaction with a human being is at a relatively slow rate anyway. If the logic is fast enough, you can do things serially and still have them work out fine.

So, that's really how it got started. I've played around with a lot of different things besides the microprocessor, but it's probably been the most publicized area I've worked in.

INTERVIEWER: *What are some of the other areas you've worked in?*

HOFF: Well, one of the first things I patented was a railroad signaling device. When I got out of high school, I got a summer job at the General Railway Signal Company in Rochester, New York. During something like my second summer there, I was working with a group of engineers who were building what's called an audio frequency track circuit. It used the high frequencies and inductance of the tracks to essentially detect the presence of a train. This basic concept had already been developed, but in the course of designing the circuitry for it I made a number of contributions, actually fundamental contributions, to the final product.

One contribution of mine was making the receiver for this unit totally passive—in other words, with no gain components in the receiver. It was much more reliable because it reduced the number of modes by which it could fail. If you have an amplifier, for example, the amplifier might break into oscillation and generate spurious warning signals. Then, you have a much tougher problem to figure out: how to prevent that from causing the circuit to malfunction. In railroad systems you're always worried about failure modes.

I also developed the method for tuning the system so that it gave a much better defined circuit. My name was one of three that went on that patent. The following year, I worked on a lightning protection scheme for it and patented that.

When I came to Stanford for graduate school, I worked with a professor there and we developed a kind of analog memory cell based on electroplating. I also patented a scheme for a digital filter.

INTERVIEWER: *Did you work on any inventions while you were at Intel?*

HOFF: When I started with Intel, I worked on a number of things other than the microprocessor. For example, we were doing work on dynamic memory, and I suggested some changes in the memory cell to make it work better. I also developed a type of memory cell for a bipolar programmable read-only memory. It was the kind of memory cell that can be programmed in the field.

I actually worked on the microprocessor at Intel from 1969 through about 1973 or 1974. After that, my charter was to look at places to use Intel technology. I was asked to look at the telephone industry, so I started to get active in the telecommunications area. That led to a telephone CODEC [coder-decoder] and a variety of techniques for implementing analog functions in MOS [metal oxide semiconductor] technology. I did some things that hadn't been done before in that area, and several of those have been patented. I've puttered around in a lot of different areas.

> *Knowledge only becomes a problem when technology changes and people don't change their outlook.*

INTERVIEWER: *Some people tell me, "Oh, I have a few patents, but I'm really an engineer." Do you think of yourself as an inventor?*

HOFF: Yes. I like to solve problems, and I like to work puzzles. Invention, in fact, is often something along the same lines. It's nice to have a new and unique way of doing something. In that sense, I like to think of myself as an inventor.

INTERVIEWER: *You mentioned you worked in Rochester during your summers in high school. Did you grow up there?*

HOFF: I grew up in Rochester, New York. I did my undergraduate work at Rensselaer Polytechnic Institute in Troy, and I graduated from there in 1958. Then, I came out to Stanford to do graduate work. I got both my master's and my Ph.D. in electrical engineering from there. I got my Ph.D. in 1962.

I stayed on at Stanford for about six years working as a research associate for Professor Bernard Widrow, primarily in adaptive systems, pattern recognition, and adaptive antennas. The Intel position came along in 1968 and sounded very interesting.

INTERVIEWER: *Was there anyone in particular, either at Stanford or before then, who inspired you to be an inventor?*

HOFF: I can look at a lot of people and say they were inspirations. To start, my father was in railway signaling. I think it was right after World War II, and his company had all this scrap—relays and other stuff. The circuits were not the type that the company used in railway signaling, but I guess they'd been working on aircraft control, and they were throwing out this junk. My father brought some of it home, and we played around with the relay circuits.

My uncle was a chemical engineer with Kodak, and he also was an influence. I was very interested in chemistry and, in fact, almost went into chemistry instead of electronics. He used to encourage me, and he gave me his books on chemistry, which I read on my own. By the time I was in high school, I knew quite a bit about chemistry. I passed the New York State Chemistry Regents Exam as a freshman in high school without even having taken the course.

Bernie Widrow at Stanford was also a great inspiration. We worked together quite closely the whole time I was there. I had been there for a year, and I approached the head of the department and talked with him about what I should do to get a thesis project started. He said, "Oh, there's this professor who's just joined us, Bernie Widrow. You should go talk to him." So, I was one of Bernie's first graduate students. It was a very good working relationship. We worked together for quite a few years. Even after I left Stanford to work at Intel, I continued to work with him until my schedule got impossible.

In one class, he started a lab project that gave students a chance to work on some very interesting projects directly. Bernie had a lot of contacts in the medical school. In many cases, these contacts were people who had computers but who didn't necessarily have the staff to work on them. In the engineering school we had eager and very capable young students, so it made an ideal working relationship. These students were often taking on research projects that were right up there with the most advanced activities. They got to work on some great things, and many of them were able to use that work as the basis for Ph.D. work later on. We did a lot of interesting work in medical electronics.

INTERVIEWER: What do you think it takes to make a successful inventor? What traits should a person have?

HOFF: Curiosity. You've got to be curious and keep questioning, "Why does this work? Why does that happen?" You've got to keep that small-child idea—always wondering why a thing works a certain way or what happens if you put two things together. Before you can invent something, you need what I call a tool kit, and I think the bigger the tool kit you have the better. You need to know how things work. An invention comes about

1	LDM	DATA	DBL	2ND WD	LOAD DATA INTO ACCUM.
2	ADD	REG NO.			ADD CONTENTS OF DESIGNATED REG TO ACCUMULATOR
3	SUB	REG NO.			SUB CONTENTS OF DESIGNATED REG FROM ACCUMULATOR
4	STO	REG NO			STORE ACCUMULATOR IN DESIGNATED REGISTER
5	INC	REG NO			INCREMENT CONTENTS OF DESIGNATED REGISTER
6	JUN	A_1	Y	A_2, A_3	JUMP TO A_1, A_2, A_3
7	JCN	COND	Y	A_2, A_3	JUMP TO $A_2 A_3$ IN SAME PAGE IF COND IS MET (NOT, GT, ODD, ZERO)
8	JMS	A_1	Y	A_2, A_3	JUMP TO SUBROUTINE
9	ISZ	REG NO	Y	A_2, A_3	INC CONTENTS OF DESIGNATED REGISTER JUMP TO $A_2 A_3$ SAME PAGE IF ≠ 0
10	SID	REG PR	0		TRANSFER CONTENTS OF REGISTER PAIR TO DATA REGISTER SELECTOR
11	JIN	REG PR	1		JUMP TO ADDRESS CONTAINED IN SELECTED REGISTER PAIR, SAME PAGE
11	RDS				READ SIGN CHARACTER (INTO ACC) OF SELECTED DATA REGISTER
	WRS				WRITE (FROM ACC) INTO SELECTED SIGN CHARACTER
	RDD				READ DEC. POINT
	WRD				WRITE DEC. POINT
	LDC				LOAD CONTENTS OF CHAR BUFFER INTO ACC
	ADC				ADD CONTENTS OF CHAR BUFFER INTO ACC
	SBC				SUBT CONTENTS OF CHAR BUFFER FROM ACC
	WRC				WRITE CONTENTS OF ACCUMULATOR INTO CHAR BUFFER
	WDR				WRITE CONTENTS OF ACCUMULATOR INTO DISPLAY REGISTER
	WPD				WRITE CONTENTS OF LOB OF ACC INTO D.P. DISPLAY REGISTER
	WRO				WRITE ACC INTO ROM OUT REG.
12	CLA				CLEAR ACCUMULATOR
	CMA				COMPLEMENT ACCUMULATOR
	IAC				INCREMENT ACCUMULATOR
	DCA				DECREMENT ACCUMULATOR
	CLC				CLEAR CARRY
	STC				SET CARRY = 1
	CMC				COMPLEMENT CARRY
	BBK				BRANCH BACK (CONTINUE FROM LAST JMS)
	SHL				SHIFT LEFT ACC + CY
	SHR				SHIFT RIGHT ACC + CY
	RKB				READ KEY BOARD INTO ACC
	RMK				READ PGM PROG KB INTO ACC
	DAA				DEC ADJ ACC, IF >10, OR IF CARRY=1, ADD 6 TO ACC
	XCC				CLEAR ACC, SET ACC=1 IF CARRY=1, CLEAR CARRY
	XCD				CLEAR ACC, SET ACC=6 IF CARRY=1 CLEAR CARRY
13	FTI	RDEST	RS		CONTENTS OF REG PAIR + ADDR TO ROM, CONTENTS OF ROM (SM PAGE) TO REG PR & RDEST
14	HLT1				HALT UNTIL T1 PULSE ARRIVES
15	HLT5				HALT UNTIL T5 PULSE ARRIVES

A section from Ted Hoff's notes for the Intel 4004 microprocessor instruction set.

when you know about something but still find a little bit that you don't know about. It's when you study those parts that you don't know about that you find a new process.

Most of the inventions I've patented have been in areas that fall between disciplines. If you go into almost any university, you will find that it is organized along all these disciplinary lines. In some ways, you know, our whole society is set up that way. Either you are an electrical engineer or a chemical engineer. Or you are a mathematician or a computer scientist.

The most interesting areas to work in are between two disciplines— when you have something that requires a skill in both areas. I don't think we're as good at teaching that. We don't teach people how to be a little more general or how to bridge disciplines. But there are a lot of areas within those cracks between disciplines for coming up with new ideas.

Consider, for example, this analog memory cell that I came up with and that made use of electroplating. It was a mixture of chemistry and electrical engineering, and it was all done for adaptive concepts that we were doing via computer simulation. It was an interesting blend of skills and technologies because I had had all this chemistry as a kid and was able to solve what was nominally an electrical engineering problem.

INTERVIEWER: *But does too much learning or intellectual baggage preclude invention? Can you get such a big tool kit that you spend more time sorting through your tools than inventing?*

HOFF: No, I don't think it's a matter of having too much intellectual baggage. Knowledge only becomes a problem when technology changes and people don't change their outlook. Actually, some of the funniest incidents in this respect came about because of the microprocessor.

You have to understand some of the background behind all this. When a computer was a million-dollar piece of equipment, people worried about putting that much money into one piece of equipment. What do you do when you don't have a problem that needs to be done on your million-dollar machine? What do you do when that thing is idle? That's crazy. So, you develop all this structure to keep your computer busy. Then, along came the ten-dollar computer, and people didn't adapt that quickly. They couldn't accept it. The technology had changed, but all the rules that people had developed for managing computers hadn't changed yet.

Once, for example, I was talking to somebody about the microprocessor, and he was asking me questions having to do with repair. It quickly became evident to me that he felt microprocessors might not be practical because they would be too difficult to repair. He thought that if there was some flaw in it, he would have to go down inside the chip and try to bond a few wires or something like that.

When it dawned on me where he was going with these questions, I said, "No, no! It's not like that at all. It's like a light bulb. You just unscrew it from the socket, throw it in the garbage, and plug in a new one." This person had a total mental block about throwing away a computer. After it had been depreciated for twenty years, he might think about throwing it away, but certainly not before then. This was just a new concept.

Somebody once asked Bob Noyce if all this discussion about high-performance microprocessors wasn't just nonsense. "How would you feel," Bob asked him, "if your IBM 360 computer fell through a crack in the floor?" He thought about it for a bit because the 360 is a very expensive piece of equipment. Then Bob said, "Well, if your computer only cost a few cents, would you really care all that much?"

INTERVIEWER: *Cheaper computers really forced people to change their perceptions about them?*

HOFF: Oh, yes. Before the microprocessor came along, the computer was in the ivory tower. It was in the glassed-in room down the hall, and nobody but the technical elite was allowed anywhere near it. Now, the computer is something you play around with at home or have on your desk at the office. The microprocessor definitely made the computer a more democratic device.

As human beings we tend to latch on to the old and familiar. When things are new and different, it's sometimes a challenge to keep up. I think people have a tendency to go through phases. Supposedly when people are young, they're flexible, and as they get older, they get more rigid. It's a challenge as you progress in years and try to remain creative. The only way to do it is to keep reading as much as possible and try your best to keep up with everything that's happening.

INTERVIEWER: *Is knowing the business or knowing how to sell your idea as important as having a good idea?*

HOFF: I used to tell the engineers who worked for me that ideas were a dime a dozen. In many cases, that's true. To be an inventor you not only must have the idea, but also must believe in it so strongly that you're not going to take "no" for an answer. You have to push for it and argue for it. That may mean that you will have to go out and start up your own company or that you may have to get somebody else to fund you so that you can pursue the idea. But if the idea is as great as you think it is, then you should be more than willing to take those risks and put that effort into it.

INTERVIEWER: *Was Intel a good place to be an inventor? Are companies good in general? Or is it better to be on your own?*

HOFF: Well, it's probably much more difficult to invent when you're on your own. For one thing, I think the stimulation you get in a company from having a

The microprocessor definitely made the computer a more democratic device.

variety of problems thrown at you gives you a larger number of areas to work in than you might find on your own.

You also need good resources to be able to work on inventions in my field. You have to have the facilities, the test equipment, and so on to really check out an idea and develop it. That makes it somewhat more difficult if you're working strictly on your own.

INTERVIEWER: *What kind of projects are you working on?*

HOFF: Well, I'm interested in things like electronics, software, and computers. I'm particularly interested in the use of computers, including such things as control, robotics, and the like. These things are a fascinating challenge—we have a long way to go before we make computers really interactive with humans.

I'd certainly like to develop a really useful robot. Let's say a useful robot for the home—something that isn't a toy but that does the day-to-day chores that you would rather not do. Like cleaning, if that's something you don't like to do. But it shouldn't do the chores you really want to reserve for yourself.

INTERVIEWER: *As far as making computers more interactive with humans, do you mean making them more user-friendly or do you have a broader goal in mind?*

HOFF: When we first introduced the microprocessor, we probably didn't appreciate the degree to which the computer would move into ordinary, nontechnical circles. There was talk of the home computer, but there was some question as to what it would actually do. To some extent, I think that still is a question.

We seem to have identified a few areas where the computer is doing useful things in the nontechnical world: some database processing, some word processing, and tasks such as helping out with income tax, and so on. But the computer is probably still not what you would call a day-to-day companion, and I think we're a long way from having that. In some sense, however, I think that's the direction we want to work in.

What you find is that certain ways of doing different operations have simply evolved over the years. One of the arguments I make is that we still tend to carry around pens and pencils. When you have an idea, you tend to jot it down on a piece of paper; you don't sit down at a computer and just start typing.

In many cases, transferring these operations to a computer is a difficult and tedious task. For example, you have your checkbook and a whole bin full of records, and you have to put the information into your computer to get a run for your taxes. Somehow, I think we've got to solve that problem, and it's one I'd like to solve. It may take a whole new way of organizing society. Certainly, computers are much more user-friendly today than they used to be. But we still have a long way to go.

INTERVIEWER: *A big part of making computers user-friendly was also making them accessible and affordable. The microprocessor really opened the door for that. Did you ever foresee its implications or imagine that it would branch out as far as it has?*

HOFF: There were some things that we definitely saw. We certainly saw that it had a lot of potential applications. We came to that conclusion very early on because a number of us in the lab had projects we were working on. We found ourselves saying, "Gee, if that chip were available today, I'd be able to use it in this project I'm working on." As an engineer, I knew I would be a customer for this chip if it was available at a reasonable price. Fortunately, we were suitable prototypes, and many other engineers felt the same way. That part of it was certainly recognized.

The first Intel advertisement for the microprocessor, dated November 1971. (Reprinted with permission of Intel Corporation © 1971.)

When we first started selling the 4004 microprocessor, people used to write to us with information about the different applications they had come up with. One group had actually installed microprocessors on cows (laughs). They were apparently recording when the cows drank, when they ate, and when they went to the salt lick. In effect, they were correlating this information with milk production. That really appealed to us. Here was a case where a chunk of computing power was going right out into the field (laughs). I mean, really in the field.

INTERVIEWER: *Do you think of the microprocessor as your most important invention?*

HOFF: Certainly that was it. But from the point of being unique, some of the work I've done in the MOS analog area was probably more creative or perhaps took a newer way of looking at things. With an invention, I'm more interested in the thought process that goes into it: the "Aha" moment, as opposed to what the results are. But certainly the microprocessor had the biggest impact.

INTERVIEWER: *What is your favorite invention?*

HOFF: I guess the one that I really liked was a concept I came up with for a digital-to-analog convertor that would be integrated into our MOS technologies.

The idea for that convertor came about because I asked a question of one of our engineers who was working with one of these processes. I wanted to know how well the resistors that were made in this process matched each other. His answer was, "They don't match very well."

"I don't care how badly they match," I said, "I only want a number." That was when I found out that nobody had ever measured the number. So, I started to measure resistors on the wafers. It turned out that they matched beautifully. From wafer to wafer they might vary considerably, but on one wafer from one position to the next they hardly varied at all. On the test wafer I was measuring, however, the resistors were still about a quarter of an inch apart. I wanted to estimate how well they would match if they were right beside each other. I made some assumptions and actually plotted the resistor values and estimated that they matched to within a half of a percent of each other. When we ran tests, it was borne out that this was a pretty good estimate. Later, we used that information as the basis for making a digital-to-analog convertor.

But that whole process was one of asking the right question and finding out that nobody had ever looked at this piece of information before. The fact that the resistors didn't match was sort of like folklore. It was something everybody believed, but nobody had ever tested. Then, when I tested it, I found out the folklore was wrong.

INTERVIEWER: *How do you go about inventing? Do you read up on a problem and gather background information or do you just delve into it?*

HOFF: Generally, I read up on a problem; I study and try to be sure I understand what's going on. If possible, I try to get to the most fundamental level. I think that's probably the most important thing.

Mathematics, for example, can be exceedingly useful for working out relationships. But sometimes you can get so carried away with the abstraction of the math that, even though it helps you solve the problem, it doesn't necessarily give you any insight into understanding what's going on. Sometimes you get lazy and work the equations without stopping to think about what they mean. I like to work back a level. When I see a term in an equation, I want to know why it's there. It's the same kind of curiosity I've talked about. If I know why a term is there, I'm more likely to have a better handle on what's going on.

There are two parts to filing a patent. In the first part, you describe what you've done, and in the second part, you describe what you're claiming as your invention. Usually, you'd like to have as broad a claim as possible in that second part—you'd like to cover your invention in the most generic way possible. To do that, it helps to have an idea of fundamentals, an idea of what is fundamentally different about your approach.

INTERVIEWER: *Were your own patents important to you?*

HOFF: I think patents are probably of somewhat limited usefulness to the inventor. They're probably more useful to the business that's producing the product the patent refers to—unless you happen to be in a position where you are inventing and selling your ideas on a royalty basis. Being an independent inventor, however, is a very difficult business to be in, but some people are successful in doing it.

It's more likely that when someone files a patent, they are staking a claim to it. A patent serves notice to the rest of the business community that this idea means something to me and I'm likely to defend it. It tells competitors that they should be careful before they try to copy a product. Patents are useful as a warning. But patent laws and patents themselves are so numerous and so complex that it gets very difficult to absolutely nail something down and stop anybody else from making a product.

When you start doing follow-up work on a patent, you find that there's very often another way of doing something. Years later, another patent may come up that looks like it has some similarities to yours, and you can be put in the position of having to explain to some referee in the Patent Office why your patent is really different from another patent. Sometimes differences become very subtle. An awful lot of patents are valuable because of only minor details.

> *To be an inventor you not only must have the idea, but also must believe in it so strongly that you're not going to take "no" for an answer.*

In many cases, you have people working all over the world on certain projects. The laws of nature are much the same all over, so people will come to similar solutions to a particular problem. Of course, the key is to be the first one to come up with it. Or, if you're not the first, to be the best. You want to come up with the best way and a unique way of solving the problem.

INTERVIEWER: *Were other people following you closely with a microprocessor of their own?*

HOFF: Work was going on towards using large-scale integration— LSI—for computers. It was mostly oriented toward the military market and high-performance computers—not necessarily making a computer on one chip, but perhaps making a dozen or perhaps thirty chips that could be used to build a computer. But that work would have led to expensive, complicated systems.

Our approach of trying to simplify the computer to one chip was, in some sense, unique. For example, people were working on calculator sets for making inexpensive calculators, but the chips they were designing were very specifically meant for calculators. After Intel established its position with microprocessors, some companies tried to offer those calculator sets as an equivalent to the microprocessor, but they didn't have the same flexibility and compatibility as ours and generally weren't successful.

In that sense, I think we were unique. If one had followed in the direction of LSI, perhaps these more complex computers would have been put on one chip. But it probably would have happened in 1980 instead of 1970. I like to think that our work really made it happen.

INTERVIEWER: *Some people prefer to come up with big ideas and let others work out the details. Do you think of yourself as a hands-on inventor, or do you prefer to come up with the basic concept and let others work out the details?*

HOFF: I like to work with my hands. I like to work at the bench once in a while and actually see the wave forms on the scope. I like to actually watch something operate and compare that performance against what it should be theoretically. Again, that's because I want to understand all the fundamentals.

We moved to a new house a few weeks ago, and I chose it because we have a nice large downstairs area where I can have a reasonably good lab of my own and a machine shop. In fact, I've got a Bridgeport mill and a metal lathe down there so that I can dabble in some of my ideas. If I want to check something out, I can try the idea out.

INTERVIEWER: *How involved was the military in developing the first microprocessors? How important is military support when it comes to basic research?*

HOFF: They weren't important in developing the microprocessor and, in fact, I don't think Intel had any military involvement at the time on any of its projects.

On the other hand, projects I worked on at Stanford had been funded by the military. I left Stanford to join Intel at about the time that there was a lot of unrest on campus. There was a movement to get away from military support for research, and classified research was pushed off campus. The people who were fighting it, however, didn't have the foggiest idea what classified research was all about.

In the areas I was working in, we were doing a little bit of work in pattern recognition. Having access to classified data allowed us to work on real problems as opposed to theoretical ones. When classified research was moved off campus, it meant that on-campus researchers no longer had access to that data; they had to go to industry if they wanted to work on real problems. I guess the groups who were fighting classified research thought they had scored some major victory for freedom of information on campus, but they were just eliminating a certain amount of it.

Overall, the military has certainly had beneficial impacts on research. Much of the work we did at Stanford was directed that way, and a lot of the work in integrated circuits was sponsored by military funding. Even so, the military is often kept from using the latest technology because of their stringent requirements. Procurement in the military takes five years, and technology is changing so fast that by the time a product developed by the military hits the market, it's five years old.

INTERVIEWER: *Did other people play an important role in turning your ideas into inventions?*

HOFF: Oh, very much so. A lot of the patents I filed had more than one name on them. In many cases, I've found that the idea for the invention itself happened because I was working with someone. During the mode of interaction, you might ask someone a key question and get an answer you didn't expect. The answer triggers another way of thinking. You keep that process going, and it really is mutually beneficial—getting two minds stimulating each other rather than having one work in a vacuum.

That was certainly true of the microprocessor. We never really patented the microprocessor, per se. What we patented was one particular implementation, the first implementation. Several people contributed to that, so they have their names on the patent as well.

INTERVIEWER: *Is invention in the future limited to high-tech discoveries or to people with technical backgrounds? Could someone get the needed background without a formal education or advanced training and a Ph.D.?*

HOFF: To some extent you can teach yourself. There are libraries and books around, but that route takes a lot of self-discipline. It's probably easier to learn if you have someone pounding it into you. Certainly, some inventions can be done with very little training, but others take a great deal. It depends on the invention. There are a lot of areas for invention.

Remember, a lot of interesting inventions take place in areas of new technology. In other words, someone makes a breakthrough—such as the process for making integrated circuits—and that becomes an area that's ripe with new possibilities.

Now, if that new area takes highly specialized equipment or is an area in which it's difficult to verify that something actually works until you've done something in the way of actual fabrication of a component, it's probably going to be more difficult to operate alone. You need resources. When

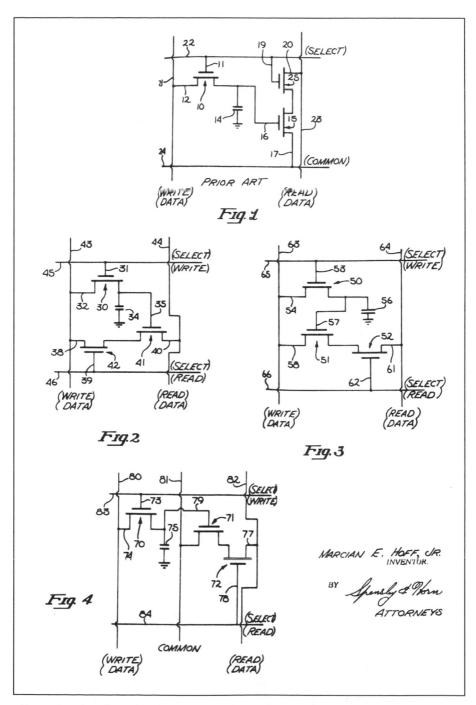

Patent drawings for Ted Hoff's cell for MOS (metal-oxide semiconductors) random-access integrated circuit memory (dated July 13, 1971).

you invent an integrated circuit, for example, an awful lot of people play a role in making that circuit become a reality. I may have patented the idea for a D-to-A convertor, but I never ran wafers through a furnace. That was something other people did. A whole army of people are required to actually make a circuit.

Some things, however, can be done with very modest resources. If you've got a clever idea, it may not take all that much to check it out and see if it works. But I suspect that there's a higher probability of finding areas for new inventions if the technology is new.

INTERVIEWER: *Can skepticism destroy an invention? How do you react to negative feedback on your ideas?*

HOFF: I like the negative challenge sometimes. That's like laying down the gauntlet. Then, I want to prove to somebody that they're wrong.

I suppose it doesn't always work that way. It depends on who the negative feedback comes from. If it comes from too much of an authority figure, I could see it being a demotivator. But if they point out something that you totally overlooked, it may be a help. In that case, it's back to the old drawing board to take another look at the problem.

INTERVIEWER: *What about the microprocessor? Did you get a lot of negative feedback?*

HOFF: We had a pretty good idea that it would be manufacturable, based on the other chips we had been working on. The bigger problem was that Intel, like any other company, was not going to go ahead with a new product unless there was a market for it. And how do you establish that there's going to be a market for a product that hasn't existed before?

Our marketing fellow told me the microprocessor would never sell. His logic, I had to admit, was absolutely irrefutable. It went something like this: "Look, this year they'll sell maybe twenty thousand minicomputers. Total." This was back in 1969, you have to remember. "We're latecomers to that market, and if we put this product out, we'll be lucky to get ten percent of the market. That would mean two thousand chips a year. It just isn't worth the hassle of trying to support a computer for a crummy two thousand chips a year." That was his logic. If they were $50 chips, that would have been only a $100,000 market.

It was difficult to prove him wrong because he was in charge of the marketing department. We had to have him on our side before we were even going to get the resources we needed to develop the product. Fortunately, we had a customer at the time—Busicom—who was willing to support the development of the chip.

Then, our marketing department said, "Well, we're never going to want to sell these microprocessors to anybody else. We're just going to sell everything we make to this one customer." The customer said, "We'd like to have the rights to this." And we said, "Sure, that's fine. We'll just sign them right over." It wasn't until much later that we finally had the rights to sell the microprocessor to other customers.

Once the product was announced and there was a large amount of interest, we had the feedback we needed to get everybody in the company behind the idea. After that, we could really make progress.

This kind of situation is also true of the media. When we started trying to publicize the microprocessor in 1972, it was difficult to get an audience.

We even had a hard time hiring people into the company to work on these new microprocessors. I can remember one kid

> *With an invention, I'm more interested in the thought process that goes into it: the "Aha" moment, as opposed to what the results are.*

who came in. He was still in college, and he was looking at places where he might work after graduation. We were interviewing, and the first question he asked me was, "What size 360 do you have?"

"Well," I said, "we don't have a 360. That's not what we're talking about. We're talking about a much smaller computer." And he said, "I'm not interested," and we wrapped up the interview. In those days, prestige was measured by how large a computer you had to work on. Because we weren't working on at least a certain model or higher, this guy wasn't about to stoop that low.

Of course, a lot of that changed when the microprocessor became really big in the media. First, it was discovered in the technical media, but even that took maybe a year. When our customers started to come out with equipment that contained these chips, the technical media started to notice.

"Hey, here's this equipment with these new interfaces, and they have computers in them." Then, maybe two or three years later, when the semiconductor companies were starting to get noticed because of all this activity in microprocessors, it hit the financial media. That really started in 1975. A few years after that, it finally started to hit the popular media—and everyone did the Silicon Valley–story spread. But it's interesting how long it takes. We're here talking about it today, and when you think about it, it all started in 1969. That was eighteen years ago. That's a long time.

INTERVIEWER: *Still, everyone seems to imagine that the computer revolution happened overnight.*

HOFF: No, it was really a long time coming. One of the fundamental steps that led to this was the integrated circuit. Look how far back that goes. If you go back farther, the whole field really started from the development of so-called planar processes: this business of applying diffusion processes to silicon to make transistors. I think that goes back to around 1955. What we're seeing now is the result of some thirty years of effort.

INTERVIEWER: *It started with Bob Noyce's work at Intel and Jack Kilby's work at Texas Instruments?*

HOFF: Yes, they were responsible for the integrated circuit, but I believe this goes back before that. In effect, thirty years of development stand behind the microprocessor, and it all goes back to the transistor, which really stimulated all the work in solid-state electronics.

It started when someone discovered a solid-state phenomenon that could be useful in electronics—the transistor. Then, someone discovered how to improve the method for making these devices. Once a good method for making transistors was discovered and a really good material was found, people discovered that they could make not only single devices but whole systems on a single wafer of silicon. Each level was built on the one before it, and each one expanded the utility of the original function.

INTERVIEWER: *What have you been doing since you left Intel?*

HOFF: I was at Intel for fourteen years, and I had the position of Intel fellow when I left. I had been doing some work in speech recognition there, but I thought I had been in one place so long that it was time to do something a little different. This interesting opportunity at Atari came along, and I took it.

At the time I joined Atari, I don't think anybody saw how many problems the company had, but there was a very interesting group working there under Alan Kay. They were doing some absolutely fascinating work in the use of computers and in applications. Atari was exploring some of the same problems I addressed earlier: how to make a computer more of a companion, more useful, more friendly.

We had some very interesting times at Atari and some very interesting discussions. Unfortunately, Atari's problems began to grow. I guess the seeds had been sown before, but they really sprouted with a vengeance sometime after I joined. Eventually, Warner sold Atari, and I left at that time. Even during the time I was there we had to undergo some shrinking to bring costs under control. It's a shame it didn't last because some fascinating projects were going on. We might have really made some earthshaking changes if the company had been able to continue. Of course, after it was sold, the company had a very different focus and philosophy. Both the new company and I agreed that the new focus was not for me.

Since that time, I've been doing mostly consulting. In fact, one of the people I worked with at Atari, Gary Summers, started a consulting company called Teklicon, located in Mountain View, California, and I've done a fair amount of consulting work through that company, plus a number of independent jobs. The consulting keeps me in contact with what's going on, but allows me to control my time much better so that I still have time to work on my own projects at home. Except it seems that there's never enough time.

INTERVIEWER: People seem to move freely from company to company in the Silicon Valley. Is that flexibility a plus or minus?

HOFF: Moving around from company to company very definitely helps put things in perspective. You don't want to move too much, but it can help. I think one of the pluses is this spirit of trying new things and the willingness on the part of venture capitalists to back new products. In fact, I begin getting a little nervous when I see venture capitalists getting conservative and backing the same thing they backed the year before. When that happens it's time to watch out. That spirit of changing technology and of trying to do things a little differently is what makes it really exciting. It keeps things going, and it's a good atmosphere for people to get into.

The work ethic is another part of this area. People have looked at it very negatively. They look at all the long hours people work and so on, and they write horror stories about how browbeaten people are. But I think that's what it takes to do something different. You've got to be dedicated to it. You can't do it eight hours a day and then turn it off.

The other thing is that this kind of dedication is also what it takes to make a company succeed. You have to realize that no small part of the motivation is financial. Maybe the only way to become financially indepen-

> *The issue with invention is to pursue it.... Otherwise, the idea is just a flash, and it's gone.*

dent is to start a company or get involved with a successful company that's just growing up. If you take a position with an old, established company, you're likely to be a working engineer your entire life.

But if you take a job with, for example, a Silicon Valley start-up company and get in on the ground floor, you may be in a much better financial position in a few years. It's the kind of success story you read about: the fellow who's an inch away from poverty one year and is on Forbes's list of the one hundred wealthiest people the next.

If you can pick an area that you consider to be really fun, where you enjoy putting in long hours, and where you can be financially rewarded if you're successful, then you have the best of both worlds.

But I think the motivation part has often been overlooked by other countries who come here and want to know how they can copy Silicon Valley. In some cases, I've seen them come away with the idea that the motivation is going to come entirely from the government. They totally overlook the personal motivation involved. I don't think you can do that.

INTERVIEWER: *Is the ability to invent a rare gift? It would seem to be more than training, because not every engineer can invent.*

HOFF: Part of it is probably recognizing that you can invent. Probably one of the most significant experiences I remember was meeting a few entrepreneurs who had been successful. It wasn't necessarily that their ideas were any better than anybody else's. The difference was that they were motivated to pursue them. Motivation actually seemed more important than the idea. I think that's probably true in invention as well.

The issue with invention is to pursue it. If you're always waiting for that wonderful breakthrough, it's probably never going to happen. Instead, what you have to do is keep working on things. If you find something that looks good, follow through with it. I suspect many people don't train themselves to think about their good ideas, or they just filter them out. Once you come up with an idea, you have to find a way to utilize it. You have to keep your creative juices working and do something with it. Otherwise, the idea is just a flash, and it's gone.

GORDON
GOULD

*I*N A flash of insight, Gordon Gould conceived of
the laser in 1957. On the first page of his notebook
he coined the term laser, *for Light Amplification by the Stimulated Emission of Radiation.
But while his term became common usage for
the coherent beam of light created by his invention, the United States Patent Office did not
issue a patent for his optically pumped laser until 1977—after what it called a "continuation"
of the patent application process.*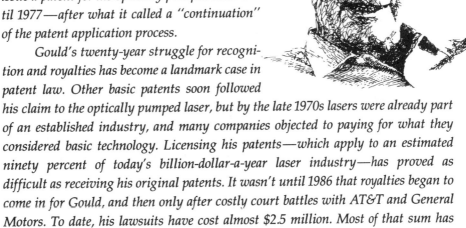

*Gould's twenty-year struggle for recogni-
tion and royalties has become a landmark case in
patent law. Other basic patents soon followed
his claim to the optically pumped laser, but by the late 1970s lasers were already part
of an established industry, and many companies objected to paying for what they
considered basic technology. Licensing his patents—which apply to an estimated
ninety percent of today's billion-dollar-a-year laser industry—has proved as
difficult as receiving his original patents. It wasn't until 1986 that royalties began to
come in for Gould, and then only after costly court battles with AT&T and General
Motors. To date, his lawsuits have cost almost $2.5 million. Most of that sum has
been paid for by the Patlex Corporation, in exchange for a sixty-four-percent share of
his expected royalties.*

*Gould conceived of the laser while studying for his Ph.D. at Columbia Univer-
sity with the Nobel Prize-winning physicist Polykarp Kusch. It was a heady time to
be at Columbia: Seven other future Nobel Prize winners were there at the time, including Charles H. Townes and Arthur L. Schawlow, who were issued a patent on a
laser in 1960 and, until recently, generally credited as the inventors of the laser.
Townes and Schawlow did not use the term laser to describe their invention, but*

preferred the term optical maser—*following Townes' invention of the maser in 1951—for Microwave Amplification by the Stimulated Emission of Radiation.*

Gould left Columbia in 1958 to work on his ideas full-time. Under the mistaken impression that he had to have a working model to apply for a patent, he did not file his claims until 1959. In the meantime, Townes and Schawlow filed their first claims for a laser in 1958. That same year, Gould joined the Technical Research Group, Inc., on Long Island, where his ideas helped TRG capture a million-dollar research contract to develop laser weapons. Gould, however, was unable to get security clearance to work on his own project.

In 1965, TRG was merged into Control Data Corporation. When Control Data liquidated its laser business in 1970, Gould became the sole owner of his laser patents and applications. It would take seven more years of legal work before he was issued his first commercially significant laser patent. Today, Gould holds several basic patents in the field, including a patent on industrial applications of the laser. Another basic patent for gas-discharge lasers—which covers almost fifty percent of the current laser market, including the helium-neon laser used in supermarket checkout systems—will be issued in November 1987.

Gordon Gould was born in New York City in 1920. He graduated from Union College in Schenectady, New York, in 1941 with a B.S. in physics. In 1943, he received an M.S. in physics from Yale University. From 1943 to 1945, he worked on the Manhattan Project in New York City with the scientists developing the atomic bomb. He co-founded Optelecom, a Maryland-based research and development firm and manufacturer of fiber-optic equipment, in 1974. He is a member of the Institute of Electrical and Electronics Engineers (IEEE) and the American Association for the Advancement of Science (AAAS). He was the president of the Laser Industry Association from 1971 to 1973. In 1978, he was named the Inventor of the Year by the Patent Office Association for the Advancement of Invention and Innovation.

INTERVIEWER: *Do you remember when you first thought of the laser?*

GOULD: In the middle of one Saturday night in the fall of 1957, the whole thing—the concept of the Fabry–Perot resonator,* together with the laser amplifier—suddenly popped into my head, and I saw how to build a laser. That night when I thought of it, I was electrified. Almost immediately I realized what the applications were going to be. I knew it would be the

---

* The pair of mirrors at each end of a laser which help shape the laser beam.

most important work of my career. I spent the rest of the weekend writing
down as much as I could and got it notarized.

But that flash of insight required the twenty years of work I had done
in physics and optics to put all the "bricks" of that invention in there. The
process of invention is fascinating in any case, and it's a process that is not
fully understood by anybody, least of all me. But I have learned that it is
necessary to have all the materials of an invention in your head.

I think the mind is unconsciously churning away, putting all these
things together like a jigsaw puzzle. If your
mind has been properly trained, ideas that *I held several*
don't work just never come to the surface.
Every once in a while, however, something *misconceptions.*
really clicks, and an idea will spring into *One of them was*
your mind. It only seems that it was *that you need*
instantaneous.

INTERVIEWER: *So, it was your back-* *a working model*
ground that led you to invent the laser?
GOULD: When I was in high school, or *of an invention*
even earlier, I knew that I wanted to be an *before you can get*
inventor; somehow it was in my blood, and *a patent on it.*
in pursuit of that, I went to Union College
in Schenectady, New York, and got a degree in physics.

In 1941, I went to Yale to start on my Ph.D. Of course, that was right
when the war started, so I was at Yale for only two years before I had to
leave. I worked on the Manhattan Project—the A-bomb project—in
Manhattan for the rest of the war.

Even though I was only at Yale for two years, what I learned there contributed to my ability, many years later, to think of the laser. I chose Yale
because it was well known for spectroscopy research in light and research
in the interaction of light with matter. I had already fallen in love with light
at Union College, where I was inspired by a very good professor, Dr. Frank
Studer. It was a field of physics that really fascinated me. A few years after
the end of the war, I went to Columbia University to finish my Ph.D.

It was very exciting to be at Columbia in the 1950s. About six Nobel
Prize winners came out of the university during that time, and the maser
was actually invented there by Charles Townes—or as his story goes, the

idea came to him while he was sitting on a park bench in Washington, D.C.

At Columbia, the field they were on top of was microwave spectroscopy. The field was really founded by I. I. Rabi, Townes, and the others at Columbia, and it was the world's leading laboratory in that area.

My research project was in microwave spectroscopy, and it had to do with exciting thallium atoms into a metastable state in what's called an atomic beam machine. After trying several different techniques to get enough atoms into a metastable state for my experiments, all of which were unsuccessful, I tried a new technique called optical pumping at the suggestion of I. I. Rabi. That technique worked, and I was able to do my research on thallium. I learned a lot about optical pumping and the interaction of light with atoms through that research. Combined with my earlier work in classical optics at Yale, the work with optical pumping and microwaves prepared me for the laser. I certainly had no idea that was what I was heading for, but I think that background—and I'm talking about experimental experiences, not theoretical—enabled me to pull everything together into what's called the laser.

INTERVIEWER: *Inventing the laser required more than just a theoretical understanding of optics and microwaves?*

GOULD: You have to have the hardware to embody an idea. Einstein had predicted the kind of stimulated emission seen in the laser. A theoretician would know about Einstein's stimulated emission coefficient, but he wouldn't have the faintest idea how to make it work. To come up with a fundamental invention like the laser, you have to have both a theoretical understanding and especially an experimental understanding of the way things work.

My idea to use a Fabry–Perot resonator to build a laser was thought up independently by two other people: Charles Townes and Arthur Schawlow (who happened to be brothers-in-law). Townes was the "father" of microwave spectroscopy and knew the microwave side of the laser, but he didn't know anything about optics. Schawlow had received his Ph.D. studying the Raman effect,* which does require optics, and he had a lot of experience with optical equipment.

---

* A phenomenon, named after the Indian physicist, Raman, who first studied it, observed in the scattering of light as it passes through a transparent medium. The light undergoes a change in frequency and a random alteration in phase due to a change in rotational or vibrational energy of the scattering molecules; a.k.a. Raman scattering.

Each of them brought a part of what was necessary for the laser. When Schawlow was a visiting professor at Columbia, they were thrown together and came up with their version of the laser.

What Schawlow and Townes did not realize, however, was the tremendous power one could get out of the laser and what it would mean. It had implications not just in communications, but in the handling of materials as well. With the laser, it was possible to control and deliver power in a concentration that was never conceivable before. In my first notebook on the laser, I calculated that you could heat up a substance to the temperature of the sun in something like a millionth of a second with a laser. I also calculated that a laser could heat up substances to temperatures far beyond those anyone knew about—namely, up to the hundreds of millions of degrees that are required for fusion power and that are being experimented with today.

After I thought about this invention and its implications, things began to change for me. I got thrown into an entirely different life, as it were. Within a month or so of the time I first thought of the laser, I knew it was the most important thing I would ever be involved with. Even though my thesis wasn't yet written, I knew I had to do something with it immediately. In early 1958, I left Columbia for TRG, or the Technical Research Group. I had the idea that I could come back and finish my thesis after the laser was launched. Of course, I never went back.

INTERVIEWER: *Was that sense of urgency why you left Columbia?*

GOULD: I knew I couldn't work on the laser at Columbia because my professor, Polykarp Kusch, was a purist as far as basic research was concerned. Anything like the laser was anathema to him. With Charlie Townes, that wasn't so; he thought developments like the maser and the laser were important and worthy of work at Columbia. But not Kusch. And because I had worked with Kusch, I wouldn't have been able to do anything about the laser if I had stayed. I knew something had to be done in a hurry, or it would be out of my hands. It was in the air—as many inventions are.

INTERVIEWER: *I've read that you knew Townes was getting close to inventing the laser himself when he called and asked you some critical questions about your thallium project. Did his interest also convince you that you had to develop your ideas soon?*

GOULD: He did call, and from the questions he asked, I knew he was thinking along lines that I had already been thinking about: how to create a population inversion between states that corresponded to light frequencies. That call still didn't galvanize me into doing anything, however, until I thought of using a Fabry–Perot resonator to build a laser. When I thought of using that, I knew that I had an apparatus that would generate a coherent beam of light. That's what galvanized me. Townes and Schawlow didn't get around to thinking about using the Fabry–Perot resonator for another few months or so.

> *You would be surprised how many people think the laser is actually that beam of light instead of the machine that produces it.*

In the meantime, I failed to really take advantage of my ideas and write a patent application. However, what I did do in 1958 proved to be very useful. I didn't really believe strongly in the optical pumping method that I had proposed in my first notebook, but by early 1958, I thought up half a dozen ways to power a laser, which were proven to work and provided much more powerful excitation mechanisms. In fact, the original type of optical pumping—which was also proposed by Townes and Schawlow—has never worked. In any case, that year of work was not wasted in the sense that the patents I have today are actually on those processes I thought up in 1958.

INTERVIEWER: *You mentioned that you failed to take advantage of the situation and write a patent application for your first ideas on the laser. Why didn't you patent those early ideas?*

GOULD: When I left Columbia for TRG in March of 1958, I held several misconceptions. One of them was that you need a working model of an invention before you can get a patent on it. I don't know how I had such a misconception. I had actually visited a patent attorney in January to try to clarify what I had to do, but somehow I came away from him with the wrong idea.

That move started me into the world of contract research and development at TRG. It wasn't long before I discovered the chilling effect of trying to find money to do things in research and development. Unable to get started on the laser immediately, I spent most of that year writing up a much more detailed notebook, and I invented a number of different laser processes including the gas-discharge laser and several others. I also had a number of auxiliary inventions such as Brewster-angle windows, which are low-loss windows for a beam of light, and the Q switch.* In the middle of 1959, all that work resulted in a big contract for TRG to develop a laser. The president of TRG thought his figure was pretty high when he asked for $300,000, and you can imagine his shock when the government came back and offered $1 million. It doubled the size of the company in one fell swoop.

INTERVIEWER: *With laser scanners and laser discs, "laser" has become a familiar term. Most people picture a laser as a powerful red beam. But how does a laser actually work?*

GOULD: You would be surprised how many people think the laser is actually that beam of light instead of the machine that produces it.

To understand the physics behind the laser, you first have to realize that quantum mechanics predicts that isolated atoms can be stable only in certain energy levels, not in a continuous range of energy levels.

If you compare the planets going around the sun to electrons going around the nucleus of an atom, the orbits of the planets are not constrained by those limits defined in quantum mechanics, and they can have any arbitrary energy level or any arbitrarily shaped orbit. When you get down to the atomic scale, however, only particular shapes of orbits are available, and those shapes are really standing waves of electrons around the nucleus. They are complicated standing waves, but they are standing waves (analogous to water waves sloshing back and forth in a bathtub).

Although there are certain restricted orbit shapes, electrons can make a transition from one level to another—for example, they can move into a higher level and then back. If the atom is left in isolation in an excited state, it will eventually get back to its original state by spontaneously emitting a photon that has an energy level equal to the difference in energy levels between the two orbits.

Now, some transitions are easily stimulated by light. Others are more difficult, and they're called "forbidden." In the case of the laser, let's just look at allowed, or semi-allowed, transitions.

Einstein had predicted both the stimulated absorption of light and the stimulated emission of light. Stimulated absorption means that when a light

---

* A device in a laser by which a "giant pulse" of light can be released.

of the right frequency passes through an atom, it "tickles" the atom and causes it to jump to the higher energy state and absorb that quantum of energy contained in the light.

With stimulated emission, if the atom is already in a higher energy state, the same tickling process causes it to undergo a transition from the higher state to a lower state and give up a photon of light. It gives up that photon—in addition to the photon that tickled it, to start the transition—which means that it has added light to the beam. In fact, it not only adds light, it adds light coherently—it doesn't change the shape or phase of the original beam. It just adds intensity, and this is what happens in a laser.

From this point of view, it's easy to see why you need a population inversion, or more atoms in an upper, or excited, state than in a lower state, in order to create a laser beam. If a cluster of atoms has more atoms in a lower state than an upper one, which is normal, those in the lower state will simply take light energy out of the system by absorbing the photons being given off by the excited atoms.

The big problem is how to create that population inversion. It turns out that it's not all that hard to create that inversion and that a variety of pumping mechanisms are capable of doing it. It is hard, however, to create a system where the efficiency is high or the power is high, or with various other characteristics you would like.

INTERVIEWER: How did your work on optical pumping help your invention of the laser?

GOULD: I could see from my research work on optical pumping that it was possible to produce a population inversion in gases with an optical pump. That technique was kind of marginal, as I've said, but I did think of better and better ways of doing it during my early work in 1958.

But as far as making the laser is concerned, the actual stimulated emission of radiation itself doesn't do the job for you. Stimulated emission itself would have the effect of amplifying the light in every direction from a light source. It really wouldn't be very different in its effect than an ordinary fluorescent lamp. Shaping a long, thin amplifier to provide directionality was an important first step.

When I conceived of the laser, I realized that it was possible to select one direction of light out of all the infinite number of directions available from such a source. That one direction could also be fed back and forth by feedback, as it were, through an amplifier and built up to a very intense beam. Out of the infinity of directions, one direction could be built up and would eventually dominate the system.

If you selected one perfect beam, you could build it up without spreading out—even if the original beam was very, very weak. It's inherent in the stimulated emission process that atoms give off light in the same phase and direction of the light that stimulated them. That particular process, which is called coherent amplification, was the key to the laser.

The maser, by comparison, likewise provided coherent amplification of microwaves, but it was only apparent as temporal coherence. In other words, when you added energy by amplification, it would be in phase with the stimulating radiation, but because microwaves are so much larger than light waves, you couldn't see the spatial effects.

Government regulations are even worse than industrial lab regulations at deadening invention, and they certainly deaden entrepreneurship.

INTERVIEWER: *But with the laser, the spatial effects could be seen because light waves are so much smaller?*

GOULD: With the laser, it became clear to me that this spatial coherence would occur, which meant that light could be generated in a form that could give you tremendous concentrations of energy if you focused it. It also meant that laser light could travel tremendous distances before it spread out, if it was used as a straight beam.

Well, I didn't realize every application, but I could see the forms those applications were going to take. I have patents on a variety of actual uses for the laser that cover such things as welding, evaporation in machining, and cauterizing. I was conscious of those possibilities from a very early point.

I also knew that the energies involved would be bigger than those in microwaves, for the simple reason that each photon of light is a hundred thousand times more energetic than a photon of microwave energy. In this case, the quantum of energy given off is equal to Planck's constant* times the frequency. It's just a simple factor, but the frequency of light is so much

---

* A constant, h, that gives the unvarying ratio of the frequency of radiation to its quanta of energy and that has an approximate value of 6.625×10^{-27} erg second (gem ^{2} per second).

greater that every atom gives off one hundred thousand times as much energy in the form of light than it gives off in the form of a microwave.

The coherent amplification of the laser and the amount of power one could get from the laser were the two things that made it so important. I knew I had to go after this thing. I couldn't just let it sit in a notebook.

INTERVIEWER: *How did you envision the first laser? Was it a solid-state laser like Ted Maiman's?*

GOULD: Although my original patent described solid-state lasers, including ruby lasers, I first envisioned a gas laser when I thought of the laser.

My patent had said that ruby had a high quantum efficiency, and TRG had started to study ruby crystals, but Irwin Wieder came out with a paper saying that its quantum efficiency was only one percent. A quantum efficiency of one percent means that only one percent of the light absorbed will be converted into emitted light, which meant that ruby wouldn't be a good material for building a laser. After Wieder's paper came out, Schawlow gave a lecture at TRG that reinforced that view. As a result, the people running the project at TRG dropped it. I wasn't in the project because I couldn't get security clearance. Six months later, Ted Maiman built the first solid-state laser using a ruby crystal.

Maiman was dissatisfied with what he read in Wieder's paper on the quantum efficiency of ruby and decided to study it. He spent a year measuring and studying the ruby to get a better measurement of its quantum efficiency and came up with a figure of ninety-five percent—all because of some errors in Wieder's work.

After that, he built his laser. He made calculations, measured the intensities of the flash lamps he was using, and knew all about the system before he pressed the button. He proved it would work before he pressed the button, and it worked the first time.

Ali Javan, William Bennett, and Donald Herriott used the same approach when they built the first helium-neon laser in 1960. They spent two years studying the fluorescence of neon before they felt confident enough to touch the button.

A year or two later, however, there was a report of several new lasers that had been discovered by the Services Electronic Research Laboratory in England using a very different approach.

Some rough calculations on the feasibility
of a LASER: Light Amplification by Stimulated
Emission of Radiation.

conceive a tube terminated by optically flat

partially reflecting parallel mirrors. The mirrors
might be silvered or multilayer interference
reflectors. The latter are lossless and may
have an arbitrarily high reflectance
depending on the number of layers. a
practical achievement is 98% in the visible
for a 7-layer reflector. Flats with
closer tolerance than 1/100 λ are not available
so if a resonant system is desired, higher
reflectance would not be useful. However
for a nonresonant system, the 99.9% reflectance
which are possible might be useful.

Consider a plane standing wave in the tube. there
is the effect of a closed cavity; since
the wavelength is small the diffraction
and hence the lateral loss is negligible.

† O.S. Heavens, "Optical Properties of Thin Solid Films"
Butter worths Scientific Publications. London 1955, P.220.

First page of Gordon Gould's laser notebook, notarized November 13, 1957.

That electronic lab was the old radar lab from the Second World War. It was run by a guy by the name of Sir Harry Boot, who dashed around in an old beat-up Rolls Royce. Boot was one of those heroes who got radar working at the beginning of the war and was a very exciting character.

Boot and the other researchers at the lab decided that they wouldn't be able to live on radar for the rest of their lives and, with that in mind, decided that they had to get on with whatever new thing was coming along—which was lasers.

Their first effort consisted of getting a great big, fat tube with windows on the end and slamming it with a klystron* power supply of the kind used to send out radar pulses. Lo and behold, fifty different wavelengths oscillated, and this was just *air* in the tube. They just whopped it with this klystron power source, and every kind of atom in there lased.

That kind of shocked the laser community. Up until then, you built a laser the way a physicist would do it—namely, you studied the thing to death and learned everything about it until you were confident that it would work. But, as Boot showed, you didn't have to do that. All you had to do was slam something with a large power source, excite it, and a lot of things would happen. That's an engineer's approach. Actually, it's not even something an engineer would do. It's an approach a guy like Sir Harry Boot would use (laughs).

Other theories relating to the power and efficiency of the laser were also developed in those first two or three years. Most of the work was done by people at Bell Labs, and they deserve a lot of credit for it. I guess somebody at the top in Bell Labs decided that lasers were going to be important after Maiman demonstrated his ruby laser and Bennett, Javan, and Herriott built their helium-neon laser. The company must have put aside a big budget, because as early as 1961 or 1962 at least fifteen people were working on lasers at Bell Labs.

INTERVIEWER: *Did you ever wish you had been able to work at a place like Bell Labs?*

GOULD: My first job was with Western Electric. I worked for them one summer in 1941, and after that summer I realized that it wasn't for me.

They liked me when I got there. I had a B.S. in physics, and they wanted me to stay. And they went through their standard procedure of

---

* An electron tube used to amplify or generate radio waves of microwave frequency by means of velocity modulation.

introducing their likely young men to the various superiors. I was working in a test lab at the time, and each week or so, I met another executive on the next level up. Finally, I got up to the vice president of Western Electric in charge of the plant where I was working. That was eleven layers up.

As you went up the ladder, things were a little better; you'd find a rug on the floor, a secretary, and a mahogany desk (laughs). As I met them, the executives also got grayer and grayer. The last guy was about sixty-five years old. I thought to myself, Man, I just can't imagine spending my life climbing that ladder. So, I left there, and I never wanted to be part of a big company after that.

Bell Labs has some of the same aspects: There is a bureaucracy, and there are rules you have to live by. I prefer a small, lively laboratory where I have more say about what I do and what I work on and where I can also make money.

INTERVIEWER: Although the salaries are good, you can't become indepen-dently wealthy as an engineer or scientist at an established company?

GOULD: No. You can't make money at a big place like Western Electric. Only the stockholders make money. But if you found your own company, there's a chance to make a million bucks, as I did make with my last com-pany, Optelecom. At TRG, the president gave me stock options when I brought in that first laser contract. When the company was merged with Control Data, I made $300,000. That never could have happened at a place like Bell Labs.

When I got that first $300,000, the prudent thing would have been to invest it in something. But at that point, I was so confident of the outcome of all these patent suits that I bought what turned out to be a great cruising boat. I don't know how I was able to do it at the time, but after buying the boat, I would take off for six weeks at a time every year and go cruising in the Caribbean. I'm really glad I did that. Of course, it was many more years than I expected before I began to make money from my laser patents, but that boat was great fun.

INTERVIEWER: Are small companies inherently more innovative than larger ones?

GOULD: The process goes on decade after decade: Companies are founded around a new idea or a new angle to a service, and then they're merged into bigger companies. Why is it that the bigger companies just stop growing? After they get to a certain size, companies seem to grow only by merging, and some of them slip backwards. Look at what happened to U.S. Steel or Penn Central Railroad or some of the other spectacular failures.

Little companies keep getting slurped up by bigger companies, but in the end they still constitute seventy-five percent of all the businesses in the United States.

It's no accident that none of the traditional optical companies like Bausch & Lomb or Perkin-Elmer ever made it in the laser business. The only big company that managed to get a substantial amount of laser business was Hughes Aircraft. They make carbon dioxide lasers and a few other types of lasers, and I think they do a few million dollars' worth of business each year. But that's still small compared to companies like Spectra Physics, which began as a start-up company. There's just something about a big company that snuffs out the entrepreneurial spirit that's needed in a wholly new field.

> It's only very recently that a scientist could patent a living organism created by genetic engineering.

The only way big companies seem to be able to get into a new area that's fairly unrelated to their previous business is to merge with a company that's successful. But even in that case, the majority of those mergers result in failure. TRG was an example of what I'm talking about.

The merger with Control Data normally would have had a better chance at success than most mergers because Control Data itself was founded by a successful entrepreneur, William Norris.

The problem was that he had contradictory reasons for buying TRG. Norris wanted the glamour of a laser company as part of his stable of companies, and he also wanted to work that technology into computers. He wanted TRG to help the company remain a leader of new technology in that area. His other requirement, however, was that TRG continue to make money.

Those last two requirements are contradictory. If you're going to spend time internally developing laser applications for the computer world, you can't be out there making money. The fact that we had to show a profit and do these other things at the same time was impossible. TRG had been making money every year since its inception, up until its merger with Control Data in 1965. After that, it never made any money again. The financial climate for research and development work got steadily worse in the late 1960s, and in 1970, Control Data liquidated its entire aerospace division, which included TRG. I had already left the company in 1967.

INTERVIEWER: *Where did you go after you left TRG?*

GOULD: I left to become a professor at the Polytechnic Institute of New York in Brooklyn. I took five people with me from the laser research lab at TRG, and we started a whole department there. Unfortunately, we started in an era when the previously lavish funding for research and development by the government began to go downhill.

The Polytechnic Institute did not have a big endowment, and for graduate students to have any funds for their research, professors had to get R and D contracts, which were getting harder to come by. At the same time, the number of science and engineering students declined, which meant that there was also a decline in tuition income. Economies were required all around, more work was required from everybody, and I just got sick of it.

In 1973, I left to form Optelecom with Bill Culver, who's been a friend of mine since 1959. That company was devoted primarily to optical communications—both fiber optics and through-the-air links. It was modestly successful, and I retired about two years ago [1985].

INTERVIEWER: *Are small companies better at turning inventions and ideas into successful products because of their flexibility?*

GOULD: Starting up and building little companies requires an entrepreneurial drive, an alertness, and an adeptness that you just don't find in big companies. I'm not saying that there aren't individuals in those companies who can think of important ideas and inventions; the problem is that most big companies are unable to make a business out of those ideas.

A few wise people in some of the larger corporations are beginning to understand that. They know they can't found a new company under the aegis of the big company, so they sponsor entrepreneurial types who want to start a company of their own, and then they acquire it after it has been built up. A perfect example of this would be Intel [Development Corporation], or rather its predecessor, Fairchild Semiconductor.

INTERVIEWER: *The "traitorous eight" who left Bill Shockley?**

GOULD: That's right. I happen to know Bob Noyce** because he was a roommate of one of the people I worked with at TRG.

Noyce realized that Bill Shockley wasn't going to go anywhere in the semiconductor business because he knew nothing about business; he was only in it for the ego. So, Noyce decided to gather a bunch of guys from Shockley's company and start their own semiconductor company. He went around to various people with his idea and eventually went to Sherman Fairchild. He put on a big presentation for Fairchild, and after an hour or two Fairchild said, "Stop talking to me! I don't want to hear any more! I'll tell you what I'll do: I'll give you a million dollars to start this company, and the only proviso is that I get to buy it at ten times its earnings in five years." And that's what happened. In five years, it was already a multimillion-dollar company. That semiconductor division turned out to be the biggest money-winner of Fairchild's whole group of companies.

INTERVIEWER: *An inventor obviously can't start a company at a government lab, but there are a tremendous amount of resources at government facilities like Brookhaven National Laboratories or Los Alamos. What do you think of a government lab as a workplace for an inventor? Are there too many restrictions and too much red tape?*

GOULD: There are certainly times of emergency when the government can attract the best people to government projects, as it did with radar development and the A-bomb project. But those top people don't stay with the government, and I think it's because of all the dead weight created by all that red tape. Government regulations are even worse than industrial lab regulations at deadening invention, and they certainly deaden entrepreneurship.

Big projects can get done in government research labs, but you don't see much inventiveness. The government does, however, try to hire people to be inventive. And that's why you see these "Beltway Bandit"† companies like Optelecom, which I started, doing contract research and development work for the government.

---

* Nobel Prize-winner who, in 1955, founded Shockley Semiconductor in Palo Alto, California.
** Then-president of Intel Development Corporation and co-inventor of the integrated circuit.
† High-tech firms, usually located on the "Beltway" (freeway circling Washington, D.C.), that do consulting for the government, usually on defense issues.

INTERVIEWER: *What is the best environment for an inventor?*

GOULD: Universities are the best place. But then there are universities and there are universities. And if you're stuck in a university that doesn't have a big endowment and can't fund professorial chairs with a research budget, you're stuck with the specter of having to find funding on your own. You can spend half your time doing that—as I know from the time I spent at Brooklyn Polytechnic.

But at places that do have endowed chairs—or in state universities like [the University of California at] Berkeley with big budgets—there's freedom for an inventor. It's not easy to get into those places. You have to follow the academic track carefully and make a name for yourself before you can get that kind of subsidy. In that setting, however, an inventor can work on inventions that are fundamentally new and different.

INTERVIEWER: *Looking back, do you regret leaving Columbia instead of establishing yourself as a scientist in the academic world?*

GOULD: There is something that distinguishes inventors from scientists. A lot of important inventions are made by scientists, but there's a distinction. For me—and

> *One hysterical person called me up and said, "People are running up and down Connecticut Avenue shooting people with lasers! You've got to do something about it!"*

I think for many other inventors—an invention has to be useful or important to have appeal.

On the other hand, the usual goal for scientists is to understand things better and create knowledge. An invention's effect on the economics of an industry or a country doesn't have much appeal to scientists. I don't mean to put down science; we couldn't do anything without it. But it wasn't for me. I was never interested enough in basic scientific research to want to stay with it for the rest of my life. I was more interested in inventions and having that flavor of importance in what I was doing.

INTERVIEWER: *What do you consider a great invention?*

GOULD: A great invention is one you don't quite see. You can't work on this type of invention as you would other inventions because you don't even know what the problem is.

Most inventions are discovered by problem-solving. Millions of ordinary problems can be solved just by grappling with them and thinking about them. However, I don't think this approach leads to the most fundamental and important inventions. You can get close to what I consider a great invention through problem-solving, especially with a team of people, but great inventions can really only happen when someone with a particular range of knowledge is playing around. And often, the applications of a great invention may not be apparent for several years.

The light bulb, for example, was certainly an important invention, but its applications were obvious. The triode is a better example of what I'm talking about. It was invented in 1910, but it took years before a vacuum tube was ever sold commercially. Nobody knew what to do with them. They just knew that a triode provided a wonderful way to control a current with an electrical signal instead of a mechanical switch.

Like the triode, the laser is also a very basic and important invention. But for the first five years or so of its life, there was a saying that the laser was "a solution in search of a problem."

INTERVIEWER: *Has the range of knowledge in science become so great that important inventions of the future will be made by groups and teams of people?*

GOULD: It's certainly true that the amount of knowledge in almost any field of science is getting enormous, and that tends to support the idea of teams. But there are still a few areas where I can imagine big breakthroughs coming about through the work of one or two individuals. I think it's likely to happen in a field like genetics where individuals work on their own or with a couple of assistants. There's lots and lots of room for development in that field.

INTERVIEWER: *Some people argue that genetic engineering isn't really inventing.*

GOULD: One reason for that attitude may be that it's only very recently that a scientist could patent a living organism created by genetic engineering. But that kind of work is certainly an invention in my book.

I guess people have this old-fashioned view that if you're not like Edison, you're not an inventor. Well, the nature of invention basically hasn't changed, but the kinds of things you work with are changing all the time.

Inventing a new algorithm for a computer? Is that inventing? If you go way back to Samuel Morse, he invented the first digital transmission a long time before there were any computers. But only relatively recently has it been possible to copyright a computer program, yet I think it takes a lot of creativity to write a program.

INTERVIEWER: *Would you use the word inventor to describe someone like Einstein?*

GOULD: People like Einstein are very creative, but I would hesitate to use the word inventor to describe him. However, his breakthroughs in thought and the theories he developed to fit the contradictory experimental results of his day are monumental acts of creativity on the highest level.

With respect to the laser, there's a term in his equations that predicts the process that is known today as the stimulated emission of light. It was known at the time that there was spontaneous emission of light and absorption of light. It was not known that there was an inverse of the absorption process or that stimulated emission had to exist.

In his paper, however, Einstein proved that there had to be this process of stimulated emission. He was able to show that all the light inside a container at equilibrium—a red-hot one with absorption and emission processes going on all the time—would disappear in a flash without stimulated emission. Absorption would dominate without stimulated emission. So, to balance out the known forces of spontaneous emission of light and absorption of light with what was observed in nature, it was necessary to have another term in the equation. It was a very short and very logical paper, but it was many years later before it was used in the maser principle. But even though Einstein only wrote one paper on the subject, he said it all.

INTERVIEWER: *Do you think inventors have any common traits? What do you think it takes to be an inventor?*

GOULD: A lot of people think they've invented something when they've *thought* of something to invent. "Wouldn't it be nice if we had this? Oh! I've invented something!"

All this publicity I've had with the laser has produced some unpleasant side effects. One is the number of people who call up and want help with their inventions. It's bothersome that many people believe that they have a perfect right to all my time.

Some really wild things have come to my attention. I remember one hysterical person called me up and said, "People are running up and down

Connecticut Avenue shooting people with lasers! You've got to do something about it!" Another time, a guy wrote me a letter asking me to help him
with his invention: He wanted to use lasers to drill holes through icebergs
and attach chains to them to tow them to Saudi Arabia. Well, that's not an
invention!

As far as being a successful inventor is concerned, I think an important characteristic is being self-critical. You have to weed out all the aspects
of an idea that aren't going to work or reject the entire idea in favor of some
new idea. You have to be able to look criti-
cally at what you've thought up and refine
it to only those things that work.

For the first five years or so of its life, there was a saying that the laser was "a solution in search of a problem."

It's somewhat like art—like painting
or writing a musical composition. If you're
just going to slap something on a canvas,
no criticality is involved. Look at Jackson
Pollock. Even in his work there has to be
some kind of self-criticism at work. A
painting may not be designed to work like
a mechanical invention or an electrical invention, but it has to "work" for the people
who look at it.

INTERVIEWER: *But can someone be too self-critical to invent?*

GOULD: I've met people at both extremes. It's true that if you're too
self-critical, nothing will ever get a chance to flourish. Some professors I've
known are so well trained in the art of being rigorous that they never have
an original idea in their lives. Their ideas never get a chance to sprout
amidst all the rocks of the rigor. They are only good at taking someone
else's ideas and looking at them very critically.

I think you have to have the right balance between self-criticism and
creativity. You have to be able to reject the ninety-nine percent of your ideas
that aren't any good—and do it before you even become conscious of
them—without suppressing any of the creative activity going on in your
mind. At least that's how I see myself when I compare myself to people who
haven't been successful inventors.

Another thing I think an inventor has to have is confidence. I think

Jacob Rabinow has this to a T. He has no doubt that if he keeps working on a problem long enough he's going to come up with a neat answer.

INTERVIEWER: *Can anyone be an inventor?*

GOULD: I think you can probably look into the background of any inventor and find that somebody somewhere stimulated them and got them to think.

To develop self-criticism without extinguishing creativity, someone has to pat you on the back when you do something right. You have to be encouraged to try things even if they don't work. That proper balance between creativity and criticism may have to be established way, way back as an emotional set.

It may not be universally true, but the advantage of growing up in a family where there is stimulation is tremendous. Imagine what your limitations would be if you grew up in a family that didn't read and had no books in the house. Suppose you didn't even learn to read until you were in the seventh grade—what a drag that would be. You wouldn't even imagine going to college or anything like that.

INTERVIEWER: *Did you grow up inventing?*

GOULD: My mother was a mechanical person even though she didn't have any formal training, and when I was three years old, she bought an Erector Set for me. She used to put various things together with it, and I used to take them apart. By the next year, I was putting them together and leaving them for her to take apart.

I also went through all those childhood phases of fixing clocks for people and so on. It was just in my blood. My brothers and I were always building and moving towards inventing.

INTERVIEWER: *This is probably something the Titans asked Prometheus, but how concerned should an inventor be about the effects of an invention? You worked on the Manhattan Project during the Second World War, for example, and the laser is now being considered as a weapon as well. Have you ever had any reservations about those uses of your invention?*

GOULD: Well, I take a pragmatic view of that. If some new invention can be used for a new military application, it's going to be done somewhere. Therefore, we damn well want to be first. I don't have any qualms about that. I don't normally invent for military purposes, although I have done contract R and D that relates to the military. I accept that, and I have no problem with it if the United States can do it first.

As far as lasers and Star Wars are concerned, that Star Wars idea goes back a long way. It goes back to 1959, when TRG's proposal to the Defense Advanced Research Projects Agency [DARPA] was received with such open arms. All those colonels got really excited when they thought about all those photon bullets (laughs).

My reaction to that, as well as the reactions of many other physicists, was as follows:

The trouble with light, no matter how concentrated it is, is that it's a wave phenomenon and diffraction will occur. You may be able to do a lot better at reducing the effects of diffraction with a laser beam than with something like a focused arc lamp, but it's still going to spread out. For a beam weapon, you'd really like to have extremely short waves so that the diffraction effects would be small.

Now, how can we develop extremely short waves? There are, you know, matter waves. Solid particles and matter also have wave properties, and they can be diffracted, but their waves are very small. In fact, why not just make a little cylinder with a point on the end of it that's made up of those tiny matter waves? Then, it wouldn't spread out at all, at least not by anything measurable. Why not make...a bullet! (Laughs.)

My attitude has been that a bullet or a missile is the best weapon to build if you want to hit a target at a long distance and keep the energy concentrated. However, I was not averse to receiving funding from DARPA because I could see plenty of good applications for lasers in the military. But not that one. The military's been very persistent about laser weapons, and eventually they may have something. But it didn't start out being the right sort of thing, and it's still not very good.

INTERVIEWER: *I'm amazed by the fact that you were unable to get security clearance to work on TRG's laser contracts with DARPA—especially when the whole project was based on your ideas. Although researchers working on the project were forbidden to tell you what they were working on, they were allowed to ask you questions. It's a rather enigmatic way of doing research. Do you think it contributed to TRG's disappointing performance on laser development?*

GOULD: I think that problem could be blamed for the fact that TRG did not develop the first laser—and for the fact that TRG was not able to make as much of a commercial business as they might have otherwise. Over the next several years, Spectra Physics was started and became very successful. Ted Maiman started the Korad Corporation, and it became a reasonably successful company until it was ruined by Union Carbide—in the way that big companies often squash the little treasures that they buy up (laughs).

There were no fewer than four different companies spawned by people from TRG. So, one can't say that the project was of no use. But it could have been much more important than it was.

Another problem was that the people running the project wasted money doing things they shouldn't have been doing. They simply weren't smart in what they tried to do. For example, a good deal of that original grant was spent learning how to grow crystals to serve as hosts for different laser materials. Instead of learning how to build lasers, they were learning how to grow crystals. A big opportunity was lost or minimized.

INTERVIEWER: When did your interference* cases start?

GOULD: The interference cases actually took place in the 1960s, when the patents were owned by TRG and Control Data. The company paid for those cases up until 1970.

There were a total of five interferences. An interference can take a long time because once the case has been heard by the Patent Office Board of Appeals, it can be appealed up and into the federal court system. That appeal process can go on for five or six years.

My case took longer because I had five. One was with Schawlow and Townes over the use of a Fabry–Perot resonator in a laser. The second was over the Q switch. The third interference was over gas-discharge laser oscillators. The fourth was with Irwin Wieder over the optically pumped laser oscillator. And the fifth was over my Brewster-angle invention with two people at Bell Labs.

INTERVIEWER: What happened to your patents when Control Data decided to liquidate TRG?

GOULD: Because I had come to TRG with these laser ideas and because of my original agreement, I retained some rights. Among other things, the company couldn't sell any patents separately from the laser business. When Control Data decided to liquidate TRG's business, they located a buyer, a former TRG employee who went on to start Hadron. He wanted the laser

---

* An action instituted by the Patent Office when the patent applications of two different inventors overlap.

business, but he didn't want the patents because he didn't have the money to do what was necessary for them.

Because of my original agreement, Control Data could not sell the laser business to Hadron unless something could be done about the patents. One day, one of Control Data's vice presidents called me up and said, "Hey, make us an offer!" I was somewhat at a loss as to what kind of offer to make. I talked to a lawyer and friend of mine, who was in Paris at the time, and he said, "I'll tell you what....Offer them one dollar and ten percent of everything you ever make from those patents...up to $100,000." (Laughs.) Control Data said, "Sold!" Many years later, I had the pleasure of going to lunch with a vice president of Control Data and handing him a check for $100,000 and saying, "It could have been $200,000."

INTERVIEWER: *Were the interferences resolved when you bought the patents back from Control Data in 1970?*

GOULD: Actually, the last one was not completed until 1973. Because I hadn't found anyone to work with and didn't have enough money of my own, I had to drop one of the interferences that I think I could have won— the one with Bennett and Javan on the gas-discharge laser. Eventually, I raised money by selling a part of my interest in the patents to Patlex.

After that last interference was finished in 1973, my patent application had to go back to the examiner for sorting out, and that took a lot more effort. When the examiner is reviewing your claims, you have to keep interacting with the Patent Office while your lawyers are writing briefs. Eventually, the examiner decided that my patent should be divided into six different applications. It wasn't until 1977 that the first of those patents was actually allowed and issued. That meant that in 1977 I had reached the point where I could start suing people for infringement.

INTERVIEWER: *So, seventeen years after your original patent application, you were finally able to start licensing.*

GOULD: But nobody was about to take a license without a fight. What was, and still is, required was a win that was credible to the whole industry. When that happens—or maybe it's already happened—then most everybody will take a license.

Control Laser elected itself the first company to be sued by immediately announcing that it was going to band together with the other laser companies and fight my patent claims. But they have been slippery, and the case has still not gone to trial.

In 1982, a law was passed by Congress that allows inventors or other individuals to ask the Patent Office to reexamine their patents to determine whether or not any prior art exists that applies to their inventions. The law was designed to help inventors cope with the big cost of patent litigations. Presumably, once the Patent Office had reaffirmed a patent, an inventor could license an invention without having to go through infringement suits.

Somewhat mysteriously, however, Control Laser, General Motors, and AT&T applied to have the same patents reexamined: my patent on the optically pumped laser amplifier and my patent on industrial applications of the laser. General Motors put together a book which was more than a foot thick; it detailed all the prior art they found that had not been looked at by the previous examiner. Part of that art included Archimedes' use of a mirror to focus light on a ship and set it afire.

From that point, it took four years. We then took the case to the Patent Office Board of Appeals, and they reversed the examiner's decision and reaffirmed the patents.

But when that patent was reaffirmed by the Patent Office Board of Appeals in a case against General Motors and AT&T—and believe me, those companies poured plenty of money into that case—it was a stunning victory. After that, nobody in their right mind would resist taking a license. But then, Control Laser is not in its right mind.

Our trial with them will begin in September of 1987. If we win, that will probably be one of the last cases. And after that, most people will probably sign up. Some people already have signed up. But it wasn't until this past year [1986] that royalties started to come in.

INTERVIEWER: It took twenty-seven years for you to be in a position to collect royalties on your patents. Would you like to see any changes in the patent system?

GOULD: I think you have to be careful in proposing any changes so that you don't make things any worse than they are. Obviously, something is wrong with the system if it takes twenty-seven years to get to this stage. However, I can think of some little changes that could be made to improve things.

For example, the five interferences were all sequential, which means that it took fourteen years to get to the end of that process. Whatever is left of your patent after that—if you've won a couple of claims—goes back to the examiner, and he starts all over again trying to sort out what claims you should and shouldn't get. If they had run all my interferences concurrently, it would have taken only three or four years. That's one obvious improvement that could have been made. Not every patent gets into an interference case, however, so that wouldn't affect most inventors.

Also, why should it take so long for even one interference to get done? I guess I can't complain that it takes so long in the Patent Office if, in fact, it takes just as long or longer to get through the courts once you get there.

What I hope will be my last big trial is scheduled to begin in September of 1987 against Control Laser. That suit was filed in 1977. It's not only the Patent Office that takes a long time if there's anything important involved. You can perhaps see why it takes a long time for an antitrust suit against AT&T or IBM to wend its way through the courts, but actually, those cases were finished in a considerably shorter time than mine.

There's something ponderous about our legal system, and the worst aspect of it to me is the amount it costs. An individual inventor could never pay for the costs of all the proceedings I've gone through—or even one of them. After it gets to trial, a full-blown case costs a quarter of a million dollars. I was lucky that I was able to team up with people who could raise that kind of money and had the talents to put it to use. It costs an arm and a leg to get justice in our court system. The average person can't do it, so full justice is not open to him.

INTERVIEWER: *So, do you think your problems with the patent system are unique, or are others going through the same struggle?*

GOULD: After the royalties began coming in on the laser patents, Dick Samuel, the president of Patlex, said, "Well, this looks real good. I think we can build this company on the Gordon Goulds of this world. We'll go in there and fight the battles for them and do the licensing." When they made a search, they didn't come up with anyone. The only other inventor in a comparable situation was a guy who had invented a special kind of concrete reinforcing.

Actually, very few situations are like mine. It's not because I'm anyone special, but because of the peculiar history of my patents on the laser and the fact that I was able to get my patents back from Control Data. Whether they're important or not, most patents are usually owned by a corporation. To have an inventor receive a batch of patents from a corporation because of a peculiar history of agreements is practically unheard of.

HAROLD ROSEN

*I*N 1964, television viewers were able to watch the Olympic Games live from Tokyo, Japan, via satellite—television's first continuous satellite broadcast. It was not so long ago that the words "live via satellite" were regularly flashed across TV screens during satellite broadcasts. Today, these broadcasts are taken for granted. Satellites are so commonplace that it is hard to imagine worldwide communication without them.

The key to satellite communications is the geosynchronous satellite—a satellite whose orbit around the earth is synchronized with the earth's rotation so that it stays in a fixed position relative to the earth. Like the manned space program, developing the world's first geosynchronous satellite required a team of people. The idea for a spin-stabilized satellite, however, was first conceived by Harold A. Rosen, now a vice president of Engineering for the Space and Communications Group of Hughes Aircraft.

In 1957, Rosen and his colleagues in Hughes' radar division were asked to look into new projects. When Sputnik was launched, Rosen began thinking about communication satellites. Others, of course, were thinking about the same thing and the idea of a geosynchronous satellite was not new; as early as 1945, the well-known science fiction writer Arthur C. Clarke outlined the benefits of a geosynchronous communications satellite.

In retrospect, Rosen's solution for the geosynchronous satellite is wonderfully simple. Other researchers had come up with complex designs that worked fine on paper, but were too heavy for the launch vehicles of the early 1960s. Rosen's approach was to use spin-stabilization—the same rotational force that keeps a football quarterback's spiral passes or the spinning artillery shell from a rifled gun on target—to *hold the satellite on course. The inherent stability of the system, coupled with improvements in the satellite's control and communication systems by Rosen and his colleagues, led to a geosynchronous satellite small enough to be launched into orbit: Syncom I.*

Not everyone was impressed. After a demonstration of Syncom's capabilities from atop the Eiffel Tower during the 1961 Paris Air Show, cynics wryly noted that the Eiffel Tower was "as high as it will ever get." Two years later, however, the first successful Syncom satellite, Syncom II, went into service as an international telephone link. In 1964, Syncom III provided the first continuous transoceanic television broadcast, and Intelsat—the International Telecommunications Satellite Consortium—was established in the same year. Eight years later, Intelsat had eighty-three member nations and more than eighty earth stations. By 1984 the limitless expanse of space was so crowded with satellites that the allocation of "parking spaces" on the 22,300-mile-high geostationary orbit had become an international political issue.

Today, satellites provide a link for everything from commercial television to lifesaving medical information. Instantaneous worldwide communication is possible via satellite; it has made the world a smaller place.

Harold Rosen was born in New Orleans, Louisiana, in 1926. He received a bachelor's degree in electrical engineering from Tulane University in 1947 and his master's and doctorate degrees from the California Institute of Technology in 1948 and 1951.

He joined Hughes Aircraft Company in 1956 and did his first work in the development of antiaircraft missiles, fire control systems, and radar. He has received worldwide recognition for his conception of the geosynchronous satellite. In 1976 he was awarded the L. M. Ericson Prize in International Communication, presented by the King of Sweden. In 1982 the Institute of Electrical and Electronic Engineers awarded him the Alexander Graham Bell Medal for "pioneering contributions to, and leadership in, geostationary communication satellites." In 1985 he received the National Medal of Technology, presented by President Ronald Reagan.

INTERVIEWER: *How important was the competition between Russia and the United States when it came to actually developing the first geosynchronous satellite? Did the fact that the Russians beat the United States into space with the first satellite in 1957 push the program along?*

ROSEN: Well, that was very important. That's actually what got me started. My colleagues, Tom Hudspeth and Don Williams, and I were all in Hughes' radar department at the time and had been charged to look into advanced communications systems and a new project. When the Russians launched *Sputnik* in October of 1957, we decided to look for a space project, and this is what came out of it.

INTERVIEWER: *How did you come up with the idea of a spin-stabilized satellite? Did it occur to you in a flash or did the idea develop over several months?*

ROSEN: I quickly decided that I would like to work on a communications satellite and that, furthermore, it should be a geostationary satellite. I ruminated about the idea of a geostationary satellite for a year or two before this spin-stabilized configuration occurred to me.

INTERVIEWER: *How did that particular idea develop?*

ROSEN: The boosters we had available at the time were relatively small, and to get a satellite into geostationary orbit the satellite also had to be very small. I felt geostationary orbit was the only practical orbit for communications satellites, although there was controversy at the time.

> *I thought it was very difficult to get the support we needed to get the thing going. But looking back… it actually happened pretty fast, although at the time it seemed like an eternity.*

I also noticed what others were trying to do to solve the same problem. The government-sponsored program, for example, had such cumbersome communication and control systems that their satellite was too heavy to be launched by any available booster. And even if it could have been launched, it wouldn't have lasted long enough to be useful.

But they proceeded with it anyway and tried to develop a booster powerful enough to get it into orbit. It seemed to me that it would be easy to do a lot better than that configuration. So, that project was kind of a good negative example.

In order to make the satellite small I had to consider all the functions it had to perform: It had to communicate, it had to have an antenna beam that reached and encompassed the earth, and it had to have a power system and a control system.

It occurred to me that the easiest way to achieve all those objectives in a lightweight configuration would be to use a spinning body with solar cells around its periphery, with an antenna pattern that was a figure of revolution so that it always encompassed the earth as the satellite spun, and with a control system that took advantage of the spin—using spin-phased impulses—so that fewer thrusters would be required. If the control system could be designed to fire at different times during the revolution of the satellite, one thruster could take the place of two or more.

Those were the elements of the spin-stabilized satellite that really got us started.

INTERVIEWER: *Did all those ideas evolve together?*

ROSEN: Well, this arrangement that I mentioned using spin stabilization, the antenna pattern, solar cells, and spin-phased impulses (to control the velocity and the orbital plane) all came together at once.

But all those elements have been evolving since then. At the time we were developing the *Syncom* communications satellite, the control system really got a big boost from Don Williams. The control system evolved rather slowly. In the beginning we didn't know that attitude control would be required continuously throughout the life of the satellite. We thought that it would be satisfactory to set it spinning at the right attitude when it was put into orbit.

But when we had a chance to look at it, we could see that the solar radiation pressure would cause it to precess slowly. We also discovered that the gravitational effects of the earth and sun and moon would require continuous control as well. We had thought that if we positioned it properly initially, the satellite would just stay there.

First I thought I would use spin-phased impulses—"bullets"—to control the initial orbits. That evolved into a gaseous system that would be more continuous, and then into a liquid system. Finally, we went to an arrangement of jets that required only two jets to do all the attitude and velocity control needed by the satellite.

The antenna stayed the way it was for quite a while, until we were able to advance to a pencil-beam antenna that had more directivity and gain. That, however, had to be de-spun relative to the spinning satellite so that even though the satellite was spinning, the antenna was in a fixed position relative to the earth. It was a major advance when we got to that.

INTERVIEWER: *Science fiction writer Arthur C. Clarke proposed a geosynchronous satellite in the 1940s. A number of people credit him with having a tremendous influence on the direction and goals of space exploration. Were you at all influenced by his proposals?*

ROSEN: It was in discussions with some of my colleagues here at Hughes that I first heard about the geostationary orbit, and they referred me to Arthur C. Clarke.

He had a visionary description of it from many years earlier. It was written in 1945. He thought it would be a pretty great idea, but at that time the technology didn't exist for accomplishing it, and he didn't know how to power it. I think his version, for example, had men in it to repair the tubes and the repeater. It wasn't clear how that was going to be accomplished.

It was extremely ambitious—but it was visionary and extremely interesting. That's where I first heard about the properties of a geostationary satellite.

INTERVIEWER: *How about your idea of spin-stabilization? Did any part of your background or training lead you to look into that?*

ROSEN: In a physics class at Cal Tech [California Institute of Technology] I had a teacher—a Nobel Prize winner, in fact—named Carl Anderson. He had discovered the positron. When we were studying dynamics, I asked him if he could explain in a simple way the effectiveness of spinning in stabilizing such objects as footballs in a spiral pass and shells coming out of a big gun with rifling in it. We kind of worked it out together in class.

If you compare the effects of an external force on a body that's spinning and one that's not spinning—say, you apply a torque for a certain time and see how much the spinning body will precess and compare that to the attitude change in a nonspinning body—you get a simple result.

The ratio of motion can be expressed like this: The disturbance to the spinning body is down by a factor equal to the angle that the spinning body spins through during the time that the torque is applied.

So, if you slowly apply a torque over a time during which the spinning body makes, say, 100 revolutions—that would be 628 radians of turn—its motions are down by 628 times those of the nonspinning body with the same mass properties.

So, that's why football quarterbacks spiral their passes and navy guns spin their shells. And that's why we started out with a spinning satellite. It was an easy way of getting a lot of stability over long periods of time. At the time it was the simplest and only practical way of doing it.

INTERVIEWER: *How important were other people's ideas to* Syncom II?

ROSEN: They were very important. Tom Hudspeth, whom I'm still working with very closely, designed a communications repeater that was light enough to fit in the small spacecraft of the time. It was really a tour de force for its time, because it was very difficult to do with the components then available. That was in 1960—we started work in 1959.

> *I'm an engineer who has a number of inventions to his credit.*

It was also difficult to make solid-state microwave receivers at the time, but we were able to do it. Don Williams, as I mentioned earlier, worked with me continuously on the control and guidance system.

We also had to design a traveling-wave tube that was suitable for space applications. It had to be light and rugged. That was originally designed by Dr. John Mendel, who's still with us.

INTERVIEWER: *With some inventions it seems that all its parts come together: the right people working together, the right technology available, and so on. Do you think* Syncom II *could have been invented somewhere else? Were there a lot of people following close behind?*

ROSEN: I'm not saying it couldn't have happened elsewhere, but it would have taken a rare combination of talents.

For example, we had John Mendel, who knew how to make a lightweight, rugged traveling-wave tube suitable for space. Not very many people in the country could have done that.

There was also the very important element of building a lightweight repeater—ours had a solid-state receiver and the traveling-wave tube transmitter. The government was making its repeater using triodes. Triodes were discovered or invented by De Forest* in 1906. They were so inefficient

---

* Lee De Forest (1873–1961) was an American inventor and pioneer of radio whose inventions include the audion and the four-electrode valve.

SYNCOM I GENERAL ARRANGEMENT

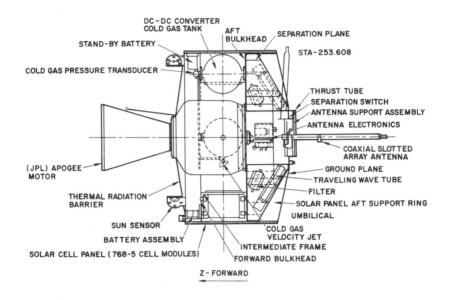

Z - FORWARD

SECTION A-A

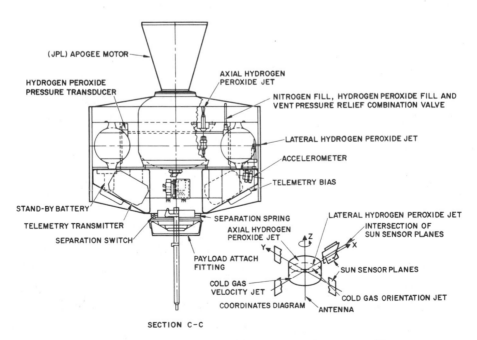

SECTION C-C

Engineering drawings of the Syncom I *geosynchronous satellite.*

that they required a huge power and thermal system to support them. The traveling-wave tube was much lighter and more efficient and was a major element in being able to make our system small. If Mendel's version of the traveling-wave tube had not been around, we might not have been able to design the repeater so small.

Don Williams was a prize. There were not too many like him in the world, and Tom Hudspeth is a brilliant engineer. I don't know. We had a very unusual collection of people.

INTERVIEWER: *A number of inventors I've talked to prefer working with a small company or independently. Obviously the geosynchronous satellite would have been difficult, if not impossible, for a small company or individual to do. Even so, what were some of the pluses and minuses of working on it at a large corporation like Hughes?*

ROSEN: The plus was that we had all the necessary skills available. We could find people who were experts in almost anything we could think of. The diversity of talent was an essential requirement.

I'm not sure it was a minus, but at the time I thought it was very difficult to get the support we needed to get the thing going. But looking back on it from my mature age (laughs), I can see it actually happened pretty fast, although at the time it seemed like an eternity.

INTERVIEWER: *Was federal or military funding of much importance when it came to getting the* Syncom *project off the ground?*

ROSEN: As far as the satellite was concerned, the initial money came from Hughes' own internal research and development program. When it came to going from prototype to actual flight, the basic money came from NASA with some help from the Department of Defense. I would say our prime contract was with NASA.

I think it would have been hard to develop *Syncom* as a private venture. I had some thoughts of trying—in fact, I tried to interest the company in going the whole way as a commercial venture—but that was too much.

INTERVIEWER: *Did you think there would be less government bureaucracy to deal with if the company funded it?*

ROSEN: I was getting discouraged trying to get government support for it. I thought that if Hughes actually put up the first satellite we could start a commercial operation like *Comsat,* which did eventually pay for its development through proceeds. As a matter of fact, AT&T—Bell Labs—put up a communications satellite a year before *Syncom II* called *Telstar*, which was the first to transmit television. This satellite was in a low orbit, however, and the transmissions were intermittent rather than continuous. This project was paid for by AT&T.

INTERVIEWER: *What was the turning point that finally interested the government in the project?*

ROSEN: In my view it was a visit by the director of Defense Research and Engineering, John Rubel, who had previously worked here. He knew us, and he knew the government program, which happened to be his responsibility at the time. He could see what bad shape it was in, costing them hundreds of millions of dollars, and he didn't see how it would ever get to its final resolution.

Technical training or creativity? I don't know. In my experience it has been a mixture of the two.

He was here on a visit to look at other things, and we showed him our geosynchronous *Syncom* prototype. He caught on right away, and to him it looked like it might be a way out of his problem. So, he became a strong advocate of it—and he also happened to be sitting on a joint NASA–Department of Defense committee set up to prevent duplication in space efforts.

NASA and the Department of Defense eventually worked out a jointly supported program where NASA had the lead in satellite development. That happened in the summer of 1961.

INTERVIEWER: *Was it a big setback to the program when* Syncom I *exploded before making it into final orbit?*

ROSEN: That was a terrible blow. That was a crushing blow. After all those years of effort! We started in the summer of 1959, and after three and a half years of struggle—which seemed like an awfully long time—all had come to naught. And it got some very bad press.

But we recovered in a short time. That was in February, and it took us five months after that to get *Syncom II* up in orbit.

INTERVIEWER: *Did you feel like you had the problem licked and that this was just one unexpected small hurdle? Or was the explosion overwhelming?*

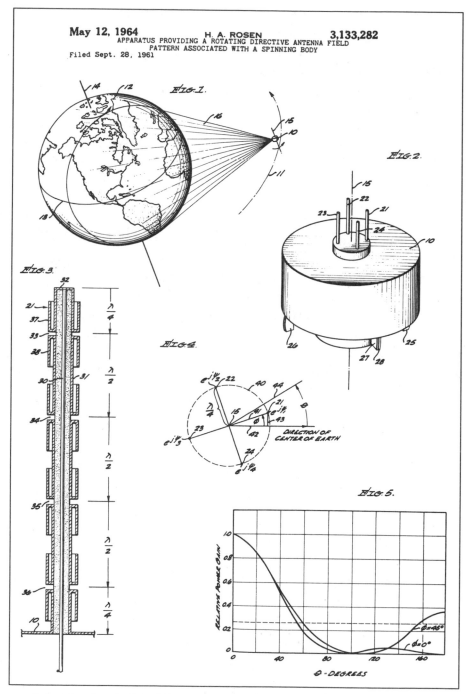

Patent drawings for Harold Rosen's directional antenna system designed for a spin-stabilized satellite (dated May 12, 1964).

ROSEN: I thought we had the problem licked and that it was a small hurdle. Everything's got to work, and in the case of *Syncom I* only ninety-nine percent worked. I knew we'd be able to get it. I was more concerned about the discouragement of others—our sponsors and such.

We were able to overcome the problem eventually. The launch was just more dramatic when it worked. Circus performers sometimes miss the first time on their most difficult stunts to let the audience know that it's really tough—so that when they do it, they get an even bigger round of applause. But we didn't lose *Syncom I* for that reason (laughs). It wasn't intentional.

INTERVIEWER: *It would have been an expensive publicity stunt.*

ROSEN: Yes. (Laughs.) But it had that result. When it worked, it was even more appreciated.

INTERVIEWER: *Did anyone encourage you to become an engineer?*

ROSEN: When I told my father I'd like to be an engineer, he really tried to dissuade me. At the time it was the middle of the depression, and I was a little kid. The only engineer he knew was someone he went to school with, and he was driving a taxicab in New Orleans. He thought that's where I would end up. But I felt that's what I wanted to do.

INTERVIEWER: *Do you think of yourself as an inventor or primarily as an engineer?*

ROSEN: I'm an engineer who has a number of inventions to his credit.

INTERVIEWER: *In your own experience with design and invention, what's been more important: creativity or technical training?*

ROSEN: Technical training or creativity? I don't know. In my experience it has been a mixture of the two.

There's more to technical training than just a formal education. I also had technical training at work. I worked at the Raytheon Company on some early guided missiles and learned various methods of controlling vehicles. I worked here at Hughes on radar, which uses a transmitter and receiver not unlike those found in a communications satellite.

But I don't know how to describe creativity or how to define it. It's just putting a bunch of ideas together.

INTERVIEWER: *What was your first invention?*

ROSEN: My first invention was for Raytheon; I don't think it was patented. It was an improved homing guidance system for the Sparrow missile that improved its effectiveness. It made the missile more versatile—made it work at a wider range of altitudes without reprogramming. I discovered a way of using the velocity information that was available in the homing radar in conjunction with accelerometer feedback to have an optimum approach to the target. I think that was my first biggie.

By the way, I did develop a desk model personal computer while I was at Raytheon. It wasn't a digital computer; it was an analog computer. I only used it in my work; I never promoted it.

INTERVIEWER: *Did you ever see potential in it for a personal computer market?*

ROSEN: (Laughs.) Oh no. It was for working on missile trajectories: homing and guidance trajectories. It had a bunch of electronic integrators, and the information was displayed on a strip chart. I could see the desired approach to the desired trajectory, and I could find the miss distance if it was a miss.

It involved having resistors and capacitors of the right values in the feedback loops of the integrators to assimilate these various functions. To do that, we had a bin of capacitors and resistors and a soldering iron attached to the machine. If I wanted to set up a problem, I just soldered in the resistors at the right terminals and the capacitors and let her go.

INTERVIEWER: *It wasn't particularly user-friendly?*

ROSEN: It sounds cumbersome, but it was a hell of a lot faster than programming a modern digital computer to solve the same problem. It would take me a few minutes to set up a problem that way; but to program a digital computer to do the same problem would probably take a few days.

INTERVIEWER: *Satellite communication has changed the world in a number of subtle and not so subtle ways. Did the pace of development or satellite applications ever surprise you?*

ROSEN: The pace of development didn't surprise me. When the first geosynchronous communications satellite went into operation, long-distance communications hadn't really advanced very far since Marconi.* I thought there was a lot of room for improvement in that particular field, and I thought satellites could play a major role, as they have.

---

* Guglielmo Marconi (1874–1937) was an Italian inventor and Nobel Prize winner (1909) who successfully experimented with wireless telegraphy in Italy and England and succeeded in sending signals across the Atlantic in 1901.

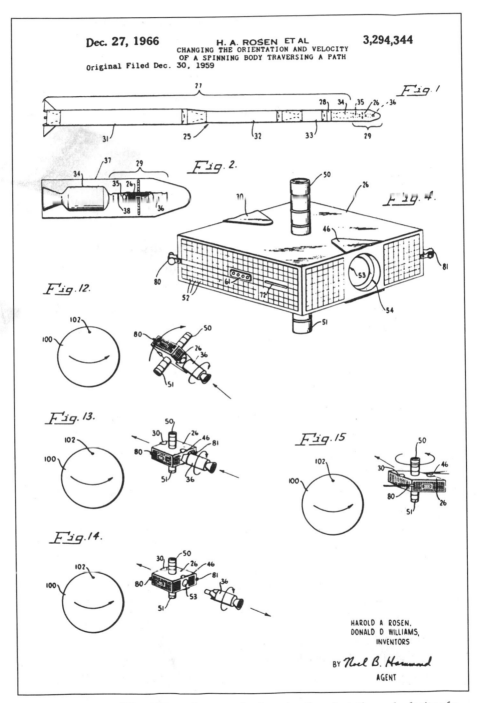

Dec. 27, 1966

H. A. ROSEN ET AL
CHANGING THE ORIENTATION AND VELOCITY
OF A SPINNING BODY TRAVERSING A PATH
Original Filed Dec. 30, 1959

3,294,344

HAROLD A ROSEN.
DONALD D WILLIAMS,
INVENTORS

BY *Noel B. Hammond*
AGENT

Patent drawings of Harold Rosen's system for changing the orientation and velocity of a spinning satellite (dated December 27, 1966).

I did not foresee the domestic applications, such as communications to extremely small terminals, that could serve a variety of purposes.

INTERVIEWER: *Did they fill a need or create one?*

ROSEN: Satellites filled a need. Long-range communications were pretty tough then. In the 1960s the first telephone cable had just been opened across the Atlantic, and it was working satisfactorily. Maybe forty channels of transatlantic communication were satisfactory. Before that there was only radio transmission, and it suffered the whims and vagaries of the ionosphere. You had to be reasonably lucky to get a path through when you wanted it. The transatlantic cable was a big advance.

> *When the first geosynchronous communications satellite went into operation, long-distance communications hadn't really advanced very far since Marconi.*

But even the first experimental communications satellite, called *Intelsat* or *Early Bird I*, had a lot more capacity than all the cables that had been laid up to that time. There was a big need. At that time cable provided only forty channels; now, tens of thousands of channels cross the oceans of the world.

Also telephony was expensive then. Dollars were worth something in 1960, and it cost a lot to make a transatlantic phone call—maybe $10 or $20, which would be equivalent to $100 or $200 today. Now, I can make a transoceanic call for a few dollars. That's not only due to the satellite, but also due to the improvements in cable that the satellite has helped accelerate.

INTERVIEWER: *Did you ever foresee live television broadcasts via satellite when* Syncom II *went up?*

ROSEN: As a matter of fact, I did. The Olympics in 1964 were the first major event televised transoceanically. *Syncom II* was not really designed with television in mind.

Our NASA and Department of Defense sponsors were so conservative and skeptical that they felt they wanted only one or two voice channels. That's all they thought it could accommodate. They had a bunch of communication experts who had grown up with ionospheric communications, which is kind of erratic, and they were used to putting very large margins on their communications links. The satellite had a lot more inherent capacity than they were calculating. They just hadn't gotten around to taking into account what a fine transmission link it was—free space, that is. It's ideal.

But on *Syncom III* we were able to make a few modifications and changes that permitted satisfactory television, using a specially constructed receiver for an earth terminal near Point Mugu, California, to receive it. We did what wasn't foreseen at the time. It was a very happy experience to watch the Olympic Games come in.

INTERVIEWER: *How do you feel about television? In the course of doing the interviews for this book I've heard many negative comments about it.*

ROSEN: Well, it's certainly capable of improving education. First of all, I'm a television fan. I love it. I have a giant screen; I watch football games, and I watch movies. With thirty channels to select from, there's often something I want to watch.

As far as educational television is concerned, I think the reason why it hasn't progressed as fast as it might—in terms of education in the general population—is that professional educators don't like it. They might see it as career-limiting. There is not a great deal of enthusiasm among professional educators to use television as a medium, where one educator could replace hundreds or thousands.

Private industry is using it a little more. IBM, for example, trains its field representatives with an interactive educational television system. Hughes Communications provides the networking services for them. I think educational television has progressed faster in that area than in the general population. I think it ought to be promoted as an educational medium for the general population.

INTERVIEWER: *Is there anything you'd like to invent?*

ROSEN: Before the space shuttle disaster I invented something that I really liked, but I was just in the early stages of being able to promote it. It was a reusable upper stage to the shuttle. It's something that NASA had dreamed about since the beginning of the shuttle program, but they couldn't find a satisfactory configuration. Along with some of my colleagues, I worked out a pretty good configuration that would take a communications satellite from the shuttle bay on the low-altitude shuttle orbit and transport it into the geostationary orbit. Then the stage would return it-self to the shuttle. It could be reused for many missions.

Now, there's no application for it because, by national policy, commer-cial satellites aren't going to be launched from the shuttle anymore.

Another invention was brought to me a few months ago, and I would like to find a way of working on it if we can finance it. This invention is a way of extending the life of satellites that are currently in orbit and operat-ing satisfactorily but running out of station-keeping fuel.

The idea is to bring up an orbital-control package that would attach it-self to the dying satellite and essentially rejuvenate it. The control package would be self-contained with its own power system, thrusters, telemetry system, fuel tanks, and command system. It would be economical because they could launch quite a few of these packages at a time so that they could service at least four satellites with one launch. It would be fun to develop and operate.

I keep hoping that someone will discover a lower-cost launch method, but I don't have any ideas on that subject—just a desire.

INTERVIEWER: *What about the push into space? Are there any frontiers you'd like to see the United States pursue?*

ROSEN: I don't think too much of the space station, if you want my view. I think there is a use for the things the space station is intended to do, but I don't think they're worth the cost. It's been sold to the public as a way of manufacturing crystals or pharmaceuticals or metallic compounds—something that's hard to do on earth—but I would be very much surprised if the value of those products could justify the cost of the enterprise.

However, one of the things they're talking about doing on the space station—and I don't know how much emphasis the idea's getting—could be valuable: as a refueling port for satellites or space probes that require higher-energy orbits than the space station.

I think there should be a low-altitude shuttle orbit refueling capability. We could transport fuel up at bulk rates once we have a heavy-lift vehicle—and some day we will. One terrific application would be to transport pro-pellent fuels into low-altitude orbit that could then be used to fuel a spacecraft intended for geostationary orbit or space probes going to Mars or

Jupiter. The spacecraft itself would be much cheaper to launch. Eighty percent of the mass of a spacecraft is the fuel required to go from the shuttle orbit into geostationary orbit. That could be done with or without the space station, but it's something I'd like to see in NASA's plans.

INTERVIEWER: *Is there anything else out there that interests you?*

ROSEN: I was really extremely pleased with *IRAS*, the multinational infrared astronomical satellite that mapped out the sky in the infrared region of the spectrum. And I'm looking forward to the space telescope, if we ever get to launch that. I'm in favor of an extensive exploratory mission to Mars.

I'd also like to see more effort spent on trying to receive signals from other civilizations. This isn't something you necessarily do in space. You can have the receiving equipment on earth. So far it's been only a token project on the part of NASA because they keep being joshed at by Senator Proxmire.

INTERVIEWER: *The "Golden Fleece Award"?*

ROSEN: Yes, he gave it the Golden Fleece Award, whereupon the proponents of the program gave him their "Flat Earth Society Award."

It gets very little attention. I think most people are afraid to promote it because they're afraid of being joshed at. But I think it would be fascinating—either answer is interesting. If we make an extremely sensitive listening station and if, after a long period, we do *not* end up with anything that sounds as though it comes from an intelligent civilization, that will tell us how rare we are—which is something I would like to know. If we ever did detect anything…I think that would be the most astounding and profound thing in the history of civilization.

NAT WYETH

*I*N A *family full of artists, Nat Wyeth decided to become an engineer. Given that decision and his family, it's not surprising that Wyeth also became an inventor.*

His father was Newell Convers Wyeth, the famous American artist and illustrator. Like his contemporary and fellow artist, Howard Pyle, N. C. Wyeth settled in the Brandywine Valley near Chadds Ford, Pennsylvania, to paint and to raise his family.

But while Nat's brother, Andrew, and his sisters, Henriette and Carolyn, studied art with their father, Nat disassembled clocks and used

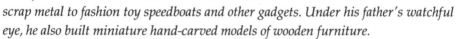

scrap metal to fashion toy speedboats and other gadgets. Under his father's watchful eye, he also built miniature hand-carved models of wooden furniture.

At the urging of an uncle who had been recruited by his father to look over engineering schools, Wyeth attended the University of Pennsylvania. Later, after working briefly for the Delco Company in Dayton, Ohio, a company started by the inventor Charles F. Kettering, Wyeth joined the Du Pont Corporation in Wilmington, Delaware.

Once his abilities as an inventor were realized, Wyeth was transferred to Du Pont's mechanical development laboratory. He spent the rest of his career in that division, designing everything from dynamite-cartridging machines to weaving and bonding machines for synthetic fibers.

His best-known invention is the ubiquitous plastic soda pop bottle. Curious as to why ordinary plastic bottles could not hold carbonated beverages, Wyeth perfected the process of cold-stretching plastic to make bottles that were both tough and lightweight.

Wyeth was a senior engineering fellow for the Du Pont Corporation before he retired in 1976. He has been selected as one of the University of Pennsylvania's distinguished alumni. We talked on a clear and sharp spring day at his home near Chadds Ford. The delicate and detailed wooden furniture he built as a child still fills a sideboard in his dining room.

INTERVIEWER: *Were you always interested in building and creating things? Did you ever think that you would be an inventor or an engineer?*

WYETH: I was always interested in this area. In fact, my father knew it too. He had a very good sense of what I wanted to do. He even decided to change my name because of it.

When I was a baby, my parents noticed that my hands or my mittens were always greasy when they brought me in from taking my nap in the baby carriage out on the front porch. "Where he's getting this dirt from in the coach?" they wondered. So they made a point of watching me.

They put me out on the porch to take a nap right after lunch one day, and they kept an eye on me. Then, they noticed me lean over the side of the coach, reach down, and move the wheels with my hands. I could move them against the brake just by turning them. I'd go from one end of the porch to the other and back again. I'd do this over and over again, and I guess I was always smart enough to end up where I was put originally, so no one had ever noticed it before.

My father said, "You know, I don't know why we should encumber this boy with an artist's name when he's undoubtedly going to be an engineer. Look at his understanding of those wheels and the way he's moving that coach!"

So, they changed my name. I was named after my father at first: Newell Convers Wyeth. They changed my name to Nathaniel Wyeth, which was my uncle's name. He was an engineer. How's that for—what do you call it—perception? I was only three or four years old, and my father said, "He's going to be an engineer." And by god, I was.

INTERVIEWER: *Did other people help you or encourage you to become an inventor?*

WYETH: No, everybody was surprised. They'd say, "How come you're not an artist?"

I'd say, "I didn't want to be an artist."

"Oh," they'd say, "didn't your father want you to start painting and drawing like your brother and sisters?"

"Look," I'd say, "Father was very much interested in what we wanted to do. The only thing he insisted on was that whatever we did, we should do it with all our hearts, with all our might."

When I was old enough to start thinking about college and my father saw that I wanted to be an engineer, he got in touch with his youngest brother, Stimson Wyeth. He was a Harvard graduate and lived in Needham, Massachusetts. My father asked him to go around to look over different colleges for me. He was instrumental in picking the University of Pennsylvania for me; he thought it was a good place to go for my technical training.

It's not only that I feel more productive when I'm working alone, it's a hell of a lot of fun too.

INTERVIEWER: *What was your first invention?*

WYETH: I worked on all kinds of things as I was growing up. I guess the biggest area of work was in model speedboats. I don't know how many clocks, how many windup alarm clocks, I dismantled so that I could use their guts to drive speedboats.

I'd make pontoon boats with airplane propellers, and I made other boats with underwater propellers. I was also on a universal joint kick. I was fascinated by the way universal joints operated. I used to build models clustered with universal joints. I'd purposely make the drive shaft come out in the wrong direction so that I would have to run one shaft this way and one shaft the next way. I had universal joints all over the place. I made them by cutting the pieces out of a tin can and soldering them together, and they worked very well.

Of course, I was wasting a lot of energy because a universal joint is not particularly efficient unless it's a constant velocity joint as you see today on the front end of front-wheel-drive cars. But I couldn't have made a constant velocity joint with a tin can and a soldering iron either.

INTERVIEWER: *In a recent TV show on your family I saw that you also developed a hydroplane while you were growing up. What's the story behind that?*

WYETH: Let me tell you some of the background of that boat. Up in Maine my father always had a tender, a rowboat really, that we towed behind our power boat. If anything went wrong with the engine, we could get in the rowboat and row.

But the rowboat was pretty heavy, and it wouldn't plane; that is, it wouldn't get up on top of the water. "Gee," I said, "I'm going to build something that will let this thing plane." So, I built this little sea sled. Its cross section looked just like a sled. It was only about six feet long, and it had a straight top and a curved bow. I put an outboard motor on the rear end of it, and we used it in place of the old rowboat.

I don't know if I invented the name for it or not, but we called it Ex-Lax because it moved so fast (laughs). I remember one day when the family was going out to Monhegan Island. I decided to take the sea sled and follow the family boat. Monhegan Island is about ten miles out to sea from where we used to stay. On the way out there I just zipped around them in circles because I had speed to play with. Well, the local paper wrote about it, and it came out that I had taken Ex-Lax and gone to Monhegan. It sounded terrible.

Later, I was at the University of Pennsylvania, and I got to thinking about the sea sled. I thought about how it curved up at the front: Why not continue that curve right up and make an airfoil out of the whole boat? I thought maybe I could use the lift of that airfoil cross section to help lift some of the boat's weight and get it out of the water. And as it turns out, that's just what I did.

The boat I eventually built from that idea was a twenty-foot hydroplane, as they called it. It didn't have an outboard motor in it, but a Ford V-8 engine. Originally, it was silver colored, so we named it the *Silver Foil*—after the airfoil design and the silver color of the boat.

INTERVIEWER: *What did your family think of the project?*

WYETH: We had a lot of fun with that boat. When I first started working on it—at about age eighteen—I tried to rush the thing. I had even picked up a secondhand Model A Ford four-cylinder engine to power it. My father said, "Look Nat, let's not rush this; let's do it right. If you just slow down and take it easy, I'll get you a new Ford V-8 to put in next year."

Well, he only had to say that once. And as it turned out, I really needed more power. Even the V-8 wasn't enough. I don't know what would have happened if I had put the four-cylinder engine in it.

I wasn't very old then, and I had a mechanic come down to help me hook up the engine. I'll never forget the first night we started it up in the barn where I was building the boat. It had two huge exhaust pipes without mufflers coming out the top, one from each bank of four cylinders. Oh, the sound of it! It was impressive to me just to hear the engine idling.

INTERVIEWER: *Did your father help with the design as well?*

WYETH: Father had a lot to do with the layout of the boat. There were louvres cut in the sides of the boat, which gave it a nice, eye-catching design.

It was a thrilling experience when we launched it. There were a lot of people on the dock, and Father came down wearing his usual plus fours with a bottle of champagne to christen the boat.

He just walked right out into the water—and you know that Maine water is terrible, just above freezing—and right up to the boat. The boat was lightly built out of white pine with a white ash frame, so he couldn't break the champagne bottle on it. He held a rock in his hand and hit the bottle on it so that the bottle broke and the champagne ran down over the boat. He was so excited that he even forgot to take his watch out. He had a lovely Waltham watch in his pocket, and it just got soaked in salt water.

INTERVIEWER: *Was the launch a big day for you as well?*

WYETH: I was trembling. I wasn't even sure the boat would float. I'd never had it in the water before. The only thing I knew was that it wouldn't tip over because it was flat-bottomed.

INTERVIEWER: *How fast did the boat go?*

WYETH: We got forty-five to fifty miles per hour out of it, which was pretty good for a Ford V-8 on a boat that big. What a racket it made! We kept changing propellers on it to try and get enough power out of it so that we could shift into high gear. It had a manual transmission, and we just couldn't shift it fast enough. As soon as we'd take the power off, it would settle right back down in the water.

But it was a lot of fun. I learned a lot from it. In fact, *Pathé News* even came up to do a newsreel story on it.

INTERVIEWER: *How did that happen?*

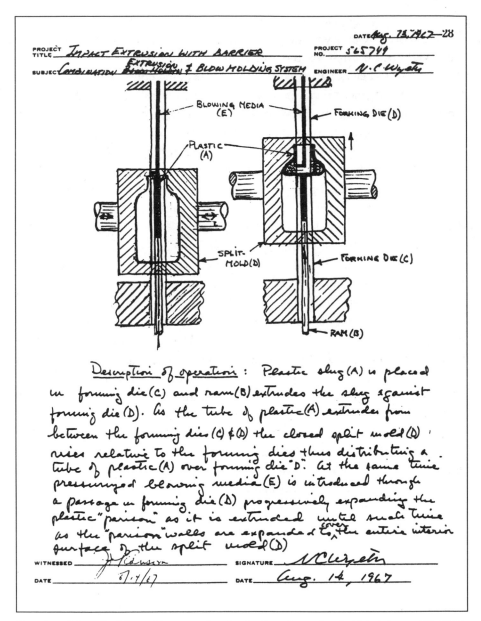

Page from Nat Wyeth's working notes for the plastic soda pop bottle (dated August 13, 1967).

WYETH: Father was doing the illustrations for Kenneth Roberts' book *Trending into Maine*, and Roberts had come up to see some of the pictures he was doing.

Of course, Father was always proud of anything we kids were doing, so he brought him down to the barn where I was working on my boat. I had taken over the barn with my boat; we couldn't even keep our cars in there.

Well, he brought him into the garage, and Kenneth Roberts said, "Dammit, *look at that!* I've never seen anything like this. I've got to get in touch with Dick Sears, the cameraman for *Pathé News* down in Boston and get him up here to see this."

Well, he called him long-distance and got him to come up the next day. We took lots of film. I remember I damn near lost the guy. He stood on the back of the boat—you know it had that sloping back—and he almost slipped off with his camera and everything.

Well, it didn't make the news. All this happened when the big war in China broke out, and my story got pushed to the back with everything else. But we got a wonderful movie out of it, and it was front-page news in all the papers in Maine. I remember some of the titles under the front-page pictures: "Is it a whale or a boat?" And there was a picture of the boat without any people on it, just a side profile, and it looked a little bit like a whale. It was a lot of fun.

INTERVIEWER: Did you start working at Du Pont right out of college?

WYETH: No, I first went to work for the Delco Company in Dayton, Ohio. It's part of General Motors. I had gotten several offers from different companies, but I went there because my Uncle Nathaniel, the one I'm named after, thought Delco would be a good place to work.

My uncle was a very interesting guy. He worked in the creative end of automobile design. The chief engineer of General Motors used to say that my uncle probably had one of the best ass-ometers in the business. Even when my uncle went to Chrysler, the man who was in charge of research at Cadillac used to call him up and say, "Nat, are you busy? How about coming over on Sunday for a ride in our new Cadillac?" Whenever he wanted to find out what was wrong with the ride of one of their new cars, he would get my uncle to test it. Nat could just sit in a car and ride around in it and tell what was wrong with the suspension system or the steering. He didn't even have to get underneath the car.

INTERVIEWER: *When did you get your first big break at Du Pont and have a chance to show your inventiveness?*

WYETH: I guess the first time I showed my ability as an inventor was when I came up with a new valve for a production machine. That valve helped to get me transferred to the department I originally wanted to be working in when I came to Du Pont.

A valve kept plugging up in a new operation that involved using a by-product from another product to make—of all things—Sani-Flush. And Sani-Flush is a pretty rough material, particularly when you're making it, because there's a certain phase where it's very hygroscopic—it picks up moisture out of the air. It's also got a lot of acid in it. I remember when we were starting up the plant, so much dust from this stuff was in the air that it would get on our hands and even down between our pants and rear end. Every so often, we'd back in under safety showers and just soak our pants because our rears were burning from all the acid (laughs). Well, that's beside the point.

> *I learned very early on that you can use negative reactions as stepping stones.*

So the valve kept plugging up with this material, which was in a semi-solid state but was fluid enough to keep flowing through the valve most of the time. Every so often, though, the valve would plug up, and we'd have to pull the whole damn thing apart.

What in the heck are we going to do to keep that thing from plugging up? I asked myself. I looked at the valve design—it was a gate valve, kind of like a sliding door. When you turned a handle the gate opened, and the material flowed through. The gate had to slide all the way across the opening for it to work properly.

I learned that you could unbolt this gate, so I decided to rebuild it with two gates or valves, each with a handle to open it, that met in the middle of the opening. When you turned the handles, both of them opened. These changes were not expensive, and they worked. The valve never plugged again. When it started to plug up, we'd just open both sides and it would clear its own throat, so to speak, and unplug.

Right after that happened, I got a call to come over to the Du Pont Building. They didn't mention the valve, but I knew my boss had been impressed by this valve trick. What they did tell me was that they wanted to transfer me to the mechanical development laboratory to work on new mechanisms and new concepts. That's just the area I wanted to get into when I came to Du Pont.

INTERVIEWER: *What were some of your first projects there?*

WYETH: In my early days of creating new things, one of the first places I worked in was a plant that made dynamite. I'm sure you've seen the tubes of cardboard with "dynamite" and the little Du Pont oval written on the tube sides.

Well, this was in the days when I was just getting started, and I designed and built a model of an automatic dynamite-cartridging machine. I built that machine out of wood and brass with the help of a German carpenter who worked for me.

The older machines for cartridging dynamite required a lot of manual labor and the problem was that the operators were exposed to the nitroglycerin powder used in making dynamite. Nitroglycerin dilates your blood vessels and gives you terrible headaches. Du Pont wanted to keep the operators away from this operation as much as possible, so one of my objectives was to mechanize it.

I drew out all the plans for the cartridging machine, and the carpenter built the model the way I wanted it. It had lots of levers and linkages that were kind of tricky as well. The carpenter really took great pleasure in building these things because he could see his workmanship come to life in the machine. However, he couldn't always visualize what the whole machine would look like, so, when we were working together, I always drew him a complete, isometric drawing of what the finished machine would look like. He loved those drawings. Once, I gave him some drawings for a machine and didn't include an isometric sketch. He looked at them and said, "I don't know what it is. Where's your drawing?" So, I had to go back and draw one for him. He got spoiled by all those isometric drawings.

I'll never forget when my boss, Charlie Johnson, the director of machine development, came by to see the experimental dynamite-cartridging machine. He was a phenomenal guy with a tremendous number of patents and with ideas just oozing out of him. He came around to see the machine with the head man from the explosives department. It was pretty tricky— the way it opened automatically to receive the cartridges, the way it moved, the way the shuttle closed on the cartridges, and so on. Parts of the design were unusual. And Charlie didn't even have to bend down to look at it; he knew how it operated just by watching it at a distance.

As he was explaining it to the explosives man, I will never forget the great pleasure I had in watching that machine go through its paces without missing a trick. I could see he was happy with it and that the other guy was impressed too. Charlie turned to me as he left. "Nat," he said, "see me in Wilmington on Monday morning, and we'll talk about getting a project started to design a final machine."

That was music to my ears. When they left, I did a dance right there in the room, jumping up and down. I'd been working on that machine for quite a while, and it performed just beautifully.

To see an idea finally go into motion is one of the most gratifying experiences I think anybody can have. There's nothing like it.

INTERVIEWER: *Was the plastic bottle your first big invention, or did you work on other products as well?*

WYETH: Well, I've also got some patents on products that are widely used, but not so well known as the bottle. One product, for example, that very few people know about is Typar. That's the trade name for a fabric made out of drawn polypropylene.

It's what we call a nonwoven fabric because you don't use a loom or a shuttle or anything like that. The polypropylene fibers are simply laid down at random on a moving screen like a Fourdrinier wire on a paper-making machine. Then, this crude fabric is stripped off the screen and run between two heated rollers to stick the fibers together. You can make a fabric a lot faster and a lot cheaper that way than by weaving.

The machine that I got a patent on in this process was the bonding machine that's used to stick the fibers together. It was really a simple way of bonding them together using heat and pressure.

INTERVIEWER: *What are some of the uses of Typar?*

WYETH: Well, one of the uses is right here on this rug at my feet. The backing on this rug is probably a Typar material. It's a very inexpensive, but tough, backing material, and it's now used in place of woven jute.

Luckily, when we brought Typar out on the market, there was a strike in the shipping industry, and because almost all of the jute came from abroad, there was no longer a supply of it. Those circumstances gave us the

ENGINEERING DEVELOPMENT LABORATORY

DATE 8/25/67

PROJECT TITLE *Impact Extrusion with Barrier* PROJECT NO. 565744

SUBJECT *Combination Extrusion & Blow Molding System* ENGINEER *N. C. Wyeth*

In discussing the process concept described on page 28 of this D & C book with J. B. Roberts and explaining the critical nature of the blowing operation as regard to avoidance of container wall rupture, Roberts suggested that the use of a moveable* mold bottom might reduce the criticality of the blowing operation by controlling ~~the~~ and balancing the expansion of the plastic parison to the walls of the container mold — see sketch below:

NOTE: THE SPRING(S) LOADED MOLD BOTTOM WOULD HAVE STOPS ON FORMING DIE(C) TO LIMIT ITS VERTICAL TRAVEL. ALSO THAT SURFACE OF THE MOLD BOTTOM (M) WHICH IS IN CONTACT WITH THE PLASTIC SHOULD BE PERMANENTLY COATED WITH A LOW-FRICTION MATERIAL SUCH AS TEFLON.

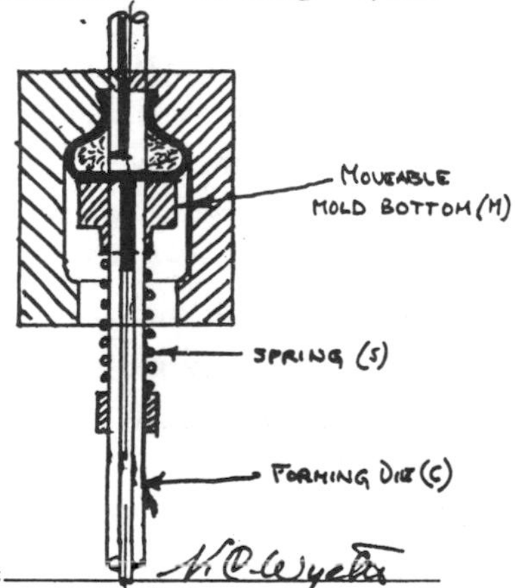

MOVEABLE MOLD BOTTOM (M)

SPRING (S)

FORMING DIE (C)

* Moveable relative to the mold

WITNESSED _____ DATE 8/25/67

SIGNATURE _____ DATE Aug. 25, 1967 4799 —29

Page from Nat Wyeth's working notes (dated August 25, 1967) for the plastic soda pop bottle.

perfect opportunity to bring Typar into the market. And once people got used to using Typar, the jute market disappeared.

It has other uses as well. For example, it's used as a bagging material, and in construction, it's used for a base when they're pouring concrete in a wet or muddy area.

So, it has a big market, but the material had to be cheap to produce. You couldn't afford to weave it—weaving only goes in inches per minute, not thousands of feet per minute. Of course, polypropylene is also one of the cheapest fibers around.

INTERVIEWER: *How did your bonding process work?*

WYETH: It was a simple way to bond the fibers together with heat and pressure. One of the developments that came out of it was a calender. Do you know what that is?

INTERVIEWER: *I don't think so. You aren't talking about a calendar that you keep dates on, are you?*

WYETH: No, this is a calender with two rolls that press something like paper or cloth between them. I think it's spelled with an "er" at the end rather than an "ar." A calender is very much like the rollers on old washing machines—the wringer that squeezed the water out of clothes.

Well, a calender is really a large wringer. As fabrics and paper became wider, the calenders became almost too cumbersome to handle. Newsprint machines, for instance, were twenty feet to forty feet wide. If you tried to put any sort of pressure on the rollers, they'd bend in the middle because they were so long.

I began to look into this problem. The solution I came up with is a good example of Kettering's* motto, which was, "Get off Route 35." In other words, don't get into a rut and keep following the same old ways to solve a problem.

The problem was that they were making the Typar in thirty-foot widths. The rolls were so long that we had to make them six feet in diameter so that they wouldn't bend. It's not feasible to try and handle something that big—particularly where you're trying to run off two thousand to three thousand feet per minute of fabric.

All that was used to squeeze the rolls together was pressure. The rolls were anchored at both ends with bearings, and to tighten the roll, you'd

---

* Charles Franklin Kettering (1876–1958), American electrical engineer and inventor.

bring the bearings together with a screw or something. But when you did that with long rolls, they tended to deflect or bend, and the material would end up thicker in the middle than at the edges. You could prevent that, but only by making the diameter so big that the rolls were ungainly.

So, I thought, There must be a better way of pushing those rolls together. I considered using a Zinzimmer mill, which is used to roll aluminum and squeeze it down to the thickness of aluminum foil. The problem with that approach is that to get any decent pressure, you have to put backup rolls on top of the main rolls in the center to hold them together and keep them from bending. Well, those backup rolls usually make a mark on the main roll and that mark makes a mark on the product. The Zinzimmer mill works fine for aluminum foil because the rolls aren't wide; you can make backup rolls that cover the whole width. But for longer rolls you can't do that. You can't have that mark from the backup rolls on paper, and we couldn't have that mark on Typar either.

> *I used to tell my father that an engineer, a development engineer like myself, has a much tougher job than an artist.*

Well, I thought to myself, Why not use a magnet and draw those two rolls together magnetically? I don't know if you've heard of Cott rolls on a textile machine, but the rollers on that machine are actually held down by a coil like a solenoid.

I thought, Let's make the two rolls magnetic so that one has a southern polarity and the other one has a northern polarity. That way, they'll be attracted to each other. We built a small roll and put windings around it so that we could run current through it and turn the roll into an electromagnet. To get more pressure between the two rolls, all you had to do was increase the amount of current running through the wire. It was very simple. Of course, because one roll was pulling the other toward it all the way across its length—with a uniform pull—there was no problem with deflection.

You see, this is an idea that had been around for a long time. Solenoids had been around for a long time. You've seen the electromagnets used to load scrap and pick up pieces of steel: A big magnet is lowered into a pile of scrap, and a lot of materials are drawn to it and fasten on to it. When the load is over the truck, the magnet is turned off, and the scrap drops.

Although this idea has been around for years, no one ever put it on a calender. It was just a case of getting off Route 35 and thinking a little differently. I think we got four or five good, solid patents on that. It was sort of like child's play when you think that this idea's been around for years and nobody used it.

INTERVIEWER: We've talked only indirectly about your plastic bottle. Do you consider it your most famous invention?

WYETH: Well, it's something people can understand easily because it's a product they use every day. There's nothing vague about it. It was really the epitome of an invention.

One of the first experiments I did was really rather amusing. I used to ask our people, "Why isn't plastic used for beverage bottles?" And they said that it couldn't hold carbonated beverages because the bottle would blow up. Well, I still wasn't convinced.

On the way home from work one night, I picked up a bottle of detergent at a supermarket. I got home, dumped the contents out, and filled the bottle with ginger ale. Then, I screwed the top back on and put the whole thing in the refrigerator. I thought I would give it a break by keeping it cold. I knew that the plastic would be a little bit stronger in the cold, and I thought it wouldn't expand quite as much.

Well, I came down the next morning and I remember that my wife was really concerned. The bottle was swollen so big that it wouldn't come out; it was solid in there. It had expanded so much that it was caught between the refrigerator cooling unit and the wall.

Well, I got it out by unscrewing the cap and bleeding the pressure off, bit by bit. And I realized, "No wonder they don't put carbonated beverages in plastic bottles. They're too weak."

INTERVIEWER: What was the secret of your bottle?

WYETH: Very early in my work with plastics I noticed that when you molded something, certain portions of the plastic were stronger than others. This was particularly true of things molded in an injection mold, where you squirt molten plastic into a mold. Of course, I wondered right away why you couldn't make all the plastic stronger. Then, you could use less plastic and make things cheaper and lighter.

At the same time, I was very much aware of the work Wallace Carothers had done with nylon. He was a Du Pont man and the inventor of nylon. You make a nylon thread by spinning the material or squirting it out of a tiny hole. Carothers found that by stretching the fibers as you made them, you could make them much stronger because the molecules would align. They would all line up in the direction of stretching.

I like to think of it as the way people line up at a rope in a tug-of-war. If the people on one side are all pulling in different directions, they won't be able to pull as hard as they could if they all pulled in one direction. You get greater force when everybody's pulling in one direction. With nylon, Carothers was lining the molecules up so that they all pulled together.

When I understood that, I said, "Well, we can orient these molecules so that instead of pulling in all directions—making the stuff rather flabby—they can pull together so that it's strong enough to hold carbonated beverages."

Then, I realized that the way to align these molecules was a little tougher than aligning them in thread. In thread you only have to orient them in one direction. In a bottle you've got to have them circumferentially oriented and axially oriented. If you only orient them circumferentially, the diameter of the bottle won't expand, but it will get longer. To make a uniformly strong plastic bottle, we had to get biaxial orientation.

Well, that was done very easily by what turned out to be a patentable process and product. We did it by extruding the plastic into what's called a preform that you could blow up. We had to extrude the preform so that we got crisscrossed flow lines. Then, we blew it up so that it could expand both lengthwise and about its diameter. Well, we did that and we had it. We had a bottle that could take the pressure.

INTERVIEWER: *Was it a quick step from the realization that you needed biaxial orientation to a working bottle?*

WYETH: It took a lot of experimentation. The first time we made a bottle, we were using a little handpress. The day we finally got it to work— when we opened the mold and saw our first model—we were completely amazed. In fact, we couldn't even find the bottle. We were so used to seeing just globs of plastic. "Did you put a slug in there?" I asked the technician. "Sure!" he said. It was poorly lighted in the room where we were working, so we got a flashlight and pointed it into the mold, and there it was!

The bottle was almost sitting there laughing at us, secretly hiding. We took it out and looked at it, we looked at each other, and then we went out and had the best spaghetti dinner I've ever had, just to celebrate.

After we made the first bottle, we got that machine running so that we were making eight bottles a day. Eight! It would take us an hour to set up to blow each bottle. Now, when I see these bottles coming off giant machines at a rate of ten thousand an hour, it's almost unbelievable.

INTERVIEWER: *Do ideas just come to you?*

WYETH: Very seldom do they come out of nowhere. It's usually a culmination of one thought after another that leads one to a solution and to a complete understanding of the problem.

INTERVIEWER: *So, to invent something you really have to stick with it?*

WYETH: You have to have a tremendous amount of patience and not give up easily. Even when a problem had been bugging me for weeks or months, I would go to work every morning with a good, clean slate and feel that I was starting afresh—using my failures and the knowledge of things that wouldn't work as a springboard to new approaches.

If I hadn't used those mistakes as stepping stones, I would never have invented anything. I would have said, "Well, if it doesn't work the first time, forget it." I've found that it's very important to keep your mind open. The brain has a phenomenal ability to come up with new ways of doing things. There's an infinite supply of new approaches. You just don't run out of material. If you think you have run out of material, there's something wrong. You'd better stop working on a problem. You'd better stop working as an inventor too, because you'll never invent anything.

INTERVIEWER: *Do you think of yourself as an inventor or an engineer?*

WYETH: I don't see any real need to distinguish between the two. I know, for example, that I've got several reasons for putting "Doctor" in front of my name, but I feel that's just sort of window dressing. I've been given honorary degrees, but so what?

Oh, it's nice to be recognized as an engineer. One of the guys at work asked me, "What are you getting an honorary doctorate for? You didn't get a doctor's degree in college." I guess his nose was out of joint. "No," I said, "I got it the right way. This one's for actual experience. That's what it's being awarded for. That's just book learning you got a doctor's degree for." (Laughs.) I was also being a little irritating myself.

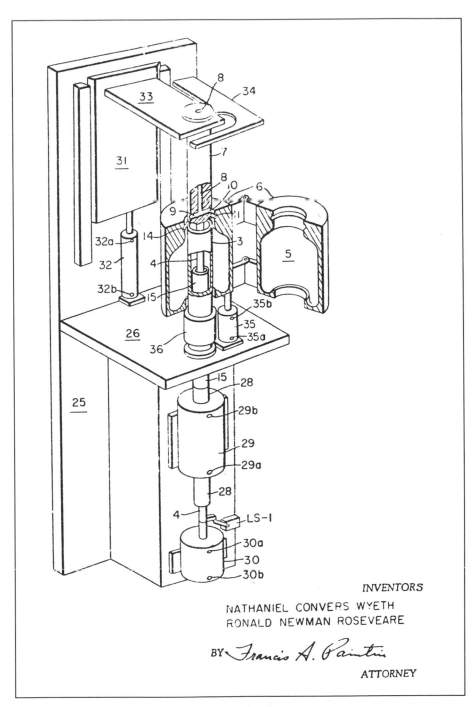

Patent drawing for Nat Wyeth's plastic bottle (dated May 15, 1973).

INTERVIEWER: Is inventing a solitary art? A friend of mine who's a painter says you have to be selfish to paint.

WYETH: My brother also says that you've got to be selfish to paint. I think you do, up to a point, in inventing as well. But the stimulus that you can get by discussion, the catalytic results, can help you get off that Route 35 that Kettering was talking about and help you solve a problem. Sometimes it's very helpful to talk to other people. They'll drop one remark, you know, and it will break through some veneer that's been surrounding your thoughts.

Now, if I'm in the middle of something and it's unfolding, then I don't want to be talked to. I want to be alone. It's not only that I feel more productive when I'm working alone, it's a hell of a lot of fun too.

But, sometimes when you're in the middle of something and things start going wrong, it's nice to have someone around. When we were in the middle of the bottle tests, it was frustrating, and I was thankful to have somebody there. You want to have somebody there to help you absorb some of the frustration in a situation like that so that you don't feel you're being sort of queer. "What did we do wrong here?" I would say. "The last sample we made didn't look too bad, but this test went sour."

I remember bringing some of those samples over to my boss, Ray Crittendon, who was then director of the lab. I'd bring over this terrible-looking sample and call it a bottle. He'd look at it and ask, "Is this all you've done for $50,000?"

"Yeah," I said, "but it's oriented, and it's hollow."

"But what a terrible-looking bottle," he said. "It looks like something dug up out of the ruins of Carthage." But he still had confidence in our work, and he kept supporting us.

INTERVIEWER: Are ideas or inventions fragile? Can too much criticism destroy an idea?

WYETH: I learned very early on that you can use negative reactions as stepping stones. I found that they gave me even more inspiration to say, "Well, dammit, I'll show them."

I remember going out to the laboratory and telling these guys that I was trying to cold-stretch the bottle, and these diehards told me, "You're wasting your time." One guy even went so far as to say, "You know what you're doing? You're doing something that's as hard to do as balancing a steel ball on the point of a needle." Well, that's just impossible. And that was all the inspiration I needed. Great. "I don't need your kind of help," I told him. (Laughs.)

Then, I went back to work. That remark just poured more coal on the fire. I started to really look into why the bottle had failed and why it was always rupturing in the same direction. I found out that the lines of extrusion were still in the tube, or the polymer, that I was using. Every time we tried to stretch it, the bottle would burst. No wonder we couldn't stretch the damn thing. It would break along the original flow lines.

It's fascinating when you think about it: how little we have invented.

I found out that when I made my preform of the bottle—which actually looked like a test tube with screw threads on top—I had to extrude it with crisscrossed lines of flow so that the lines were self-reinforcing. As soon as I discovered that principle, it didn't rupture.

Another problem was that the plastic, polypropylene, we used to make the early bottles wasn't a self-balancing elastic. An elastomer can be stretched and when it starts to get stiff, it starts to resist. Once it's to the point where it won't stretch any further, it starts stretching someplace else. It's self-balancing. But these preforms of polypropylene wouldn't do that; they'd keep right on stretching until they'd rupture. They weren't like the elastomer.

Now, polyethylene-terephthalate, commonly called PET, which is the polymer we finally used in the bottle, had some of the stretching characteristics of an elastic. In the amorphous form, it would tend to stretch until it reached some internal limit, and then it simply stretched somewhere else until it had balanced itself. When we started using that polymer, it was duck soup. The bottle was self-balancing and tough. In addition, it was clear: beautiful, like glass. And the more you stretched it, the clearer it got.

INTERVIEWER: You have a lot of hands-on experience working with things and refining them. How important do you think those hands-on, practical skills are to being a successful inventor?

WYETH: Well, it's had a great influence on me. I was only ten or twelve years old when I started learning how to use tools.

My father was quite a craftsman, and when he would discuss something with me, he always pointed out mistakes and ways to do a thing better. "Well," he would say, "you should have done it this way." He wasn't just talking through his hat; he could do it himself. He could take my jack-knife and carve something just the way he said to. "Now, this is the way it should be, see?"

He helped me with sincerity and with the ability to back up what he said. He taught me a great lesson: Rather than doing a thing poorly, it would be better not to do it at all. So, if you're going to do something, do it the best way you can.

When I started making models of furniture, I would get halfway through one and do something wrong, or I'd realize that I wasn't happy with it. So, I'd take it apart and start all over again. Sometimes I would have to do it several times. It took a lot of perseverance and patience, but I got over wanting to finish something in a hurry just to see what it would look like. It was always so rewarding to do it well.

But I learned a lot about design from building models. I remember the first model I built was a ladder-back chair. Father came in and looked at it. "That's very good, you know," he said. "But right here you should have...." And he very quietly told me what a lousy job I'd done. But he did it with real compassion. He was trying to get a point across.

When he left the room, tears started to run down my face. Oh, I didn't let him see, of course. I put that model chair onto the floor and just stamped it into little pieces. I was so mad at myself. And I started to build it again, and what a difference! Beautiful! Beautiful chair! That lesson really registered with me, and I never forgot it. No matter what I've done, I've always felt that was a wonderful lesson to learn. My father never missed an opportunity to do that, with all of us.

This lesson has been something that has carried through in my work. You might ask, "How can working in wood have anything to do with developing a plastic bottle or this and that?" But it was that idea—"No, now wait a minute, there's a better way to do it. Let's take a little longer and think about it and maybe experiment a bit until we get it right." That was what was so important.

I also learned a lot about design from other models I worked on. Once I built a quarter-scale model of a foot-operated garbage pail—the kind with a foot pedal to open the lid. My sister has a doll house that is all quarter-scale, so I built her this garbage pail.

In building this thing, I found out a lot about why it was built the way it was. To my surprise and amazement, I found that some of the parts were made from pieces of stampings left over from another part. I'd take a part, flatten it out in a drawing to get its dimensions, and find out that it was stamped out of a piece from the hole for the foot pedal and used to make one of the levers. It taught me a lot about ingenuity and why things are designed the way they are.

INTERVIEWER: *I guess as an inventor you have to have both some creativity and some technical skills—some building blocks to work with.*

WYETH: I think I can liken it to something that is understood in the atmosphere of my family—an artist's atmosphere. It's like what Father always said, "Before you can do a really good job at anything, you've got to be well trained in the basics."

Father learned very early the importance of being able to draw. Oh, I don't think you have to have a photographic eye to draw well, but if something was drawn with some sense of understanding, you can feel it.

Take my brother, Andrew, for instance. When my father was teaching him, he said, "What you do on your own time is all right with me. But when you're working for me as a student, you're first going to learn how to draw. You're going to learn the basics of drawing things as they are."

For years, Father made him come to the studio and draw, in charcoal or pencil, very simple objects—cubes, spheres, pyramids—over and over again, to get his eye established. Andy was almost driven up a wall.

But you can see that kind of training in Andy's work: the beautiful proportions and accuracy. He has an eye like an eagle. His pencil sketches of a rope or the limb of a tree are simply phenomenal. It didn't just come by saying he wanted to do it. He had to work at it.

In much the same way, I think an engineer has to have a very fundamental training and understanding of, for example, the various laws of physics before he can start using them. This is particularly important when you're using your skills in fields or areas where you're really exploring for the first time. We have enough to do and enough problems without moving in false directions because we haven't learned the basics in engineering.

Boy, did we have examples of it at Du Pont. People were hired who would build gadgets that would practically fall apart when put into operation. These people just didn't understand or didn't visualize what in the heck was going on when the particular gadget they were working on went through its paces. Some of the mistakes were very simple things that anyone with an understanding of mechanical engineering would never have made.

I remember one very obvious example. It was almost pathetic. This guy had built a very elaborate machine out of wood for the manufacture of dynamite. Wood is safer to use with dynamite. If one piece of metal strikes another, you can strike a spark and ignite the nitroglycerin.

You mark my words: One of these days we're going to understand gravity.... Isaac Newton would go nuts if he heard me talking.

INTERVIEWER: *Which isn't really a good thing at all.*

WYETH: No (laughs). No, it isn't. Well, the machine this fellow had built was made all out of wood. But he really showed his complete lack of understanding on his engineering drawings for some of the machine parts: He had limits on the dimensions of plus or minus one one-thousandth of an inch.

Whoever thinks that wood can hold those kinds of tolerances needs to have his head examined. Wood grows and shrinks tremendously with changes in temperature and moisture. But he was putting dimensions on this wood as if it were metal. And, it was costing Du Pont money to get these dimensions and they weren't any good! The machinists were just throwing up their hands. "How do we get these dimensions? They'll be here today but gone tonight, and tomorrow they'll all be different." That engineer just didn't have any feeling for what he was doing. But there again, that's basics.

INTERVIEWER: *So, it helps to have an almost intuitive understanding of what you're trying to do?*

WYETH: It's almost more than that. Andy once did a picture. This is sort of an extension of what we've been talking about, but it's indicative of the kind of training I'm talking about.... Andy did a picture of Lafayette's headquarters which is down here on Route One near Chadds Ford. It's a beautiful, old building, built before the Revolutionary War, and in his picture was a huge sycamore tree coming up from behind the building with all its beautiful branches. You could see part of the trunk coming up over the roofline.

When I first saw the painting, he wasn't quite finished with it. He showed me a lot of drawings of the trunk and the gnarled roots going into the ground, and I said, "Gee whiz, where's that in the picture?" "It's not in the picture," he said. And I looked at him.

"Nat," he said, "for me to get the feeling that I want in that tree, the part of that tree that's showing, I've got to understand and know very thoroughly how that tree is anchored to the ground in back of that house." It never showed in the picture. But he could draw the part of the tree above the house with a lot more authenticity because he knew exactly the way that thing was anchored in the ground. Isn't that remarkable?

To me, this was all very indicative of what my father trained into us in whatever we were doing: to understand what we were doing.

A lot of my ideas came about when I was lying in bed. Or I was sitting in a chair just thinking. Often, I didn't even have a pencil in my hand, and an invention or idea would come to me. I'd think, I've got to do this or I've got to do that. Or I won't do that. Many times, I can think far enough ahead to save myself a lot of trouble. I may say to myself, That will never work that way. But that's part of that training, that understanding of what's going on in there.

INTERVIEWER: *What do you think is the best environment for an inventor? Du Pont worked out extremely well for you, but do you think big companies are the place to be?*

WYETH: One thing that's hard to replace is the seemingly infinite fund of money and the equipment you can get at a large corporation.

That simple little machine that we built to make the first bottle turned into a very complex operation. You ought to have seen the equipment and instrumentation that we used. The reason it took us so long to produce the first bottle was that there were all kinds of critical aspects to the operation. Temperature and timing were very important. The timing had to be just right when you were extruding that little preform cylinder and when you were introducing air to blow the preform. The kind of timing we needed could only have been done with very sophisticated equipment. I had a guy working with me, Ron Roseveare, whose name actually appears on the patent, who was instrumental in making that equipment as sophisticated as it finally had to be.

It turned out that the simplest way to make the bottle was to make a preform of amorphous, relatively high molecular weight PET, heat it up to one hundred degrees centigrade, just below the boiling point of water, and blow this preform into the bottle mold.

Our original concept had been to extrude it and blow it while we were extruding it. According to the polymer chemists, that method would give us a perfect bottle from the standpoint of uniform orientation. But it was much simpler to reheat the preforms. We didn't need to have a perfect bottle anyway because we already had enough of a safety margin in strength.

On your own, doing all the work necessary to get to that point would have cost a lot of money, and you would have had to worry about where your money was going to come from and what your family was going to live on.

INTERVIEWER: *Do you think there are any similarities between the creativity involved in being an artist and the creativity involved in being an inventor?*

WYETH: I think there are. I used to tell my father that an engineer, a development engineer like myself, has a much tougher job than an artist. I tell Andy that every now and then too. My father didn't agree with it.

I remember my father saying, "What do you mean, a tougher job?"

"Well," I said, "we not only have to draw the picture of what we want, but then we have to build it and it has to work. If it doesn't do what we planned it to do, we're out of work. We're out of business. You guys just paint a picture and you're done."

He sort of looked at me sideways.

"No," I said, "it's true. You see people draw pictures of a person sitting down with his feet on the floor, but if you really spaced off his legs in the drawing, they'd be about half as long as they should be. If the guy stood up, he'd look like a dwarf. But we can't get away with that. If our things don't work, we're out of business."

I didn't drive it too hard because I think he got the point. My father would say, "Well, a good artist wouldn't draw something like that."

"No," I said, "but there sure are a heck of a lot of people who get away with it." (Laughs.)

INTERVIEWER: *Do you have anything you'd like to invent?*

WYETH: There's a number of things I've tried to invent. For a number of years, I tried to design a vacuum cleaner that would use the vacuum to operate a pounding mechanism that would beat the rug as you swept it.

I also tried for quite a while to make a lawn mower, the type with a spiral blade, not the kind with a blade that spins on a vertical shaft.

INTERVIEWER: *You mean the old push type with the spiral blades?*

WYETH: Yes, the old push type. I always wanted to make one that would cut tall weeds. Usually, any kind of tall grass is just pushed down by the spiral-blade type of lawn mower and never gets cut.

"Anything new is special. Don't let this go to sleep," I said, pointing to my head.

I had all kinds of ideas for sweeping tall grasses into the spiral blades, but I never came up with anything that worked. Finally, I ended up buying a rotary-type cutter. Of course, those things are rather hazardous; they throw rocks and twigs, and they're easy to catch your hand in, if you don't watch out. There have always been little things like that that bothered me.

INTERVIEWER: *Do you think it's getting more difficult to be an inventor? A lot of would-be inventors seem to feel that everything's already been invented.*

WYETH: That kind of thinking is the mark of a narrow mind. There's so much out there. Saying everything's already been invented is like saying you've breathed all the air there is.

It's fascinating when you think about it: how little we have invented. We've done some remarkable things. We've done some things we probably shouldn't have done, such as the atomic bomb. But when I think of the understanding we have now, we've just barely scratched the surface.

I'm glad we're still exploring the stars, the planets, and so on. I'm sure there are concepts out there that will lead us to new materials and to things that are way beyond our feeling for gravity. They will give us a whole new approach. You mark my words: One of these days we're going to understand gravity. God help us if we do, because it could unlock some pretty vicious and awesome powers.

You can't see gravity, but there's something that's pulling us towards that floor. Some people say, "Oh yeah, that's just centrifugal force." Well, it isn't centrifugal force. It's not magnetic either because we're nonmagnetic, so what is it? Just think if we understood it.

One of my pet inventions used to be finding a way of negating gravity by just rotating something. In other words, to find a way to put centrifugal force to work—to have all the centrifugal force pointing in one direction—just by mechanically manipulating something. So, if you started to spin something, it would just lift, and it would move in whatever direction you aimed it. Think how it would change things if you could negate gravity. It's unbelievable.

Just think of a house: It could be floating. You would have to have an understanding of how to make the house stay on the ground, but it would weigh a lot less. In the future, you could use materials like balsa wood to build houses. You wouldn't need all these great, big, heavy things we move around now—with a great expense of energy—because we think the weight is necessary or that we have to live with it.

Well, that's just one minor detail. Isaac Newton would go nuts if he heard me talking.

INTERVIEWER: *No more dropping apples.*

WYETH: (Laughs.) Right. But with thoughts like these, what you're really getting into is the essence of invention. It's like Thomas Edison's invention of the light bulb. He realized that oxygen made things burn. So, he thought that if he heated up a wire, until it was white hot, inside a glass bottle—and kept out the oxygen so that it wouldn't burn—the wire would glow to make light. Well, he was right.

INTERVIEWER: *Are you saying he had an intuitive understanding of physical laws?*

WYETH: He understood them, and he applied them. He put them to use. A lot of people say, "Oh, he didn't invent the light bulb. His lamp only lasted ten seconds." Of course he invented it. The guy who eventually came up with the steel-alloy filament that would last wouldn't even have thought of doing it if it hadn't been for Edison. His work gave people a whole new start, a whole new playing field.

INTERVIEWER: *A lot of engineers graduate from college with all the right course work behind them, but they still can't invent. When it comes to applying their technical knowledge, a lot of well-trained people just can't comes to grips with it. What's wrong?*

WYETH: Well, they went through the whole thing, but it was just a course in memory to them. It didn't have any meaning to them.

I remember giving a talk on creativity at a college, and a student raised his hand before I even got started.

"Mr. Wyeth," he said, "I'm very interested in hearing about creativity. But what's your incentive? Everything that's going to be invented has been invented. All the patents have been granted."

"Do you really believe that?" I asked.

"Oh yes," he said. "Everything's been done."

"Well, alright," I said, "let me tell you about something that is new, and it hasn't been patented yet. Three professors got together and thought they'd try to develop an automatic oyster shucker...."

He cut me off with: "Well, that's nothing special; all you've got to do is mechanize it."

"Well now, wait a minute," I said. "I want you to listen. Don't think about what you're going to say. Just listen. Be a good audience."

And I continued, "These professors thought it over, and do you know what they came up with? They first punched a hole in the oyster, right in the pivot in back—broke the hinge, in fact—so that they could see the oyster. Then, they took a muscle relaxant, put it into a hypodermic needle, and injected it into the part of the oyster exposed by the hole. In several minutes, the shell opened up completely—no pressure on it. And the oyster was in complete, good shape. From that point on, it was easy to mechanize it. Now, you tell me that's been done before?"

"Oh, now wait a minute; that's something special," he said.

"They're all special," I said. "Anything new is special. Don't let this go to sleep," I said, pointing to my head. "You've got a brain up there with ideas that are just bursting to get out if you'd just use it."

Well, he sort of looked around and shuffled his feet. I could see he was embarrassed. I didn't mean to embarrass him, but the guy had it coming. Can you imagine? What if everybody thought that way? (Laughs.)

Actually, the guys who invented that machine didn't do such a good job at first. They hadn't done their homework. There were a few pitfalls they had to get over. The biggest one was that, with the muscle relaxant they were using, anyone who ate those oysters would have to get a prescription from their doctor.

There are relaxants you can use that don't have that effect. But isn't that a good approach? Instead of fighting that oyster's muscle, make it work for you. With that machine, they could shuck oysters faster than you could eat them.

INTERVIEWER: *Can you make people think creatively?*

WYETH: Creativity is not easy. It's not like falling off a log. It's not easy to get people to think along new lines, but it can be done.

Of course, I have to preface what I say about creativity with the importance of getting your basics down. A lot of people think that if you're creative, you don't have to go to school. But that's not true. I always cite my brother's case. He was made to learn how to draw before he became an artist. It wasn't just lucky that he became one of America's most famous artists. It came by hard work. He was made to learn how to draw, and that's a good model for engineers and inventors too.

Before you can put your creative juices to work and make an invention, you've got to know enough about the area you're interested in. If you're going to invent like I did, you've got to know about the engineering field. That background is very important. It has to be learned.

INTERVIEWER: *But to be an inventor one has to combine that knowledge with creativity.*

WYETH: Oh, I know creativity is essential. The disappointing thing is that everybody has that ability, but some of us don't use it. We don't wear it on our cuff, so to speak. We keep it under cover. Most of the time we don't even think about it.

APPENDIX

Reproduced in its entirety on the following pages is Roman Szpur's patent for a waffle maker (dated May 31, 1977).

United States Patent [19]

Szpur

[11] **4,026,202**

[45] **May 31, 1977**

[54] APPARATUS FOR AUTOMATICALLY PRODUCING WAFFLES AND SIMILAR FOOD ARTICLES

[76] Inventor: **Roman Szpur**, 2685 Culver Ave., Dayton, Ohio 45429

[22] Filed: **Nov. 24, 1975**

[21] Appl. No.: **634,363**

[52] U.S. Cl. .... 99/355; 99/341; 99/404; 99/431; 99/443 C; 198/599; 426/498
[51] Int. Cl.² A47J 37/12
[58] Field of Search .... 99/404, 405, 341, 352, 99/353, 354, 355, 356, 407, 409, 416, 443 C, 431, 442, 427; 425/436 R; 198/28, 131, 185; 426/439, 498, 512, 515, 474, 389

[56]   **References Cited**

UNITED STATES PATENTS

1,781,411	11/1930	Reiber	99/427
2,576,633	11/1951	Naylor	198/28
2,614,485	10/1952	Sinkwitz	99/404
2,786,430	3/1957	Robbins	99/442
3,267,836	8/1966	Yepis	99/427
3,490,392	1/1970	Ver Hoeven	426/498
3,747,508	7/1973	Elam	99/442

Primary Examiner—Billy J. Wilhite
Attorney, Agent, or Firm—Jacox & Meckstroth

[57]   **ABSTRACT**

An elongated endless conveyor unit extends in a horizontal plane and successively carries a plurality of article forming molds from a batter coating station through a hot oil within a cooking vessel located under the conveyor and then to a discharge station where the articles are successively removed from the molds. Each of the molds is connected to the conveyor by a corresponding arm assembly including a cam element which is actuated for rotating the arm to remove the mold and article from the oil. The batter is recirculated from a removable reservoir container to an overflow container removably supported within the reservoir container, and the overflow container has an adjustable side wall for precisely selecting the level of the batter relative to the path of the molds. Air is introduced into the batter supplied to the overflow container to maintain the batter at a uniform consistency, and the removal of the cooked articles from the molds is produced by impacting each arm and then passing the mold between a set of flexible stripping elements spaced on opposite sides of the mold path. The entire machine is constructed for convenient disassembly and reassembly to simplify cleaning of the machine.

13 Claims, 8 Drawing Figures

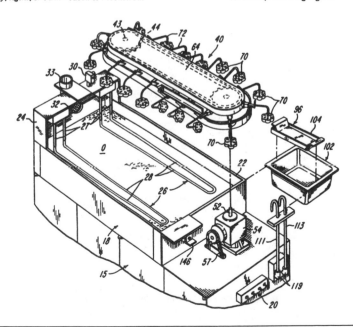

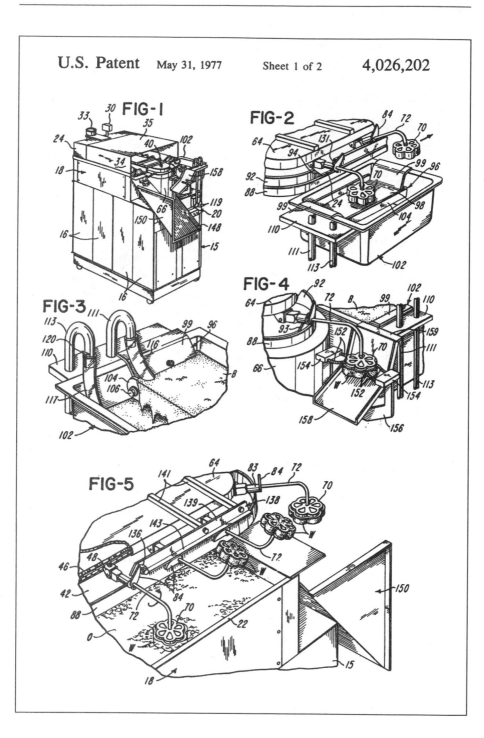

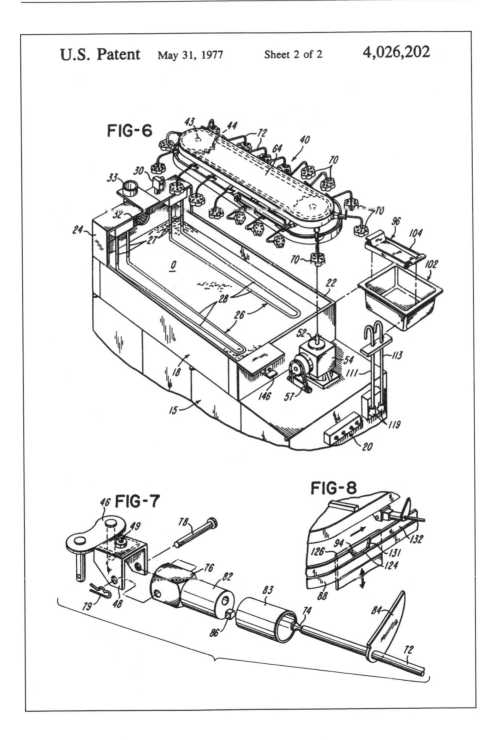

U.S. Patent   May 31, 1977   Sheet 2 of 2   4,026,202

FIG-6

FIG-7

FIG-8

4,026,202

1

APPARATUS FOR AUTOMATICALLY PRODUCING WAFFLES AND SIMILAR FOOD ARTICLES

BACKGROUND OF THE INVENTION

The present invention relates to apparatus for automatically forming and cooking food articles such as commonly referred to as "circus waffles" and which are formed by dipping a heated metal mold into a fluid batter and then immersing the mold and coated layer of batter within a hot cooking oil for a predetermined time period. More specifically, the invention relates to improvements in the general form of apparatus disclosed in U.S. Pat. No. 2,614,485 which issued to J. C. Sinkwitz and applicant as coinventors. In such an apparatus, it has been found desirable for the apparatus or machine to have a high dependability of operation so that the operating and maintenance labor can be minimized and one operator can handle a plurality of machines. It has also been found desirable to minimize the floor space required for the apparatus and to provide the apparatus with components which can be quickly and conveniently disassembled and reassembled to facilitate cleaning. As another important feature, the machine should provide for precisely controlling the level of the batter with respect to the path of each mold when it is dipped or lowered into the batter and depending on the viscosity of the batter to assure that each mold is not submerged within the batter. In addition, it is desirable for the machine to provide for continuously aerating the batter so that is maintains a uniform consistency during the continuous operation of the machine.

SUMMARY OF THE INVENTION

The present invention is directed to an improved apparatus or machine for efficiently forming and cooking batter-type food articles and for successively delivering or discharging the cooked articles to a receiving bin or container with a minimum production of unacceptable articles. The apparatus of the invention further provides all of the desirable features mentioned above and, in addition, is convenient and simple to operate. These advantages and features are provided in the illustrated embodiment wherein an elongated chain conveyor is positioned in a horizontal plane with a major portion of the conveyor extending over a rectangular pan or vessel containing hot cooking oil.

A plurality of molds, corresponding to the configuration of the food article, are connected to the endless conveyor chain by corresponding rotatably supported arms each having a radially projecting cam element. As the molds travel around a generally oval path, the molds are successively dipped into a overflow container which receives a continuous supply of batter from a pump having an inlet connected to a reservoir container surrounding the overflow container. The overflow container is removably supported within the reservoir container and incorporates an adjustable side wall for precisely controlling the level of batter relative to the path of the molds. After the layer of batter on each mold is cooked in the oil for a predetermined time, the mold is rotated out of the cooking oil by actuation of the cam element and is delivered to a discharge station where the arm rotates and impacts a stop member. Flexible spring fingers then engage oppo-

2

site sides of each mold and assure that the cooked article is stripped from the mold.

Other features and advantages of the machine will be apparent from the following description, the accompanying drawings and the appended claims.

BRIEF DESCRIPTION OF THE DRAWINGS

FIG. 1 is a perspective view of apparatus for producing waffle-type food articles and which is constructed in accordance with the invention;

FIG. 2 is a fragmentary perspective view illustrating the position of each mold and its support arm relative to the overflow and reservoir containers;

FIG. 3 is a fragmentary perspective view of the apparatus and illustrating the flow of batter from the overflow container into the reservoir container;

FIG. 4 is another fragmentary perspective view of the apparatus and illustrating the operation of stripping a cooked food product or waffle from its forming mold at the discharge station;

FIG. 5 is a further fragmentary perspective view of the apparatus and illustrating the operation of automatically removing the cooked waffles or food products from the cooking oil;

FIG. 6 is an exploded perspective view of the apparatus and illustrating how the apparatus is disassembled for cleaning;

FIG. 7 is an exploded perspective view of a typical mold support arm assembly and showing its connection to the endless conveyor chain; and

FIG. 8 is another fragmentary perspective view of the apparatus and showing the mechanism for by-passing the batter supply container with the forming molds.

DESCRIPTION OF THE PREFERRED EMBODIMENT

Referring to the drawings, the automatic forming and cooking apparatus illustrated in FIG. 1 includes a rectangular metal base cabinet 15 which encloses a storage container (not shown) for cooking oil, a motor drive pump for supplying oil from the container, and also encloses a main drive motor and a motor driven recirculating pump, as will be described later. The base cabinet 15 has pivotally supported side doors 16 to provide for convenient access to the oil storage container, the drive motor and the motor driven pumps. A rectangular open top pan or vessel 18 is constructed of stainless steel sheet metal and is supported by the base cabinet 15 which is somewhat longer and projects to the front of vessel 18.

The cooking vessel 18 defines a rectangular chamber for receiving a predetermined volume of cooking oil which is supplied to the chamber through a line connected to a motor driven pump (not shown) having an inlet connected by flexible tube to the oil storage container within the base cabinet 15. The pump is controlled by a switch on the main control counsel 20 mounted on the front of the base cabinet 15. The cooking vessel 18 has an inwardly projecting and peripherally extending top flange 22 (FIG. 6), and a stainless steel sheet metal housing 24 is mounted on the rearward portion of the flange 22.

The housing 24 supports a pair of elongated sheath-type heating elements 26 (FIG. 6) each of which has an L-shaped configuration formed by vertical portions 27 which depend into the vessel 18 and support horizontal portions 28. The electric heating elements 26 are automatically controlled by a thermostat 30 which may be

4,026,202

3

adjustably set by rotation of a control knob. The housing 24 also defines an exhaust outlet 32 which is connected to the inlet of a motor driven blower 33 mounted on the rear wall of the housing 24 for exhausting any smoke or fumes produced during the cooking operation. A pair of stainless steel sheet metal side panels 34 are also mounted on the top flange 22 of the vessel 18 and project forwardly from the housing 24 to support a removable transparent cover member 35 which provides for conveniently observing the cooking operation.

An elongated generally oval-shaped endless chain conveyor unit 40 (FIG. 6) extends horizontally with a major portion positioned over the open top cooking vessel 18. The conveyor unit 40 is supported by the front wall of the vessel 18 and a set of depending legs (not shown) which rest on the bottom wall of the vessel 18. The conveyor unit 40 includes an elongated oval-shaped base wall 42 on which is mounted a pair of bearings for rotatably supporting corresponding shafts 43 which carry a pair of end sprockets 44. An endless bicycle-type flexible chain 46 extends around the sprockets 44 and has generally parallel spaced horizontal runs. The chain 46 carries a set of longitudinally spaced U-shaped brackets 48 (FIG. 7) each of which is attached to a chain link by a screw 49.

The forward semi-circular end portion of the conveyor unit 40 projects forwardly of the cooking vessel 18, and the shaft 43 supporting the forward end sprocket 44 projects downwardly through the base wall 42 and is connected by a socket-type coupling to an upwardly projecting output shaft 52 of a right angle gear reduced unit 54. The input shaft of the reducer unit 54 is driven by an endless chain drive 57 connected to the shaft of an electric conveyor drive motor which is enclosed within the base cabinet 15 and is controlled by a switch on the control console 20. As illustrated in FIG. 6, the endless conveyor chain 46 is covered by an elongated oval-shaped sheet metal cover member 64, and the gear reducer unit 54 is enclosed by a semi-cylindrical sheet metal housing 66 (FIG. 1) which extends downwardly from the forward end portion of the conveyor unit 40 to the top wall of the base cabinet 15.

Each of the U-shaped brackets 48 secured to the endless conveyor chain 46 carries a waffle forming mold 70 which is preferably formed of cast aluminum and has a configuration corresponding to the desired shape of the waffle-type food product W. Each of the molds 70 is supported by a corresponding J-shaped support rod or arm 72 which has one end portion threadably connected to the mold 70. The opposite end portion of each arm 72 has a circumferential groove 74 (FIG. 7) and is rotatably supported within a bore formed within a corresponding support block 76. Each block 76 projects into the corresponding bracket 48 and is pivotally connected to the bracket 48 by a corresponding pin-like shaft 78 which also extends tangentially through a portion of the groove 74 of the corresponding arm 72 to retain the arm within the support block 76.

Each pivot shaft 78 is releasably retained by a snap pin 79 which extends through a hole within the end of the shaft and permits each mold and arm assembly to be quickly disassembled for cleaning. Each arm support block 76 includes an integral cylindrical portion 82 which provides a bearing for a roller sleeve 83. The sleeve 83 is retained on the cylindrical portion 82 by a

4

blade-like lever or cam member 84 which is rigidly secured to the arm 72 in a radial plane. Rotation of the arm 72 and the corresponding mold 70 is limited to approximately 225° by engagement of the cam member 84 with a stud 86 which projects axially from the cylindrical portion 82 of the support block 86 and is formed as an integral part of the support block.

When the conveyor chain 46 is driven in a counter-clockwise direction (looking down from the top) and the molds 70 are advanced in a generally oval path around the conveyor unit 40, the roller sleeves 83 normally ride on a peripherally extending rail or track 88. An arcuate cam track 92 is secured to the track 88 and projects upwardly from the forward end portion of the track 88. The cam track 92 has an inclined end surface 93 (FIG. 4) which serves to pivot each arm 72 upwardly adjacent the forward end of the conveyor unit 40 for successively elevating the molds 70.

The cam track 92 has a downwardly sloping opposite end surface 94 (FIG. 2) which provides for successively lowering the arms and molds 70 into a supply of batter B (FIG. 3) which is supplied to an overflow container 96. The overflow container 96 includes a formed tray-like sheet metal bottom wall 98 which extends to form a pair of upwardly and outwardly projecting ear portions 99 positioned to rest on an upper flange of a batter reservoir container 102. The side walls of the overflow container 96 are formed by a U-shaped metal frame 104 which has its ends pivotally supported by screws 106 (FIG. 3) secured to a bar attached to one of the ear portions 99 of the bottom wall 88. The frame 104 is thus pivotally supported by the screws 106 for precisely adjusting the level of the batter B within the overflow container 96, and the frame 104 is frictionally retained in a selected position.

As shown in FIG. 6, the flange of the reservoir container 102 is supported on one end by the top flange 22 of cooking vessel 18 and on the other end by a plate 110 which is mounted on a pair of vertical metal tubes 11 and 113 each having an inverted U-shaped upper end portion. As illustrated in FIG. 3, the batter for producing the waffles is added to the reservoir pan or container 102. To prevent the batter from settling, it is recirculated from the reservoir container 102 to the overflow container 96 where the batter is maintained at a preselected level by precisely adjusting the U-shaped frame 104. The upper end portions of the tubes 111 and 113 are connected by corresponding flexible transparent plastic tubes 116 and 117 which extend into the overflow container 96 and reservoir container 102, respectively. The lower end portions of the tubes 111 and 13 are connected through support fittings 119 (FIG. 6) to the inlet and outlet of a motor driven recirculating pump (not shown). The pump preferably incorporates a flexible vane rubber-like impeller which effectively pumps the batter without significantly changing its consistency.

As shown in FIG. 3, a T-shaped needle-like 120 is inserted between the upper end portion of the supply tube 113 and the surrounding end portion of the flexible plastic tube 117 to define small axially extending air passages on opposite sides of the pin 120. Thus as the batter is sucked from the reservoir container 102 through the tubes 113 and 117, air is sucked into the batter which flows to the recirculating pump, thereby assuring that a desired amount of air is maintained in batter. The flow of air is adjustable simply by adjusting the pin 120.

4,026,202

5

Referring again to FIG. 2, as the roller sleeve 83 of each mold support arm assembly rolls or moves down the end ramp surface 94 of the cam track 92, the corresponding mold 70 is lowered or dipped into the batter B which is retained within the overflow container 96. Preferably, the level of the batter is maintained so that it is a fraction of an inch below the top surface of each mold 70 after the corresponding sleeve 83 moves downwardly into the notch or recess 124 extending from the end surface 94. As illustrated in FIG. 8, when it is desired for the forming molds 70 to bypass the batter overflow container 96, for example, when it is desired to shut down the machine, a lever (not shown) is actuated to move a by-pass rail or track 126 upwardly adjacent the recess 124 so that the mold support arms 72 do not move downwardly in the area of the batter supply container 96.

As the molds 70 and their support arms are advanced past the batter supply container 96, the roller sleeves 83 successively engage a ramp or cam end surface 131 of another cam track 132 (FIG. 2). The end surface 131 is effective to pivot each arm 72 upwardly so that the corresponding mold 70 is lifted from the batter supply container 96 and advances to a position over the cooking vessel 18 with a coated layer of batter. The cam track 132 has an inclined opposite end surface which lowers each arm 72 and its corresponding mold 70 with a coated layer of batter down into the hot cooking oil O (FIG. 5) within the vessel 18.

Referring to FIG. 5, as the molds 70 advance along the oval path of the conveyor unit 40, the coated layer of batter on each mold 70 is deep-fried or cooked within the oil to form a food article or waffle W (FIG. 5). As the molds 70 and their support arms 72 advance or move forwardly at the end of the cooking period, the cam element 84 on each support arm 72 engages a roller 136 which is supported by one end portion of an elongated horizontal track 138. The track 138 includes a vertical flange 139 which is supported by a pair of parallel spaced bracket members 141 secured to the cover member 64 for the chain conveyor unit 40. When each cam element 84 engages the roller 136, the corresponding arm 72 is rotated counterclockwise (FIG. 5), thereby rotating the corresponding mold 70 and the waffle W to a retracted position where the mold 70 and waffle W are positioned on an inclined angle above the level of the oil within the cooking vessel 18. The track 138 also includes a bottom horizontal flange 143 which is flush with the bottom surface of the roller 136 and serves to hold each cam element 84 in its rotated position while the corresponding mold 70 and waffle W are advanced forwardly from the cooking vessel 18 to a discharge station adjacent the forward end of the machine.

When each mold 70 and the waffle W formed thereon arrive at the discharge station, the cam element 84 of the corresponding support arm 72, advances past the forward end of the track 138 so that the arm 72 is free to rotate back to its normally stable position, as shown in FIG. 5. As each arm 72 rotates, it engages or impacts a stop member 146 (FIG. 6), and the impact vibrates the mole 70 so that the waffle W is released from the mold. In response to the impact, the waffle may drop downwardly onto an inclined wire rack 148 (FIG. 1) which is supported by an inclined metal discharge chute 150 releasably attached to the forward end portion of the cooking vessel 18 and resting on the base cabinet 15.

6

In the event that waffle W does not drop from its forming mold 70 when the mold support arm 72 impacts the stop member 146, the waffle is stripped from the mold 70 as the mold passes upwardly between a set of flexible stripping elements or coil compression springs 152 (FIG. 4) when the corresponding roller sleeve 83 engages the end surface 93 of the cam track 92. The stripping springs 152 are arranged in opposing pairs on opposite sides of the path of the molds 70 and are supported by a pair of blocks 154 mounted on a U-shaped bracket 156. An inclined sheet metal chute 158 slopes downwardly through the bracket 156 under the stripping springs 152 and has an upper flange 159 which rests upon the top flange of the reservoir container 102. The lower end portion of the chute 158 overlies the chute 150. Thus if a waffle remains adhered to a mold 70 after the mold support arm impacts the stop member 146, the stripping springs 152 are effective to peel the waffle from the mold 70 as it passes upwardly between the springs, as illustrated in FIG. 4. The stripping springs thereby assure that each cooked waffle is removed from its forming mold for discharge down the chutes 150 and 158 into a receptacle such as a container lined with a plastic bag.

From the drawings and the above description, it is apparent that a machine or apparatus constructed in accordance with the present invention, provides desirable features and advantages. For example, the configuration and support of the endless conveyor unit 40 relative to the cooking pan or vessel 18 not only provides for automatically and efficiently producing a high volume of waffle type food products but also provides for conveniently disassembling the conveyor unit 40 to facilitate cleaning of the apparatus. In addition, the construction and assembly of the mold support arms and their connections to the endless conveyor chain also provide for convenient disassembly and reassembly for cleaning. As another advantage, the elongated endless conveyor system provides for quickly advancing or moving the molds 70 at a higher velocity around the forward semi-circular end portion of the conveyor unit 40 and through the discharge station so that the molds have a minimum heat loss during the time period they are removed from the hot cooking oil.

Another desirable feature is provided by the simplified means for introducing air into the recirculated batter which is supplied to the overflow container 96, by simply inserting a needle to stretch the flexible plastic tube 117 to form small venturi-type air passages. A further desirable feature is provided by the use of the cam elements 84 for rotating each mold support arm to remove the corresponding mold from the hot cooking oil and for holding the mold and cooked waffle in a position for effective drainage while the mold and waffle are advanced from the cooking vessel 18 to the discharge station. This structure also permits each arm 72 to be quickly disassembled and reassembled for cleaning purposes.

As mentioned above, the flexible stripping elements or springs 152 also assure that each finished waffle is removed from its forming mold and is not redipped into the batter supply. In addition, the construction and arrangement of the overflow container 96 within the reservoir container 102 not only provide for convenient disassembly for cleaning but also provide for precisely adjusting the level of the batter within the overflow container so that the batter flows to a predetermined height on each mold 70. This adjustment is

4,026,202

7

especially desirable with changes in viscosity of the batter in order to maintain the batter level at a constant elevation. As is also apparent from FIG. 6, the entire apparatus may be quickly and conveniently disassembled for cleaning so that maximum sanitation can be maintained.

While the form of apparatus herein described constitutes a preferred embodiment of the invention, it is to be understood that the invention is not limited to this precise form of apparatus, and that changes may be made therein without departing from the scope and spirit of the invention as defined in the appended claims.

I claim:

1. In apparatus for automatically producing waffles or other food articles, and including means defining a cooking chamber for receiving a volume of cooking oil, means for heating the oil within said chamber, container means for receiving a supply of batter, means for maintaining the batter at a predetermined level within said container means, a plurality of article forming molds, power driven means for moving said molds along a path where said molds are successively immersed into the batter and then into the cooking oil and then delivered to a discharge station, and means at said discharge station for removing each cooked article from its corresponding mold, the improvement wherein said means for moving the molds along said path comprise an elongated endless conveyor, a plurality of arms connected to said conveyor at spaced intervals and supporting corresponding said molds for rotation relative to said conveyor, lever means connected to each of said arms for rotation therewith, and means positioned to engage said lever means on each said arm to effect rotation of said arm and mold for removing each cooked article from the cooking oil.

2. Apparatus as defined in claim 1 wherein said conveyor has generally parallel spaced horizontal runs extending over said chamber for receiving the cooking oil.

3. Apparatus as defined in claim 1 including meanns for introducing air into the supply of batter within said container means for maintaining the batter at a substantially uniform consistency.

4. Apparatus as defined in claim 1 wherein said container means comprise an overflow container disposed generally within a reservoir container, said overflow container includes adjustable means for selecting the level of batter within said overflow container and at which the batter overflows into said reservoir container, and means including a pump for recirculating the batter from said reservoir container into said overflow container.

5. Apparatus as defined in claim 4 wherein said adjustable means for selecting the level of batter within said overflow container comprise a vertically adjustably siide wall on said overflow container.

6. Apparatus as defined in claim 1 wherein said conveyor has generally parallel spaced runs extending generally horizonatally above said cooking chamber and includes a semi-circular end portion projecting horizontally outwardly from said cooking chamber and adjacent said discharge station, and means disposed under said end portion of said conveyor for driving said conveyor.

7. Apparatus as defined in claim 1 including a plurality of flexible spring-like elements located at said discharge station in spaced relation and positioned to

8

receive said molds therebetween to assure removal of each cooked article from the corresponding said mold.

8. Apparatus as defined in claim 1 wherein said means defining said cooking chamber comprises an elongated generally rectangular vessel, and said conveyor comprises an endless chain having generally parallel spaced runs extending over said cooking chamber.

9. Apparatus as defined in claim 1 wherein container means for receiving the batter comprise a reservoir container having an open top, an overflow container removable mounted on said reservoir container and depending into said reservoir container, and said overflow container includes means for conveniently adjusting the level of batter within said overflow container.

10. In apparatus for automatically producing waffles or other food articles, and including means defining a cooking chamber for receiving a volume of cooking oil, means for heating the oil within said chamber, container means for receiving a supply of batter, a plurality of article forming molds, power driven means for moving said molds along a path where said molds are successively immersed into the batter and then into the cooking oil and then delivered to a discharge station, and means at said discharge station for removing each cooked article from its corresponding mold, the improvement wherein said means for moving the molds along said path comprise an elongated endless flexible conveyor having opposite generally U-shaped end portions connected by generally parallel-shaped side runs extending above the level of the cooking oil within said cooking chamber, one of said end portions of said conveyor projects horizontally outwardly from said cooking chamber adjacent said discharge station, and means disposed adjacent said one end portion for driving said conveyor.

11. In apparatus for automatically producing waffles or other food articles, and including means defining a cooking chamber for receiving a volume of cooking oil, means for heating the oil within said chamber, container means for receiving a supply of batter, means for supplying batter to said container means and for maintaining the batter at a predetermined level within said container means, said batter supplying means including a power operated recirculating pump connected to said container means by a batter suction line and a batter supply line, a plurality of article forming molds, power driven means for moving said molds along a path where said molds are successively immersed into the batter and then into the cooking oil for a predetermined time and then delivered to a discharge station, and means at said discharge station for removing each cooked article from its corresponding mold, the improvement comprising means defining an air suction passage connected to said batter suction line and effective for asperating air into the batter supplied to said container means for maintaining the batter at a generally uniform consistency.

12. Apparatus as defined in claim 11 wherein said batter suction line comprises a flexible tube, and said means defining said air suction passage comprises an elongated pin extending generally axially into said flexible tube.

13. In apparatus for automatically producing waffles or other food articles, and including means defining a cooking chamber for receiving a volume of cooking oil, means for heating the oil within said chamber, container means for receiving a supply of batter, means for maintaining the batter at a predetermined level within

4,026,202

9

said container means, a plurality of article forming molds, power driven means for moving said molds along a path where said molds are successively immersed into the batter and then into the cooking oil and then delivered to a discharge station, and means at said discharge station for removing each cooked article from its corresponding mold, the improvement wherein said container means comprise an overflow container overlying a larger reservoir container, a pump container, a pump connected to recirculate the batter from

10

said reservoir container to said overflow container, said overflow container including a bottom wall disposed adjacent a side wall, said side wall being separate from said bottom wall, and including means whereby said side wall of said overflow container is vertically adjustable relative to said bottom wall for precisely adjusting the level at which the batter flows over said side wall of said overflow container into said reservoir container.

* * * * *

KENNETH A. BROWN

A native of Dayton, Ohio, Ken Brown graduated from Stanford University in 1983 with degrees in geology and English. He received his master's degree from Columbia University's Graduate School of Journalism in 1984. He has worked as a reporter in both Africa and the United States.

Other titles from Tempus Books

Computer Lib/Dream Machines

This is a time whose book has come.

First published in 1974, COMPUTER LIB became the first cult book of the computer generation, predicting the major issues of today: design of easy-to-use computer systems, image
synthesis, artificial intelligence, and computer-assisted instruction. Ted Nelson's vision of a
nonsequential way of storing data — hypertext — is particularly relevant today with the
emergence of CD ROM. Republished by Tempus Books, COMPUTER LIB's wildly Utopian
introduction to computers is now available to a new generation. Included is new material
from Ted Nelson — commentaries, insights, updates, and reconsiderations — all in his char-
acteristically opinionated, startling, uplifting, and informative style.

Ted Nelson, 336 pages, $18.95 softcover

The Pursuit of Growth
The Challenges, Opportunities, and Dangers of
Managing and Investing in Today's Economy

Success stories of phenomenal business growth — IBM, Du Pont, Proctor and Gamble — have
been well publicized, as have spectacular growth failures — Atari, Bendix, People Express.
What is this peculiar obsession with growth at any cost? When does it serve the best interests
of managers, investors, politicians, and the community? And when is it a formula for disaster? The authors provide a highly readable and insightful analysis of growth as an underlying
tenet of business and government.

G. Ray Funkhouser and Robert R. Rothberg, 274 pages, $17.95 hardcover

Machinery of the Mind
Inside the New Science of Artificial Intelligence

"An ideal presentation of what artificial intelligence is all about."
Douglas Hofstadter, author of *Gödel, Escher, Bach*

Focusing on the work of giants in the artificial intelligence field — including Marvin Minsky,
Roger Schank, and Edward Feigenbaum — George Johnson gives us an intimate look at the
state of AI today. We see how machines are beginning to understand English, discover scientific theories, and create original works of art; how research in AI is helping us to understand
the human mind; and how AI affects our lives today. Captivating reading for anyone with an
interest in science and technology.

George Johnson, 352 pages, $9.95 softcover

Available wherever fine books are sold, or place your credit card order by calling 1-800-638-3030.

The manuscript for this book was prepared and submitted to Microsoft Press in electronic form. Text files were processed and formatted using Microsoft Word.

Cover design by Don Wright
Interior text design by Darcie S. Furlan
Portraits by Charles B. Solway
Principal typographer: Russell H. Steele
Principal production artist: Becky Geisler–Johnson

Text composition by Microsoft Press in Palatino with display in Palatino Italic, using the Magna composition system and the Linotronic 300 laser imagesetter.

10⁹⁵

OPiuss

Fn

ISBN 1-55615-123-3

51795

PP Science